# STUDIES IN PHILOSOPHY

*Edited by*

## Robert Bernasconi
University of Memphis

A ROUTLEDGE SERIES

# STUDIES IN PHILOSOPHY

ROBERT BERNASCONI, *General Editor*

# ART AS ABSTRACT MACHINE
## ONTOLOGY AND AESTHETICS IN DELEUZE AND GUATTARI

Stephen Zepke

Routledge
New York & London

Published in 2005 by
Routledge
Taylor & Francis Group
270 Madison Avenue
New York, NY 10016

Published in Great Britain by
Routledge
Taylor & Francis Group
2 Park Square
Milton Park, Abingdon
Oxon OX14 4RN

Printed in the United States of America on acid-free paper
10 9 8 7 6 5 4 3

International Standard Book Number-10: 0-415-97155-1 (Hardcover)
International Standard Book Number-13: 978-0-415-97155-3 (Hardcover)

**Library of Congress Cataloging-In-Publication Data**

Catalog record is available from the Library of Congress

Taylor & Francis Group
is the Academic Division of T&F Informa plc.

Visit the Taylor & Francis Web site at
http://www.taylorandfrancis.com

and the Routledge Web site at
http://www.routledge-ny.com

# Contents

# Abbreviations

AO      Gilles Deleuze and Félix Guattari, *Anti-Oedipus, Capitalism and Schizophrenia,* translated by R. Hurly, M. Seem, and H. R. Lane. Minneapolis: University of Minnesota Press, 1983.

Gilles Deleuze and Félix Guattari, *L'Anti-Œdipe.* Paris: Minuit, 1972.

ATP     Gilles Deleuze and Félix Guattari, *A Thousand Plateaus,* translated by B. Massumi. London: Athlone, 1988.

Gilles Deleuze and Félix Guattari, *Mille Plateaux.* Paris: Minuit, 1980.

B       Gilles Deleuze, *Bergsonism,* translated by H. Tomlinson and B. Habberjam. New York: Zone Books, 1991.

Gilles Deleuze, *Le bergsonisme.* Paris: Presses Universitaires de France, 1966.

C1      Gilles Deleuze, *Cinema1, The Movement Image,* translated by H. Tomlinson and B. Habberjam. Minneapolis: University of Minnesota Press, 1989.

Gilles Deleuze, *Cinema 1: L'Image-mouvement.* Paris: Minuit, 1983.

C2      Gilles Deleuze, *Cinema 2: The Time-Image,* translated by H. Tomlinson and R. Galeta. Minneapolis: University of Minnesota Press, 1989.

Gilles Deleuze, *Cinéma 2. L'Image-temps.* Paris: Minuit, 1980.

Chaos   Félix Guattari, *Chaosmosis: an ethico-aesthetic paradigm,* translated by P. Baines and J. Pefanis. Sydney: Power publications, 1995.

Félix Guattari, *Chaosmose.* Paris: Galilée, 1992.

DR             Gilles Deleuze, *Difference and Repetition,* tranalated by P. Patton. New York: University of Columbia Press, 1996.

Gilles Deleuze, *Différence et Répétition.* Paris: Presses Universitaires de France, 1968.

ECC           Gilles Deleuze, *Essays critical and clinical,* translated by D. Smith and M. Greco. Minneapolis: University of Minnesota Press, 1997.

Gilles Deleuze, *Critique et Clinique.* Paris: Minuit, 1993.

EPS           Gilles Deleuze, *Expressionism in Philosophy: Spinoza,* translated by M. Joughin. New York: Zone Books, 1992.

Gilles Deleuze, *Spinoza et le problème de l'expression.* Paris: Minuit, 1968.

FB             Gilles Deleuze, *Francis Bacon: the logic of sensation,* translated by D.W. Smith. London and New York: Continuum, 2003.

Gilles Deleuze, *Francis Bacon logique la sensation.* Paris: Seuil, 2002.

LS             Gilles Deleuze, *The Logic of Sense,* translated by M. Lester with C. Stivale, edited by C.V. Boundas. New York: Columbia University Press, 1990.

Gilles Deleuze, *Logique du sens.* Paris: Minuit, 1969.

NP            Gilles Deleuze, *Nietzsche and Philosophy,* translated by H. Tomlinson. New York: Columbia University Press, 1983.

Gilles Deleuze, *Nietzsche et la philosophie.* Paris: Presses Universitaires de France, 1962.

REA           Félix Guattari, "Ritornellos and Existential Affects," *The Guattari Reader,* p. 158-171, edited by G. Genosko. Oxford: Blackwell, 1996.

Félix Guattari, "Ritournelles et Affects existentiels," *Cartographies Schizoanalytiques.* p. 251-267. Paris: Galilée, 1989.

SPP           Gilles Deleuze, *Spinoza: Practical Philosophy,* translated by R. Hurley. San Francisco: City Lights Books, 1988.

Gilles Deleuze, *Spinoza Philosophie pratique.* Paris: Minuit, 1981.

TF             Gilles Deleuze, *The Fold: Leibniz and the Baroque,* translated by T. Conley. Minneapolis: University of Minnesota Press, 1993.

Gilles Deleuze, *Le Pli, Leibniz et le baroque.* Paris: Minuit, 1988

WP          Gilles Deleuze and Félix Guattari, *What Is Philosophy?*, translated
            by H. Tomlinson and G. Burchell. New York: Columbia
            University Press, 1994.

            Gilles Deleuze and Félix Guattari, *Qu'est-ce que la philosophie?*.
            Paris: Minuit, 1991.

References in the text give the page number of the English translation, followed
by the page number of the French edition. References to other texts by Deleuze
and Guattari are given in the notes. The title and page number for other quoted
sources are given in the notes, with full details found in the bibliography. When
a book is quoted which is not listed in the bibliography, full details are given in
the notes.

# List of Figures

All efforts have been made to locate the rights holders for the stills from Dreyer's *La Passion de Jeanne D'Arc* and Antonioni's *Deserto Rosso.* If anyone has information regarding the copyright for these images, please contact Routledge.

# Acknowledgments

As is always the case, this book has been an exercise in group production. It has emerged from an assemblage of influence and cooperation to which many people have contributed. Paul Patton, Éric Alliez, Dan Smith, and Brian Massumi all read and gave important feedback to earlier versions of the text, and their own work on Deleuze and Guattari has been a constant source of inspiration. Eva Brückner, Scott Hayes, Yves Mettler, Claudia Mongini, David Quigley and Arturo Silva gave valuable assistance in the preparation of the text, for which I am most grateful. Thanks also to my family, Nick and Linda, Gaynor (Mum), Jeanette and Joshua, and my friends Ralph Paine and Karma Percy. Finally, Anita Fricek has given her support and love through the long process of writing, and is this book's real condition of possibility. Many thanks to all of you.

S.Z.—Vienna

Introduction

# Art as Abstract Machine

> And the question is still what it was then, how to view scholarship from the
> vantage point of the artist and art from the vantage of life.
>
> —Friedrich Nietzsche, *The Birth of Tragedy.*

"Art as abstract machine" (ATP, 496/619). This book's title is not a description
but an imperative. It urges an action, an undertaking, a perpetual departure, for
wherever we start, it remains to be done. A machine has to be constructed, and
art as abstract machine will require an artist adequate to the task: a mechanic.
For each machine its mechanic: "The painting machine of an artist-mechanic."[1]
We are already—as always—in the middle of things, a swirling cacophony of
questions: A mechanic? A machine? Who? What? When? And given all that,
what does this machine produce? And for what reasons? But these questions are
the necessary conditions for any construction, for their answers will be the components of new machines that will themselves depart, to test out new directions.
The abstract machine is nothing but this unfolding of complexity, a fractal en-
gineering inseparable from life, a blooming of multiplicity.

But let's step back from this complexity that will nevertheless remain the
condition of our investigation. We don't want to crash and burn, not yet. Let's
try taking one question at a time. If our title is an imperative what does it bid
us do? To construct an abstract machine, obviously, but how? And to risk another question, already, what does it do? (We will see how these questions, to
immediately step into Deleuze and Guattari's vocabulary, will become indiscernible.) Deleuze and Guattari give what seems a straightforward answer: "The
diagrammatic or abstract machine does not function to represent, even something real, but rather constructs a real that is yet to come, a new type of reality"
(ATP, 142/177). Art as abstract machine's first principle: it is real and not a representation. Deleuze and Guattari, whether discussing art, philosophy, or anything else, will not stop coming back to this first principle.[2] And as such, it

*1*

immediately implies another—its necessary compliment—that constructing an abstract machine is to construct construction itself. The abstract machine is the vital mechanism of a world always emerging anew, it is the mechanism of creation operating at the level of the real. Here, a new world opens up, a living world in which nothing is given except creation. To open a world, to construct a new type of reality, this is the ontological foundation of the world—of *this* world and of all the others—on an abstract machine guiding its becoming.

The abstract machine creates a new reality, constructs new ways of being, but although inseparable from this innovation of existence, it has no being. The abstract machine is the entirely immanent condition of the new, and thereby receives its Nietzschean definition: its being is becoming. For now we will unfold the implications of this ontology rather rapidly, any beginning must involve a certain reckless plunge . . . The abstract machine doesn't represent anything because nothing exists outside of its action, it is what it does and its immanence is always active. In the middle of things the abstract machine is never an end, it's a means, a vector of creation. But despite the abstract machine having no form, it is inseparable from what happens: it is the "non-outside" living vitality of matter. (But is it an inside? As we shall see the question marks a certain limit to an old and no longer useful topological vocabulary.) As a result, abstract machines are neither ideal identities nor categories of being, and remain entirely unaffected by any transcendent ambitions.

But before we get into the intricacies of this technical philosophical terminology we should remind ourselves that we are speaking of practical matters, of machines and their constructions. Building an abstract machine is more DIY than techno-science, and requires a bit of the mad professor.[3] Deleuze and Guattari, mad professors no doubt, adopt the language of the construction site, an earthy directness reflecting the pragmatism required by the job at hand. Machines eat and sleep, they remind us, they shit and fuck. (AO, 1/7) We are, no mistake, machines. "Everything is a machine" (AO, 2/8). Our task—to be done with techno-paranoia—is to turn these machines creative, to liberate their parts in an explosion that remakes the world. The mechanic is, to use another of Deleuze and Guattari's colorful phrases, "the cosmic artisan: a homemade atomic bomb" (ATP, 345/426). "There is a necessary joy in creation," Deleuze says, "art is necessarily a liberation that explodes everything."[4] But the abstract machine is not an expression implying technophilia either, and is inseparable from a mechanics of the flesh, an example of Deleuze and Guattari's avowed materialism: "The abstract machine is pure Matter-Function" (ATP, 141/176). The world is a plane of matter-force, a material process of experimentation connecting and disconnecting machines. On this plane abstract machines act as guidance mechanisms—

"*probe-heads*" (*têtes chercheuses*, ATP, 190/232)—steering the world on its "creative flight" (ATP, 190/233). The abstract machine is therefore both vital and material, it exists, Deleuze and Guattari write, as the "life proper to matter as such, a material vitalism that doubtless exists everywhere but is ordinarily hidden or covered, rendered unrecognizable, dissociated by the hylomorphic model" (ATP, 411/512). Hylomorphism is an operation that moulds matter into forms according to an ideal model, an operation by which the world appears as obedient and predictable representations. Once more, the abstract machine *against* representation.

We have already sketched—at a speed that no doubt calls out for a subsequent slowness—the underlying structure of this book's diagram. First, not only the echo of Nietzsche in the abstract machine's *against*, but Deleuze and Guattari's mobilization of his ontology of becoming. Second, the necessity of Spinoza to any philosophy of immanence. Spinoza will be the permanent signature of Deleuze and Guattari's immanent machinery, of its expression and construction. Third, a materialism inseparable from a vitalism; in other words, Bergson. These are the abstract co-ordinates of Deleuze and Guattari's philosophical machine, and are mapped in the first three chapters of this book. These chapters lay out the basic components of Deleuze and Guattari's ontology, while seeking to show how they work, how they must be put to work in constructing an expression of the living materiality of the world, in constructing an abstract machine. Understanding this ontology will therefore confront us with the immediate necessity of understanding its appearance in and as life, an understanding inseparable from an experience of the new realities that are forever being created. At this point it becomes obvious that the ontology of the abstract machine implies an aesthetic, because its existence is indiscernible from its appearance in and as experience.

What then, to ask the question of aesthetics, are the conditions of this experience? This question calls to account another of Deleuze and Guattari's philosophical interlocutors: Kant. Unlike Nietzsche, Spinoza and Bergson however, Kant is less a "fellow traveller" than an adversary, and the site of combat will be the aesthetic. For Deleuze and Guattari aesthetics is not the determination of the objective conditions of any possible experience, nor does it determine the subjective conditions of an actual experience *qua* beautiful. Aesthetics instead involves the determination of real conditions that are no wider than the experience itself, that are, once more, indiscernible from *this* experience. Aesthetics then, is inseparable from ontology, because experience is, for Deleuze and Guattari, irreducibly real. To construct an abstract machine will mean constructing a new experience indissociable from a new reality. The sensible, like the thinkable, is nothing but the temporary conditions from which an abstract machine departs, following Spinoza's "war cry" (the phrase is Deleuze's) "we don't even know what a body can do" (EPS, 255/234). This introduces another of our constant concerns, how can we create a new body, a new sensibility adequate to a life of ontological innovation? Art emerges here as a privileged site of corporeal experimentation. Art as abstract machine gives a genetic definition of art, one that transforms both its ontological and aesthetic dimensions. "Everything changes once we determine the conditions of real experience," Deleuze writes, "which are not larger than the conditioned and which differ in kind from the categories: [Kant's] two senses of the aesthetic become one, to the point where the being of the sensible reveals itself in the work of art, while at the same time the work of art appears as experimentation" (DR, 68/94). An abstract machine determines the real conditions of experience, conditions neither subjective nor objective (they have become abstract), and that can only be experienced in the work of art (in a machine). A work entirely experimental, inasmuch as art is a permanent research on its own conditions, and is always constructing new machines. Feedback loop. Once more, this will be an overarching concern of this book, to understand the necessary and active immanence of abstract and actual, infinite and finite in the machine of art. The work of art understood in this way will give a real experience, an experience of its real conditions, an experience of and as its immanent abstract machine in the process of (re)constructing reality. Which is to say—or what can be said before we say everything else—art is an experience of becoming, an experiential body of becoming, an experimentation producing new realities. The implications are obvious: there is neither an ontology of art nor an aesthetics of art, each in its own realm of competency, each with its own all too serious professors. There are artists constructing abstract machines, mechanics engaged in the pragmatic practice of *onto-aesthetics*. Cosmic artisans everywhere setting off their atom bombs.

Our diagram has already grown quite complex. The co-implication of ontology and aesthetics in art as abstract machine—the onto-aesthetics of art—involves a redefinition of experience by which its objective and subjective conditions are dissolved in the real, the reality of the world as it becomes nothing else than itself. Art in these terms is an autogenesis expressing the world (its real conditions) by constructing experience (its real experience). And what is this experience? A simple question that it will take a whole book (and no doubt not just this one) to answer. Art is, before all else, and as Deleuze and Guattari put it, a sensation. A sensation of this work, but this work, this sensation, it does nothing if it does not restore us to our constitutive infinity by creating the world anew. Deleuze and Guattari's understanding of art as sensation will set off from

Nietzsche's statement serving as the epitaph above, to view scholarship from the vantage of art—it means our investigations only begin when we start to create—and art from the vantage of life—meaning our creations must become alive. Art will be nothing (at least not for us) if it is not this ongoing expression of life in the construction of living machines.

Expression and construction are the doubled dimensions of art as abstract machine. The abstract machine expresses the autogenetic and infinite processuality of its real conditions (the infinite, a cosmic world), which appear as the construction of *this* reality, *this* art-work. But, once more, doubled, the abstract machine expresses the infinite, but also constructs it, right here right now: "The field of immanence or plane of consistency must be constructed." Deleuze and Guattari write: "It is constructed piece by piece, and the places, conditions, and techniques are irreducible to one another. The question, rather, is whether the pieces fit together, and at what price. Inevitably there will be monstrous crossbreeds" (ATP, 157/195). To express an infinite world in constructing a finite art-work, to make art in other words, is a process by which the becoming of the world is expressed in a construction which works upon its own conditions, which operates at the level of its constitutive mechanism. Any construction of art then, any sensation, emerges through an abstract machine to express an infinite plane by way of an actual becoming whose very specificity and precision involves or infolds a change in its real conditions. The world is this genetic plane of immanence, a Bergsonian multiplicity, which in being expressed in a finite construction, an art-work, a sensation, changes in nature. At this point it is not a question of distinguishing expression and construction as two dimensions or moments of sensation, because they have become indiscernible on the single multiplied plane of onto-aesthetics. All that remains is to affirm their identity, construction=expression.[5]

This affirmation will be another theme of this book, echoing in its different terminologies. It appears as Nietzsche's interpretation and evaluation of will to power, as Spinoza's affects of joy and beatitude in God/Nature, as the actual and the virtual dimensions of duration in a Bergsonian cinema, as traits of content and expression in the abstract machine, and finally as the affect and the percept in sensation itself. In all these cases it is the affirmation of becoming that puts immanence to work in a feedback loop of construction and expression, making becoming the being of a work of art that, as Deleuze and Guattari put it, "wants to create the finite that restores the infinite" (WP, 197/186).

We could well ask, as some already have, whether Deleuze and Guattari are offering us a modern version of Romanticism here, whether onto-aesthetics is simply art expressing nature. Certainly Deleuze and Guattari pass through Romanticism, and although they find a stopping place in the inhuman rupture of the sublime—a rupture and rapture—they do so only by changing its Nature. A change that rejects the sublime's Kantian conditions, removing art from any romantic analogy with the divine, and placing it back among the animals. All this will be developed later of course, but I mention it here as the first qualification of what is the necessary correlate of the construction=expression equation, an "atheistic mysticism." This is a phrase employed by Deleuze to describe Spinoza's philosophy of immanence, and is the only way to understand Deleuze and Guattari's ironic deification of Spinoza as the "Christ of philosophers" (WP, 60/59). Spinoza is the philosopher who thought the "best" plane of immanence, the "best" God, because through the attributes the plane's (God/Nature) expression in the joy of affectual assemblages is nothing but the ongoing construction of an infinite and divine *here and now:* God yes, but *Deus sive natura.* Spinoza's revolutionary formula introduces an atheist God to philosophy—an atheism inseparable from a true philosophy of immanence—because reason is the way to express God/Nature constructing itself, and immanence achieves nothing without this identity of expression and construction. To put it simply, Spinoza overcomes transcendence because, as Deleuze puts it, "expression is not simply manifestation, but is also the constitution of God himself. Life, that is, expressivity, is carried into the absolute" (EPS, 80–1/70).

This strange atheism that in Spinoza never stops speaking of God, and in Deleuze and Guattari never stops seeking to become adequate to becoming itself, will be the consistent aim of a *practical philosophy.* Philosophy, like art, is a construction site, a workshop producing abstract machines with cosmic ambition. Deleuze and Guattari are continually coming back to this mystical practice, the production of what Michel de Certeau has called, "the infinity of a local singularity."[6] From the Nietzschean simulacrum as the superior form of everything that is to the seed/universe of the cinematic crystal image, from the visions of cinema's seer to Bacon's BwO, from Goethe's differential color theory to Leibniz's imperceptible waves infolding perception in the ocean of experience, Deleuze and Guattari describe the atheistic mysticism of a philosophy of immanence, the construction and expression by an abstract machine of a *"local absolute"* (ATP, 382/474). This vision of a mystical Deleuze and Guattari is, I am well aware, regarded with suspicion by many commentators.[7] Nevertheless, with the important addition of its atheist condition, this seems to me the best way to approach the profusion of mystical formulations in Deleuze and Guattari's work, and their consistent attempts to find our real conditions on a cosmic plane of production.

Mystical atheism is the real condition of Deleuze and Guattari's pragmatic philosophy. Mysticism is the experience of immanence, of the construction/expression of the at once infinite and finite material plane on which everything happens. Thus, mysticism as an experience of immanence is necessarily atheist, because it cannot involve transcendence of any kind (where to?). Atheist mysticism replaces transcendence with construction/expression, first of all as a construction of the body—atheism *against* asceticism. Mysticism is a physical practice: how do you make yourself a body without organs? Furthermore, mysticism is a creative process that, whether in the realm of philosophy, art, or somewhere else, is inseparable from affirmation. Deleuze and Guattari identify the same philosophers as philosophers of affirmation as they did the philosophers of immanence, the holy trinity: Nietzsche, Spinoza, and Bergson. It's no accident of course, as in each case it is by affirming the immanence of a fundamentally creative life that the joy proper to mysticism will explode on its lines of flight, all the way to infinity. Deleuze reads Nietzsche's affirmation of will to power, the affirmation of affirmation as he puts it, as the practical mechanism of overcoming, the door through which we eternally return. Similarly, it is the Spinozian affect of joy that constructs the rhizomatic compositions of power constituting the ever increasing All, and culminating in the mystical affect of beatitude, the love by which God/Nature loves itself. In Bergson Deleuze finds in the intuition of the *élan vital*, an intuition Bergson associates with artists and mystics, an affirmation capable of entering into the creative process itself. "If man accedes to the open creative totality," Deleuze writes of Bergson, "it is therefore by acting, by creating rather than by contemplating" (B, 111/118). Deleuze suggests as a slogan, and it's a joke, but perhaps only half a joke, "It's all good, but really."[8]

Affirmation is the mechanism of immanence, the means by which to construct a joyful expression. No doubt Deleuze's affirmation of affirmation also has a serious philosophical function as the antidote to that other notable philosophical double-banger, the negation of negation (just as overcoming in this context is the overcoming of *Aufhebung*). But it is also the guiding thread of Deleuze and Guattari's work in a practical sense, for they very rarely discuss artwork, at least, which they do not *like*. (And in a wider sense this would be the rational behind Deleuze's refusal to specifically deal with the philosophy of Hegel.) But behind this seemingly banal observation lies an important new element to Deleuze and Guattari's abstract machine, and that is its ethical dimension. Affirmation is an ethical choice, a choice for the creative energies of life, first of all our own. This will be an ethics that will immediately appear in our first chapter on Nietzsche, where affirmation returns will to power eternally, a return that will be our own overcoming. Here affirmation takes on a critical function, because a true affirmation of immanence will involve the destruction of nihilism, of all the resentful negations defining the human, all too human. As

Nietzsche said, and it is a slogan that will accompany us through the course of this book: no creation without destruction. A motto for the artist first of all. Affirmation, and the mystical onto-aesthetics it enables, is nothing if not critical. It is, in fact, the creative process of critique, and involves violence and cruelty, and their correlate: pain. Just like nature. Any creation worth its name will therefore encompass the destructions necessary to set it free, an explosion that destroys negation and propels its liberated matter into the new. Affirmation is therefore like a leap of faith, a leap into the chaos of the world in order to bring something back, in order to construct something that expresses life beyond its sad negation. And how could it be anything else? Because from our subjective perspective, from within its narrow and blinkered vision, the life of matter, the cosmic infinity of our here and now is what cannot be experienced or thought, at least not without some recourse to mollifying images of a transcendent beyond. This unthought of thought, the insensible in sensation, this is the impossible aim of Deleuze and Guattari's project. Not, once more, to transcend the world, but to discover it as it is, to create a thought, a sensation, a life that participates in the world's joyful birth of itself: a dancing star. This, Deleuze writes, "is the impossible which can only be restored within a faith. [ . . . ] Only belief in the world can reconnect man to what he sees and hears" (C2, 172/223).

To reconnect man to what he sees and hears, this is nothing less than the project of art. A critical project for sure, because art has been overcoded with so many merely human ambitions, so many representational limitations. Let us not forget: "No art and no sensation have ever been representational" (WP, 193/182). First, we need a machine to clear the canvas (or the screen, the page, the compact disc) of all the clichés which prevent a creation. Second, we need an affirmation that is strong enough to actually create something, because a constant risk of destruction is that nothing new will emerge from it. Nothing is sadder than a void, nothing so ugly as a black hole. And art can just as easily be these things, a soporific or worse, a poison. Art as abstract machine therefore involves an ethical choice, a selection and conjugation of those matter-flows which are in the process of escaping from themselves, it must affirm only what is the most deterritorialised. Art must be critical enough to divert its contents and expressions back to the plane of consistency, to achieve an absolute deterritorialisation. But then, something must happen, something must emerge, the creative life of this plane must be expressed in a sensation. And sensations must be created, as any artist knows, for the machine to work.

In this way the abstract machine operates at the interstice between finite and infinite, it deterritorialises the concrete world, breaking matter out of its overcoded forms, to put it back into contact with its vitality, with its living flows, its inhuman and inorganic nature. This is art's infinite material dimension, and here, absolutely deterritorialised, the machine begins to work, "flush with the real" as Deleuze and Guattari put it, constructing flows of matter-force into expressive sensations. This is the bacchanaal of art, immersed in the real, affirming its own creative ecstacies. Deleuze is a laughing Dionysus: "Yes, the essence of art is a kind of joy," he affirms, "and this is the very point of art."[9]

Here art will become a politics of lived experience, a realm of experimentation that opens life up to alternative modes of being, affirming new realities, new communities, and new methods of self-organisation. Art becomes a kind of bio-politics, an experimentation with life as it is lived, a contestation in the realm of experience with everything that seeks to prevent us from affirming our power of composition. Art is a mechanism to increase our power, to liberate ourselves from the limits of representation (and the political operation of these limits is a constant subtext of Deleuze and Guattari's discussion). Art is the freedom to experiment on our conditions of existence, and is the ethical condition of any revolution. Art as ethics, and as bio-politics, serves to emphasise the fact that art is always concerned with very practical problems. In this sense Deleuze and Guattari offer a philosophy of art-*work,* and it only begins—*for real*—when we put it to work for *and against* ourselves.

Finally we have arrived at what has no doubt been a puzzling absence to this introduction. Art, I mean art as it is normally understood, pictures and things. Of course it was never absent, because the path so far taken was necessary in order to open the question of what art means for Deleuze and Guattari, ontologically, aesthetically and ethically. It is the question to which this book will try to provide some answers. But nevertheless, and following Deleuze and Guattari, much of this book will talk very specifically about art, about artists, their work, and about how art works. Each chapter—with the exception of the second on Spinoza, where the introduction of art examples to a discussion of a thinker who barely mentions art at all seems a little far-fetched—contains a more or less lengthy discussion of an art-work, an artist's work, or an art movement. In each case the general philosophical argument of the chapter is taken up in an example appropriate to it: Andy Warhol's "Death and Disaster" series in relation to the Nietzschean simulacrum (Chapter One); cinema in terms of Bergson's ontology of time (Chapter Three); Venetian Renaissance painting as an abstract machine (Chapter Four); Jackson Pollock's "middle" period as a diagram for Abstraction opposed to his American modernist champions (Chapter Four); the readymades of Marcel Duchamp as machines of chaosmosis (Chapter Five); and the work of Francis Bacon (Chapter Six). In each case the aim is to show how it is meaningless to isolate Deleuze and Guattari's discussions of art from their wider philosophical concerns, and further that their discussion of art can only be fully understood within this wider context. This is to say that Deleuze and Guattari offer us an onto-aesthetics, but more importantly it is to show it in action, to get close to the explosions it ignites, its destruction of inherited opinions about aesthetics and art, and the joyful affirmations it offers in their place.

This is finally simply to follow what I have outlined above, a Deleuzeo-Guattarian *practice,* a practice in which life is both expressed and constructed, and by which art restores the finite to its infinite dimension. It means that in attempting to understand art as abstract machine we will have to understand its onto-aesthetics, its mystical and yet utterly actual processes of creation. This, as Guattari put it, will be our, and art's "dance of chaos and complexity" (Chaos, 88/123).

Chapter One

# The Artist-Philosopher: Deleuze, Nietzsche, and the Critical Art of Affirmation

> The notion of a "beyond" is the death of life.
> —Friedrich Nietzsche, *The Antichrist.*

> It is not without profound sorrow that one admits to oneself that in their highest flights the artists of all ages have raised to heavenly transfiguration precisely those conceptions which we now recognise as false: they are the glorifiers of the religious and philosophical errors of mankind.
> —Nietzsche, *Human, All Too Human.*

> Our religion, morality and philosophy are decadent forms of man. The *countermovement: art.*
> —Nietzsche, *Will to Power.*

## NIETZSCHE, DELEUZE AND THE NEW

Deleuze's reading of Nietzsche is in the spirit of Zarathustra's words to his disciples: "One repays a teacher badly if one always remains nothing but a pupil."[1] Nietzsche does not want followers, he wants those capable of creating something new. He wants to produce, in other words, artists. Deleuze's reading of Nietzsche is therefore artistic; in the spirit of Nietzsche he creates a new Nietzsche. This practice of creative interpretation affirms an important element of Nietzsche's aesthetics, that art is not representational, but is an experimental process by which the form of representation is overcome, and through which something new emerges. The emergence of the new is, for Nietzsche as for Deleuze, nothing less than the movement of life, the genetic process of life expressing itself. Consequently, Nietzsche's aesthetic is inseparable from the ontology that animates it. The creative movement of life is "entirely different," Deleuze writes, "from the imaginary movement of representation or the abstract

*11*

movement of concepts that habitually takes place among words and within the mind of the reader. Something leaps up from the book [or art work] and enters a region completely exterior to it. And this, I believe, is the warrant for legitimately misunderstanding the whole of Nietzsche's work."[2]

Misunderstanding before representation! This cry sounds strange to philosophical ears, although perhaps not so strange to artistic ones. Creative misunderstanding (what, as we shall see, Nietzsche calls affirmation) overcomes the old to produce something new, a creative process inseparable from art and an art inseparable from life. This onto-aesthetic ecology inspires Nietzsche to introduce another odd conjunction as its agent: the *"artist*-philosopher" (Nietzsche's emphasis). Artist-philosophers *practice* a creative life, a practice— common to thought and the plastic arts—by which they "survey all the strengths and weaknesses of their nature and then fit them into an artistic plan until every one of them appears as art."[3] Art, embodied by the artist-philosopher, is first of all a process of self-creation, an ethical and ontological practice as much as an aesthetic one. This, Nietzsche claims, is a "Higher concept of art"[4] that no longer simply describes an object, nor a subjective process, but the mechanism by which the creativity of life, the "will to power" as Nietzsche calls it, is expressed in a life.

The problem for the artist-philosopher—the same problem for art and for philosophy—is how to express the will to power despite the forces of a human, all too human culture that seeks to deny it? How, in other words, is it possible to live as the affirmation of will to power, or, more simply, how can life create art? The answer is found in Deleuze's reading of Nietzsche's method of critique. Critique is a "higher concept of art," a vital practice of evaluation and selection through which life is returned to us in a radically revalued art-work, what we shall see Deleuze call a "simulacrum." The simulacrum is produced by critique as an expression of will to power, and will to power lives as this expression.

## CRITIQUE

Will to power is an ontological energy, the living power of everything; it is, Nietzsche writes, "the unexhausted procreative will of life" (Z, "Of Self-Overcoming"). This living will seeks to increase its power, to grow, and doing so means overcoming whatever resists it. "Every living thing,' Nietzsche claims, "does everything it can not to preserve itself but to become more" (WtP, 688). The will to power is therefore essentially creative, but this creation involves the necessary destruction of whatever seeks to oppose and negate it. To create means to become more powerful and requires an affirmation of will to power, but, and it's sadly obvious, most people are not creative and prefer to protect their banality by denying will to power's violent vitality. Will to power, Nietzsche argues, is embodied along these two trajectories of expression: "Every individual may be regarded as representing the ascending or descending line of life. When one has decided which, one has thereby established a canon for the value of his egoism."[5] The point is two-fold. Humans gain or lose power, ascend or descend depending on whether they live an affirmative or negative life. But these values are neither pre-given nor fixed, and are themselves the product of an evaluation ("when one has decided . . .") by which will to power is expressed in and as our life. This "notion of value," Deleuze argues, "implies" a "*critical* reversal" (NP, 1/1). Our values are no longer derived from pre-existing transcendent truths and moral laws, but are instead created by our own evaluations, our own affirmations and negations of will to power. This leads to another reversal: for Nietzsche the problem of critique is no longer to criticise given values, but is to create them (NP, 1/1). Critique is the art of creating values as the direct expressions or "symptoms" of will to power.

"Critical philosophy," Deleuze writes, "has two inseparable moments: the referencing back of all things and any kind of origin to values, but also the referencing back of these values to something which is, as it were, their origin and determines their values" (NP, 2/2). The first moment is "interpretation," which establishes the "meaning" of things according to whether they have an active or reactive value, according to whether the forces they embody overcome their limits to become something new, or react against this power to confirm things within their limits. Interpretation analyses things as symptoms of force, and requires, as Nietzsche famously puts it, a physician of culture. Force, Nietzsche writes, "requires first a *physiological* investigation and interpretation, rather than a psychological one; and every one of them needs a critique on the part of medical science."[6] We will examine this physiological aspect of interpretation a little later, but staying with medical metaphors we can say that interpretation, by producing a thing's value, is a creative "symptomatology," and as such, Deleuze writes, "is always a question of art."[7]

Interpretation however, is inseparable from the second moment of critique, for a forces value only emerges through an evaluation that creates it. This second moment is a "re-valuation of value" that makes of the individual's interpretation of forces an affirmation or negation of the will to power. Evaluation is therefore pre-individual, and expresses will to power in "perspectives of appraisal," (NP, 1/1) perspectives which reveal the individual as a resentful human negating will to power, or as the human overcome, an *Übermensch* whose values are alive with joy. This is the extraordinary value of the artist-philosopher; their evaluative perspective—the value of their values—is affirmative.

Affirmation is the Nietzschean condition for the creation of art, and affirmative evaluation defines the perspective of the artist-philosopher, who creates (that is interprets) active things or forces. This is a new critical art which encompasses both an affirmative process and the active things it creates. Art is procreative for Nietzsche, it is a critical practice by which things increase their power, by which things become new, and as such is indiscernible from life. "Art and nothing but art!" he writes, "It is the great means of making life possible, the great seduction to life, the great stimulant of life" (WtP, 853, ii). We have quickly reached the necessary immanence of ontology and aesthetics in Nietzsche's philosophy of art, for, as Deleuze puts it, "Nietzsche demands an aesthetics of creation" (NP, 102/116).

For Deleuze, as for Nietzsche, the ascending line of critique embodies an "artistic will," because its creative power is "always opening new 'possibilities'" (C2, 141/185).[8] On the descending line however, there is a completely different method of evaluation. Here "*ressentiment* itself becomes creative and gives birth to values" (GM, I, 10). This resentful creation, Nietzsche writes, is "the *other* origin of the 'good,' of the good as conceived by the man of *ressentiment*" (GM, I, 13). These resentful men and women interpret the strength required to overcome as *evil,* so that they, the weak and overcome, will appear good. Thus their evaluation negates the creative energy of will to power, and establishes a truth and moral system that transcends and judges the life of will to power. Nietzsche pours scorn on all such evaluations, based as they are on "the belief that *the strong man is free* to be weak and the bird of prey to be a lamb—for thus they make the bird of prey *accountable* for being a bird of prey" (GM, I, 13). This morality of good and evil requires the fallacy of understanding physiological strength according to a psychological cause. The man of *ressentiment* imagines that the eagle chooses to kill the lamb, when in fact that is its function and necessity, its strength and active force.[9] In judging the eagle to be evil the sweet little lambs justify the "goodness" of their own impotent negations of will to power. These moral judgements are symptoms of an evaluation based on different ontological assumptions to those of the artist-philosopher. The ontology of sheep, of the "herd" as Nietzsche calls them, projects "ascetic ideals" to justify their moral judgements, ascetic because they are removed from life and attributed to a transcendent God, a divine "beyond." This moralistic and mortified metaphysics justifies the *ressentiment* of the herd by privileging the negation of will to power over its active strength. Here it is not will to power that lives, but God.

Nietzsche assumes an immanent will to power as the genetic condition of life, but its ascending and descending lines of valuation give different ontological expressions of its vitality. Depending on the perspective, evaluation produces values (interpretations) that either affirm or deny life. To negate will to power means to deny life and results in nihilism, whereas to affirm is to create, and so participate in life's vital becoming. Whichever way we look at it, there is no extra dimension in which our evaluations and actions are judged. We are what we do, and we get the life—and the art—we deserve depending on our perspective. Nietzsche explains it this way, "popular morality," he writes, "separates strength from expressions of strength, as if there was a neutral substratum behind the strong man, which was *free* to express strength or not to do so. But there is no such substratum; there is no "being" behind doing, effectuating, becoming; the "doer" is merely a fiction added to the deed—the deed is everything" (GM, I, 13). The strong man or woman, the artist-philosopher, is defined by their act, an action that overcomes human nihilism and the delicate ego it seeks to protect, just as it overcomes the herd's resentful morality. Man overcome, or the Overman, is no longer made in God's image, for God—the ultimate nihilist—is dead, and with him the moral laws that judge man's actions from "beyond." The art of critique frees life from its divine judgement, from its human limitations and moral determinations, and affirms (that is embodies) the will to power as creative life. As a result, art must be critical because it is only through the critique of man and his values that something new and truly beautiful can be created. No creation without destruction, as Nietzsche put it, "whoever must be a creator in good and evil, verily, he must first be an annihilator and break values. Thus the highest evil belongs to the highest goodness: but this is creative" (Z, "Of Self-Overcoming"). Neither Nietzsche nor Deleuze can be understood apart from this fundamental aggression.[10]

The artist-philosopher, and the art he or she creates, affirms will to power in the face of everything—God, man, culture, morality—that tries to negate it. This is the difficult critical affirmation by which ascetic ideals, as the determining truths the "good" man represents, are destroyed and an active "perspective" of will to power emerges. To understand how, we must enter further into Deleuze's reading of the Nietzschean world of force. The universe, Deleuze argues, is made up of forces. But a force exists only through its difference to other forces, these forces themselves existing through differences, their ramifying relations encompassing, at their limit, everything. A force's quality (the object it constitutes) therefore appears as active or reactive, noble or base, good or bad, according to the quantitative differences between the forces that constitute it. "Forces," Deleuze writes, "express their difference in quantity by the quality which is due to them" (NP, 53/60). It is interpretation that fixes a force's quality, and so gives meaning to an event, but it is the evaluative perspective of will to power that has first put the forces into contact and established their quantitative relation. As Deleuze puts it: "The relation of force to force is called 'will.'"[11] In critique "force is what can, [and] will to power is what wills" (NP, 50/57). Force and will (the qualities and quantities of interpretation and evaluation) are therefore inseparable, the interpretation of forces expressing the will to powers "fluent, primordial and seminal qualitative elements" (NP, 53/60) of affirmation or negation. But a quality is never fixed once and for all, because a force's constitutive quantitative relation is rising and falling as it overcomes other forces, or is overcome. In other words, a force is a quantitative becoming before it is a quality, a (human) being or a fact. Differential relations of force embody ascending or descending lines of evaluation (affirmation and negation), becomings active or reactive, and these give rise to interpretations of qualities and their accompanying actions or reactions. The rise and fall of will to power, its becoming, therefore develops through the linked operations of interpretation and evaluation in critique. Critique is either "artistic" in affirming the differential becoming of forces as will to power, and produces something new, or it negates a force's becoming, giving it an identity, a being, in order to "arrive at a semblance of affirmation,"[12] in mans nihilist affirmations of a moral truth. As Deleuze rather dramatically puts it, reversing the Christian trajectories Nietzsche attacks: "Affirmation takes us into the glorious world of Dionysus, the being of becoming and negation hurls us down into the disquieting depths from which reactive forces emerge"(NP, 54/61).

## PERSPECTIVES

The will to power appears as a force's quality because appearance (quality) necessarily implies an interpretation of a quantity of force as active or reactive, and this interpretation in turn requires an evaluation—the affirmation or negation—of and by will to power. Each quality therefore embodies a perspective, an affirmation or negation of will to power that encompasses the differential infinity that makes it up. In this way interpretations are perspectives constituting the processes of life. Critique is therefore the expression of will to power, and life is nothing if not critical. Consequently, we cannot interpret by comparing forces to outside (transcendental, moral) criteria, and critique cannot give a judgment that stands as a "true fact." Interpretation cannot be conceptually distinguished from the becoming that gives it value, for the evaluation it embodies, as the becoming active or reactive of will to power, is its real and immanent condition. Will to power is what constructs meaning and value, at the same time as meaning and value express its 'seminal elements.'[13] This has radical epistemological consequences, for the world as will to power is the permanent becoming of ideas as much as things. Knowledge, as Nietzsche put it, is "Interpretation, the introduction of meaning—not 'explanation' . . . There are no facts" (WtP, 604). An understanding of the world is always a question of creative interpretation and the evaluation it implies. For Nietzsche, as Deleuze puts it, "*creation takes the place of knowledge itself*" (NP, 173/199).[14]

Critique is the creation of knowledge and things through the interpretation of qualities, according to an evaluation of and by will to power. Evaluation is in this sense a mode of being, and the ontological ground of those who interpret. "This is why," Deleuze argues, "we always have the beliefs, feelings and thoughts we deserve given our way of being or our style of life" (NP, 1/2).[15] Critique is the production of our feelings and thoughts (interpretation) according to their immanent will to power, the mode of existence they embody (evaluation). As a result, Deleuze tells us: "Fundamentally it is always a question 'What is it *for me?*'" (NP, 77/87). The answer to this question will embody a perspective; at once the value of my life and an expression of the will to power. As Deleuze writes: "Willing is the critical and genetic instance of all our actions, feelings and thoughts. The method is as follows: relating a concept to the will to power [interpretation] in order to make it the symptom of a will [evaluation] without which it could not even be thought (nor the feeling experienced, nor the action undertaken)" (NP, 78/89). An evaluative perspective is produced by and as will to power, and is expressed in interpretations. This means life *qua* will to power, is inseparable from a life that lives it.

The critical question in regard to the art-work is therefore not "what is it?" nor "what does it mean?" but "what is it for me?" Obviously, art always awaits its critique, indeed it requires it, because critique poses the ethical-ontological problem of who is able to affirm, before it answers questions as to meaning or value. The question posed by the art-work ('what is it for me?') is nothing but the question of who is able to be an artist-philosopher. In asking "what is it?" we assume a metaphysics of essence and truth and an object that represents them. The question "what is it for me?" however, asks "what are the forces which takes hold of a given thing, what is the will that possesses it? Which one is expressed, manifested and even hidden in it?" (NP, 76–7/87). The question "what is it for me?" therefore implies another, about what this "me" is. It implies a critique of any assumed subjective unity, as does any "thing" or object. In this way critique detaches experience from the subject/object relation as much as from subjects and objects as categories of thought. As Nietzsche puts it: "The origin of 'things' is wholly the work of that which imagines, thinks, wills, feels. The concept 'thing' itself just as much as all its qualities. Even 'the subject' is such a created entity, a 'thing' like all others: a simplification with the object of defining the force which posits, invents, thinks, as distinct from all individual positing, inventing, thinking as such" (WtP, 556). In other words, "subject" and "object" are interpretations that attempt to detach a thought from thinking as a force, and are negations. For Nietzsche the personal is only ever a symptom or expression of the impersonal will to power and must be revalued as such. It is only in such a revaluation that we will overcome our human nihilism and emerge as artist-philosophers. Henry Miller poses this problem of a transvaluative criticism precisely: "Why are we so full of restraint? Is it fear of losing ourselves? Until we do lose ourselves there can be no hope of finding ourselves. We are of the world, and to enter fully into the world we must first lose ourselves in it."[16] All objective interrogations of the form "what is . . . ?" must be revalued in answering the question "what wills?" a question whose answer in turn revalues the subjective question "what does this mean to me?" We lose ourselves in finding the answer, for the answer is neither a subject nor an object, but something existing between them, a becoming—active or reactive, an affect. Nietzsche puts it in this way:

> The question "what is that?" is an imposition of meaning from some other viewpoint. "Essence," the "essential nature," is something perspective and already presupposes a multiplicity. At the bottom of it there always lies "what is that for me?" (for us, for all that lives, etc.) A thing would be defined once all creatures had asked "what is that?" and had answered the question. [ . . . ] One may not ask: "who then interprets?" for the interpretation itself as a form of the will to power, exists (but not as a "being" but as a process, a becoming) as an affect. (WtP, 556)

Any perception of an object is always an interpretation of forces, necessarily different each time, which gives an answer to the question "what is it for me?" in a becoming-active or reactive, in an expression of the will to power in an affect, in a rise or fall of power. This means that the art of critique will be, as we shall see, necessarily physiological.

In Deleuze's Nietzschean aesthetics, will to power's affirmative or negative evaluations are expressed in the active or reactive forces of life. But these forces appear in an interpretation that lays hold of them, and constructs their differential quantity. This quantity, as quality, emerges from an in principle infinite series of differential relations that at their limit encompass the entire genetic conditions of will to power, co-extensive with life. In being interpreted each force receives a value only through the construction of the differential series that composes it. At the same time however, this construction is the expression of will to power in an evaluative perspective. Each force therefore constructs a world, the world of will to power, the world each force expresses. Will to power exists in and as this ongoing critical construction, and as affirmation it creates new and by definition active forces (this is Deleuze's interpretation of Nietzsche's eternal return), as its own becoming-active. This means, as Deleuze writes: "The conditions of a true critique and a true creation are the same: the destruction of an image of thought [or art] which presupposes itself and the genesis of the act of thinking in thought" (DR, 139/182).

Becoming-active will therefore be Nietzsche's critical definition of art, a definition as much ontological as aesthetic, and succinctly expressed by Nietzsche's famous statement: "To impose upon becoming the character of being—that is the supreme will to power" (WtP, 617).[17] Art and philosophy as critical affirmation, and embodied in the artist-philosopher, do not represent a life outside them, but affirm life as will to power, in a becoming-active, in their active affects. In the ontology of will to power there is no "being" behind "doing," and this insight will be developed by Deleuze both in terms of an inorganic vitality, and the affects that its becoming produces. With no "being" in the background there is no truth, meaning aesthetics cannot be a science of representation, because quite simply there is nothing to represent. Art without truth; it means that art is nothing but the creation of falsehood. This is one of Nietzsche's most important insights about art, which Deleuze repeats:

> The world is neither true nor real but living. And the living world is will to power, will to falsehood, which is actualised in many different powers. To actualise the will to falsehood under any quality whatever, is always to evaluate. To live is to evaluate. There is no truth of the world as it is thought, no reality of the sensible world, all is evaluation, even and above all the sensible and the real. (NP, 184/191–2)

We get the truths, values, and affects we deserve according to the way we live, the way we evaluate, and the perspectives we create. As Nietzsche writes: "All seeing is essentially perspective, and so is knowing" (GM, III, 12).

## THE PHYSIOLOGY OF THE ARTIST-PHILOSOPHER

Bodies, whether human or otherwise, are the mechanisms of critique because, Nietzsche claims, "all sense perceptions are permeated with value judgments" (WtP, 305). Sense perceptions are interpretations of forces, vision for example emerges from what he calls "the value-positing eye" (GM, I, 10). This is a Nietzschean empiricism that is inseparable from a critical art, because "art" is always an empirical question, a question of what something is for me *as will to power*. But the "I/eye" of the subject perceives the identity of things too quickly, and only sees itself through the negation of will to power. Human vision is, to steal a line from T. S. Eliot, "eyes assured of certain certainties."[18] This is the tenacious insistence of human nihilism, its self-fulfilling negations find themselves confirmed in every experience appearing under its terms.

"Only we have created the world *that concerns man*" (GS, 301), Nietzsche writes. But what exactly is this world, and how have we created it? For Nietzsche it is human rationality which determines our perceptual certainty through its power of negation, a "no" which preserves the human, as much as each human, by separating us from what we are not. "Slave ethics," Nietzsche argues, "begins by saying no to an "outside," an "other," a non-self, and that no is its creative act" (GM, I, 10).

Deleuze claims that the philosophical method of negation is the dialectic, because the dialectic understands the differential forces of will to power (difference itself) as a power of the negative. "We already sense the form in which the syllogism of the slave has been so successful in philosophy:" he writes, "*the dialectic.* The dialectic, as the ideology of *ressentiment*" (NP, 121/139). The dialectic enslaves life because it is unable to affirm the constitutive difference of will to power. Instead the dialectic represents difference as negation, assuming that the essential activity of life is its power of negation. This is nothing but the negation of Nietzschean empiricism in thought, because for Nietzsche interpretation is the affirmation of a forces constitutive difference—an action producing becoming—whereas the dialectic establishes identity only through negating differences—a reaction which cannot be creative.[19] The dialectic therefore negates will to power's constitutive difference by representing it as the negative itself. Inasmuch as dialectical negation is creative then, it is so only within the confines of a human thought that makes negation its essence and principle of existence (NP, 9/10). Both thought and art labour under this nihilistic ideology and its dialectical method in attempting to represent the truth of life, in attempting to transcend life (i.e. negate it) by giving a representation of truth. For Deleuze dialectical representation "poisons" philosophy, and as the product of the slave it is one of his most consistent targets (NP, 81/92). Nietzsche also attacks the nihilism of representation, often directly in terms of the fine arts. "The profession of almost every man, even that of the artist," he writes, "begins with hypocrisy, with an imitation from without, with a copying of what is most effective."[20]

Nietzsche claims to "possess an instinctive distrust of dialectics,"[21] and he extends his distrust to the dialectic's avatar, the artist of negation, the sick and decadent "anti-artist" as Nietzsche calls him or her. These artists, in producing the "arts of man," merely create aesthetic confirmations of their human sensibility and its metaphysical consolations. Within this loop, Nietzsche argues: "Nothing is beautiful, only man: on this piece of naivety rests all aesthetics, it is the *first* truth of aesthetics. Let us immediately add its second: nothing is ugly but degenerate man—the domain of aesthetic judgment is therewith defined" (TI, "Expeditions of an Untimely Man," 20). What is beautiful confirms man because it represents his higher Being, and what is ugly denies this higher truth. Thus the arts of man are fundamentally moral, and aesthetics is a realm of moral judgment identifying the heavenly truths—unchanging and essential—that act as transcendent standards by which art is both produced and assessed. As a result, what is most beautiful in man is that which is beyond him, the ascetic ideals by which he confirms the beauty of his negations, his own perceptions, and his own art. Once more, the stakes in aesthetics are shown by Nietzsche to be ontological, for with the anti-artist "we have made the 'real' world a world not of change and becoming, but one of Being" (WtP, 507).[22] In this way anti-artists have always functioned as "the glorifiers of the religious and philosophical errors of mankind" (HH, 220). In the critical art of the artist-philosopher however, in their affirmations of will to power, in their artistic constructions, as Deleuze simply puts it, "there is no longer any place for another world" (NP, 175/201). But to arrive in this new world—which has no other world—we will need a new sensibility adequate to will to power's active affects, and a new thought able to revalue our values. The artist-philosopher will require an entirely new physiology.

For Deleuze dialectical systems and their negation of difference (i.e. difference *as* negation) are "powerless to create new ways of thinking and feeling" (NP, 159/183). New thoughts and feelings can only emerge from affirmation, as Deleuze writes: "For the speculative element of negation, opposition or contradiction, Nietzsche substitutes the practical element of *difference,* the object of affirmation and enjoyment [*jouissance*]" (NP, 9/10). Deleuze, like Nietzsche, will turn to a critical art capable of transvaluing negation through the affirmation of difference, in order to introduce a new body and new thoughts and feelings into philosophy and art. In this way we could say Deleuze and Nietzsche, like Francis Bacon—whose phrase it is—are cerebrally pessimistic ("We deny," Nietzsche writes, "that anything can be done perfectly so long as it is done consciously."[23]), but nervously optimistic. This optimism extends to nihilism, which Nietzsche argues still has the will to power as the living pulse of its sad life. "If we say no," Nietzsche writes, "we still do what we are" (WtP, 675). In other words, will to power appears in its negation as an affirmation denied, and this at least implies the possibility of a critical transvaluation. As Nietzsche explains: "We negate and must negate because something in us wants to live and affirm—something that we perhaps do not know or see as yet.—This is said in favor of criticism" (GS, 307). In favour of the artist-philosopher whose creative interpretations change the value of the world in which we live, offering new perspectives, new worlds, or more accurately, a world which is forever becoming new. In Nietzsche thought becomes truly creative, and as such becomes a question of sensibility.

"In knowing and understanding, too," Nietzsche writes, "I feel only my will's delight in begetting and becoming" (Z, "On the Blissful Islands").

Art is in this sense the artist-philosophers *"pure contempt of man"* (A, 54). Although this sounds harsh, it's not. Man justifies himself through negation, and this is the object of the artist-philosopher's contempt. But this contempt is the destructive side of an affirmation in which man overcomes himself to become something new, the Overman. Not the negation of negation, but the affirmation of affirmation.[24] "The aim of critique," Deleuze writes, "is not the ends of man or of reason but in the end the Overman, the overcome, overtaken man. The point of critique is not justification but a different way of feeling: another sensibility"(NP, 94/198). The contempt of the artist-philosopher is not a negation but a strength, an aggression, an ability to affirm to the point of overcoming man. This will mean the reinvention of man, and—Deleuze makes the point again—*"a new way of feeling"* (NP, 163/188). The human, all too human, was only good for feeling himself, a reassuring masturbation. The artist-philosopher, the overcome man, has as Nietzsche puts it: "New ears for new music. New eyes for what is most distant. A new conscience for truths that have hitherto remained unheard" (A, preface).

This new sensibility, Nietzsche argues, requires a physiological transformation creating an inhuman body. Through the artist-philosopher's critique of man's rational nihilism, Nietzsche proudly announces, "we have dropped him back among the beasts" (A, 14). The revalued physiology of the artist-philosopher is no longer human, and has become animal. Critique thereby frees a new sensibility, an "'animal' sensibility" (WtP, 800) as Nietzsche calls it, a sensibility that isn't opposed *to* the human but is the animal sensibility *of* the human, the sensibility of a vital will to power capable of affirming what human consciousness has until this point negated. The revalued physiology of the artist-philosopher, of animal-man, is what enables him or her to affirm will to power, and create the new. As Nietzsche writes, this feeling "of animal well-being and desires constitute the aesthetic state" (WtP, 801). The artist-philosopher's animal vigour is the antidote to the poison of representation and human rationality; it overcomes anti-artistic nihilism to restore life to its animal health. Animal sensibility affirms active force in its interpretations, constructing perspectives no longer rational and conscious, but operating through, Nietzsche writes, "the perfect functioning of the regulating, *unconscious* instincts" (GM, I, 10). The animal vitality of the artist-philosopher will emerge once we have freed our sensibilities from the nihilist task of knowing, once we have become an animal capable of living the un-known, capable of enjoying it, and capable, finally, of embodying becoming as being. D. H. Lawrence knew the feeling: "You've got to lapse out before you can know what sensual reality is, lapse into unknowingness, and give up your volition. You've got to do it. You've got to learn not to be, before you can come into being."[25] The artist-philosopher-animal will therefore embody critique in physiological becomings inseparable from the production of art. Nietzsche puts it clearly: "Art reminds us of a state of animal vigor; it is on the one hand an excess and overflow of blooming physicality into the world of images and desires; on the other, an excitation of the animal functions through the images and desires of an intensified life;—an enhancement of the feeling of life, a stimulant to it" (WtP, 802).

Art and artist are, in these terms, two poles of an animal perspective that constructs itself, and continually overcomes itself, in its own affirmation, creating a feedback loop of/as will to power. As Nietzsche sings: "I drink back into myself the flames that break from me" (Z, "The Night Song"). Instinctual interpretations construct an art-work as a new singularity, a singularity that affirms (expresses) all of will to power in its differential genesis, and eternally returns all of will to power in the living becoming of its differences, in a construction of the art works intensified life. Deleuze explains art's feedback loop like this: "According to Nietzsche we have not yet understood what the life of an artist means: the activity of this life serves as a stimulant to the affirmation contained in the work of art itself, to the will to power of the artist as artist" (NP, 102/177). But we haven't understood, we haven't become active, become artists, and so from our still human perspective a transvalued and animal art appears as a "play of mirrors"[26] between art and artist, a paradoxical and irrational mystery. Indeed we cannot "understand" it, and the inseparability of an art of critique from the art-work it produces, an inseparability of an aesthetics and an ontology of will to power, will produce an inhuman state of animal health which Nietzsche calls intoxication: "the effect of works of art is to *excite the state which creates art*—intoxication" (WtP, 821). To make art we must get out of it, a Nietzschean practice many artists have taken literally. But only if such intoxication gives birth to the animal, the inhuman, *in the work,* does it stand up, and indeed, as Deleuze and Guattari often stress, does it have the sobriety to do so.[27]

Art and artist, producer and product, are inadequate terms to describe the new physiology required to create art. We need a new concept in which artist and art-work can be understood as the becoming of an intoxicated animal body. This concept arrives in Nietzsche's figure of Dionysus.[28] Dionysus is neither subject nor object, because Dionysus cannot tolerate any personal identities based on human negation. Dionysus is the animal-artist in the middle of things, as the affirmation that creates their simultaneous immanence and singularity. Dionysus, the artist, Nietzsche writes, "stands in the midst of the universe with a joyful and trusting fatalism, in the *faith* that only what is separate and individual may be rejected, that in the totality everything is redeemed and affirmed— *he no longer denies. . . . .*" (TI, "Expeditions of an Untimely Man," 49). In no longer denying, in affirming the will to power in a cosmic construction, Dionysus creates a new totality. Dionysus no longer denies, he creates. In Dionysus the will to power lives as becoming, and in the Dionysian art-work this creative power is unleashed. This is the way we are able to understand the art-work as expression, that is, as the constructive force of a creative will to power, as a Dionysian art. Under these conditions, Nietzsche notes: "The work of art appears without an artist, e.g., as body, as organization (Prussian officer corps, Jesuit order). To what extent the artist is only a preliminary stage. The world as work of art that gives birth to itself" (WtP, 796). The art-work is an individuation of the world, an interpretation constructing a singularity in which the will to power is expressed as an evaluation that constructs itself. With the destruction, or transvaluation of the ontology and aesthetics of a nihilist anti-art, the Dionysian artist-philosopher introduces art as the material process of life, an expressive vitalism expressed in art, as the affirmative will to power itself. This is finally the artist's answer to the question "what is it for me?" As Deleuze puts it: "Dionysus, the will to power, is the one that answers it each time it is put" (NP, 77/88).

In affirmative critique the artist-philosopher becomes animal, because his or her actions are physiologically rather than psychologically determined. The artist and art-work are nothing but affects, and as such embody the will to power immediately, expressing it without mediation. "One takes," Nietzsche writes, "one does not ask who gives; a thought flashes up like lightening, with necessity, unalteringly formed—I have never had any choice" (EH, "Thus Spoke Zarathustra," 6). How could artists have a choice when their affects are determined by the vital feedback mechanism of art, in an interpretation expressing will to power giving birth to itself? We construct the world we deserve. . . . The artist-philosopher is in this sense, and as Nietzsche writes, an "involuntary co-ordination" of will to power, "a kind of autonomism of the whole muscular system impelled by strong stimuli from within" (WtP, 811). Impelled by an affirmative will to power the artist affirms, and this creates art. The physiology of the artist expresses the necessity and beauty of life in what they create, and so what they create is necessary and beautiful. "I want to learn more and more to see as beautiful what is necessary in things," Nietzsche writes, "then I shall be one of those who make things beautiful. *Amor fati* let that be my love henceforth" (GS, 276). Here is a new canon for beauty, and a new aesthetic for art. Art's beauty is no longer judged by external standards or formal criteria, or by transcendental faculties through which they would operate. Art is necessary, it is the creation necessary for life, and in seeing this necessity, in feeling it, the artist-philosopher is drawn into its affirmative loop, to become with it, and to construct will to power once more, embraced in its eternal return. "*The world is perfect,*" this for Nietzsche is "the instinct of the man who says yes to life" (A, 57).

We can contrast the necessity of the work of art formed in and by critique with the work of the art critic, another nihilist anti-artist. Jacques Derrida describes the nihilism of the art critic, who, "face to face with art, never abandons his positions in front of art, who never actually ventures to lay his hands on it, who, even though he at times fancies himself an artist producing works, is content merely to gossip about art."[29] We could imagine Deleuze agreeing on this point. Practicing the art of critique, for Deleuze and for Nietzsche—as artist-philosophers—is to embody will to power *as* will to power. Will to power is art and art work, indiscernibly the affirmation which creates a singular work and the work which expresses all of will to power in its becoming, in its evaluative perspective. There are many artist-philosophers and many art-works, but in the necessity of their construction, each time anew, they express will to power *again* as the eternal return of its differential infinity. The artist-philosopher is the singular animal life that affirms will to power, and through which will to power creates art—beyond good and evil and true and false. Art is not the true, because, as we have seen, there is no truth. Similarly, art represents nothing because there is nothing to represent. Art becomes, and as a result it needs a new name, a name Deleuze gives it—the simulacrum.

## SIMULACRA

Deleuze suggests the concept of the "simulacrum" as a new image of art, one that meets the ontological, aesthetic and ethical requirements of the artistic methodology of affirmative critique. Critique transforms the representational forms of nihilism into the affirmative and animal bodies of will to power, and these bodies are what Deleuze simulacrum.

Plato originally suggested the concept of the simulacrum as the bottom rung of his metaphysical ladder. On top were "Ideas," pure immaterial essences as the truth of things, and absolutely distinct from the images that represented them. These images, or things, existed in the material world and were the mere copies of the essences that determined them. Finally, lying beneath things were the degraded simulacra produced by the arts, nothing but dangerous copies of copies that could cause us, through the feelings they evoked, to treat them as real and so ignore the Ideas. In the Idea Plato created the definitive structure of metaphysical transcendence and founded, Deleuze claims "the entire domain that philosophy will later recognise as its own: the domain of representation" (LS, 259/298). In this domain an "appearance" only exists in relation to the ideal "beyond" it represents and the philosopher will only arrive at truth by transcending this world to arrive at its immaterial essence. The critical powers of Plato's philosopher are therefore spent judging this world according to a truth found in an ideal beyond. In this sense, Deleuze writes, Plato's Idea's were, "a moral vision of the world" (DR, 127/166). This metaphysical structure was adopted by Christianity, which made full use of its moral implications. In Christianity as in Plato, our world represents a fall, and contains the danger of illegitimate and evil images distracting us from a divine truth. In Christianity Deleuze argues, man is made in God's image, but through the fall our good image turns to bad, and our sin does nothing but affirm material life. In sin then: "We have become simulacra" (LS, 257/297).[30] The demonic simulacrum is inferior to the copy because it has no true model, its model being found in an already impure matter. Plato's metaphysics as much as Christianity's condemn the body in privileging the transcendent, and it is no surprise that Nietzsche's animal artist announces the death of God as the necessary condition for a living body. Atheism and art, as we shall see, are continually co-implicated in Deleuze's thought. Plato was in fact one of Nietzsche's most cherished targets, he was, Nietzsche writes, "the greatest enemy of art Europe has thus far produced. [ . . . ] the deliberate transcendentalist and detractor of life" (GM, III, 25). Unsurprisingly Plato is also Deleuze's enemy, and escaping Plato's system will be a consistent feature of the philosophical lineage Deleuze creates: "In truth," he writes, "only the philosophies of pure immanence escape Platonism—from the Stoics to Spinoza or Nietzsche" (ECC, 137/171).[31]

For Deleuze, the simulacrum is the affirmation of a power that escapes the Idea, and embodies Nietzsche's explicit attempt to reverse Platonism's philosophy of representation.[32] "The simulacrum is not a degraded copy," Deleuze writes, "It harbors a positive power which denies *the original and the copy, the model and the reproduction*" (LS, 262/302). Against Plato, and with Nietzsche, the simulacrum is for Deleuze the image of a univocal will to power, an expression of life beyond, not only good and evil, but also beyond the "beyond" of Christo-Platonism. In this sense, "the copy is an image endowed with resemblance, the simulacrum is an image without resemblance" (LS, 257/297). The simulacrum is Deleuze's response to Nietzsche's explicit aim of living in semblance, it expresses life as semblance undetermined by any idea of truth. The results of this overturning of Platonism are dramatic, for with the disappearance of essence appearances as representations also disappear.[33] As Nietzsche puts it, *"with the real world we have also abolished the apparent world"*

(TI, "How the 'Real World' at last Became a Myth"). Without essence as its transcendent determination, the simulacrum is free to continually become something else. As such the simulacrum is art, because it is the appearance of becoming (will to power) itself. As this power of the false, Nietzsche writes, "art is *worth more* than truth" (WtP, 835, iv).

The simulacra are critical, first, in being destructive, in abolishing the true world of Ideas along with their appearance as representations. Simulacra are non-representative, because there's nothing beyond this world of representation. Second, the simulacrum as "a Dionysian machine" (LS, 263/303) is a creative surface of interpretation that affirms will to power in escaping the transcendence of truth. Here art gains its active onto-aesthetic dimension. As Pierre Klossowski puts it, Nietzsche proposes "a positive notion of the false, which, as the basis of artistic creation, is now *extended to every problem raised by existence.*"[34] The art of simulacra now begins to take on a political dimension as the ethical lie (which shouldn't be confused with usual political practice). This is the art of politics in the most creative sense, where lying—as art—is the ethical practice of affirmation, the affirmation of life.[35] Art is an affirmative lie for Nietzsche, a creative and radical politics, "whenever man rejoices [i.e., affirms], he is always the same in his rejoicing: he rejoices as an artist, he enjoys himself as power, he enjoys the lie as his form of power" (WtP, 853).[36]

The art of appearances, the creation of simulacra, nevertheless requires a technique. This technique will be critical, and will be, Deleuze argues once more following Nietzsche, a question of selection. "For the artist appearance no longer means the negation of the real in this world but this kind of selection, correction, redoubling and affirmation." The artist-philosopher selects (interprets) what is active in the world, thereby affirming will to power, and actively overcoming nihilist art and thought. Selection is therefore the artistic construction of new truths as the creative expression of life. Deleuze writes: "Then truth perhaps takes on a new sense. Truth is appearance. Truth means bringing of power into effect, raising to the highest power. In Nietzsche, 'we the artists' = 'we the seekers after knowledge or truth' = 'we the inventors of new possibilities of life'" (NP, 103/117). Appearance as construction (interpretation) and expression (evaluation) now exist on a single plane of immanence—will to power—which is both existence and essence, a univocal formula Spinoza also uses and which we will come back to in the next chapter. Nietzsche's own formulation is similar: "What is 'appearance' for me now?" he asks, "Certainly not the opposite of some essence. What could I say about any essence except to name the attributes of its appearance!" (GS, 54). To name the attributes of appearance means to interpret, to select and affirm active forces, and so to construct an affirmative expression of and as will to power. Expression of the will to power in appearance is therefore inseparable from its construction as appearance. "The joy in shaping and reshaping—a primeval joy!" Nietzsche cries, "We can only comprehend a world that we ourselves have made" (WtP, 495). Not a world made in our image, or in God's, but a world without image and without truth, except as pure appearance. The simulacrum is the appearance of this world's essence, but this essence only exists as its appearance in an art-work. This means the simulacrum cannot exist in a dimension "beyond" the human, but is the mechanism by which the human, all too human, world is overcome in being created anew.

The simulacral art-work is a repetition of constitutive differences (forces) in an individuated series, a series that is constantly becoming-other as it continues to affirm (repeat) its difference from itself. "Simulacra," Deleuze explains, "are those systems in which different relates to different *by means* of difference itself. What is essential is that we find in these systems no *prior identity*, no *internal resemblance*. It is all a matter of difference in the series, and of difference in the communication between series" (DR, 299/383). Each series is constituted through, and includes all the others, the simulacral art-work being the simultaneous unity and irreducible multiplicity of a new point of view on/of the world. An art-work therefore, "is" nothing, because it is, under the impetus of evaluative affirmation, a simulacrum always "becoming" something else. But it is not "becoming" in a simple sense, as if this was a simple statement of the type "everything changes." Rather the art-work as simulacrum exists only when "everything *is* change." At this, the ontological affirmation operating in and through the transvaluative power of critique: "Everything has become simulacrum" (DR, 69/95).

The ontological transvaluation of aesthetics marks another important Deleuzian break, this time within the tradition of aesthetics as it is more usually understood. Plato's metaphysics of representation defined the transcendental conditions for all possible experiences, and Kant subsequently maintained these conditions while dividing aesthetics into two realms, one in which the sensible in general appears according to categories of possible experience (in his *Critique of Pure Reason*), and another in which the beautiful was defined according to the conditions of real, or actual, experience (in the *Critique of Judgement*) (DR, 68/94). In this way aesthetics is divided on the one hand into a theory of sensation describing the objective conditions of experience, and on the other as a theory of the beautiful defining the subjective conditions of experience. With the simulacrum however, we can only have a real experience undetermined by any subjective or objective conditions. There is no "outside" determining experience (whether this is imagined to be a transcendent essence, as with Plato, or an immanent transcendental faculty, as with Kant), because the simulacrum expresses

only its own immanent conditions, as the repetition of its constitutive difference in an ongoing series or becoming (Deleuze also calls this a "sign"). The conditions of the sign's real experience (will to power) are therefore the same as the
sign's real experience (will to power). As Deleuze puts it, the will to power "is an
essentially *plastic* principle that is no wider than what it conditions, that changes
itself with the conditioned and determines itself in each case along with what it
determines" (NP, 50/57). The Kantian division of aesthetics is therefore overcome by Nietzsche, because will to power as the being of the sensible, as the eternal return of difference in the simulacrum, only exists in and as the appearance
of the work of art (DR, 68/94).[37] The simulacrum appears as a singularity without identity, without subject or object, as the sensation of/as repetition, of/as the
eternal return of difference, as it overcomes itself. Once more any distinction of
the artist and art work, as separate identities, is impossible. As Deleuze puts it:
"To every perspective or point of view there must correspond an autonomous
work with its own self-sufficient sense" (DR, 69/94). The art-work is an action,
an affirmation in which artist and work are entirely immanent in the sensation,
and that appears in the revalued physiology—no longer defined subjectively or
objectively—adequate to this "affect."

## THE SIMULACRUM AS ETERNAL RETURN

Critical art therefore destroys as it creates; on the one hand its interpretations
overcome the world of man, and on the other it expresses the cosmic dimension
of will to power constructing itself. Art begins as the transvaluation of representation, as the overcoming of "anti-art" and its "sad" repetitions, all the banal and
stereotypical re-productions of habit and cliché. Art once more emerges here in
its ethical modality, because its action, its affirmation, produces simulacral signs
that construct the world. Deleuze puts it in his own anti-Platonic terms:
"Things are simulacra themselves, simulacra are the superior forms, and the difficulty facing everything is to become its own simulacrum, to attain the status
of a sign in the coherence of eternal return" (DR, 67/93). In Nietzsche then, aesthetics attains its properly political and ethical dimension, a dimension equally
ontological, where art must overcome man in creating a simulacrum, to eternally return us to what we already are—the becoming of will to power.

The artist-philosopher is what we could call will to power's "operative,"
he or she is the one capable of giving an interpretation that constructs simulacra as the affirmative evaluation of will to power itself. In simulacra in other
words, the conditions of a real experience (the "seminal" constitutive differences of will to power) are entirely immanent to that experience, and fulfil
the Deleuzeo-Nietzschean conditions of onto-aesthetics: "It is a matter of

showing," Deleuze argues of the one who wills, "that he could not say, think or feel this particular thing if he did not have a particular will, particular forces, a particular way of being" (NP, 78/88). This means that the simulacrum as particular thing, as interpretation, is so only on condition that it expresses a particular will, an evaluation, as the genetic differential relation of forces constituting the becoming of its world. "Each difference passes through all of the others," Deleuze writes, "it must 'will' itself or find itself through all the others" (DR, 57/80). As a result, the simulacrum expresses its genetic differential conditions through affirming them, but affirmation necessarily unleashes an overcoming, an on-going becoming inseparable from the eternal return and that constructs the world anew. This is the "highpoint of the meditation" for Nietzsche: "That everything recurs is the closest approximation of a world of becoming to a world of being" (WtP, 617).[38]

The simulacrum gives a perspective of will to power, but this perspective doesn't "represent" will to power, as in a snapshot, it is the sensation of the becoming—the eternal return—of will to power. The simulacrum is the series produced through the repetition of its own constitutive differences, as these extend to encompass the world. This means, as Deleuze argues: "Every thing, animal or being assumes the status of the simulacrum; so that the thinker of eternal return [ . . . ] can rightly say that he is himself burdened with the superior form of everything that is" (DR, 67/92). The simulacrum is the continual creation of the world, the becoming of a world constructed into mobile series, differentiating and differentiated. In this sense, "the eternal return concerns only simulacra" (DR, 126/165). In the simulacrum, Nietzschean transvaluation is not achieved simply by changing something's value, but by achieving a new, affirmative and artistic way of evaluating. The simulacrum is not a new truth, because it transvalues "truth" as the element from which the value of value derives, replacing it with a power of the false, a vital power inseparable from an artistic life. This finally is the transvaluation of the creative artist, who is no longer content to simply create things or to express themselves, but constructs a world of simulacra (i.e. interprets the world) through an evaluation that eternally returns the world, as the affirmative and creative will. For Nietzsche, as for Deleuze, "only the Dionysian artist takes the power of the false to the point where it is realised, not in form, but in transformation" (ECC, 105/133). Finally, the immanence of expression and construction in the artistic affirmation of the will to power means, as Deleuze puts it: "Between the eternal return and the simulacrum, there is such a profound link that the one cannot be understood except through the other" (LS, 264/305).

For Deleuze it is to the credit of modern art, before philosophy, to have rejected representation in favour of producing simulacra. All that we have just seen, therefore, defines the Nietzschean artist-philosopher as the practitioner of a truly modern art. Deleuze argues that the creation of divergent series, as divergent and in a single work, "is, without doubt, the essential characteristic of the modern work of art" (LS, 260/300). Modern art is the affirmation of a creative becoming, creating divergent series in which the art-work is continually becoming-other. "Art does not imitate," Deleuze argues, "above all because it repeats; it repeats all the repetitions, by virtue of an internal power (an imitation is a copy, but art is simulation, it reverses copies into simulacra)" (DR, 293/375). In this sense, Deleuze believes, modern art shows the way to philosophy, for "when the modern work of art develops its permutating series and its circular structures, it indicates to philosophy a path leading to the abandonment of representation" (DR, 68–9/94). Modernism renounces art's ancient metaphysics of true and false, of original and copy, and announces its embrace of the repetition of difference in the eternal return.

Although Deleuze's examples in *Difference and Repetition* are Mallarmé's *Book* and James Joyce's *Finnegans Wake,* Nietzsche is also privileged in the genesis of the "modern image of thought" as the one who "succeeded in making us understand, thought is creation, not will to truth" (WP, 54/55). But Nietzsche makes a further claim to the invention of a truly modern art in being one of the few philosophers to have managed to "slip in" to the realm of art. Zarathustra, Deleuze and Guattari argue, is not only a "conceptual persona" but an "aesthetic figure," a creator of sensations, and in the serial wanderings of Nietzsche's eponymous hero affects as well as concepts are produced (WP, 217/205). Nietzsche's concepts of will to power and eternal return are therefore already at work in aesthetics' realm of experience, and it is in modern art's complication of its intense "divergent series" that the Nietzschean physiology of the artist-philosopher is fulfilled, and Zaruthustra dances. The repetition of difference as the compositional principle of modern art produces, Deleuze claims, an "internal resonance," a "forced movement which goes beyond the series itself" (LS, 260–1/300–1). This "forced movement" is the affect or "affective charge" (LS, 261/301), a sensation of becoming (i.e. of a repetition) coextensive with the differential life of will to power. This affective charge is intoxicating, and overcomes the object experienced as much as the subject experiencing it. The identity of the object is dissolved in the divergent series constituting the affect (art-work as an expression and not an object), and the identity of the subject is dissolved in the multiplicity of differences the affect at once infolds and unfolds (artist as a force under construction and not a subject). But nothing is lost, Deleuze argues, because each series exists only in the return of all the others, and modern art appears only at this point of transvaluation, when everything has become a simulacrum

(DR, 69/95). Modernism is therefore defined by the dismemberment of every thing which separates art from the life of will to power, every thing which prevents its eternal return. What would prevent the eternal return, according to Deleuze, is to only understand art in terms of the artist (pure construction), or only in terms of the conditions under which the art work appears (pure expression).[39] The eternal return "repudiates these and expels them," Deleuze writes, "with all its centrifugal force. It constitutes the autonomy of the product, the independence of the work" (DR, 90/122). Deleuze was obviously not the first to define the modernist art work as autonomous, but unlike the classical modernism of Clement Greenberg for example, this autonomy will not be defined by a formal purity, but by its formal vitality.

## THE ART-WORK AS SIMULACRA

Given this profound link between the simulacra and eternal return, how should we approach art works as they normally appear? This is a problem of immediate urgency, not just to gain an understanding of our own "real experience," but also to bring Nietzsche's onto-aesthetics into affect within the politics of the everyday. This is entirely necessary as both Deleuze and Nietzsche condemn any aesthetic philosophy separating art from life.[40] Indeed, as Deleuze dramatically puts it, "there is no other aesthetic problem than that of the insertion of art into everyday life" (DR, 293/375). Deleuze immediately proposes an example: "Warhol's remarkable 'serial' series" (DR, 294/375). Given the publication date of *Difference and Repetition* (1968) Deleuze's example must refer to the so-called "screen-print" paintings Warhol begins in 1962 and developed over the next five years in what is known as the "Death and Disaster" paintings.[41] We have already seen Deleuze suggest that modern art's use of repetition in composing series is simulacral, but here he elaborates this suggestion in terms of his concrete example of Pop. "Even the most mechanical, the most banal, the most habitual and the most stereotyped repetition finds a place in works of art," he writes, "it is always displaced in relation to other repetitions, and it is subject to the condition that a difference may be extracted from it for these other repetitions" (DR, 293/375). This passage clearly affirms Warhol's use of commercial reproduction techniques and their media aesthetic as an insertion of art into life, which is not in itself such a controversial claim about Pop art. More controversial however, is Deleuze's suggestion that Warhol's use of repetition does not repeat (represent) a model, but produces a real and simulacral experience coextensive with the creative repetitions of life.[42] This suggestion is a good example of Deleuze's critical method, and repays exploration. Deleuze is certainly not alone in claiming that Warhol reinserts art into life by using the aesthetics of consumerism.

But Deleuze provides an ontological interpretation of this "insertion" by affirming it as the creation of simulacra, the production of "a canvas whose very operation reverses the relationship of model and copy, and which means that there is no longer a copy, *nor is there a model.* To push the copy, the copy of the copy, to the point at which it reverses itself and produces the model: Pop art."[43]

Deleuze reads Pop art, and specifically Warhol's work, as the emergence of mechanical repetition immanent to modern processes of mechanical reproduction, and hence as an art form 'inserted' into everyday life. It is obvious, looking at Warhol's *Triple Elvis* (1963, Virginia Museum of Fine Arts) for example, that he transforms a mechanical reproduction through its repetition.[44] This transformation is achieved through a mechanical technique (the screen print) which retains the in principle infinity of its "original," which it "copies," and therefore side-steps any appeal to the mythology of the artist's subjectivity as the guarantor of artistic value.[45] Indeed, Warhol's whole mediatized personality, even if ironic, sought to engage and deconstruct such mythologies—in this he was utterly "modern." Warhol's repetition of the process of mechanical reproduction is not "critical" in any subjective sense, and is instead an affirmation that revalues painting itself. Painting is no longer "expressive," but—in a Warholian sense—repetitive. As he said: "The reason I am painting this way is that I want to be a machine."[46] Warhol's painting process, as a mechanical reproduction, takes in the case of the *Elvis* paintings an "original" (a postcard of Elvis as he appeared in the film *Flaming Star*), which is itself a "copy" (of a studio promotional photo, it is not an image originally in the film). Each painting is therefore a copy of a copy, and affirmed in its very mode of appearing as such, it is a simulacrum, and is elaborated in an in-principle open (the principle of mechanical reproduction) series.[47]

The Warhol-machine understood perfectly that the work of art had lost its aura as original in the age of mechanical reproduction. But he refused to mourn this loss, and instead embraced the living power of repetition it introduces. He did so by using reproduction technology to produce "original" art works that had, through this process, and their inevitable appearance in series, attained an entirely modern "aura," that of the simulacrum. But this still must be explained, as obviously Deleuze is interested in Warhol's images, and not just any old photo of Elvis. Warhol succeeds in producing simulacrum by foregrounding the way an image's repetition introduces necessary differences. Each work in the series differs from the others, but this difference is not a consistent object that structures the work (as it would be in Frank Stella's paintings or Donald Judd's work, or in much conceptual art, such as Sol Le Witt's sculptures, for example), but is the genetic element immanent to their production, the differing difference which does not stay the same (it is not a "grammar"), and in

**Figure 1** Andy Warhol, *Triple Elvis,* 1963, Virginia Museum of Fine Arts. © 2004 Andy Warhol Foundation for the Visual Arts / Artists Rights Society (ARS), New York

fact rejects the same from the process of serial repetition. The first things we notice are the differences. Warhol's series are in this way a repetition, or eternal return, of what is already different from itself. Elvis as simulacrum. Elvis as object has no identity in Warhol's paintings, and exists only as the always differing repetition of himself as "sign." The eternal return is in this way affirmed in the middle of the everyday process of consumption, a point we will pick up again later.

The *Elvis* paintings, like all Warhol's series of the time, dissolve their "subject" and themselves as "objects" in being emptied of any extra dimension outside that of their own production. What appears on this surface of evaporation is their own genetic and vital force, they affirm the will to power as it continually overcomes itself. As their serial production has no beginning (no "original") nor an end (it is in principle open) it is composed only of a self-differing repetition (the technique does not allow homogeneity between paintings) as both subject and object of its multiple affects. This is why Deleuze emphasizes the serial nature of Warhol's work, because it is in the series that the repetition of difference becomes visible, even, or perhaps especially when this seriality is seen in a single work (*Elvis Eight Times* or *Elvis (Eleven Times)* for example).

Warhol is not therefore, a proto-post-modernist, as some would have it.[48] His series do not multiply perspectives in order to deny any possibility of presence, but instead foreground presence as the differential process appearing as the real experience of mechanical reproduction itself. Painting for Warhol is not a play of signifiers forever deferring presence, but the evaporation of the signifier in the presence of the self-differing sign, a perspectival art work adequate to the serial processes of the everyday. This is Warhol's dramatic (and of course utterly banal, Warhol's genius was to be able to combine these elements so effectively) revaluation, from signifier to simulacrum, and from representation to repetition. Just another Elvis comeback. As such Warhol's series are the perfect elaboration of Deleuze's theory of modern art:

> each composing repetition must be distorted, diverted, and torn from its centre. Each point of view must itself be the object, or the object must belong to the point of view. The object must therefore be *in no way* identical, but torn asunder in a difference in which the identity of the object as seen by a seeing subject vanishes. Difference must become the element, the ultimate unity; it must therefore refer to other differences which never identify it but rather differentiate it. [ . . . ] Divergence and decentring must be affirmed in the series itself. Every object, every thing must see its own identity swallowed up in difference, each being no more than a difference between differences. Difference must show itself to be *differing*. (DR, 56/79)

Pop art produces a Nietzschean perspectival critique in which the eternal return as repetition of difference (i.e. as simulacral art-work) appears in the midst of the modern everyday.

Warhol inserts the simulacrum into everyday life by using a commercial production technique and aesthetic to make images of the people and events already being infinitely reproduced in the media. In using already recognizable images Pop art was, as Warhol said, "for everyone." But this availability nevertheless carried with it a transformative charge, for it made visible the way mechanical processes extended from "form" to "content" in popular culture, which effectively produced an image with nothing behind it—a pure surface.[49] "Once you 'got' Pop," he said, "you could never see a sign the same way again. And once you thought Pop you could never see America the same way again."[50] This is Deleuze's point, that the transformation in our perspective achieved by Pop art operates at once on the level of the ontology of the sign (as surface), and within the commercial economy of that sign, within, in other words, everyday life. Warhol succeeded in bringing these levels together to show how life was nothing more (but also nothing less) than the creation of difference through mechanical repetitions. Warhol thereby affirms the eternal return of will to power in life, as *our* life.

Warhol succeeded in transforming mechanical reproduction into mechanical repetition, by affirming the former to the point where the distinction of model and copy are lost in productive difference. In this way Pop art exemplifies Nietzsche's own artistic strategy, "we want to be poets of our life—first of all in the smallest, most everyday matters" (GS, 299). Perhaps, given Warhol's use of pop culture technologies and subject matter we could say he was the poet of his life in the *smallest, most everyday* manner. Warhol is the artist of the little difference, but his affirmation of mechanical repetitions nevertheless produced a new relation between art and the world. Warhol's *Death and Destruction* series produced simulacrum, and in these simulacrum the destruction of man is necessarily connected to the creation of this vital life of the everyday. Deleuze makes this link explicitly:

> The more our daily life appears standardised, stereotyped and subject to an accelerated reproduction of objects of consumption, the more art must be injected into it in order to extract from it that little difference which plays simultaneously between other levels of repetition, and even in order to make the two extremes resonate—namely the habitual series of consumption, and the instinctual series of destruction and death. (DR, 293/375)

From the sublime to the ridiculous: *Marilyn Munroe* to *Tuna Fish Disaster*.

The relation of repetition to death in Warhol's work can be understood in terms of Deleuze's discussion of Freud in *Difference and Repetition*. There Deleuze reinterprets Freud's grounding of symptomatic repetition in the death drive. Deleuze argues that this drive is not a return to a pure inanimate matter, as most interpretations of Freud would have it, but is instead the genetic principle of repetition which operates 'beneath' its symptomatic representation and which this representation represses. As such, death is the realm of instinctual drives—the Freudian term for the 'seminal qualitative elements' of the will to power. These drives can only be lived by being repressed, because they are by nature a-subjective. But this repression is their repetition in disguise, and they have no reality other than becoming disguised. The death instinct is then, the return of the repressed as disguised, and as what disguises, making death (*qua* the unlivable) the genetic principle of repetition itself. As Deleuze puts it:

> Repetition is truly that which disguises itself in constituting itself, that which constitutes itself only by disguising itself. It is not underneath the masks, but is formed from one mask to another, as from one distinctive point to another, from one privileged instant to another, with and within the variations. The masks do not hide anything except other masks. (DR, 17/28)

This last sentence would seem an appropriate description of Warhol's celebrity series, but rather than their repetition of masks being a critique of either the morbidity or the entropy of popular culture as some have argued,[51] the repetition of masks is the living reality of the genetic power, *qua* death.[52] The mask as simulacrum does not disguise a reality behind it; rather, it is the only possible repetition, the only possible lived reality, of genetic difference. Warhol's "Death and Disaster" series affirm this in foregrounding the mask as a repetition of difference (eternal return) inseparable from death.

It is interesting to speculate at this point about the disappearance of the term "simulacrum" from Deleuze's work after *Difference and Repetition*. Could we link this disappearance to Deleuze and Deleuze and Guattari's move towards articulating art's modernity through the question of color? This hypothesis is strengthened by the fact that Deleuze makes no further reference to Warhol, apart from the brief discussion of his films in *Cinema 2*.[53] Indeed, after *Difference and Repetition* and coinciding with his collaboration with Guattari, Deleuze moves away from many of the terms and formulations of *Difference and Repetition* he had connected to Pop art. For example, in *Difference and Repetition* Deleuze emphasizes the role of disguise in any appearance of the repetition of difference, which draws a line between it and its instantiation and radicalises its appearance as death.[54] This is one way Deleuze tends to elaborate difference as being cancelled in its extensive representations.[55] This means genetic forces tend to be repeated in forms (masks) which dissipate their becoming, and only very few exemplary art works are able to reveal the vitality of masks themselves, in simulacra. While this argument seems to fit with Warhol's "Death and Disaster" series, it also tends to locate genetic will to power in an otherworldly sphere in relation to our own experience (i.e. as death). It is this aspect of *Difference and*

*Repetition* that Deleuze moves away from after meeting Guattari, who introduces a less disguised/disguising value to onto-genesis.[56] I have also tended to avoid this interpretation in my reading of the simulacrum, in line with Deleuze's later work. In the realm of art this shift introduces the centrality of color for Deleuze and Deleuze and Guattari as the locus of a sensation that is understood as a living embodiment of difference.[57] We will be turning to this philosophy of color in later chapters, but here it is worth noting how this assemblage of terms Deleuze uses to articulate Pop art—masks, repetition, eternal return, series, simulacra and death—along with Pop art itself, all fade from his work. Many of them, however, remain important thematics for Deleuze (the centrality of Nietzsche and the powers of the false in *Cinema 2* for example), but these thematics are rethought and so require a new vocabulary.

Nevertheless, it is also possible to follow another trajectory through the Nietzschean assemblage of Pop art that emphasizes its critical, and therefore transformative, possibilities. To do this we must return to Deleuze's reference to "different levels of repetition" (DR, 293/375) which is in fact a reference to his theory of the three syntheses of time. The first, habit, operates the material repetitions necessary for the functioning of organic processes, and fixes life in a pure present that passes. The second, memory, creates a past which the present becomes, and through this repetition institutes the realm of consciousness and thought. The third, the eternal return, is the time of the future, where repetition produces "complete novelty" (DR, 90/122). In the third synthesis time is the repetition of what is to come, dissolving subject and object in a pure difference that refuses any identity and is "precisely" the death instinct (DR, 111/147). As we have seen, Deleuze's equation of the simulacrum and eternal return implies a radical transformation inseparable from death, and Warhol's death and disaster paintings seem the perfect expression of this conjunction. But death is not a pure outside; it is what disguises as it is disguised. The critical question for art would therefore be how to produce the third synthesis of time as it appears (i.e. as it disguises itself) in the other two, immanent to the banalities of material and subjective life. Deleuze argues the third synthesis must affirm the other two, but in doing so it operates its law of eternal return, beyond its living cancellation, as the freeing of difference in the genetic repetition of a living future. This will finally be where the simulacrum, the eternal return and repetition find their paradoxical politics—in the death necessary for life. This is the "critical and revolutionary power" of art, Deleuze argues, and it is exemplified in Warhol's paintings of Elvis. These paintings embody the resonance between the everyday habits of consumption and the eternal return of mechanical repetition produced by the simulacrum. This resonance is what *may* "lead us from the sad repetitions of habit to the profound repetitions of memory, and then to the ultimate repetitions of death in which our freedom is played out" (DR, 293/375). This then, would be Deleuze's affirmation of Warhol's *Death and Destruction* series, they are nothing less than an overcoming of human sadness, an overcoming of our memorial sentiment, in a work of art that eternally returns the inhuman vitality of will to power, that eternally repeats its difference in a simulacrum inseparable from our own death. And this indiscernibility, indiscernible that is from *Life,* is finally the very freedom of art.

Despite this (only seemingly) morbid end for the Nietzschean artist-philosopher in the simulacrum's eternal return of death, and despite Deleuze abandoning its vocabulary, much of what we have seen him develop here remains the focus of our ongoing exploration of an onto-aesthetics. Specifically the univocity of will to power as both critical and genetic principle, and its construction and expression in the art-work, will continue to be a focus of our discussion. Similarly, the destruction of representation will remain the "eternal truth of painting"[58] throughout Deleuze and Deleuze and Guattari's work. Affirmation as the necessary "motor" of a vital repetition of difference will also be a feature of Deleuze's onto-aesthetics we will continually come back to. Nevertheless, much of the Nietzschean assemblage does drop out of Deleuze's account, and is replaced by a much stronger emphasis on the philosophy of Spinoza, to which we will now turn.

# Chapter Two
# Spinoza: Mystical Atheism and the Art of Beatitude

The more we understand singular things, the more we understand God.
—Spinoza, *The Ethics.*[1]

I am God most of the time.
—Félix Guattari.[2]

## INTRODUCTION

"There is," Deleuze writes, "a philosophy of 'life' in Spinoza; it consists precisely in denouncing everything that separates us from life" (SPP, 26/39). Already the tone has changed from the death and disaster of Warhol's simulacrums. Spinoza's philosophy of life understands the individual as an expression of God, a God Deleuze describes in an old mystical formulation as, "a circle whose centre is everywhere and circumference nowhere" (EPS, 176/160). Again, we seem far from Nietzsche's overcoming of man through the death of God. But perhaps not, for in Deleuze's reading of Spinoza God exists only as the continual transformations and creations of the actual world. The world is expressive, and God exists only in being expressed in life. This means, as Deleuze writes, "expression is not simply manifestation, but is also the constitution of God himself. Life, that is expressivity, is carried into the absolute" (EPS, 80–1/70). Once more, art understood as expression will be inseparable from a process of construction, and this very indiscernibility will be the principle of a creative life. Of course with Spinoza the terminology will change, but nevertheless the univocity of being, as what is both expressed and constructed in becoming, will be the common ontological insight Deleuze draws from both Nietzsche and Spinoza. For Spinoza God is immanent and univocal, meaning its essence is its existence and, to make the obvious connection to the previous chapter, God's being is becoming.

Expressionism is Deleuze's term for the univocity of becoming, a becoming of life inseparable from the being of Spinoza's univocal and immanent God.

We saw in the previous chapter how Nietzsche's concept of art attacks artists who produce nihilistic cultural expressions. These, he argued, must be gone beyond in the critical process by which art overcomes its rational and re-active forms, and truly begins to live. Art, as the process of construction express-ing will to power, defines a way of living, and so Nietzsche's aesthetics are equally an ethics. In Spinoza we will find the definitive formulation of this eth-ical-aesthetics, even though he does not consider traditional aesthetic questions, nor discuss "art" in any specific sense. Consequently Spinoza does not set his ethics against art as a cultural product and practice in the way Nietzsche does, nor does he privilege certain aesthetic practices as "ethical." Indeed, if in the first chapter we were immediately placed within the context of a critical art practice, then this one will step back from the explicitly artistic realm to explore its ethi-cal and "mystical" dimensions. As a result, most of this chapter will move through the key concepts of *The Ethics,* and refers to art only as an implicit ex-ample of the ethical world of expression. Nevertheless, at certain points I will try to show how these concepts can be used to think about art works as mech-anisms of expression.

## SUBSTANCE

There are three basic distinctions in Spinoza's ontology: Substance, Attribute and Mode. Each of these describes a necessary aspect of a philosophical system in which, Deleuze writes, "univocal being is said immediately of individual dif-ferences or the universal is said of the most singular independent of any media-tion" (DR, 39/57). Substance describes being inasmuch as it is everything, the One-All of God, but this being is univocal, and is understood in all its forms as through itself. God, in Spinoza, is not a supplemental dimension. Spinoza writes: "By Substance I understand what is in itself and is conceived through it-self, that is, that whose concept does not require the concept of another thing, from which it must be formed" (Ethics, I, D3). If God as Substance is under-stood only through itself, as *causa sui* or cause of itself, then our understanding of God will always be a part of God. This is what we could call Spinoza's mys-tical "head-start," that God is necessarily immanent in its expressions, because an immanent cause is only present in its effects. God, Spinoza argues, has an ab-solutely infinite power of existing (Ethics, I, P11s), and whatever exists cannot be conceived without God. (Ethics, I, P15) Simply, every actual thing (or mode) is an expression of God, and God or Substance is the essence of all existing ex-pressions. But this distinction of essence and existence only appears within the ongoing process of expressionism, a process in which, as Spinoza famously puts it: "God's existence and his essence are one and the same thing" (Ethics, I, P20). This is an aesthetic formula, as we shall see, because it means my existence is an expression of God, and as Walt Whitman writes, "a song make I of the One form'd out of all."[3] There is no better understanding of Deleuze's declaration: "Spinoza and Us."

The univocity of being is expressive because of the role played by the attributes. God as Substance consists of an infinity of attributes, each one expressing an eternal and infinite essence of God (Ethics, I, D6). Modes express Substance in an actual and determinate way, each mode being a modification of Substance, expressed according to the essence of each attribute. So in a schematic sense, Substance expresses itself, attributes express its essence, while modes are expressions within the attributes, and hence expressions of the essence of Substance.[4] Modes in relation to the attributes are, as Deleuze comments, "an expression, as it were, of expression itself" (EPS, 14/10). That is, the expressed (Substance) has no existence outside of its expression (modes), because modes express the essence (attributes) of what expresses itself. This means, Spinoza writes: "God must be called the cause of all things in the same sense in which he is called the cause of himself" (Ethics, I, P25d). God is therefore absolutely non-hierarchical, and in univocal being, as Deleuze comments, "all things are in absolute proximity" (DR, 37/55).

In the *Tractatus Theologico-Politicus* Spinoza argued that it is through the things of this world that God is known, rather than through his revelation in scripture. This radical departure from traditional Christian theology is implied by Spinoza's univocal ontology, which argues that God only exists as expressed in Nature. This gives rise to Spinoza's heretical formula *"Deus sive natura,"* or God/Nature. For Spinoza, Nature is the infinite unfolding of what expresses itself, the explication of the One in the many. But this process is simultaneously an implication, by which the One is constructed by its multitudinous expressions. Accordingly "one" and "many" become two ways of describing the same thing, the genetic, or vitalist process of becoming, the infinite (un)folding of being in life. For Spinoza, Nature is becoming because God's expressive essence exists only in its action: "That eternal and infinite being we call God, or Nature," he writes, "acts from the same necessity from which he exists. For we have shown that the necessity of nature from which he acts is the same as that from which he exists" (Ethics, IV, Pref.). God exists as active expression in the modes, which exist as the continual inter-action—the continual construction— of Nature. Substance, attributes and modes therefore comprise the systematic immanence of essence and existence in expressive and univocal being. As Spinoza writes, "the whole of nature is one individual, whose parts, that is, all bodies, vary in infinite ways, without any change of the whole individual" (Ethics, II, P13L7s). Clearly then, Spinoza's Nature is nothing to do with the "natural," and eludes any distinction between nature and culture. Nature is instead a name for a vital and inorganic Substance, and its living expressions can be equally "natural" or "unnatural."

## ATTRIBUTES

Attributes animate Spinoza's system, they are both expressions of God, and what is expressed. Spinoza writes: "By attribute I understand what the intellect perceives of a Substance, as constituting its essence" (Ethics, I, D4). Essence is infinite, and each attribute is an unlimited quality of Substance. Substance (God/Nature) does not pre-exist its attributes, just as it does not pre-exist its actual expressions. The attributes are the immanent formal elements that constitute God's absolute nature, but in being the formal constituents of God's essence they are also the mechanisms of God's expression in differentiated things. Attributes are the way in which God remains One/All, *in* its individual expressions. "The unity of Substance, and the distinction of attributes," Deleuze writes, "are correlates that together constitute expression. The distinction of attributes is nothing but the qualitative composition of an ontologically single Substance" (EPS, 182/166). Attributes are therefore common to Substance and modes, according to what Deleuze calls the "rule of convertibility" whereby "the essence is not only that without which a thing can neither be nor be conceived, but is conversely that which cannot be nor be conceived outside the thing" (EPS, 47/38). This convertibility of the attributes means they simultaneously constitute God's essence, and God's existence. The attributes form the qualitative composition of an ontologically single Substance, each essence (attribute) being an unlimited, infinite quality of Substance. Within the attribute the mode, in its essence and as God's existence, is always a certain degree or quantity of this quality. The philosophy of expression then, begins and ends with an entirely active and affirmative Substance, whose qualitative essences are expressed in its attributes, and whose quantitative existence is expressed in the actions of its modes. As Spinoza puts it: "God's power is nothing except God's active essence. And so it is impossible for us to conceive that God does not act as it is to conceive that he does not exist" (Ethics, II, P3s). God's essence and existence are expressed in and through the attributes.

The affirmative activity of Substance will be the occasion for Deleuze to extend his critique of "that imbecile Hegel" and his dialectic, which we introduced in relation to Nietzsche in the last chapter.[5] Hegel claimed Spinoza did not understand negation, and this reading was very influential in the subsequent philosophical demonisation of Spinoza as an atheist.[6] Deleuze's reading of Spinoza's expressionism as implying an entirely active essence and an entirely affirmative existence, rejects Hegel's claim that we need negation in order to understand being, or to act. As Deleuze rather bluntly puts it: "When Hegel says, against Spinoza, "ah that one never understood anything of the labor of the negative," it's perfect, the labor of the negative is a load of crap."[7] For Deleuze, this is the beauty of Spinoza's philosophy, in it "negation is nothing, because absolutely nothing ever lacks anything" (SPP, 96/125). The absence of dialectical negation in Spinoza's ontology means, as we shall see, that negation becomes purely epistemological, existing only as an incomplete understanding of Substance's expression.[8]

Spinoza claims we only know two attributes, extension and thought, because we can only conceive as infinite those qualities—body and mind—that constitute our essence. Thought and extension are parallel attributes for Spinoza because, as he puts it, "the mind and the body are one and the same thing, which is conceived now under the attribute of thought, now under the attribute of extension" (Ethics, III, P25). As a result, there is no connection or causality between attributes, as each is conceived through itself (Ethics, I, P10). God is the cause of all things and all ideas, these modifications occurring in the same order in two parallel series. The parallelism of the attributes means neither mind nor matter, ideas nor bodies are privileged over the other. This opposes what Deleuze calls, "the moral principle" (EPS, 256/235) running from Plato to Descartes (and beyond) in which the mind or soul is imagined to be what determines the body's actions. Spinoza puts it simply: "The body cannot determine the mind to thinking and the mind cannot determine the body to motion, to rest, or to anything else" (Ethics, III, P2). This implies an "epistemological parallelism" (EPS, 117/102) as Deleuze calls it, where every affect of my body corresponds to an affect in my mind. This parallelism has important consequences, for, as Spinoza writes, "in proportion as a body is more capable than others of doing many things at once, or being acted on in many ways at once, so its mind is more capable than others of perceiving many things at once" (Ethics, II, P13s). As ideas and bodies are strictly parallel, and the intellect cannot produce true ideas about Substance without Substance expressing itself in these ideas, the more we experience, the more we know about God (SPP, 91/118–19). Consequently, reason provides a way of understanding God not as an object outside of us, but as an immanent and constitutive infinity, expressed in the affectual relations of my body and ideas. This does not, Deleuze argues, mean a devaluation of thought in relation to the body, but a devaluation of moral consciousness as the intentional and guiding mechanism of an otherwise inert body—the body is set free. Spinoza provides a new body, along with new ideas to understand it.

## ATHEISTIC MYSTICISM

The aim of Spinoza's ethics will be to know God—God as Nature—but, once more, this means that God exists as, and only as, its expressions. This project of knowing God, despite surface similarities, differs radically from the traditional Christian concept of a transcendent God. The Christian God builds on the Platonic concept of the "Good," and the neo-Platonic concept of the "One."[9] The "Good" and the "One" are transcendent terms from which our lives are de-rived, and against which they are judged, as second order realities. Spinoza, like Nietzsche, will develop his concept of a univocal and immanent God/Nature in opposition to both, and this will be his implicit "anti-Platonism." Christianity's theology of transcendence—as a religious Platonism—is exemplified by Thomas Aquinas' statement: "God is the essence of all, not essentially, but causally."[10] For Aquinas, God's essence is the transcendental cause of existence, and stands in direct contrast to Spinoza's God whose essence is entirely imma-nent in existence. Similarly, Spinoza's God departs from the neo-Platonic mys-tical tradition emerging from Plotinus, in which the whole or One is emanative. Here God is the cause of being while remaining in himself, being is his gift but not his essence. As Deleuze explains it: "Emanation is at once cause and gift: causality by donation, but by productive donation" (EPS, 170/154).[11] The One produces being, as a gift that we receive, and through which we participate in the One. But we only participate in the One through what it gives (being) (rather than our being constructing the One directly), making the One tran-scendent and insuring that, as Plotinus argues, we have with it "nothing in com-mon."[12] "The giver is above its gifts," Deleuze explains, "as it is above its products, participable through what it gives, but imparticipable in itself or as it-self, thereby grounding participation" (EPS, 171/155). Emanation gives rise to a hierarchy of being as closer or further away from the One, and laid out on a mystical path of redemption/reabsorption. This path finally transcends being because being as existence is subordinated and outside the transcendent essence of God.[13]

  Spinoza's univocal and immanent God is also an alternative to the Christian doctrine of *creatio ex nihilo,* in which God creates the world from nothing. This creation assumes a non-being pre-existing being, and implies that God as creator is outside being, as its immanent but nonetheless negative shadow. God on this account is expressed in the world in representations which cannot lay hold of his essential (non)being, and, as Deleuze puts it, "asserts and expresses himself in the world as immanent cause, and who remains inexpressible and transcendent as the object of a negative theology that denies of him all that is affirmed of his immanence" (EPS, 178/161). As Psuedo-Dionysus, an important early exemplar of this tradition puts it: "There is no speaking of it [the divine], nor name nor knowledge of it."[14] For negative theology God cannot be grasped in his essence, because this is by definition outside of human intelligence. Meister Eckhart's elaboration of this idea is the most well known example of this doctrine, and argues that any statement of the type "x is" is said of beings, and so cannot be said of God. This leads us onto a mystic path towards God seeking to leave our human being behind. This mystical spiritualism rests on a transcendental metaphysics, and is expressed in Meister Eckhart's claim: "Scripture always exhorts us to go out of this world."[15] Spinoza opposes this tradition, because for him God as Nature exists only as this world, meaning our knowledge of the world must also be direct knowledge of God. Spinoza's Substance exists as the affirmative expression of its essence, it avoids a distinction between being and non-being, as it avoids a dialectical mysticism working through negation. Finally, Deleuze writes: "Immanence is opposed to any eminence of the cause, any negative theology, any method of analogy, any hierarchical conception of the world" (EPS, 173/157).

Spinoza's God/Nature is, paradoxically, atheistic because its essence exists only as its expressions, and not in a transcendent dimension.[16] In other words, everything is God and thus God loses his place. A metaphysics of the divine cannot be maintained on the plane of univocal being. Nevertheless, and as we shall see, univocal being implies for Spinoza the mystical possibility of knowing God as God knows itself. Spinoza's univocal and immanent God is therefore the conceptual condition for what Deleuze calls, "a kind of mystical atheist experience proper to Spinoza."[17] This is a strange atheism in which Spinoza talks of nothing but God, a bit like the poet Pessoa, for whom: "Only Nature is divine, and she is not divine."[18] It was necessary, of course, for Spinoza to talk of God in the seventeenth century, although it did not prevent his excommunication from the Jewish church.[19] Deleuze argues that Spinoza's atheist "God" is in fact the condition of his "radical emancipation" from both a religious and philosophical transcendence. This is not however, to deny Spinoza's mysticism, but to affirm that in formulating a mystical understanding of God's univocity Spinoza declares his atheism. In this sense, and as Deleuze argues in relation to Spinoza, "atheism has never been external to religion: atheism is the artistic power at work on religion."[20] In other words, Spinoza's atheism is a mystical affirmation of God's immanence in life. It is creative in Nietzsche's sense, for expressionism is nothing but the construction of new possibilities for life, just as it is mystical in an atheistic sense, expressing a God/Nature entirely immanent in its expressions.[21] Spinoza's mystical atheism will therefore be the formula for an ethical-aesthetics that is critical in Nietzsche's terms, as the overcoming of religious transcendence in order to live a creative life, in order to experience our real conditions (God/Nature) as they are constructed in our expressions. Spinoza's mystical atheism is therefore Christianity's own artistic power, inasmuch as it is, as Deleuze puts it, the "transformation of constraints into a means of creation."[22] For Spinoza art must be atheistic in order to escape a metaphysics of representation, just as it must be mystical in expressing the univocity of God/Nature. As a result, my account of a Spinozian ethical-aesthetics will explore its atheistic mysticism, which, I argue, culminates in an understanding of God in which we find our highest expressive power, in the creation of God/Nature itself.[23]

## MODES AND THEIR AFFECTS.

Unlike Substance, which is being in itself, the modes are being in something else (Ethics, I, D5). They are modifications of Substance, in the form of particular things. "Particular things are nothing but affections of God's attributes," Spinoza writes, "or modes by which God's attributes are expressed in a certain and determinate way" (Ethics, I, P25c see also Ethics, III, P6d). The modes are the expression of God, as Spinoza says quite specifically: "Whatever exists expresses the nature, or essence of God in a certain and determinate way, that is, whatever exists expresses in a certain and determinate way the power of God, which is the cause of all things" (Ethics, I, P36d). Extrinsic parts (modes) form a whole, but through their constantly variable relations this is a dynamic whole undergoing continual transformation, and forming an infinitely changeable universe. As a result God, as Nature, and as expressed in the modes, is this permanent becoming, and has an infinite power of expression.[24]

In *Difference and Repetition* Deleuze seems to question the univocity of Spinoza's Substance by confronting it with Nietzsche's formulation of eternal return. This raises many interesting questions about Spinoza's relation to Nietzsche, and about Deleuze's changing evaluation of Spinoza's philosophy of immanence. Deleuze suggests that Spinoza's univocity retains a hierarchical distinction between Substance and modes, and requires a Nietzschean "correction" to become truly immanent.

> There still remains a difference between Substance and the modes: Spinoza's Substance appears independent of the modes, while the modes are dependent on Substance, but as though on something other than themselves. Substance must itself be said *of* the modes and only *of* the modes. Such a condition can be satisfied only at the price of a more general categorical re-

versal according to which being is said of becoming, identity of that which
is different, the one of the multiple, etc. (DR, 40/59)

Deleuze believes that unless Substance is said only of the modes Spinoza's God
runs the risk of re-introducing a transcendent term. In response to this problem
Deleuze posits a Nietzschean Spinoza: "All that Spinozism needed to do for the
univocal to become an object of pure affirmation was to make Substance turn
around the modes—*in other words, to realize univocity in the form of repetition in
the eternal return*" (DR, 304/389). Nietzsche appears here as the necessary
(Deleuzian) condition to understanding Spinozian Substance and its "expressive immanence." This reading would avoid the danger Deleuze indicates, of an
emanative Being, by affirming a univocal being in becoming (i.e. univocal being
as the repetition of eternal return). But as we have seen, the "categorical reversal" Deleuze requires to fully affirm Spinoza's Substance can be found in his
reading of Spinoza's attributes in *Expressionism in Philosophy: Spinoza,* published
the same year as *Difference and Repetition* (1968). The attributes both constitute
God's essence as Substance, while simultaneously and inseparably expressing
God's essence in the existence of the modes. Deleuze argues that Substance is
constituted by an infinity of attributes, and their expressions in modes exist on
the same plane, a plane of immanence, where the attributes simultaneously constitute the essence of Substance. This means Substance (being) is defined entirely in terms of the modes (becoming), which express the essence of Substance
(attributes).[25] This will allow the modal expression of Substance in existence to
be the simultaneous construction of an immanent (and therefore atheist) God
in its essence. "What is involved," Deleuze explains, "is no longer the affirmation of a single substance, but rather the laying out of a *common plane of immanence* on which all bodies, all minds, and all individuals are situated" (SPP,
122/164). Substance is, at this point, immanent to the modes and is expressed
only in and as the process of modal becoming which constructs it.

This will mean the trajectory Deleuze takes after 1968 does not follow the
"correction" of Spinoza by Nietzsche, but instead tends to privilege Spinoza's
system inasmuch as it was *already* Nietzschean. As Deleuze and Guattari put it:
"What we are talking about is not the unity of substance but the infinity of the
modifications that are part of one another on this unique plane of life" (ATP,
254/311). The ethical question of how to live therefore becomes a question of
how one constructs this plane of immanence, for, Deleuze writes, "it has to be
constructed if one is to live in a Spinozist manner" (SPP, 123/165).
Understanding what this could mean will form the bulk of what follows, but
suffice to say it is the trajectory of Spinoza's apotheosis in Deleuze's thought, a
trajectory that is, as we have seen, indiscernible from Deleuze's construction of
what he calls "the grand identity Spinoza-Nietzsche."[26]

Let's take a closer look at the modal world of becoming. Existence is composed of bodies continually coming into contact with other bodies in chance encounters. There is no prewritten divine plan, although, as Spinoza rather sarcastically points out: "Men have been so mad as to believe that God is pleased by harmony" (Ethics, I, App.III). The modes as affections (*affectio*) are determined on this infinite plane of modal interaction by their dynamic relations, every finite thing being an effect of another thing, which is itself the effect of some other thing, *ad infinitum* (Ethics, I, P28). As a result, Deleuze writes, "a thing is never separable from its relations with the world" (SPP, 125/168). Modes are determined through their continual interaction, and in this sense they are "images or corporeal traces" (SPP, 48/68) of each other. As Spinoza suggests: "The idea of any mode in which the human body is affected by external bodies must involve the nature of the human body and at the same time the nature of the external body" (Ethics, II, P16). This modal relation forms an affect (*affectus*) as either the greater (composition) or lesser (decomposition) perfection of the mode resulting from its interaction with other modes. These modal (de)compositions constitute the tenor of our lives, for, Spinoza explains, "we live in continuous change, and that as we change for the better or worse, we are called happy or unhappy" (Ethics, V,P39s). More usually, Spinoza uses the terms "joy" and "sadness" to describe these changes. "By joy," he writes, "I shall understand in what follows that passion by which the mind passes to a greater perfection. And by sadness, that passion by which it passes to a lesser perfection" (Ethics, III, P11s). Perfection is measured in terms of a mode's power of acting, the more a mode is positively affected, the more it can act. The affect of joy causes the body to be affected in a greater number of ways, (Ethics, IV, P38) whereas sadness decreases a body's power to be affected. The aim of life, quite simply, is maximum joy, which results in maximum power, and maximum action. This is what Deleuze means when he says Spinoza's is an ethics of affirmation.

For Spinoza joy is found in a process of perfection that doesn't assume a pre-existing concept of the perfect. What is perfect and therefore good is simply what increases our power to act, and this is defined only by the immanent conditions of each encounter. Spinoza's *Ethics* offers a practical program for the production of joy which is undetermined by any metaphysical concepts by which we could judge it. What is good always remains to be discovered, and is produced in the experimental relations we have with the world. As Spinoza writes, "in ordering our thoughts and images, we must always attend to those things which are good in each thing so that in this way we are always determined to acting from an affect of joy" (Ethics, V, P10s). Spinoza's *Ethics* is therefore antithetical to a morality, and is another reason it appeals to Deleuze: "Ethics, which is to say a typology of immanent modes of existence, replaces Morality, which always refers existence to transcendent values" (EPS, 269/248). Life is a question of selection and affirmation, not of judgment, which presupposes an otherworldly truth represented by metaphysical idols and moral symbols. Christianity is the obvious example of such a system, establishing God as the external authority on behalf of which one judges. But such a system is always despotic, Deleuze argues, and "condemns us to an endless servitude and annuls any libratory process" (ECC, 128/160). God's judgment descends on us from on high and damns us for our sins, it is impervious to lived particularity and demands only obedience, punishing our guilt when it is not obeyed. Thomas Bernhard gives a beautiful description of this horror: "Whenever I entered the chapel," he writes, "even at the age of fifteen or twenty, it seemed to me a place of terror and damnation, a hall of judgment, a lofty courtroom where sentence was passed on me. I could see the relentless fingers of the judges pointing down at me, and I always left the chapel with my head bowed, as one who had been humiliated and punished."[27] Spinoza's *Ethics* "Have Done with Judgment," and in this echo of Artaud kills God just as surely as we will see Artaud kill man's organism.[28]

Spinozian ethics involves making a typology of our modal affects, of our joy and sadness. But our joy and sadness are not predetermined, and our typology is always conditional on each new encounter, and appears only according to its local and singular conditions. This typology of affect can obviously be used in considering art, and this would be the starting point of a Spinozian ethical-aesthetics. We are, once again, in the heart of a participatory critical process that defines the artwork, or the *work* of art. Once more, we are required to sense the real forces at play in the artistic field, rather than judge an object through a moralistic aesthetic. Aesthetic experience in Spinoza's terms is always under construction as the ethical process of selecting those encounters that increase our power and perfection. For Spinoza as for Nietzsche, the art-work, ethically understood, is this process of construction, a process understood as an increase or decrease in power rather than as an object already determined. Importantly, this also changes our concept of the subject, as the subject is similarly processual, emerging only in the affectual selections that are made, as the changing appearance of forces that are no longer simply "subjective" in an organic or psychological sense. The art-work exists within an affectual economy of emergence, and cannot be "understood" (in the precise sense we will see Spinoza give to this term) by any kind of judgment. Deleuze is explicit on this point:

> What expert judgment, in art could ever bear on the work to come? It is not a question of judging other existing beings, but of sensing whether they

agree or disagree with us, that is, whether they bring forces to us, or whether they return us to the miseries of war, to the poverty of the dream, to the rigors of organization. As Spinoza had said, it is a problem of love and hate and not judgment. [ . . . ] This is not subjectivism, since to pose the problem in terms of force, and not in other terms, already surpasses all subjectivity. (ECC, 136/169)

To have done with judgment in evaluating art means overcoming the organization of the subject and object, and entering the artwork to construct its process of expressive emergence. The art work is constituted by modes and their affects, these affects emerging in a perception of the work that constitutes a singular body defined by its increasing or decreasing power and perfection, by the joy or sadness which defines its becoming. Art as affect is constructed in this processual life of modes, and as we shall see, it is as such that it expresses the immanent infinity of God/Nature. This implies a revaluation of the subject-object relation as it is usually understood, and as it operates in aesthetics. A Spinozian ethical-aesthetics, as he puts it, "*consider[s] human actions and appetites just as if it were a question of lines, planes and bodies*" (Ethics, III, Pref.).[29] Art is therefore an ethical practice, and as such expresses an increase or decrease in power, or force, (a becoming—"Affects are becomings" (ATP, 256/314)) and emerges in a process of participation. Art does not appear in a judgment assuming our exteriority to the work, and requiring transcendental values to maintain everything in its proper place (art in the gallery, the market, in the studio, on the wall, but not in our life, not as a question of life. . . . . . ). In Spinoza's ethical-aesthetics the question of art would be, as Deleuze puts it, "to make exist, not to judge" (ECC, 135/169). Art emerges—it is created—in our experimental relations, as what lives, as the increase or decrease in a body's power to act. This will lead us out of our human, all too human form of understanding: our imagination, and the passions it evokes. For an ethical-aesthetic will affirm joyful affects in constructing a new mode of existence, an existence that expresses God, and understands this expression as a becoming through which God constructs and so understands itself. This will be the atheistic mysticism of art. Before considering this culminating moment of understanding however, we must consider the rest of Spinoza's system.

## MODAL ESSENCE

All modes have an intensive and extensive quantity, each of which is infinite. The first constitutes modal essence, the second modal existence. The essence of a mode is immanent to its existence, but nevertheless exists independently of the modes existence. Spinoza writes: "The essence of things produced by God does not involve existence" (Ethics, I, P24). How is this possible in a univocal ontology? Modal essence, Spinoza argues, defines the mode's power to persevere in its being (Ethics, III, P7). Beyond this essential threshold a mode simply exists as something else. This essence or power is caused by and exists in God eternally, whether or not the mode itself exists. For Spinoza: "God is the cause, not only of the existence of this or that human body, but also of its essence, which therefore must be conceived through the very essence of God, by a certain eternal necessity, and this concept must be in God" (Ethics, V, P22d). This necessity is that of an idea comprised in the idea of God, that is, an idea caused by God, as opposed to an object or idea which finds its cause in relation to other objects or ideas (modes). Existence is not added to essence as a distinct actuality (for they remain immanent), but is Deleuze writes, "a sort of ultimate determination resulting from the essence's cause" (EPS, 194/176). That is, modal essence does not cause modal existence, both find their cause in God.

Modal essences form an important part of Deleuze's interpretation of Spinozian univocity, for it is essence as degree of power that will provide the mechanism by which: "Being is said in a single and same sense of everything of which it is said, but that of which it is said differs" (DR, 36/53). In other words, it is through the capacity of the modes to affect and to be affected, according to their essence or degree of power, that difference emerges in modal becoming. Existing modes are composed of an infinity of extended parts in relations of movement and rest, which express a degree of intensity (modal essence or power). The composition of extended nature fluctuates in the continuous variation of its affections and affects, but as long as a particular relation of movement and rest exists between modes, it expresses a modal essence or power. Essences all agree on their immanent plane, forming as Deleuze puts it, "an actually infinite collection, a system of mutual implications, in which each essence conforms with all of the others, and in which all essences are involved in the production of each. Thus God directly produces each essence together with all the others. That is, existing modes themselves have God as their direct cause" (EPS, 184/167 see also 198/181). Modal essences exist in a reciprocal and differential determination of each other, and form a plane immanent to all modes, which thereby find their cause in God. "Thus," Deleuze argues, "essences form a total system, an actually infinite whole" (EPS, 194/177). In understanding modal essence, we will understand the individuation of modes, but because modal essences exist on a univocal plane of being immanent to existence, understanding modal essence will mean understanding the expressive power of the infinite whole of God *in* its actual expression *as* existing modes. Consequently, Deleuze states, "each finite being must be said to *express the absolute,* according to the intensive quantity that constitutes its essence, according, that is, to the degree of its power" (EPS, 197/180). Once more, we are not far away from Deleuze's reading of Nietzsche's will to power as a quantity of force appearing in qualities. Individuation for Deleuze, in Spinoza as much as in Nietzsche, is always intensive. That is, modal essence as power is simply a certain capacity to affect and be affected, a capacity which determines the individuated limits of modes in their constitutive relations of motion and rest, and speed and slowness (Ethics, II, P13L1).

But modal existence is constantly becoming, as each mode increases or decreases its power in the vibration of inorganic life. As a result, understanding modal essence will be a matter of understanding modal relation, and this will mean understanding how the becoming of modal existence expresses the creative dynamism of God. At this point however, there remains the problem of the independence of Substance, as Deleuze posed it in *Difference and Repetition*. For in fact all modes express an essence, but not all essences involve existence. This apparent problem for univocity finds its answer in Deleuze's insistence on the mutual implication of essences, which means all modal existence expresses all the modal essences, despite the fact that not every modal essence has a modal existence. As Deleuze puts it: "They [essences] are all compatible with one another without limit, because all are included in the production of each one, but each one corresponds to a specific degree of power different from all the others" (SPP, 65/100).

Within the attribute all essences agree because they share God as their efficient and material cause, and together form God's infinite whole under that attribute or essence. Because modal essence exists in God as it does in modes, and because each modal essence is determined through its relation to all others, in knowing a modal essence we will know God. This introduces another important aspect to Spinoza's philosophy, that any means of understanding essence must be immanent to existence. This means a materialist thought as much as a materialist mysticism, and requires us to consider more closely how understanding emerges and operates. Unsurprisingly, any understanding of God will be found in the ideas, which in the attribute of thought, and as modal essence, are both ours and Gods. As Deleuze puts it, "the things we know of God belong to God in the same form as that in which we know them, that is, in a form common to God who possesses them, and to creatures who imply and know them" (EPS, 142/128). What we must now understand is the process of reason required to adequately understand ideas in their modal essence, and how they express God's immanence in existence.

The existence and the essence of the modal idea together constitute consciousness, but it is a consciousness that will no longer be subjective, and will be able to think itself as divine. How? Every idea has as its object something that exists (i.e. either a thing or another idea), and this idea can in turn become the object of another idea. This idea of an object is the objective reality of the idea. But every idea also exists in the attribute of thought as a modal essence, and as such it is independent of the mind that thinks it. This essential aspect of the idea constitutes the formal reality of the existent and objective idea.[30] These two realities of the idea coexist in any given idea as its reflexive (objective) and expressive (formal) aspects, these aspects being, Deleuze says, "one and the same thing" (EPS, 139/125). This means consciousness no longer implies a subject as a psychological character or a moral entity, consciousness being simply the affect or "trace" (objective idea) of an essence (formal reality) found in the attribute of thought. This implies—contra Descartes—a thought without an "I am." This thought, which Spinoza will develop in the third type of knowledge, operates in eternity and without a subject, without an organism-body, and without a consciousness-idea. This subjectless and eternal thought is the thought of God, and is the aim of Spinoza's mystical atheism.

## INADEQUATE IDEAS

Inasmuch as we have ideas, they are representative ideas and shouldn't be confused with the idea that we are, inasmuch as this constitutes our essence or formal reality. We don't have this idea we are immediately, and it is what we strive for in our understanding. The ideas that we have on the other hand, are those given to us through perceptions of affections and affects. As Spinoza writes: "The images of things are affections of the human body whose ideas represent external bodies as present to us" (Ethics, III, P27d). These images are what Spinoza calls inadequate ideas because they tell us nothing of our, or other essences, but are simply representations of objects relative to us (Ethics, III, P23d). Insofar as the mind has such representative ideas, it is said to imagine. It means we imagine that an artwork is beautiful, but we don't understand this affectual relation in its essence. If we wish to reach a true understanding of art according to a Spinozian ethical-aesthetics, we will have to overcome imaginative representations and the subjective consciousness that supports them. Ethical-aesthetics will therefore begin with the epistemological problem of the proper way to think, or in Deleuzian terms, the proper image of thought.

As we have seen, reflexive ideas represent our random encounters and the consequent variation of affects according to their imagined causes. This knowledge however ordered, is inadequate as it imagines our experience of the world entirely in terms of the affects of objects upon us. As a result, the process of representation operates through a human consciousness, because it requires a pre-existing subjectivity, as effected, to understand our relations to the world. The problem with this, Spinoza argues, is

> . . . that each one has judged things according to the disposition of his brain; or rather has accepted affections of the imagination as things. We see, therefore, that all the notions by which ordinary people are accustomed to explain Nature are only modes of imagining, and do not indicate the nature of anything, only the constitution of the imagination. And because they have names, as if they were [notions] of beings existing outside the imagination, I call them beings, not of reason, but of imagination. [ . . . ] For the perfection of things is to be judged solely from their nature and power [i.e. essence]; things are not more or less perfect because they please or offend men's senses, or because they are of use to, or incompatible with, human nature. (Ethics, I, App.III)

Spinoza offers a new evaluative framework for our understanding of life, one in which we will have understood nothing, of art or of anything, if we remain at the level of the human imagination. Like Nietzsche, understanding life in its real conditions will mean overcoming the false consciousness of humans.

This new way of understanding involves a radical revaluation of value, for it is only from our point of view as human subjects that a relation could be bad, and could decompose our modal integrity. From the point of view of Nature every relation is affirmative and expresses an increase, even those that are, from our perspective, disasters. Deleuze's example is a car crash in which the fire that burns, the air that escapes its compression in the tires, and the flesh combining with the dashboard, are all compositions.[31] As a result, bad things, sad affects and all other negations are simply symptoms of an inadequate and anthropocentric understanding (we could say "evaluation") of the world. This means humanity, or at least our way of imagining such negative affects, will only be a hindrance to understanding God/Nature. In Nature, in the midst of its constant compositions, there are no distinctions between the human and inhuman, just as there are none between the natural and artificial: "Artifice," Deleuze writes, "is fully a part of Nature" (SPP, 124/167). Spinoza's ontology therefore carries remarkable epistemological consequences: "There is nothing positive in ideas," he writes, "on account of which they can be called false" (Ethics, II, P33). Whenever we regard something as false, and negate it, or when we are ourselves negated and feel sad, we are simply having an inadequate idea, caught in an incomplete understanding, or imagination. As Deleuze rather wryly comments: "Sadness makes no one intelligent."[32] For in the inadequate idea of an imagination, I understand only the effect (as decomposition) and not the cause (the composition in Nature), and in this sense, according to Spinoza, I have only a *"privation of knowledge"* (Ethics, II, P35).

On the other hand, however, when I understand an effect as causing me joy, I retain this same imaginative epistemological relation. I still experience what Spinoza calls a passion, "a confused idea, by which the mind affirms of its body, or of some part of it, a greater or a lesser force of existing than before, which, when it is given, determines the mind to think of this rather than that" (Ethics, III, General definition of the Affects). This determination of what the mind thinks by an imagined outside cause, whether good or bad, indicates a lack of power, a failure to select and affirm, and an inability of the mode to actively express the power of its essence. "Man's lack of power to moderate and restrain the affects," Spinoza writes, "I call bondage. For the man who is subject to affects is under the control, not of himself, but of fortune, in whose power he so greatly is that often, though he sees the better for himself, he is still forced to follow the worse" (Ethics, IV, Pref.). Modes are captured by their imaginative representations, in which life is simply a series of causes and effects taking place between individual things. Thus we can only imagine passions, even if these are joyful, rather than understand them. As we shall see, Spinoza liberates man from the bondage of the passions and, in Deleuze's hands, this will become a liberation from the human itself. We can easily see how art exists on the level of the imagination, as the cause of our feelings of joy or sadness, and how these feelings determine our judgments of its qualities. But we can also see how art's existence as the cause of those feelings is determined by man's faculty of imagination, rather than by anything intrinsic to art. Therefore the liberation of man's understanding from its human limitations will also mark a new mode of existence for art. A new image of thought will mean a new artistic image.

## ADEQUATE IDEAS / COMMON NOTIONS

Spinoza argues that good and bad can only be understood in terms of actual modal relations. What is bad for us is contrary to, or reduces, our power of action, and what is good for us agrees with our nature and increases our power of action (Ethics, IV, P29–30). This means good and bad do not exist outside the material fluctuations of our own being, according to the quality of our affects as they express the changes in our embodied power. But what determines good and bad as the increase or decline of my power of action? As we have seen, the passions of joy and sadness always arise from the imagination, as the affect of something on us from outside. Although joy is related to what is good, the passions of joy and sadness are not the same as what is good and bad. Rather it is lack of power that is bad, and the power to act that is good. As Spinoza has it, "lack of power consists only in this, that a man allows himself to be guided by things outside him, and to be determined by them to do what the common constitution of external things demands, not what his own nature, considered in itself, demands" (Ethics, IV, P32). It will be by doing what its own nature demands, in acting according to its essence or power that a mode will do good. This is when it will truly be active, for then it is determined to action by nothing other than its own power (i.e. by its real conditions) and by an understanding that is entirely adequate (Ethics, IV, P59d).

How are we to have adequate ideas of the essence of things? The first step, typical for the seventeenth century, involves the nature of the idea. "An affect which is a passion," Spinoza writes, "ceases to be a passion as soon as we form a clear and distinct idea of it" (Ethics, V, P3). As a result, Spinoza explains: "The more an affect is known to us, then, the more it is in our power, and the less the mind is acted on by it" (Ethics, V, P3c). Thus, it is reason that separates an affect from its imagined external cause, forming a true (clear and distinct) idea of it (Ethics, II, D2). As we can only experience an affect, at least initially, as a passion, as an external body acting upon ours, our understanding of its essence will begin from an inadequate understanding of its affect. We know that when we feel joy it is because joining forces with that of another mode has compounded our power of action. Alternatively we feel sadness for the opposite reason, when our power of action has been decreased by another mode. As a result our understanding of affects, and our ethical ability to select the good ones, will come through knowing our body's "agreements, differences, and oppositions" (Ethics, II, P29s).

In understanding we turn our attention from imagined effects to modal affect, and this change introduces us to what Deleuze calls "ethology." Bodies now appear, as we have noted before, according to capacities of affect and affection rather than any pre-existing identificatory schema. Ethology takes us beyond the form to understand the affectual dynamic of life, and a thing is no longer identified by asking "what is it?" but by the question "what does it do?" what is it for me? Deleuze explains the consequences: "Concretely, if you define bodies and thoughts as capacities for affecting and being affected, many things change. You will define an animal, or a human being, not by its form, its organs, and its functions, and not as a subject either; you will define it by the affects of which it is capable" (SPP, 124/166).

Ethology starts with an understanding of the affects, and leads to a clear and distinct idea of what is shared by two modes, and what it is that enables the joyful affect they produce. What is shared in a joyful affect is a common modal essence, and when the understanding grasps this essence it has an adequate idea. As Spinoza puts it: "If something is common to, and particular to, the human body and certain external bodies by which the human body is usually affected, and is equally in the part and in the whole of each of them, its idea will be adequate in the mind" (Ethics, II, P39). It is through joy therefore, that a clear and distinct idea of what is common to the bodies in question, their "common notion" as Spinoza calls it emerges. This makes joy the prerequisite and first step towards understanding modal essence in common notions. Common notions, or adequate ideas, form the "second" kind of knowledge through which we will be able to pass to the "third," of God. As Spinoza argues, "the greater the joy with which we are affected, the greater the perfection to which we pass, that is, the more we must participate in the divine nature. To use things, therefore, and take pleasure in them as far as possible—not, of course, to the point where we are disgusted with them, for there is no pleasure in that—this is the part of the wiseman" (Ethics, IV, P45s). This leads Deleuze to clearly state the line of ethical affirmation laid out by Spinoza: "The primary question of the Ethics is thus: What must we do in order to be affected by a maximum of joyful passions?" (EPS, 273/252). And as a result: "The second principle question of the Ethics is thus: What must we do to produce in ourselves active affections?" (EPS, 274/253). These questions compose a Spinozian ethical-aesthetics; how may we create and understand joy? How may we understand the world from our own point of view (from our active force), in its essence, and as it is related to all other essences in and as God? These may seem questions unrelated or only distantly related to those of art. But in fact these questions include those concerning the production of art, and revalue them as ethical and ontological questions. This revaluation removes art from its representational and inadequate frame of the subject-object, and from the realm of the passions, and reposes the question of its function in terms of understanding its affects. The art of creating joyful affects will in this way find its "higher concept" in an understanding indiscernible from an atheist mysticism. This will be Spinoza's "higher concept" of art.

Deleuze finds this "higher concept" in what he calls Spinoza's "war cry"(EPS, 255/134), Spinoza's claim that "no one has yet determined what the body can do, [ . . . ] For no one has yet come to know the structure of the body so accurately that he could explain all its functions" (Ethics, III, P2s). For Deleuze, Spinoza offers philosophy a new model with this war cry—the body, but the body as a process of material experimentation. That is, we know nothing about a body until we know what it can do, what its affects are, and whether its relations with other bodies decompose it, or compose a more powerful body. The more affections a body is capable of the more joy it experiences, each increase gives the body more power and more understanding (for Spinoza knowledge is power), right up to the overcoming of its own limits in the mystical state of beatitude. This path to the absolute requires a rigorous program of experimentation, as experimentation is the way a body, as Deleuze puts it, "transcends

its limits in going to the limit of what it can do" (DR, 37/55). Beyond our limits we have thoughts that overcome our consciousness, thoughts in which an
unknown body as the unknown of thought emerges. (SPP, 17/28) This "unknown" is so only from the point of view of the limits of human consciousness
and organic integrity however, and Deleuze's reading of Spinoza quickly pushes
beyond such inadequate ideas. As Deleuze and Guattari succinctly put it, "pure
affects imply an enterprise of desubjectification" (ATP, 270/330). To the point
where, Deleuze says: "Experimentation on oneself, is our only identity."[33]

The path of reason, in forming common notions, overcomes the human
in its understanding of essence and ultimately of God. This path begins from
discovering our maximum possible number of affects, and as this is in principle infinite, we must live in a constant process of experimentation, forever
seeking what the body can do, in order to understand the eternal essence(s) of
God. As Spinoza writes:

> *He who has a body capable of a great many things has a mind whose great-*
> *est part is eternal.* Dem.: He who has a body capable of doing a great
> many things is least troubled by evil affects, that is, by affects contrary to
> our nature. So he has the power of ordering and connecting the affec-
> tions of his body according to the order of the intellect—consequently,
> of bringing it about that all the affections of the body are related to the
> idea of God. (Ethics, V, P39)

For Spinoza the formula is a simple one, the more affects the body is capable
of, the more knowledge it will have (Ethics, II, P14). The nature of our ideas
therefore, will always be determined by the capacity of our body to experience
life—our real conditions—and the process of understanding God (as well as
of creating art) will always be carried out through a process of experimentation with the body. This means, for Deleuze, that Spinoza's *Ethics* like
Nietzsche's thought, gives us an anti-Platonic physiology of art. "The body,"
Deleuze writes in *Cinema 2,* but in direct relation to Spinoza, "is no longer
the obstacle that separates thought from itself, that which it has to overcome
to reach thinking. It is on the contrary that which it plunges into or must
plunge into, in order to reach the unthought that is life. [ . . . ] 'We do not
even know what a body can do': in its sleep, in its drunkenness, in its efforts
and resistances. To think is to learn what a non-thinking body is capable of,
its capacity, its postures" (C2, 189/246).

The result of acting according to ethical reason, and this will have important consequences for an aesthetics constructed on its basis, will be acting according to what increases our power, according that is, to what is good. In an
art of common notions experimentation is nothing but the expression of

essence as the production, that is the construction, of a new body, a body constructed of common notions. Art, adequately understood, is nothing but this experimental construction of common notions eventually leading to ideas expressing a mystical knowledge of and as God.

When we understand our joy as the result of a common notion, we understand how it is an action, an expression and affirmation of our own power of acting (of our essence, or formal reality). As Spinoza puts it, "insofar as he is determined to do something from the fact that he understands, he acts, that is does something which is perceived through his essence alone, or which follows adequately from his virtue" (Ethics, IV, P23d). The more we know of what a body can do, the more we understand the essences it expresses. This process will culminate with the removal, or at least the radical minimization of passions (Ethics, V, P20s). As a result: *"The more perfection each thing has, the more it acts and the less it is acted on; and conversely, the more it acts, the more perfect it is"* (Ethics, V, P40). We are now in a position to understand more fully the role of affirmation in Spinoza. Affirmation is the active expression of essence, inasmuch as understanding is an affirmation of our power to act in which an imagined joy expresses a common notion. Spinoza writes: *"The mind strives to imagine only those things which posit its power of acting. Dem.:* The mind's striving, or power, is its very essence; but the mind's essence (as is known through itself) affirms only what the mind is and can do, not what it is not and cannot do. So it strives to imagine only what affirms, or posits, its power of acting" (Ethics, III, P54). For Spinoza, affirmation is the mechanism by which God is expressed, for it is through affirming my power of acting that I express myself as essence, this essence being in itself an expression of God. As Deleuze puts it, each finite being must be said to express the absolute, according to the intensive quantity that constitutes its essence, according, that is, to the degree of its power (EPS, 197/180). The degree of each things power (i.e. their modal essence) constitutes the singularity of their modal existence, this existence now being understood in its essence and hence as an expression of the absolute. Through this process of understanding thought opens out to an understanding of its own infinity.

Spinoza argues that the move from the first to the second kinds of knowledge, from imagination to understanding, involves the transformation of perceptions of objects into concepts of essence. "I say concept rather than perception," he writes, "because the word perception seems to indicate *that the mind is acted on by the object. But concept seems to express an action of the mind"* (Ethics, II, D3,Exp.). Concepts, Spinoza will argue, involve knowledge of ourselves, an understanding of our affects not as imaginative, subjective representations, but as expressions of immanent essences.[34] Understanding, on this account involves a knowledge that emerges from the affirmation of essence (concepts), and as such dissolves subjective and representational distinctions (imaginative perceptions). In this way, and like Nietzsche, Spinoza provides a way for our human, all to human subjective imagination to overcome itself, not once and for all, but in an ongoing affirmation of life. This process of understanding, in which concepts of common notions emerge through an experimentation at the limits of what a body can do, constructs a body beyond human perception which lives as the expression of its real immanent power or essence, as the expression of God.

Common notions express modal essences, but more than this the understanding that constructs common notions gives an adequate idea of an essence's formal reality in the attribute. To have an adequate idea or concept of an essence means to have an adequate understanding of all essences, as they constitute any singular essence in the attribute. As Spinoza explains:

> A true idea must agree with its object, that is (as is known through itself), what is contained objectively in the intellect must necessarily be in Nature. But in Nature there is only one Substance, namely, God, and there are no affections other than those which are in God and which can neither be nor be conceived without God. Therefore, an actual intellect, whether finite or infinite, must comprehend God's attributes and God's affections, and nothing else. (Ethics, I, P30d)

In understanding the common notion, objective and formal idea come together in the concept. In understanding therefore, modes break out of the recursive imagination of causes and effects, to express their immanent essence as the expression of God.

The more we act according to essence, and the more we understand and affirm that essence in common notions, the more we act and think as immanent expressions of God. This means that the actions of an intelligent person, being actions determined entirely by their essence, are actions always already determined by the infinite and necessary connection of essences in God, and as God. Consequently modal action properly understood, as Spinoza famously argues, dispenses with the inadequate idea of free will. It is only the consciousness of inadequate ideas which gives rise to the subjective illusion of freedom, and so free will only exists in a subject which imagines its passions as caused by outside objects. In understanding the realm of modal essence, everything is already decided, for when we understand and affirm a common notion we understand it as entirely necessary in its relation to all other essences. Spinoza puts it this way: "*In the mind there is no absolute, or free, will; but the mind is determined to will this or that by a cause which is likewise determined by another, and this again by another, and so on to infinity*" (Ethics, II, P48). The affects of the modes are generated from their chance encounters, but these affects are determined by the modal essences they express. Reason will be the way in which we may understand these affects not as effects caused by other modes, but as actions expressing the modes essence in a common notion. In understanding common notions we construct affectual assemblages expressing God/Nature, in which subjective imagination is redundant, and affects are necessary. We become, to use a term Deleuze introduces in *Cinema 2,* but which is appropriate here, a "spiritual automaton" (C2, 170/221) capable of understanding and living the necessary relation of man and the world, or of modes and the God/Nature they express.

## ART AND ETHICAL AESTHETICS

We have seen how the affectual body constructed by an understanding of common notions arises from perceptions, but cannot be understood as such. Common notions are concepts, as is art when it is adequately understood. This introduces another crucial element of Deleuze's onto-aesthetics, one we have already seen him develop in relation to Nietzsche: art adequately understood no longer appears as a representational image. Understanding art as a representational image means for Spinoza that we experience it through the affections that make it present to us. As Spinoza puts it, "the affections of the human body whose ideas present external bodies as present to us, we shall call images of things, though they do not reproduce [external] figures of things. And when the mind regards bodies in this way, we shall say that it imagines" (Ethics, II, P17s). But art adequately understood cannot be representational in this way, and has become a concept that is truly expressive.[35]

For Spinoza, expressions rather than representations are univocal, as only they give an idea that is equally in Substance and mode. Furthermore, it is expression that is adequate to the parallelism of ideas and bodies, as representation implies that one affects the other. Representation is of course, a kind of knowledge, but it is an inadequate one that must assume a position outside of its object in order to create an analogical sign for it.[36] An expression on the other hand, encompasses object and idea in expressing their essence as a common notion. As Deleuze writes:

> . . . an idea represents an object, and in a way expresses it; but at a deeper
> level idea and object express something that is at once common to them,
> and yet belongs to each: a power, or the absolute in two of its powers, those
> of thinking or knowing, and being or acting. Representation is thus located

in a certain extrinsic relation of idea and object, where each enjoys an expressivity over and above representation. (EPS, 335/317)

This means the duality between subject and object required by representation will be transformed. Expression includes neither subject nor object inasmuch as it is their common notion, or essence that is expressed. Similarly, art does not represent an object for a subject, and cannot be a signifier ("a crazy concept for Spinoza,' Deleuze comments).[37] Deleuze does not tire in making this point: "There is clearly a theory of the sign in Spinoza," he writes, "which consists in relating the sign to the most confused understanding and imagination in the world, and in the world such as it is, according to Spinoza, the idea of the sign does not exist. There are expressions, there are never signs."[38] Art for Spinoza will consist of expressions, and will be an art of common notions rather than representational signs. Art will be the construction of assemblages of affects through an ethological understanding of the world, a construction that expresses modal essence. As Deleuze puts it: "Spinoza's whole operation consists in making, in imposing a kind of *assemblage of affects* which implies likewise a critique of representation."[39] The understanding of art-works gained through this practice will be conceptual rather than perceptual. This is not to say that art transcends the body, because all understandings have their parallel in a bodily encounter from which common notions emerge, but understanding art as it appears through a bodily encounter means forming an adequate idea.

How do we reach this concept of art, and how, precisely, does it involve the body? The physical perception of objects given in an imagined image already involves an affect, and is experienced as an increase or decrease in our power to be affected. Experiencing art, even inadequately as an image, is already a dynamic experience of relation, of joy and sadness. This means that although understanding art will produce a concept expressing modal essence, imagination will nevertheless be the starting point for this process, because such an understanding must start from its joyful affects. Ethical-aesthetics always begins with what we like, with what affirms our power to act.

Spinoza introduces a new understanding of art, no longer as inadequate representation, but as adequate expression. As a result, ethical-aesthetics will not ask what an artwork means or represents, but what it is capable of, what it expresses. An expressive artist is the one who affirms new common notions, and constructs new affectual assemblages. The artist has become critical, and is simply the name for the action of affirmation that emerges from modal encounters properly understood. The artwork is, similar to last chapter, indiscernible from this action as its embodiment and expression. Only by asking what the artwork does, what joys it brings and what essences it expresses, will we understand it. But this understanding is not once and for all, and is processual, resumed each time the work is perceived or encountered. This means the art assemblage includes on the one hand the affects emerging from its encounter, and on the other remains open to connections yet to come. Art is always under construction. Aesthetics is always a question about "what happens?," about the process of composition that is expressed in a work. This is entirely appropriate given the ontological assumption that, as Deleuze puts it: "Everything in Nature is just composition" (EPS, 237/216). This is the sense in which ethical life requires a certain artistry, an ability to compose ourselves, to select the good encounters and construct from them the maximum number of joyful affections. Deleuze states this expanded concept of art clearly: "The common notions are an Art, the art of the Ethics itself: organizing good encounters, composing actual relations, forming powers, experimenting" (SPP, 119/161). But common notions are not only constructed through an ethics that could be broadly described as artistic, they are also transformative in a way we have already seen Deleuze make a condition of art. In understanding common notions life breaks free of its imaginative representations, and expresses structures that cross the boundaries of the organism, of subjects and objects, and the consciousness that maintains them.

Common notions therefore provide the beginnings of an art practice which is: 1) Specific to the body of the affectual assemblage constructed and the essence which is expressed. These assemblages are always changing as their relations change, meaning the work of art, or artwork is never separate from the becoming of the assemblages it is part of. 2) This participatory practice is capable of producing new concepts in response to new conditions. Art practice becomes an empirical experiment with what art can do, constructing an experimental body as a real expression of its real conditions, an expression of God/Nature's essence. 3) Under these conditions the criteria for successful art-work are no different than those determining any successful creation whatsoever. Aesthetics in these terms is an ethical-aesthetics, a practice rather than a theory of the object, the practice of composing affectual relations into common notions. This experimental art defines a practice, an art-work that is inseparable from the works it creates, as it is from the common notions it constructs and expresses.

The question remains, however, whether art expresses common notions in a way that could be identified as belonging specifically to something called "art." It seems to me that both in the last chapter and in this one, Deleuze is consistent in calling for an art and an aesthetics which is ethically and ontologically defined, and undetermined by any material or formal givens. Under these conditions art must be understood in terms of Deleuze and Guattari's statement, "art includes no other plane than that of aesthetic composition" (WP,

195/185). This immanent plane of composition defines art in terms of its affectual relations, in terms of what Deleuze and Guattari will call sensations. What Spinoza shows us however, is that this plane of aesthetic composition cannot be understood except as the plane of ethical action, and this means the revaluation of art within a wider frame of ethical-aesthetics. This does not however, exclude an understanding of art as a particular aesthetic practice, with its own mechanisms of expression. Indeed, Deleuze, and Deleuze and Guattari develop various typologies within specific arts in order to explain particular aesthetic processes of composition, and we shall look in detail at those developed for cinema and for painting. But art as an ethical-aesthetics in a Spinozian sense cannot be limited to these mechanisms, and gives instead the conditions by which life—including those things we commonly call "art works"—can be understood as expressive, and by which "art" becomes art.

## TOWARDS GOD: BEATITUDE, OR THE THIRD KIND OF KNOWLEDGE

Adequate ideas, or common notions express essence, and as such find their necessity in their relations to all the other essences making up the infinite attribute of thought. The less the mind is acted upon by passions the more ideas it understands adequately, leading to a point where, according to Spinoza: "The mind understands all things to be necessary, and to be determined by an infinite connection of causes [i.e. in and by God] to exist and produce effects" (Ethics, V, P6d). Adequate knowledge understands the affects as they are in their modal essence, that is, as they are in God. Such knowledge does not exist subjectively as if of an object, but immanent in God, as a part which expresses God's necessary and interconnected whole. As Spinoza explains it, "our mind, insofar as it understands, is an eternal mode of thinking [i.e. essence], which is determined by another eternal mode of thinking, and this again by another, and so on, to infinity; so that together, they all constitute God's eternal and infinite intellect" (Ethics, V, P40s). Knowledge constituted by adequate ideas is not the operation of a subject but of an "eternal mode of thought," one that affirms the idea *qua* essence in the attribute of thought. As a result, subjective consciousness is overcome in the understanding, where we do not affirm or deny anything of a thing (imagination), the revalued thing (as affectual assemblage) affirms or denies (expresses) something of itself (essence) in us (SPP, 81/79). This is an important moment in Spinoza's "mystical" thought, and means, as he puts it, "our mind, insofar as it perceives things truly, is part of the infinite intellect of God; hence, it is as necessary that the minds clear and distinct ideas are true as that God's ideas are" (Ethics,

II, P43s). In the adequate knowledge of common notions we begin to know God not from the outside as it were, in relations to the objects that affect us, but from the inside, as expressions of God, as God's modal essences (Ethics, V, P22). As Deleuze writes, *"common notions are ideas that are formally explained by our power of thinking and that, materially, express the idea of God as their efficient cause"* (EPS, 279/258). The common notions are the folds from the human to the divine, they express the immanence of modal existence and substantial essence, and as a result, "give us direct knowledge of God's eternal infinite essence" (EPS, 280/259). This knowledge of common notions emerges from the affirmation of joy, and charts an ethology in which we become active. This becoming active is the creation of a new body, one that I experience as it is in God, as God's expression. The becoming active of ethical-aesthetics makes the art of ethology the expression of God, and makes of the understanding an atheistic mysticism. It is this claim, marking the high point of Spinoza's path of reason, that we will now go on to examine further.

In the first type of knowledge, or imagination, we perceive affects as caused by outside bodies. Our ideas act as representational signs of these extrinsic determinations. In the second type of knowledge we understand what is common to our body and another, and construct an affectual assemblage or common notion, acting as an adequate idea. This idea expresses an essence, which in turn exists only through its combination with others according to the eternal laws of God/Nature. Common notions therefore express essences, but only from a modal point of view and not yet as ideas that God has of itself. That is, common notions express God's essence but do not give an adequate (clear and distinct) idea of it. Common notions remain ideas about the essences of perceived bodies and their relations, which in expressing God's essence only point towards its adequate understanding. But in doing so common notions "propel" (EPS, 299/279) us into a new domain, that of the third type of knowledge (Ethics, V, P28). "We begin," Deleuze writes, "by forming common notions that express God's essence; only then can we understand God as expressing himself in essence" (EPS, 301/280). Here our knowledge of God is no longer restricted to common notions, and we reach the beatitude of knowing how we are ourselves modal expressions of the essence of God. Beatitude is the expression of univocity in life, for in the third type of knowledge, Deleuze writes: "A reasonable being may [ . . . ] in its way, reproduce and express the effort of Nature as a whole" (EPS, 265/243).

An idea we have is essentially true, and gives the third kind of knowledge, when we understand it as an expression of God's essence rather than as an expression of a modal essence (the second kind of knowledge). To understand how this is possible we must remember certain distinctions Spinoza makes. The idea of God I have is an objective idea, and remains at the second level of knowledge inasmuch as it arises through my understanding of modal essence. This idea exists within the attribute of thought, which constitutes God in his essence, and is inseparable from his power of thinking as this constitutes the formal attribute of thought. Spinoza began the *Ethics* by assuming the univocity of God, which meant God could only be understood through itself. This in turn implies, as Deleuze has it, "the idea of God is the idea in its objective being, and the infinite intellect is the same idea considered in its formal being. The two aspects are inseparable; one cannot dissociate the first aspect from the second" (SPP, 80/90–1). As a result, God's infinite intellect, in constituting his essence in the attribute of thought, and as the formal being of his essence, constitutes the essence and existence of all ideas (Ethics, I, P17sII). Consequently, we have the opportunity to understand our thought as God's inasmuch as, according to Spinoza: "God is the efficient cause of all things which can fall under an infinite intellect" (Ethics, I, P16c1). Beatitude will mark the mystical moment of thought where an objective idea of God will be adequate to and expressive of its formal being, of God as thinking being. Beatitude will be an understanding of God such as God has of itself.

Beatitude will arrive in an idea of the absolute immanence of God and the modes, but will nevertheless maintain the distinction of Substance from modes, and of God's infinite essence from the modal essences and existences that express it (Ethics, I, P16c3). As Spinoza explains: "God's intellect, insofar as it is conceived to constitute the divine essence, differs from our intellect both as to its essence and as to its existence, and cannot agree with it in anything except in name" (Ethics, I, P16sII). This "name" is the univocal attribute of thought, in which God's essence as intellect is constituted, and the modal essence of an idea is found. Beatitude will be an idea adequate to the attribute as God's essence, and which will require the final overcoming of "our" intellect to become a singular idea God has of itself. But this overcoming will emerge from "our" intellect inasmuch as it understands, because this understanding finds its condition in the univocity of the attribute. This transformation of the understanding into beatitude obviously needs careful explanation, as it is both the culmination, and the most obscure point of Spinoza's *Ethics*. An idea has a cause inasmuch as it has an essence that it expresses, and which is thought as another idea. But every idea also has God as it's formal cause, different from the idea in its essence and existence. These two senses of idea meet in the univocal attribute of thought, "in which," Deleuze writes, "the effect is produced and by which the cause acts" (SPP, 53/78). As Spinoza has it:

> Singular thoughts, or this or that thought, are modes which express
> God's nature in a certain and determinate way. Therefore there belongs
> to God an attribute whose concept all singular thoughts involve, and
> through which they are also conceived. Thought is one of God's infinite
> attributes, which expresses an eternal and infinite essence of God, or God
> is a thinking thing. (Ethics, II, P1d)

The formal cause of all ideas is God's infinite intellect in its essence as attribute,
which is expressed in modal form as ideas in their essence and existence. The
idea giving the third kind of knowledge therefore explains its essence *qua* attribute as formal cause, in an idea expressing this cause itself.

So what constitutes this "true idea" of the third kind? God's essence is formal in the attributes that constitute his nature, God's power of acting being the
essence or "formal being of things," and God's power of thinking being the
essence or "formal being of ideas" (Ethics, II, P5d and P6d). As Spinoza explains, this simply means that the modes find their formal essence in God's attributes, that is, God is the cause of all thinking and acting things (Ethics, II,
P8). Objective ideas find their necessity and order in being caused by God's formal essence. This means, Spinoza writes, "whatever follows formally from God's
infinite nature follows objectively in God from his idea in the same order and
with the same connection" (Ethics, II, P7c). God's formal essence, insofar as we
are concerned, is its infinite intellect and body, and these compose all modal
bodies and ideas in the infinity of affectual assemblages according to their divine order. The attributes therefore constitute the formal being of all things and
ideas, and the third kind of knowledge will give an adequate idea of this divine
essence. Beatitude will only emerge in thought however, because it is only the
attribute of thought which has the capacity to express all the other attributes and
their modes in objective ideas, including the formal being of thought itself. This
is the final, remarkable, consequence of Spinoza's theory of parallelism, and
opens up the mystical power of understanding. Reason will, at its furthest reach,
comprehend God's essence in its formal being as thinking thing, as the necessary co-implication of all things and ideas within the attribute of thought. How
is this possible? First of all, Spinoza argues: "*The formal being of ideas admits God
as a cause only insofar as he is explained as a thinking thing, and not insofar as he
is explained by any other attribute. That is, ideas, both of God's attributes and of singular things, admit not the objects themselves, or the things perceived, as their efficient cause, but God himself, insofar as he is a thinking thing*" (Ethics, II, P5). As
we have already seen, there can be an objective idea of anything, including ideas.
When inadequate, these ideas understand their cause as an idea of another body,

but when they are adequate they understand and express their essence in a common notion, which necessarily expresses the interrelated co-determination of essences constituting the attribute of thought. Finally, in the third kind of knowledge an idea comprehends its formal reality, meaning it understands its cause not in terms of its own power as an essence, but as an idea of God expressing itself. In other words, the third kind of knowledge understands an idea as caused by God, in its formal essence, as expressing the whole of Nature.

Between the second and third types of knowledge therefore, we move, according to Spinoza, "from an adequate knowledge of certain attributes of God, to an adequate knowledge of the essence of things" (Ethics, V, P25d). This is a move from knowledge of essence in its attribute, to knowledge of God's essence as attribute, expressed in modal existence as an idea. In the second kind of knowledge we have an idea of God, but only through the common notions that express it, the formal reality of God not being one of these notions (EPS, 309/288). An understanding of essence in the third type of knowledge however, expresses the formal reality of God as thinking thing as the immanent cause of this idea, and so comprehends God's essence in all its attributes and modes. Pierre Macherey describes this final stage of reason nicely, "by returning into itself," he writes, "without escaping its own order, thought discovers everything contained within Substance, insofar as the latter is expressed in the infinity of all its attributes."[40] The final end of philosophy for Spinoza is the point where we understand the formal cause of our objective ideas as God's infinite intellect, which contains the infinity of attributes that make up his essence, and the infinity of modes in their essence and existences. An objective idea of God as formal cause of that idea is therefore an adequate idea of God's essence. In the third type of knowledge then, an objective idea has moved from an idea of affects, as inadequate (imagination) or adequate (understanding), to an idea of the whole of God/Nature as cause of, and expressed in, this idea (beatitude). To put it in other, more personal words (Spinoza's), it is the adequate idea of my own essence, attained in the second kind of knowledge, "which therefore must be conceived through the very essence of God (by I, A4 ['The knowledge of an affect depends on and involves the knowledge of its cause']) and this concept must be in God" (Ethics, V, P22d).

It is therefore possible for a finite intellect to know everything, to understand its own constitutional infinity as the formal being of God. At this point our power of comprehension would be the same as our power of expression, and we would know and express God as God knows and expresses itself. This is the culmination of Spinoza's mystical atheism, because it is an understanding of my own essence and existence that comprehends and expresses the infinity of all that is. This is an understanding of our existence as the univocity of God in the immanence of its formal essence and objective expression, and is the meaning of the phrase of Guattari's that began this chapter, "I am God most of the time." An idea in the third type of knowledge expresses all of God, inasmuch as God's formal essence in the attribute of thought is its cause, and includes an idea of everything. Ideas of the third kind will therefore be ideas we have of God's essence at the same time as they will be ideas of our essence as God conceives them. For in the third kind of knowledge, Deleuze writes: "We think as God thinks, we experience the very feelings of God" (EPS, 308/287). In beatitude, or an atheistic mysticism proper to Spinoza, we reach the full reversibility of Substance and mode Deleuze calls for in *Difference and Repetition.* In the third type of knowledge the modes and Substance become entirely immanent to each other on a single univocal plane. "Our essence," Deleuze writes, "is a part of God, and the idea of our essence a part of the idea of God, only to the extent that God's essence explicates itself through ours" (EPS, 309–10/288–9). In this way, as Deleuze and Guattari put it, remembering Spinoza: "The One expresses in a single meaning all of the multiple. Being expresses in a single meaning all that differs" (ATP, 254/311).

Finally then, it is the univocity of the attribute that is capable of rendering God and modes fully immanent in the third kind of knowledge, but it is expression that ensures their relation maintains their distinction while being entirely dynamic and co-determining. As a result, Deleuze writes: "In Spinoza *the whole theory of expression supports univocity;* and its whole import is to free univocal Being from a state of indifference or neutrality, to make it the object of a pure affirmation, which is actually realized in an expressive pantheism or immanence" (EPS, 333/309). This is why Spinoza calls the third kind of knowledge the "salvation of man," because, as Deleuze explains, once more evoking the mystical path of reason: "The path of salvation is the path of expression itself: to become expressive—that is, to become active; to express God's essence, to be oneself an idea through which the essence of God explicates itself, to have affections that are explained by our own essence and express God's essence" (EPS, 320/298). The salvation of man then, will be, quite precisely, the overcoming of man, because the becoming active of man is his or her becoming expressive, and this, in the final moment of an ethical-aesthetics, is a becoming-divine.

At this, the high point of reason, the thinker expresses everything in their idea of God, so expressing the "greatest human perfection" (Ethics, V, P27d) and the greatest joy. But this joyful expression of ones own perfection is beyond all affections of joy or sadness, because one's perfection is expressed through a purely "intellectual love" of God. This love is only found through ideas of the body and its essence, and is not itself an extended thing. In this intellectual love, or beatitude, all affections and images of things are related to the idea of God, (Ethics, V, P14) making the body immanent to, but distinct from the mind's love of God (Ethics, V, P16). Things exist in God, but God can only be truly expressed in the beatitude of the idea. Deleuze develops this understanding of bodies in terms of intensity. Bodies are always extended things, and although their ideas lead to knowledge, bodies are not themselves knowledge. Beatitude, as a result, will involve bodies but not be bodies, the world of ideas being purely intense. "What interests me in this mystical point," Deleuze says, "is this world of intensities. There, you are in possession, not merely formally but in an accomplished way. It's no longer even joy, Spinoza finds the mystical word beatitude or active affect, that is to say the auto-affect. But this remains quite concrete. The third kind is a world of pure intensities."[41] The concreteness of intensities is therefore quite different from that of things, and indeed this is what Spinoza argues, that extended things exist in duration, whereas essences exist eternally (Ethics, I, Def.8). As he puts it: "*Whatever the mind understands under a species of eternity, it understands not from the fact that it conceives the body's present actual existence, but from the fact that it conceives the body's essence under a species of eternity*" (Ethics, V, P29). In the third kind of knowledge it is precisely the body's essence that is understood as the eternal and infinite essence of God (Ethics, V, P29s). God's essence exists in eternity, which means it has an intense existence rather than an extended duration. As a result, in understanding our or another's essence as eternal we conceive things, through God's essence, as real and yet intense beings (Ethics, V, P30d). Again, it is the univocity of the attribute of thought which is crucial here, as it is only insofar as the mind itself is eternal (i.e. part of God's attribute of thought) that it can have knowledge of the third kind (Ethics, V, P31). This is not to finally privilege ideas over the body, for although the eternal is "a certain mode of thinking" (Ethics, V, P23s), thinking is the expression of "the essence of the body under a species of eternity" (Ethics, V, P23s). That is, in the mystical and intellectual love of God everything attains its concrete existence as intensity and in eternity.

Our greatest perfection, our salvation, will therefore leave all notions of ourselves as volitional, affective, and extended subjects behind, in becoming the thoughts of God. Any form of psychological consciousness has evaporated, leaving, as Deleuze calls it, a purely "explicative logical formalism" (EPS, 326/303). We have become purely formal elements in the systematic explication of God/Nature, spiritual automatons in which all "human" affects have been overcome, "not only that love, hate, and the like are destroyed," Spinoza explains, "but also that the appetites, or desires, which usually arise from such an affect, cannot be excessive" (Ethics, V, P4s).[42] In place of the human subjective emotions is an inhuman intellectual love that surpasses them, the impersonal joy of

God/Nature as it affirms and expresses itself. As Spinoza writes: "*The mind's intellectual love of God is the very love of God by which God loves himself, not insofar as he is infinite, but insofar as he can be explained by the human mind's essence, considered under a species of eternity; that is, the mind's intellectual love of God is part of the infinite love by which God loves himself*" (Ethics, V, P36).[43] The intellectual love of God is an action in which the mind contemplates itself, inasmuch as God is its cause. In contemplating ourselves we contemplate God, in understanding the part we understand the whole. This is what Deleuze elsewhere calls a "percept" (ECC, 148/184) or "direct vision" (EPS, 301/281) of God, and this is a term we will come back to in Chapter Five, where it play an important part in art's production of sensation. As Spinoza has it, the third kind of knowledge is, "an action by which God, insofar as he can be explained through the human mind, contemplates himself, with the accompanying idea of himself [as the cause]" (Ethics, V, P36d). Finally then, the third kind of knowledge is the formula for Spinoza's mysticism: "God's love of men and the mind's intellectual love of God are one and the same thing" (Ethics, V, P36c). Or as Deleuze and Guattari put it, we have become indiscernible because we have become the world, and entered the "impersonality of the creator"(ATP, 280/343).

## THE ART OF ATHEISTIC MYSTICISM

Knowing what the third kind of knowledge is naturally leads us to the question of how we may attain it. It is precisely the empirical compositional experiments that the body has made in discovering what it can do, that has lead to the understanding of intense essence as an idea of God. A body capable of a great many things has ethically optimised or affirmed its compositional joy. This means it is not troubled by bad affects, and does not express affects contrary to its nature. Such a body affirms its own power of acting and has succeeded in ordering and connecting its affects according to the necessary order of essences as they constitute the attribute. As ideas are always parallel to bodies, the ethical ordering of affects implies ideas that are adequate to these affects. This knowledge of the body is, as we have seen, the condition for the eternal and intellectual love of beatitude. The rarefied realm of the third kind of knowledge is therefore inseparable from an ethical-aesthetics as the critical practice of life. As Spinoza writes: "*He who has a body capable of a great many things has a mind whose greatest part is eternal*" (Ethics, V, P39). Although the third kind of knowledge is entirely intellectual, it emerges from an experimental understanding of things, and understands the essence of God only inasmuch as it involves existence. Consequently, as Spinoza puts it: "To conceive things under a species of eternity, therefore, is to conceive things insofar as they are conceived through God's essence, as real beings, or insofar as through God's essence they involve existence" (Ethics, V, P30d). Eternity is not gained by transcending the body, but through understanding its affects. The body under these conditions expresses its intense eternal essence, rather than marking our distance from essence. Spinoza's intellectual love of God is not a transcendence of the body but is the true immanence of God's essence and existence in the attribute of thought. Only in relation to this immanence of existence and essence can we understand the mind's ideas as eternal. Eternal essence is expressed in bodies but this essence *as* God, rather than simply as *expressing* God, is only understood in the mind.

The point, in relation to art, is that art cannot be thought outside the parallelism of things and ideas. Art must be the construction of ethical bodies through a critical practice, as much as the thinking of ideas expressing God's essence. The minds mystical comprehension of the essence of God, inasmuch as this emerges from the construction of affectual bodies (assemblages), offers a beatific image of art. Art is an experimental practice exploring what the body can do, and as such is the continual emergence of new expressions (new existences, new affectual assemblages, new becomings) of intense essence. Parallel to this emergence is an understanding of these expressions in a true idea of God. Together this experimental body and its intellectual understanding, produce a mystical but atheist art. This art exists as the expression of a dynamic world of affectual assemblage, and as an understanding of eternal essence as this constitutes God/Nature. Art in these terms is inseparable from beatitude, which defines the univocal expressions of an ethical aesthetics. Once more then, we return to our previous problem regarding the status of art as we would usually understand it. Clearly the mystical understanding of the intense world of divine essence does not exclude art from a beatific knowledge. Furthermore, important aspects of an ethical practice, such as selection and affirmation could be broadly defined as "artistic." None of this however, could be regarded as telling us much about art's specific forms of expression. Spinoza's ethics, considered as an aesthetics, can be seen as an affirmative creative process constructing affectual assemblages as expressions of intense essence, and whose ideas, properly understood, culminate in a mystical love of God/Nature. But ethical-aesthetics in these terms is not particular to art, even if it involves, as Deleuze says, an art of the common notions.

We can, at this point, both sum up, and look forward to the work yet to be done. The question as to arts specific modality within Deleuze's ethical-aesthetics, as it has so far emerged from his readings of Nietzsche and Spinoza, no doubt remains. Its answer awaits a consideration of art's various types of materiality, and how these form their specific affectual assemblages. This will tell us much more about how art operates within the broader definition of an onto-

ethical-aesthetics so far undertaken. As a result our attention will now turn to
Deleuze's work on cinema and Francis Bacon, as well as to his and Guattari's discussions of painting. But this promissory declaration should not detract from
what has already been achieved, most importantly the definition of a new image
of art, even if this has taken us well away from what we may have previously considered it to be.

Art thought through Spinoza's *Ethics* exists only in its compositional relations and their affectual becomings, and is understood as intense expressions of
the infinitude of God/Nature. This mystical understanding is already a liberation of art from its duties of representation, and its confinement along the sub-
ject/object perceptual axis. Michael Hardt puts it clearly when he argues that
Deleuze's use of expressionism "constitutes a polemic against semiology on ontological grounds. A system of signs does not recognize being as a productive
dynamic; it does not help us understand being through its causal genealogy.
[ . . . ] a theory of expression seeks to make the cause present, to bring us back
to an ontological foundation by making clear the genealogy of being."[44] Spinoza
offers an alternative understanding of art, one in which it expresses the productive dynamics of being, and so places its ontological foundation on the same
plane of immanence as its expressive existence. This is already a lot, and is clearly
the preparatory work necessary to the more specific examinations of a "mystical" art that are to follow.

In a broader sense however, and once more to finish in an ecstatic register
as appropriate to a discussion of Spinoza as to Nietzsche, ethical-aesthetics
transforms my relations into a question of art, it challenges me to experiment
with joy in order to create common notions which connect me to the world.
This is an art theory that gives the proper weight to the *work* of art, and gives
its proper ontological importance, its proper ethical dimension (as we shall see,
a dimension which is also political), and its properly cosmic nature, even if it
does not yet describe its specificity. Spinoza's ethical-aesthetics of experimentation expresses the intense Substance of God, and offers an understanding of the
way we are folded into the infinite. Spinoza gives a new image of art, an art of
living as a living expression of God, and an atheistic mysticism as a new belief
in immanence. Art is the expression of this living communion with God, the
construction of an immanent spiritual dimension, as life and in life. God has
appeared, as our sensation.

# Chapter Three
# We Need New Signs: Towards a Cinematic Image of Thought

My eyes are useless for they render back only the image of the known. My whole body must become a constant beam of light, moving with an ever greater rapidity, never arrested, never looking back, never dwindling.

—Henry Miller, *Tropic of Capricorn.*

## INTRODUCTION

We have seen the affect emerge within Nietzsche's physiology of overcoming and Spinoza's mystical trajectory of reason as the at once singular body and cosmic unity of art. These are, we could say, the simultaneous directions of art's constant movement. Although this movement defines the onto-aesthetic reality of art as such, there is nevertheless an art composed specifically of moving images: cinema. Cinema is a machine for the production of signs that both affect the body in a new way, and give us a new image of thought. Deleuze's two books on cinema will explore this body-brain through a highly innovative taxonomy of its signs, a taxonomy that develops a new semiotic of cinema, gives a fresh account of cinema's historical development, and as the condition of possibility of these contributions, offers a new ontology of cinema itself. Deleuze has given cinema studies new signs, and the results of his startling generosity undoubtedly remain "to come." I can't pretend to exhaust his store of explosives here, and instead will limit myself to tracing Deleuze's ontology of cinema's temporal signs, in order to explore the ways it gives us a new image of thought.

Deleuze bases his discussion of the cinema on the work of Henri Bergson. Although much of what he finds there will echo what we have already encountered in the first two chapters, Deleuze's use of Bergson in relation to cinema also has its own necessity. First, it provides an explicit ontology of perception, which Deleuze takes primarily from Bergson's *Matter and Memory*.[1] Second, this book was published in 1886, making it directly contemporary to the new artform of cinema. Deleuze will begin then, from the idea that Bergson's book gives the philosophical elaboration of cinema's great discovery: the moving-image. Cinema invents a new type of sign, and will require—indeed it almost seems to anticipate—the new philosophy of images Bergson provides. But cinema develops Bergson's philosophical insights in its own directions, acting as a kind of experimental laboratory for his ideas that soon produces remarkable new inventions. The most important is the time-image, which moves beyond Bergson and, through Deleuze's intercession, offers cinema back to philosophy as a new image of thought. It is as if the modern exemplar of Nietzsche's artist-philosopher is a film-maker, an experimenter in the realm of cine-thought.

Deleuze begins by outlining two possibilities for cine-thought, which we could call cinema's before and after. The first, Bergson's explicit position, sees cinema's photographic technology as limiting it to a "snapshot" of the present, an "immobile section" of the constantly moving aggregate of images—each acting on every other—constituting the becoming of the universe (this is what Deleuze, following Bergson, calls "duration").[2] The second, the position Deleuze finds in Bergson, sees cinema invent a new image capable of perceiving and extending this universal movement in a "mobile section of duration" (C1, 22/36).[3] This alternative repeats the by now familiar Deleuzian distinction between representation and expression, this time in the Bergsonian register Deleuze believes is appropriate to cinema.

> What is in the present is what the image 'represents'," Deleuze writes, 'but not the image itself, which, in cinema as in painting, is never to be confused with what it represents. The image itself is the system of the relationships between its elements, that is, a set of relationships from which the variable present only flows. [ . . . ] What is specific to the image, as soon as it is creative, is to make perceptible, to make visible, relationships of time which cannot be seen in the represented object and do not allow themselves to be reduced to the present. (C2, xii)

Here Deleuze succinctly defines the Bergsonian conditions of cinema's onto-aesthetics—the construction of an image capable of expressing duration in "relationships of time."

The cinema books develop in detail two cinematic expressions of time. First, the movement-image of classical cinema expresses the whole of time (duration) as its immanent cause, but indirectly, through already given conditions of possibility. Second, modern cinema breaks with these conditions and directly expresses duration in a time-image. Before examining this difference in detail, it is important to point out that the difference between these two cinematic images is neither hierarchical nor strictly chronological, but is a difference in kind—they emerge from different ontological co-ordinates. In fact, Deleuze writes: "It cannot be said that one is more important than the other, whether more beautiful or more profound. All that can be said is that the movement-image does not give us a time-image" (C2, 270/354). So although each image emerges at a specific time (movement-images before, and time-images after WWII), and due to its own historical conditions (although these remain summary and peripheral in Deleuze's account), their difference cannot be reduced to historical factors and is, in fact, ontological. This means that it is not enough for a film to be produced after the war for it to produce a time-image. In fact, Deleuze claims that Hollywood persists in using the formulas of the movement-image, which in its hands has degenerated into a politically repressive form.

This introduces another important aspect of Deleuze's cine-thought, its political dimension. Hollywood after the war, he argues, inherits the Nazi development of cinema's power of producing "psychological automaton" (C2, 264/345). The cinema of the masses, Deleuze caustically remarks, "has degenerated into state propaganda and manipulation, into a kind of fascism which brought together Hitler and Hollywood, Hollywood and Hitler" (C2, 164/214). Deleuze positions the time-image as an aesthetic intervention into this realm of the Spectacle, opposing the political passivity produced and reproduced in the consumption of mass media.[4] Cinema's interventions act as a "shock-therapy" (appropriately administered in part by Antonin Artaud, as we shall see), which create new temporal experiences forcing us to think beyond the cliché, its repressive politics, and its first and last bastion, the human, all too human.

## THINGS RE-ENTER INTO EACH OTHERS[5]

Deleuze begins *Cinema 1* with a "commentary" on Bergson's concept of movement. Bergson proposed in *Matter and Memory* that "real" movement could no longer be thought through its representation, a proposition Deleuze will test in relation to its contemporaneous instantiation, the cinema. Bergson argues that previous philosophical attempts to represent movement through abstract categories of thought failed. "You cannot reconstitute movement," Deleuze paraphrases, "with positions in space or instants in time: that is, with immobile sections" (C1, 1/9). Space and time, as categories of thought, translate movement into their abstract coordinates, and think movement as a sequential numerical passage appearing as a line drawn through space and time. Movement is thereby reduced to points on a graph. "The number t would always stand for the same thing," Bergson writes, "it would still count the same number of correspondences between the states of the objects or systems and the points of the line, ready drawn, which would be then the 'course of time'"(CE, 9). Reason produces this representation by defining movement as a difference of degree between abstract points that in themselves remain the same. Movement becomes measurement. But Zeno's paradoxes had already shown the impossibility of thinking movement in such a way, and revealed its difference in kind from this numerated, "scientific" and represented movement.[6] This (mis)representation of time by thought rests, for Bergson, on a failure to understand the difference between two sorts of time, a scientific present that is continually coming to pass, and duration as all of time co-existing with the present. As Bergson puts it: "The systems science work with are in an instantaneous present that is always being renewed; such systems are never in that real, concrete duration in which the past remains bound up with the present" (CE,22). Science deals with a present that dies and is reborn again at every instant, making of each present instant a frozen image of duration that does not reveal the changes occurring between these fixed points. In producing these "immobile sections" of time reason remains unable to think the movement of change—becoming—and is therefore unable to account for its own genetic dimension. At the same time as the movement-image appears in cinema then, a new image of thought capable of thinking it appears in Bergson's concept of intuition.[7] The temporal conjunction of Bergson's philosophy and cinema's invention takes us, Deleuze argues, beyond a scientific reason as the general and abstract condition of experience, towards a movement-image expressing its conditions of real experience (B, 27/17). Deleuze's use of Bergson in relation to cinema therefore converges with his attack on Kantian aesthetics that we have already discussed, for in the movement-image time and space no longer form the autonomous transcendental conditions of all possible experience, but "these conditions can and must be grasped in an intuition [ . . . ] precisely because they are the conditions of real experience."[8]

The conditions of our experience of movement, Bergson argues, are found in the virtual dimension of duration, which although not actual is nevertheless real, and produces the movements we perceive. Duration is the past, inasmuch as the past is no longer understood as a numbered line leading to the present, but as the immanent All, the whole of time in its continual interaction that constructs the becoming of the present. Duration is the immanent and ontogenetic life of becoming, of which the present is its expression. As Bergson puts it, "duration means invention, the creation of forms, the continual elaboration of the absolutely new" (CE, 11). Duration can't be said *to be* in space or time, because it is the *becoming* of space and time. Deleuze argues duration is an open set, or perhaps better, the open "itself," the virtual dimension both expressed and constructed anew in actual movement.[9] For Bergson the infinite movements of duration and the finite movement of images are not different in kind, for the latter are the actual expressions of the former once they have passed through the brain (B, 24/14). For Deleuze cinema functions in this way—like a brain—and constructs moving-images, as becomings, expressing their real and immanent conditions: "a change in duration or in the whole" (C1, 8/18).

When images are understood as representations of objects moving in space and time they give, Bergson suggests, *"only a snapshot view of a transition"* (CE, 302). These snapshots cancel the genetic movement of duration, and only give a frozen image of what escapes them. This snapshot depends on the mechanism that produces it, the rather too slow machinery of reason, which only by freezing movement produces its representation. Opposed to this snapshot, even if it is at 24 frames a second, Deleuze seeks a real image of duration, and this will require both a moving-image, and a new perceptual (and indeed conceptual) mechanism to produce it. Deleuze provides both, and so rehabilitates cinema within Bergson's philosophy, by shifting our perceptual mechanism from the projector and its projection of snapshots, to the screen. "The brain is the screen."[10] This changes everything, for on the brain-screen a new image and new perception—a new *intuition*—emerges. Now, as Deleuze writes: "Instead of going from the acentred state of things to centred perception, [we] could go back up towards the acentred state of things, and get closer to it" (C1, 58/85). This distinction Deleuze makes between "descent" and "ascent" is one made between two images of movement. These two images emerge from their cerebral mechanisms, reason (the projection of snapshots) and intuition (moving images on the screen). As Bergson argues: "The first only unwinds a roll ready prepared. In principle, it might be accomplished almost instantaneously, like releasing a spring. But the ascending movement, which corresponds to an inner work of ripening or creating, *endures* essentially, and imposes its rhythm on the first, which is inseparable from it" (CE, 11). As such, intuition is a "superior empiricism," one Deleuze often calls for, that would be capable of perceiving the real ontological conditions of each actual perception. This affirmation of intuition as the mechanism of a new cine-brain takes us "beyond the human condition" and its inadequate rationality, to reveal "the inhuman and superhuman" conditions of cinema and thought—duration (B, 28/19).

Deleuze calls this inhuman dimension of duration—and it is a term he takes from Bergson—a "spiritual reality" (C1, 11/22). For Deleuze, as for Bergson, the spiritual reality of duration is both atheist and mystical, inasmuch as it exists as entirely material "cerebral vibrations," (MM, 23) but these vibrations keep every thing "open somewhere by the finest thread which attaches it to the rest of the universe" (C1, 10/21).[11] This "spiritual" movement is imparted through the perceptual process of intuitive thought—the process of the cine-brain—that returns to things their living becoming in duration.

"Spirit," as Bergson puts it, "borrows from matter the perceptions on which it feeds and restores them to matter in the form of movements which it has stamped with its own freedom" (MM, 249). As a "mystical" movement similar to that we found in Deleuze's reading of Nietzsche and Spinoza, Bergson's "spirit" is immanent to life as what gives life, a type of thought utterly material, but one that takes us beyond the rational limits of human being. This life is what Deleuze believes the spirit of cinema discovers as the vital movement that animates its images. Spirit then, is not a Christian concept, and refers to nothing transcendent. It is the immanent and inorganic life of duration, expressed in the perceptive mechanism of the brain as it constructs the new. The problem for Deleuze will therefore be to show how the cine-brain "ascends" to the immanent and virtual plane of duration without transcending its actual images, to show, in other words, how the cine-brain constructs images in such a way as to express their spiritual dimension.

## A NEW PRACTICE OF IMAGES AND SIGNS

The conjunction of cinema and Bergson is an obvious one, Deleuze argues, inasmuch as for Bergson: "The identity of the image and movement stems from the identity of matter and light" (C1, 60/88). This is the simple statement by which Deleuze shifts cinema's mechanism from projector to screen. Deleuze justifies this shift by Bergson's physics, a radical physics that posits the equivalence of matter and images, and of images and light.[12] The movement-image emerges from this Bergsonian equivalence of light in its materiality and an image in movement, because as Deleuze points out, if "light is movement, [then] the movement-image and the light-image are two facets of one and the same appearing" (C1, 49/73). This is the materialism Deleuze takes from Bergson: "The movement-image is matter itself, as Bergson showed" (C2, 33/49). The materiality of cinema's moving-image is luminosity; it is a propagation of energy as light. Images, as luminous moving matter are "vibrations" (C1, 8/19), movements that express the infinite connectivity and creativity of the open and immanent plane of duration. As Deleuze puts it: "IMAGE=MOVEMENT" (C1, 58/86). Things are images (i.e. perceptions) *as* movements of matter, rather than static and immaterial representations *of* this movement. As a result, and as Deleuze suggests, the universe is cinematic, "the universe as cinema itself, a metacinema" (C1, 59/88). This is the most cosmic and cinematic formulation possible of Bergson's ontology, one that perfectly expresses Deleuze's ontological approach to aesthetics.

Deleuze, following the first chapter of Bergson's *Matter and Memory*, now dissolves rational consciousness into the universal action and reaction of images in movement. The brain too is matter in movement he argues, a series of images of duration. The cosmos-cinema therefore involves a new brain, for as Deleuze puts it: "How could my brain contain images since it is one image among others? External images act on me, transmit movement to me, and I return movement: how could images be in my consciousness since I am my-self image, that is, movement? And can I even, at this level, speak of 'ego,' of eye, of brain and of body?" (C1, 58/86). The implication is that eye, brain and body are all images, and "perception" must become the ascending movement expressing their duration. Perception has ceased to be representational, and has become expressive movement.[13]

The question now is to understand this expressive movement as it appears specifically in the cinema. Cinema's movement-image "perceives" the world in a "mobile section" of its movements, this section being composed of the shot, and its connection to other shots in montage. Montage extends (or "ascends") shots by constructing an "out of frame" they express, shots and their out of frame world being in reciprocal presupposition. But this relation is dynamic; each shot expressing changes in the world, while these changes are in turn re-constructed by the world montage has created. This makes of a film an open whole where world and image are continually interacting to compose a film's duration. This interaction is further complexified by the fact that perception is not outside this process but participates in it. The brain is a screen. This means the movement-image no longer implies a human eye at the apex of a cone of vi-sion, but a cine-brain as the fold of duration. To understand the movement-image, and the duration it both expresses and constructs we must therefore understand the cine-brain that produces it.

## CINEMA-BRAIN

Although pre-war cinema produces a new image of movement as a movement-image of duration, duration does not appear directly in this image. Deleuze (once more following Bergson closely) argues that duration is a consistent plane of images making up moving matter, and on this plane, he writes: "The move-ment-image and flowing matter are strictly the same thing" (C1, 59/87). But for "things" to exist as perceptions an image must be removed from the infinite movements of action and reaction comprising duration, and become a "sign." This happens with the introduction of an interval between the automatic move-ments constituting the plane, and it is only this interval that is capable of con-stituting a "point of view"—a perception. Deleuze puts it like this:

> The thing and the perception of the thing are one and the same thing, one
> and the same image, but related to one or other of two systems of refer-

ence. The thing is the image as it is in itself, as it is related to all the other images to whose action it completely submits and on which it reacts immediately. But the perception of the thing is the same image related to another special image which frames it, and which only retains a partial action from it, and only reacts to it mediately. (C1, 63/93)

We must be careful to keep these two sides of the thing, as image and as perception, in mind, because Deleuze will tend to use the same term—"movement-image"—for both of them. The "special image" that "frames" the thing as image, is an interval. This interval extracts the thing from its infinite relations in duration by confining the reception of these movements to one of its sides, and its reactions to the other. But in doing so the interval performs a further operation, which is to subtract from the image all the movements of duration which do not directly involve the interval's own interests. This is the function of perception that enables the interval to take the appropriate actions enabling it to develop and survive (C1, 62/92).[14] This "living" interval is, for Bergson (as for Deleuze), the brain, the operation of which remains entirely material. The brain is constituted by the "cerebral vibrations" of a things action upon it, and the analysis of this action transmits vibrations to the body enabling it to make the appropriate reaction. The brain, Bergson writes, is "an instrument of analysis in regard to the movement received and an instrument of selection in regard to movement executed" (MM, 30). The movements of duration now appear relative to the interval-brain operating as a screen, they are no longer images strictly speaking, Bergson writes, they are *"pictures"* (MM, 36). Perception represents the movement of external bodies to the brain, which then determines a corporeal response. Perception and action are the two sides and the two functions of the brain-interval, and accordingly the centre they constitute is a sensory-motor, in which, Deleuze writes: "One passes imperceptibly from perception to action" (C1, 65/95). But this passage through the interval nevertheless involves a further stage, which Deleuze (and Bergson) calls "affection," which is "the way in which the subject perceives itself or feels itself 'from the inside'" (C1, 65/96). The subtraction of a perception-image is immediately connected to memory, which relates perceived movement to a "quality" or a lived state (an affection), which will determine our reaction, or lack of it. Through this process we are able to function as organisms, as body-brains whose temporal continuity is maintained by rational processes in which, "the qualities of matter are so many stable views that we take of its [duration's] instability" (CE, 301).

Given that the brain is a screen, the sensory-motor describes cinematic movement-images as much as it does the images we in fact are. Cinema before the war, in other words, assumes the same perceptual mechanism for its actors as do our actions. Once more, it means that Deleuze's investigation into the cinema will be at once ontological and aesthetic. In fact, the basic division of the cinema's movement-image Deleuze uses: perception-images, affection-images and action-images, is that Bergson suggests in his ontological analysis of human perception. What remains for Deleuze to do, his commentary on Bergson now over, is to develop these images into a taxonomy of cinema's signs. He will do so by turning to the work of the American semiotician Charles S. Peirce.

## PEIRCE'S SEMIOTICS OF THE "SIGNALETIC MATERIAL"

"Peirce's strength," Deleuze writes, "when he invented semiotics, was to conceive of signs on the basis of images and their combinations, not as a function of determinants which were already linguistic. [ . . . ] Peirce begins from the phenomenon or from what appears" (C2, 30/45).[15] In other words, Peirce provides Deleuze with a semiotic system adequate to Bergson's ontology of the image. For both Pierce and Bergson, the image as sign is material rather than linguistic, and as a result this "signaletic material" is not reducible to representation (C2, 33/49). Peirce puts it in slightly different terms: "A sign," he writes, "must have a real physical connection with the thing it signifies so as to be affected by that thing."[16] Furthermore, the sign is for Peirce, as the image is for Bergson, inseparable from the brain and its cerebral vibration—thought. Once more this has a slightly different formulation in Peirce, who emphasises how in being thought a sign becomes a thing connected to another sign that signifies it, *ad infinitum.* "Thus," Peirce writes, "there is a virtual endless series of signs when a sign is understood."[17] This is Peirce's way of emphasising the material continuity of thought, for, as in Bergson, thought is a movement encompassing the whole of image-matter. Peirce's semiotics is therefore compatible with Bergson's ontology, as in both the sign shares a materiality with what it expresses, and is inseparable from an endless movement of thought as its condition of possibility, and as what returns it to its constitutive infinity (for Peirce and Bergson both, this is the "virtual").

As we have seen, an image is produced in the interval-brain, or as Peirce puts it: "A sign is something which stands for another thing to a mind."[18] In other words, the sign is the emergence of the movements of duration in thought. To understand how this works we must explain Peirce's most famous idea, of which the last quote was a succinct statement, that of the signs "triadic relations." Peirce begins, according to Deleuze, from the same point as Bergson, with the perception-image. As a result, the perception-image is the degree-zero of a Peircean-Bergsonian semiotics of the cinema because it is the simple fact of appearance. It is, Deleuze writes, "an image which no longer simply expresses movement, but the relation between movement and the interval of movement" (C2, 31/47). The sign's first element, its "firstness"as Peirce puts it, is a quality or power as an affect. This is a feeling which refers only to itself, "t is as it is for itself and in itself,"(C1, 98/139) Deleuze writes, and is the appearance of the affection-image.[19] Peirce's "secondness" refers on the one hand to the affect's "real physical connection" to something else, it is "what is what it is in relation to a second" (C1, 98/139). On the other hand, the "secondness" of a sign appears in the action an affect gives rise to, and is in Deleuze's terms, an action-image. "Thirdness" refers to the necessity of these two moments of the sign being interpreted in thought, which in turn returns us to firstness as this interpretation also exists as a sign, involving its own triadic relations. In this way any sign passes through thought, which does not determine the sign in an arbitrary fashion, but according to a relation or law. For Peirce, thought gives interpretations according to "a sense of government by a general rule."[20] Thirdness therefore appears in "relation-images," or "mental-images" as Deleuze sometimes calls them, which will constitute for cinema, "a new, direct, relationship with thought," (C1, 198/268) inasmuch as the relation-image gives an image of the rules governing the perceptions, affections, and actions of the sensory-motor (C1, 200/271). These images are "interpretations which refer to the element of sense; not to affections, but to intellectual feelings of relations" (C1, 197/267). Thirdness gives an image of thought as it operates in and as the movement-image, and "reconstitutes the whole of the movement with all the aspects of the interval" (C2, 32/47).[21] Relation-images, in other words, make thought itself the object of an image, showing the laws and habits which interpret and connect sensory-motor perceptions, affections and actions.

   Each moment in Peirce's triadic sign finds expression in cinema, but before discussing each sign in more detail we will look at the relation-image, because here we gain a first glimpse of the way cinema moves beyond movement-images, and so beyond Pierce and Bergson, to produce time-images. It is Hitchcock, according to Deleuze, that "introduces the mental-image into the cinema" (C1, 203/274). But Hitchcock, despite creating an image of thought, also pushes these images to their limit, where Deleuze sees something that goes beyond it. This "beyond" emerges at the limit of the mental-image, where Hitchcock's characters are "assimilated to spectators," (C1, 205/276) and in this role are able to re-examine the "nature and status" of movement-images themselves. This re-examination, Deleuze writes, is provoked by "the rupture of the sensory-motor links in a particular character" (C1, 205/277). Hitchcock's films often revolve around the struggle of the protagonist to "understand" images that confound them, images that arise from a rupture of the sensory-motor, such as the broken leg of the photographer in *Rear Window,* or the dizziness of the detective in *Vertigo.* The smooth mental functioning of these characters stumbles over a gap that opens in their sensory-motor interval, a gap that produces signs that cannot be understood within the habitual mechanisms of a coherent mental-image. These characters can no longer give a rule to the signs that confront them, and are thrust outside the interval, and thought, into "a pure optical situation" (C1, 205/276). The hero reduced to the pure uncomprehending eye of his telephoto lens in *Rear Window,* or the incredible vortex of *Vertigo,* where the whole plot seems to leap into the irrational void that opens within the detective, and makes us spin along with him. This is a change in the brain of cinema, which no longer produces signs expressing the organic and understandable relation between subject and world, but like Scotty in *Vertigo,* leaps into the chasm emerging between what is seen and what can be thought. This leap is cine-thought's escape from the sensory motor and its Peircean-Bergsonian image-sign. This is a necessary leap, Deleuze argues, because the "ground-zero" of the perception-image does not take us to the real genetic element of vision—duration—which only appears indirectly, according to the conditions of the sensory-motor. The time-image therefore emerges beyond the sensory-motor, in a cinema that ascends *directly* to an image of duration. It is in developing his theory of the time-image that Deleuze will part ways with Peirce, and by the beginning of *Cinema 2* he writes: "We therefore take the term 'sign' in a completely different way from Peirce" (C2, 32/48). Deleuze describes this crucial development as follows,

> the sensory-motor link was broken, and the interval of movement produced the appearance as such of *an image other than the movement-image.* Sign and image thus reversed their relation, because the sign no longer presupposed the movement-image as material that it represented in its specified forms, but set about presenting the other image whose material it was to specify, and forms it was to constitute, from sign to sign. (C2, 34/50)

Cinema was going to need a new brain.

As the cinema moves beyond the movement-image it moves beyond Peirce's conception of the sign (C2, 34/50). But is this also a move beyond Bergson? The answer to this can only be yes and no. Yes, inasmuch as cine-thought finds its own path beyond the sensory-motor in which indirect movement-images are replaced by a "detour through the direct" (C1, 206/278). For Deleuze, this new regime of cine-thought implies a new brain capable of thinking beyond its Bergsonian conditions: "The soul of the cinema demands increasing thought," he writes, "even if thought begins by undoing the system of actions, perceptions and affections on which the cinema had fed up to that point" (C1, 206/278). But, and here is the no of our answer, in abandoning the sensory-motor cinema ascends to its truly Bergsonian conditions, an ascension that Bergson himself couldn't make, and begins to construct images directly expressing duration itself. The brain-screen of cine-thought thereby attains new ontological conditions (and as we shall see opens out a new aesthetic set of possibilities), conditions that retain a Bergsonian duration, but one no longer thought within the conditions of the movement-image and its interpretive generation of signs. Duration emerges in the time-image for itself, and cinema discovers after the war, a Bergson beyond Bergson.

## THE CLASSIC, GRANDIOSE CONCEPT
## OF THE MONTAGE KING

Deleuze often describes the move from the movement-image to the time-image, from classical to modern cinema, as a disjunction or break. But as Deleuze's other example of the breakdown of the relation-image—the Marx brothers—suggests, classical cinema itself often undid the logic of the sensory-motor, and approached the limits of the movement-image. Indeed, Deleuze's analysis privileges these cases by always searching for the genetic element to each of cinema's Bergsonian-Peircean signs, that element that ascended the furthest. In looking at some of these examples we will understand better both the Bergsonian character of early cinema and the way cinema after the war passes beyond it.

Montage, Deleuze argues, is the "principle act of cinema," (C2, 34/51) and is the operation through which movement-images give an image of the whole, as an "image *of* time" (C2, 14/51). The movement-image is constituted on one side by single shots in which the positions of objects in space vary and on the other by a whole that "flows from montage" (C2, 35/51). In this way: "Montage is the determination of the whole," (C1, 29/46) and as such is the conceptual/perceptual operation of the interval-brain as much as of cinema. Montage then, is the mechanism of cine-thought. But the montage of classical cinema necessarily constructs an indirect image of duration, because it is "deduced from movement-images and their relationships" (C1, 29/46). This is not to say that the movement-image is a formally restrictive category, but that classical cinema worked within it as under a certain epistemological regime. The sensory-motor schema, as the brain of cinema, selected images and montaged them according to conditions it itself set, conditions which were real, but which nevertheless mediated duration's presence to itself. As a result, the creative movement of duration is transformed into a whole relative to the perceptions and actions in which it appears. The movement-image expresses duration, but it is a duration which has been produced from within one of its parts as it were, a whole produced by montage according to the interval's own laws of thought. The movement-image therefore expresses duration within an organic relation between the brain and a whole the brain constructs in its own image.

Montage, as the mechanism of this classical cine-thought, operated Deleuze writes, "a powerful organic representation [that] produces the set and the parts," through a "rhythmic alternation" (C1, 31/49).[22] These alternations take on formal characteristics in the different montage techniques, in the different rhythms of composition typical to each great school of pre-war cinema. Some of these compositional rhythms however, produce in their most exemplary moments images that exceed the sensory motor and broach another regime of cinematic images unaccounted for by the movement-image. Deleuze asks of these images, "to what extent they would be separate from movement-images, and to what extent conversely, they would be based on certain unknown aspects of these images" (C1, 29/47). This is an important question, because it distinguishes an outside *to* the movement-image, from an outside *of* the movement-image. The latter position would be occupied by images that seem to move outside the confines of the movement-image but which nevertheless retain its logic. On the other hand, images that appear outside *to* the movement-image ("separate from") would be images operating according to another logic. This distinction will prompt Deleuze to ask the question that defines his overall project: "How are we to delineate a modern cinema which would be distinct from 'classical' cinema or from the indirect representation of time?" (C2, 39/57)

We can begin to see Deleuze's answer in his discussion of the work of Dziga Vertov. Vertov's "kino-eye," exemplified by *Man with a Movie Camera* (1929), introduces a new materialism to cinema by revealing a plane of molecular and "non-human matter" (C1, 40/61). In Vertov's films, buildings, machines, humans and most importantly cinema itself, all appear on the same plane. This plane is not composed in the manner of Eisenstein, through a dialectical montage of the human and his world that both urges and assumes their organic connection, but through a dialectic *in* matter, by which "the whole merges with the infinite set of matter, and the interval merges with an eye in matter" (C1, 40/61). Vertov's montage explores an inhuman whole that exists beyond the human sensory-motor, and offers an alternative to the Soviet dialectic of man and Nature. How? Vertov's films are entirely Soviet inasmuch as they retain its quintessential theme of Nature being transformed by man into a new communist world, and its consistent aim of raising the masses' consciousness through this dialectic. But Vertov no longer identifies the camera with a human point of view. The function of the camera, Vertov argued, was to see what the human eye could not, like a telescope or microscope, and he extended this idea to montage, incorporating the freeze-frame and single-frame editing to give effects well beyond those the human eye was capable of.[23] For Vertov the kino-eye embodies a raised consciousness in which Nature and man (whole and interval) have become merged in a new material collective achieving the consciousness of matter.[24] In Vertov's kino-eye Deleuze finds an entirely material dialectic enacting the "correlation between a non-human matter and a super-human eye" (C1, 40/60). Vertov's montage thus enabled the cinema to "regain the system of universal variation in itself" (C1, 80/116) and produced an "identity of a community of matter and a communism of man" (C1, 40/60). Vertov's man with a movie camera is for Deleuze, nothing less than "the overman of the future" (C1, 83/121).

On Deleuze's account, Vertov's montage breaks with the sensory-motor interval and its indirect image of time, inasmuch as Vertov's theory of the interval "no longer marks a gap which is carved out, a distancing between two consecutive images but, on the contrary, a correlation of two images which are distant (and incommensurable from the viewpoint of our human perception)" (C1, 82/118). But to return to our initial question; does Vertov's montage technique give us images other than movement-images, or simply images which were previously unknown to the classical regime? In fact, Deleuze affirms the latter, arguing that Vertov's camera, like other privileged moments in pre-war cinema, finds a universal variation "which goes beyond the human limits of the sensory-motor schema towards a non-human world where movement equals matter [ . . . ]. It is here the movement image attains the *sublime*" (C2, 40/58, italics added). This is a material sublime, which in carrying perception into matter and action into universal interaction, "points to a 'negative of time' as the ultimate product of the movement-image through montage" (C2, 40/58). This is not, Deleuze points out, a negation, but an image that remains "indirect or derived" despite its inhuman and communist reality (C2, 288/58). It seems that Vertov, in breaking with human perception in favour of the kino-eye, produces a sublime movement-image, one that perceives an unrepresentable duration/variation, a radical outside which can only be thought as the "negative of time." The sensory-motor is discarded in favour of a machinic consciousness, but this retains the epistemological coordinates of the interval (perception and action) in overcoming their human dimensions and extending them to the entire universe (C1, 40/61). As a result, Vertov's films remain within the classical regime because, in overcoming the sensory-motor, they erect a machinic interval (the "kino-eye") which re-invents, without leaving, (and this shouldn't be read as a criticism, just the opposite) the philosophical conditions of the movement-image. A new cinema emerges after the war, with a new ontology, where duration is no longer expressed in terms of an interval, not even one that is sublime, but is absolutely immanent to the image. Modern cinema then, does not take Vertov's route of attempting to escape its human conditions to gain a radical material exteriority, but instead discovers the way the movement-image can be "shattered from the inside" (C2, 40/58).

A sublime outside of the sensory-motor is also found in expressionist cinema. There, Deleuze writes, we find images of "*[t]he non-organic life of things*," (C1, 50/75) the deep dark negation of organic life, an image in which life = 0. This negation appears first of all in the deep blacks in the image, against which light, or luminosity, defines organic forms in their distance from the black zero. But the organic cohesion of this light is forever falling back into the black and evil non-organic night. This is also the classic expressionist story-line of course (Lang's *M* (1931), or *Siegfried* (1924), Sternberg's *The Blue Angel* (1930), and even Murnau and Flaherty's sun-drenched *Tabu* (1931)) which figures duration (non-organic life) in the terms of Kant's dynamic sublime, as a formless power which overwhelms organic life. But as in Kant's dynamic sublime our destruction in this dark immensity of an inorganic Nature is simultaneously our projection into a transcendental subjectivity. As Deleuze puts it, expressionism unleashes "*a non-psychological life of the spirit*," which is "the divine part in us, the spiritual relationship in which we are alone with God as light" (C1, 54/80). We lose our organic sensory-motor in Expressionism's black and inorganic night, only to gain the "ideal summit" (C1, 54/81) of the "spiritual abstract Form" (C1, 55/81). This super-natural and supra-sensible divine light breaks with organic composition, but only to take us beyond its sublime conditions "to discover in us a supra-organic space which dominates the whole inorganic life of things" (C1, 52/77). One need only think of the ethics of the criminal community, acting no doubt under a "categorical imperative," that Lang shows provoked by the sublime evil of M. As with Vertov, then, Expressionism breaks with the organic relation of the sensory-motor and the whole it indirectly represents, only to discover a sublime world, this time ideal rather than material, in which we find a spiritual redemption which reconfirms the organic conditions of the movement-image.

## AS EXPRESSED BY A FACE

Deleuze's discussion of the affection-image, and its expression of an affect in the face, provides another example of the way the movement-image retains an indirect image of duration in seeking its beyond. The affection-image, as we have seen, is in Peirce's terms a "firstness," and is called by Deleuze "the feeling-thing," or "the entity" (C1, 96/136).[25] Deleuze goes on to elaborate Peirce's definition: the affect as firstness "is not a sensation, a feeling, an idea, but the quality of a possible sensation, feeling or idea. [ . . . ] it expresses the possible without actualising it, whilst making it a complete mode" (C1, 98/139). Peirce puts it rather nicely, explaining that the quality of a firstness is in itself, "a mere possibility. [ . . . ] Possibility, the mode of being of Firstness, is the embryo of being. It is not nothing. It is not existence."[26] The qualities of affects therefore, are "pure possibles" (C1, 102/145) which "constitute the 'expressed' of states of things" (C1, 102/145).[27] The affect doesn't exist independently of its expression, although it is distinct from it, and together affect and affection-image form, in Deleuze's Peircean vocabulary, an "icon." The icon's bi-polar composition, the "likeness" it embodies between affect and affection-image, "serves," Peirce notes, "to convey ideas of things they represent simply by imitating them."[28] The affection-image is neither an actualisation of affect in action, nor an expression of a psychological state, but a sign of a "purely possible" mode of being (the affect) expressed by a face (C1, 66/97). "The affect," Deleuze writes, "is like the expressed of the state of things, but this expressed does not refer to the state of things, it only refers to the faces which express it and, coming together and separating, give it it's proper moving context" (C1, 106/151).

Deleuze is once again combining Peirce's semiotics of signs with Bergson's physiology, for an affect is the change in state existing between an image's perception by a motor nerve (a perception-image) and its instantiation in a motor action (an action-image). The affect as a possible "power" or "quality" expressed in an affection-image therefore emerges within the sensory-motor "between" perception and action, and as a possible "break" in the smooth functioning of the movement-image of cine-thought. For the affect, Deleuze argues, is "that part of the event which does not let itself be actualised in a determinate milieu" (C1, 107/151). This exteriority of the affect, as possible, is explored and defined by Deleuze in *Difference and Repetition*. There Deleuze distinguishes the possible from the virtual, their difference being, as he rather dramatically puts it, "a question of existence itself" (DR, 211/273). The possible, he argues, exists in relation to a state of affairs that pre-exists it, in which it is actualised and expressed, while nevertheless remaining outside this state of affairs. The virtual, on the other hand, exists only as the production of existence, and does not exist outside of this event. The point for Deleuze is that the exteriority of the possible (as mere firstness or affect) appears in an affection-image, but it is this state of affairs (as the interiority of the subject, or sensory-motor) that conditions the exteriority of the affect. This distinction of possible and virtual is decisive for our purposes here, despite Deleuze employing both terms in his description of the affect. This is because although the affect is in itself a complex virtuality of singularities in variable relations, it is produced as a unity (i.e. as a possible) by "the virtual conjunction assured by the expression, face or proposition" (C1, 105/149). This then, is the specifically cinematic way the possible is always "retroactively fabricated in the image of what resembles it" (DR, 212/273). This is precisely the ontological status of the cinematic affect. "The affect is independent of all determinate space-time;" Deleuze writes, "but it is none the less created in a history which produces it as expressed and the expression of a space and a time, of an epoch or a milieu (this is why the affect is the 'new' and new affects are ceaselessly created, notably by the work of art)" (C1, 99/140). Here Deleuze defines both the ontological status of the affects "independence" from, and "exteriority" to states-of-affairs (as produced by that state-of-affairs), and indicates how this "exteriority" defines an important creative aesthetic dimension of the movement-image.

Classical cinema constantly created new affects, whose affection-images lead away from the clichés of human sensibility and actions, towards what Deleuze calls, "an inhumanity much greater than that of animals" (C1, 99/141). This inhumanity can be understood through two of Deleuze's examples which conveniently lie at opposite ends of the facial spectrum, the expression of a spiritual beyond found in Carl Theodor Dreyer's *Passion of Joan of Arc* (1928), and the nihilist sensuality of Ingmar Bergman's magnificent women. In *Passion of Joan of Arc*, "the affective film *par excellence*," there is on the one hand the historical state of affairs, the trial, Joan, her accusers and the law, but on the other there is her faith, a pure affect "outside" the historical state of affairs and expressed so beautifully on Falconetti's face. Her miniscule trembles and teary uplifted eyes are signs for her faith, "this inexhaustible and brilliant part which goes beyond its own actualisation" (C1, 106/151). The film focuses on this interruption of the spirit, and the moving way Joan attempts to remain faithful to it, to attain salvation and peace in its divine beyond. This affect is the "inhuman" content of the film's narrative, the trajectory of martyrdom, the annihilation of Joan's individuality in her becoming-saint.[29] Bergman's faces on the other hand are more monumental, expressing singular affects rather than intense movements that achieve suspensions of individuation that teeter on the edge of the void, where the affect is in a permanent proximity to death. Everything in Bergman seems to play against this backdrop of death, and his highly formalised dramas are often reduced to a simple turning toward or turning away of the face, into or away from the void. *Cries and Whispers* (1972) is surely the finest, where the women are no longer characters but pure affects-faces, locked into a series of violent pirouettes. Bergman will accelerate these savage relations to the point of an ambiguous schizophrenia merging the women in *Persona* (1966), who exchange faces in a place "where the principle of individuation ceases to hold sway" (C1, 100/142). In both Dreyer and Bergman the affect emerges for itself, suspends individuation, and creates a powerful possibility, an a-subjective outside to the sensory-motor schema.

These a-subjective affects appear in affection-images—faces—that, Deleuze writes, "go beyond the state of things, to trace lines of flight, just enough to open up in space a dimension of another order" (C1, 101/144). This new dimension is not a state-of-affairs, but opens at the limit of the lived. This new dimension appears in various ways depending on the director who creates it. In Dreyer the affection-image opens up the fourth and fifth dimensions of time and spirit (C1, 107/152). In Bergman the affection-image tends towards "the effacement of faces in nothingness" (C1, 101/144). This new and extra dimension of the affect, Deleuze suggests, is "schizophrenic," (C1, 110/156) inasmuch as the schizophrenic experience is a turning away from identity into a space of tactile boundlessness, and expresses this corporeal dissolution in a sign detached from its motor continuation in the sensory-motor (paralysis, autism, or delirium). "Schizophrenic" images no longer take place in rational time and space, nor are they the representative signs of human thought (thirdness). Schizo-images exist outside the sensory-motor interval in an "any-space-whatever," as the "genetic element" or "differential sign" of affection-images (C1, 110/156). With the "any-space-whatever" we have the unusual instance of a term traversing the two cinema books, being introduced in the first in relation to the affection-image, and being explored in the second as a crucial new element of cinema after the war, one discovered by Italian neo-realism. In both cases however, an "any-space-whatever" is a singular space that has lost any homogeneity imposed by an exterior standard of measure, making it the site of an infinite number of possible

**Figure 2**  Carl Theodor Dreyer, *La Passion de Jeanne D'Arc,* 1928, Austrian Film Museum

linkages. "It is," Deleuze writes in relation to classical cinema, "a space of virtual conjunction, grasped as a pure locus of the possible" (C1, 109/155).

We have seen Bergman create this opening through a turning away of faces onto death (perhaps most explicitly in the last scene of *Shame,* 1968). The films of Dreyer and Robert Bresson achieve it in a different way, by discovering this schizo any-space-whatever through a "spiritual opening" (C1, 117/165). Common to both is this "discovery" being indistinguishable from the act of choosing it (Dreyer's *Passion of Jean of Arc,* or *Gertrude* (1964), and just about any of Bresson's films, *Diary of a Country Priest* (1950), *Pickpocket* (1959), or *A Man Escaped* (1956) to mention a few of the most famous ones). This "opening" is sublime in "overcoming" the "formal obligations and material constraints" of physical space and the sensory-motor, but this "opening" is metaphysically determined by the "decision" which takes us "from" the subjective physical space it disrupts, "to" a "spiritual" world of the affect, operating— as pure possible—as a super-sensible Idea. This is the Kantian operation of the affection-image, and is, as Deleuze calls it, a "theoretical or practical evasion" (C1, 117/165). This "evasion" finally "restores" the metaphysics of the movement-image by elevating the "decision," or the act of choosing choice (what Deleuze calls an "auto-affection") to the point where it "takes upon itself the linking of parts" (C1, 117/165). In choosing choice the sensory-motor is opened onto its outside, onto a pure indeterminability, a pure possibility or any-space-whatever acting as a space of virtual conjunction, and where the affect is raised to its pure genetic power or potentiality (C1, 113/159). But despite its undeniable beauty and power the affection-image is not an image of duration. In opening onto this beyond of the affects, and in a Kantian manner, the super-sensible becomes, as pure possible, the re-founding of an ontological continuity between this world and its metaphysical dimension. Finally then, affects as pure possibles are determined by the limits of the sensory-motor they exceed, and in this way the directors who are their masters attain sublime movement-images.

When the sublime movement-image "goes beyond the human limits of the sensory-motor," to find "a non-human world where movement equals matter" (Vertov), a "super-human world which speaks for a new spirit" (Lang), or a purely spiritual affect (Dreyer and Bresson), it produces an opening of the sensory-motor beyond its limits, a beyond acting in a Kantian fashion as a super-sensible guarantee of the necessary unity of man and duration (however this is figured), inasmuch as it acts as "the absolute condition for movement." As a result, "the movement-image remains primary, and gives rise only indirectly to a representation of time" (C2, 40/58). A direct image of time must await a new ontology of cinema, a new ontology that will find its historical possibility after the war (C1, 120–122/168–172).

## NOTHING BUT CLICHÉS, CLICHÉS EVERYWHERE . . .

We must now briefly return to our initial discussion of Bergson's ontology, in order to understand the transition it undergoes between the cinema books. If we remember, within the mental space of an interval-brain the sensory-motor schema translates the matter/image of duration into perceptions, affections, and actions and their cinematic signs. Although at their limit these images pass into a sublime outside of the sensory-motor, this outside is nevertheless conditioned by openings produced by the sensory-motor, and remain indirect images of duration. The sensory-motor schema therefore installs a perceptual process that maintains itself even in being passed "beyond," so that even in its "sublime" moments we perceive only "what it is in our interest to perceive," once our interests have turned spiritual or super sensible (C2, 20/32). Although these images are a wonderful testament to the creativity of the movement-image, they are nevertheless exceptions and more generally Deleuze defines the movement-image as a cliché. "A cliché," Deleuze explains, "is a sensory-motor image of the thing. [ . . . ] We therefore normally perceive only clichés" (C2, 20/32). As a result, "the image constantly sinks to the state of cliché: because it is introduced into sensory-motor linkages" (C2, 21/32–3). Cinema's biggest challenge, the same challenge facing all the arts, is to produce images that are not clichés, and combat its "conspiracy." Doing so will involve not only the production of new images, but also a new image of art, an image which will allow us, Deleuze writes, to combat, "a civilisation of the cliché where all the powers have an interest in hiding images from us, not necessarily in hiding the same thing from us, but in hiding something in the image" (C2, 21/33).

What is this hidden "thing," and how can we see it? It is the image "itself," the image inasmuch as it expresses duration, in a direct image, or as Deleuze calls it, a "time-image." We perceive this image through a double movement, on the one hand, "our sensory-motor schemata jam or break" (C2, 20/32) and, "[o]n the other hand, at the same time, the image constantly attempts to break through the cliché, to get out of the cliché. There is no knowing how far a real image may lead: the importance of becoming visionary or seer [*visionnaire ou voyant*]" (C2, 21/33). The seer or visionary will be able to go beyond the sensory-motor without reconfirming its movement in a sublime outside. The figure of the visionary, as we shall see in later chapters, recurs in Deleuze's discussions of art and is always associated with a resistance to the cliché, or "opinion" as he and Guattari finally call it. In this way *Cinema 2* brings us back to the mystical and yet atheist dimension of Deleuze's ontology we have already encountered, and develops it further. The visionary artist, according to Deleuze, is able to see and produce the new directly, as an onto-genetic vision of duration's construction/expression. "Vision" operates in this sense as the absolute immanence of duration and the image, beyond the breakdown of the sensory-motor, as the production of a new image and of a new image of thought. There is, Deleuze claims, "a simultaneous change in our conception of the brain and our relationship to the brain" (C1, 210/283). The "visionaries" of cinema, those directors considered artists (i.e. *auters*), "attack," Deleuze claims, "the dark organization of clichés" and "'commit' the irreversible." These directors "extract an Image from all the clichés to set it up against them" (C1, 210/283). Modern cinema is defined by this transvaluation of its own ontology in turning its power of thought against itself; against its own clichés. In this way great directors are artists in being at once political activists (against the "dark organization of clichés"), formal innovators (breaking with the montage techniques of the movement-image), and philosophers (creating a new image of thought).

Deleuze claims the historical conditions of the new image in cinema lie in the collapse of subjective certainty after the war.[30] This collapse of the subjective and objective assumptions of the movement-image marks the condition of possibility of cinema's self-transformation. This change is however, ontological before it is historical. Here Deleuze picks up Bergson's own extension of his philosophy of vitalism into a mystical understanding of art.[31] In this sense Deleuze's vocabulary is Bergsonian when he writes: "It is necessary to *combine* the optical-sound image with the enormous forces that are not those of a simply intellectual consciousness, nor of the social one, but of a profound, vital intuition" (C2, 22/33–4). This is nothing less than a claim for the mystical immanence of actual images and virtual vital forces (duration), whose "combination" can only be "seen" in an "aesthetic intuition" or "vision" as the construction of an inhuman image expressing its own genesis, its own real conditions. In this sense Deleuze echoes Bergson, who believed the force of mysticism "is exactly that of the vital impetus; it is this impetus itself."[32] This vital impetus animates those mystics, those "visionaries" as Deleuze puts it, who go beyond the forms of man, and man's form (the sensory-motor), towards the genesis of the vital impetus itself. Such visionary artists are like mystics, Bergson claims, in seeking "the establishment of a contact, consequently of a partial coincidence with the creative effort of which life is the manifestation."[33] Mysticism, for Bergson, has a fundamentally artistic aspect, not only in its search for the creative basis of life, but also in its realization of a creative response to this imperative. Art would therefore share mysticism's task of finding new forms to express the fundamentally creative energy of life itself. Both then, in Bergson's words, "consist in working back from the intellectual and social plane to a point in the soul from which there springs an imperative demand for creation. The soul within which this demand dwells may indeed have felt it fully only once in its life time, but it is always there, a unique emotion, an impulse, an impetus received from the very depth of things. To obey it completely new words would have to be coined, new ideas would have to be created."[34] Mysticism and art therefore come together in the creative art of "visions," as in both these are created by "visionaries." Such creators, Deleuze writes in his book on Bergson, are "the great souls," the "artists and mystics," who, at the limit, "play with the whole of creation, who invent an expression of it whose adequacy increases with its dynamism. [ . . . ] the mystical soul actively plays the whole of the universe, and reproduces the opening of the Whole" (B, 112/118). So even if the Second World War introduces the historical conditions for cinema's transformation, the real impetus for this change is ahistorical, it is the vital impetus shared by artists and mystics—the impetus to create a "vision" of and as life itself. This is not to say that cinema is ahistorical or apolitical, but that its historical and political development must first be understood ontologically, as expressions of a living duration that is constantly constructing itself new. Now we must see how this mystical art appears in the cinematic image.

## THE EYE WE DO NOT HAVE

Cinema after the war, Deleuze argues, breaks with the sensory-motor schema and its movement-image, in order to explore pure optical and sound images that appear under new ontological conditions. These are images in which the virtual realm of duration is directly expressed in an actual image, once "movement has become automatic" and "the artistic essence of the image is realized" (C2, 156/203). These statements describe a new way to think as much as a new image. After the war direct images of time appear that no longer perpetuate in their delay through the sensory-motor interval, movements (action-images and affection-images) that express duration in the clichés of the human. These direct images are the visions of a new breed of characters, and of a new viewer, mutants who "saw rather than acted, they were seers" (C2, xi). Seers embody a type of experience that no longer finds its genetic conditions in perception-images, but instead produce visions of genesis. Vision becomes autonomous and active, a construction expressing duration. Art in its essence—it is a definition Deleuze will repeat in relation to painting—is the creation of visions. The painter Henri Matisse, himself influenced by Bergson, had already pointed this out, "for the artist creation begins with vision. To see is itself a creative operation."[36] What are seen/created by modern cinema, Deleuze argues, are pure optical and sound situations; automatic and unmediated images "which bring the emancipated senses into direct relation with time and thought" (C2, 17/28). These are what Deleuze will go on to call "crystal images," images of time in its pure state, images of duration appearing through a crack in the sensory-motor, and by which the cine-brain will think time itself.

The trajectory of the cinema books can perhaps be summarized by Deleuze's question: "How can we rid ourselves of ourselves, and demolish ourselves?" (C1, 66/97). The movement-image's answer to this appears in Samuel Beckett's *Film* (1965), where the escape from vision is figured by, as Deleuze puts it, "death, immobility, blackness" (C1, 68/99). This would be a kind of cinematic summation of the way the movement-image figures our escape from the sensory-motor as an opening onto its sublime outside. As we have seen, the movement-image was only able to answer the question of its limit with an image of duration that confirmed the genetic powers of the sensory-motor. In cinema after the war Deleuze finds a new image, one in which our demolition does not assume a super-sensible duration as our beyond, but is the creation of the world as it already was, the world Cézanne knew, "the world before man, before our own dawn" (C1, 68/100). Cinema after the war creates images which are adequate to a creative power "before man," before and not beyond the sensory-motor, an inhuman power of expression adequate to its vital and artistic essence. Here the mystical "ascension" of cinema toward the plane of duration cannot be separated from a simultaneous descending movement of individuation, the folding of (and not an opening onto) the plane of immanence as cine-thought. In this ascension-descension, and here we come back to the most important aspect of Deleuze's mystical aesthetics, the time-image constructs duration at the same time as it expresses it—there is no outside—and this is the creative and artistic "essence" of the vision of the seer.

Cinema constructs a new eye, an inhuman eye that is in duration, that is of matter and in matter, able to "see" time in its simultaneous emergence as the whole of the past being created in the passing present of an individuation. Thus the movement of the time-image constructs a vision of all time, and as Deleuze puts it, "time is no longer the measure of movement but movement is the perspective of time" (C2, 22/34). This is an important distinction, and implies a time-image which does not represent something pre-existing it, it has neither conditions of possibility, nor indeed any super-sensible outside which would determine it. The movements of the time-image give a perspective on all of time, a perspective which did not exist before, and whose construction exists as the continual emergence of the new, as the becoming of duration itself. In this way the inhuman eye is a new cine-brain, its images constructing (thinking) time as the expression of duration. As a result, representation is surpassed in a vision that is, Deleuze writes, "at once fantasy and report" (C2, 19/30). Deleuze argues that this thinking-eye of the visionary belongs as much to the viewer, as to the character of the film (C2, 19/30). The viewer and the character, as the poles of a single time-image they produce between them, constitute a seer who can see in life what is more than sensory-organic life, "the part that cannot be reduced to what happens: that part of inexhaustible possibility [the virtual as duration] that constitutes the unbearable, the intolerable, the visionary part" (C2, 19–20/31).[36] This is the mystical dimension of a vitalist cinema, one which follows the Bergsonian intuition: "*Wherever anything lives, there is, open* somewhere, a register *in which* time *is being inscribed*" (CE, 16).

The time-image emerges prior to the distinction of subject and object, as the immanence of vision and visionary in a seer, who no longer acts, but who "is prey to a vision, pursued by it or pursuing it, rather than engaged in an action" (C2, 3/9). This break with the movement-image is accomplished by Italian neo-realism, and the films of Michelangelo Antonioni are some of Deleuze's favourite examples.[37] For example, the disappearance of a woman in *L'Avventura* (1960) does not give rise to a series of actions leading to the resolution of this situation, but instead animates an affair between her boyfriend and best friend, whose increasingly destructive movements make them victims of the absence they are both pursuing and pursued by. The film no longer expresses duration through the actions and reactions of characters moving through an ordered and pre-existing time and space, instead the film is constructed around a genetic element (the woman's disappearance) which dislocates sensory-motor coherence (the affair is played out as a series of convulsions which exist "despite"—or to spite—the couple's rational protestations), in which the characters become the passive spectators of their own emptiness (thus exemplifying Antonioni's pessimistic assumption that Eros is sick). But this account should not lead one to think that Antonioni has structured the film around a lack. The disappearance of Anna early in the film does not make it rotate around her absence, and instead this absence becomes creative and generates a series of disarticulated and intense affects. These mark out a new temporality, and give new images of duration, not by actualising its infinite interconnectedness in a sublime break of the interval, but by opening the actual up, and dissolving the interval in a virtual infinity. This is what explains both the slowness of the film and its unpredictable trajectory. On the one hand nothing seems to happen because the narrative cohesion suggested by Anna's disappearance is quickly ignored, and in its place the lovers Claudia and Sandro seem to "wander" through disconnected any-space-whatevers. On the other, the situation existing between the lovers is extraordinary, and unfolds according to a seemingly spontaneous rhythm, "subject to," Deleuze points out, "rapid breaks, interpolations and infinitesimal injections of atem-

porality" (C2, 8/16). Time has become "unhinged," and duration as the genetic virtuality of the image (even when this is understood by Antonioni as
the sickness of chronos itself, expressed in symptomatic images (C2, 8/16))
has become the "subject" of cinema, the real conditions cinema now expresses. This is a Deleuzean vitalist cinema, where duration as the univocal genetic element of images is expressed only as it is constructed: time-image.

## THE CRYSTAL IS EXPRESSION

Bergson will introduce the philosophical framework for Deleuze's direct time-
image in a distinction he makes regarding memory. On the one hand we have
our automatic or habitual recognition, by which we recognize objects according
to the memories of our sensory-motor schema, both confirmation of and conforming to the world we live in. On the other hand, is what Bergson calls "attentive" recognition, a perception of something as truly "new," something never
seen before. The vision of a child, the visions of a visionary. . . . an image unin-
telligible to our sensory-motor schema, because it is the emergence *of,* rather
than *in,* time. Attentive memory is continually producing these images by creating new virtual connections in vision. We see an image that is continually
changing, continually under construction, vibrating in its difference from itself.
And this construction works in both directions at once, producing new actual
images that in turn construct the new virtual memories it expresses. Here
Deleuze quotes Bergson, "it will be seen that the progress of attention results in
creating anew, not only the object perceived, but also the ever-widening systems
with which it may be bound up" (C2, 46/65).

Attentive recognition produces a "recollection-image," in which virtual
and actual are perceived in dynamic and creative relation (C2, 46/64). But although the recollection image transforms itself through the process of memory,
Deleuze argues, it is not in itself virtual, but simply the actualisation of each successive virtual dimension, of each "layer" of memory it actualises, and therefore
its construction remains representational. "This is why," Deleuze writes, "the
recollection-image does not deliver the past to us, but only represents the former present that the past 'was'" (C2, 54/75). The recollection-image is therefore
already integrated into the temporal linearity along which the sensory-motor
organism moves, and its virtual relations are fed back into spatio-temporal and
subjective normality. What is truly disruptive to this, Deleuze will argue, and finally what will give us images making visible the fully reciprocal immanence of
the actual and the virtual, is the failure of memory. When the organism cannot
remember, cannot represent the virtual in a "new" actual image, a truly new
image appears, which "enters into relations with genuinely virtual elements"

(C2, 54/75). The sensory-motor has broken down, but this has produced a visionary function that becomes creative.

A "genuine relation" with the virtual will be forged in the crystal-image, "the image with two sides, actual and virtual at the same time" (C2, 69/93). Here virtual and actual are distinct but indiscernible, being "totally reversible" (C2, 69/94). This reversibility, the "continual exchange" (C2, 70/95) of the actual and the virtual, means the crystal-image is adequate to and expressive of duration. In the crystal-image the virtual and actual, the infinite and the finite, are truly indiscernible, and we have arrived at a mysticism that is entirely atheist. Deleuze suggests as much: "In the crystal-image there is this mutual search—blind and halting—of matter and spirit: beyond the movement-image, 'in which we are still pious'" (C2, 75/101). Still pious because it still seeks the super-sensible. As we have seen, the mystical expression of a vital materialism, a vision, is the Deleuzian condition of art. As Deleuze puts it, the indiscernibility of virtual and actual has "always accompanied art without ever exhausting it, because art found in them a means of creation for certain special images" (C2, 76/103).

What exactly is this "special image" and how does it appear in the cinema? Deleuze argues that the actual image is always present, but that this present passes as each new present arrives. It is the virtual dimension of the image that preserves all of the past, and so when virtual and actual are totally reversible in the crystal-image, it is an image of both the passing present and all of the past at the same time. The differential relation of these simultaneous and "heterogeneous directions" of time form the image in its "most fundamental operation" (C2, 81/108). This genetic and differential relation, Deleuze claims, is the ontological process of a "powerful, non-organic Life which grips the world" (C2, 81/109). At this point Deleuze's taste for taxonomy once more comes to the fore, as he begins the task of classifying crystal-images. He finds the first in the films of Yasujiro Ozu, and identifies one technique in the film *Late Spring* (1943), in which a shot of a vase is inserted into a sequence showing the daughter's half smile and tears. The change in the character, as actual change, appears in a differential relation to the unchanging vase as the form of time (the duration of the virtual), time itself, which does not change. "There is becoming," Deleuze writes, "change, passage. But the form of what changes does not change, does not pass on. This is time, time itself, 'a little time in its pure state': a direct time-image, which gives what changes the unchanging form in which the change is produced" (C2, 17/27).

What happens no longer takes place in time, nor does time simply measure what happens, time and its image, virtual and actual are fully reversible in a crystal-image. This, quite simply, means: "The present is the actual image, and *its* contemporaneous past is the virtual image" (C2, 79/106). The two aspects of the crystal image are indiscernible, the virtual from "the actual present *of which* it is the past, absolutely and simultaneously" (C2, 79/106–7). The crystal-image as indiscernibility, or "smallest circuit," of actual and virtual encompasses, in its largest circuit, the whole universe, all of duration itself. Crystal-images therefore, are mystical images in which, as Deleuze puts it, "one and the same horizon links the cosmic to the everyday" (C2, 17/28). They are images of the present and its own past, "the whole of the real, life in its entirety, which has become spectacle, in accordance with the demands of a pure optical and sound perception" (C2, 84/122). Deleuze describes this cosmic image with the appropriately mystical metaphor of an ocean, in which images "bathe or plunge to trace an actual shape and bring in their provisional harvest" (C2, 80/108).[38] That Deleuze's language should get particularly poetic here, where the crystal image is delineated in its mystical dimension, should be no surprise, it is a trait of Deleuze's writing which is as expressive as the image he is attempting to describe. He continues:

> The crystal-image has these two aspects: internal limit of all the relative circuits, but also outer-most, variable and reshapable envelope, at the edges of the world, beyond even moments of world. The little crystalline seed and the vast crystallisable universe: everything is included in the capacity for expansion of the collection constituted by the seed and the universe. (C2, 80–1/108)

The crystal-image is mystic inasmuch as seed and universe exist in co-implication within it, inasmuch as the crystal traverses these at once microscopic and cosmic dimensions, each constructing and expressing the other in their processual immanence. For this co-existence is in no way static. The crystal-image is ontogenetic, it constructs the universe which is expressed in the seed, as it must when, once more, *nothing is given except the to come.* Only a mystic seer can produce this image. "The visionary, the seer," Deleuze writes, "is the one who sees in the crystal, and what he sees is the gushing of time as dividing in two, as splitting" (C2, 81/109).

This visionary, inhuman, "third eye" (C2, 18/29) does not perceive things through passive sensory reception, but constructs time-images in what Deleuze calls "hallucinations." This hallucinatory perception, disengaged from spatio-temporal *a prioris,* as from the sensory-motor of a subject, constructs a vision of the virtual it expresses in an actual image. To hallucinate an object as a crystal-image is to "see" the ontogenetic split in time, as it becomes both seed and universe, as it passes in the present and includes all of the past, an actual expression that constructs a virtual universe, again. Hallucination is the art of seeing the image as actual virtuality as, Deleuze writes, the "sole decomposed and multi-plied object" (C2, 126/165). In this way a crystal-image "stands for its object, replaces it, both creates and erases it" (C2, 126/165). Hallucination constitutes the "cinema of the seer" (C2, 126/166), a materialist cinematics where the "seer" is an eye *in* matter, an eye that is no longer an interval organising the dialectic of man and Nature, but is a pure vision in which the subject and object are dissolved in an image of, and as an image as, material innovation—the universe as cinema itself. "What can be more subjective than delirium, a dream, a hallucination?" Deleuze asks, "But what can be closer to a materiality made up of luminous wave and molecular interaction?" (C1, 76–7/111). The seer has a vision, as the visuality of matter itself, as the vision matter creates for itself as it emerges in images, each time, again. The vision and the viewer come together in the seer, as the necessary condition to all art-work.[39] Art is hallucination, which is to say art is creation, and cinema after the war becomes hallucinatory. Needless to say, this visionary image can no longer be understood in Peircean or any other linguistic terms. Modern cine-thought is no longer defined by a tri-partite sign and its sensory-motor, but by a break it creates through which the brain will escape. A crystalline cine-thought emerges anew, its images rinsed of cliché and crystallising in their hallucinatory ellipses a little time in its pure state, a crystal through which the universe is refracted.

Despite the crystal bathing in the cosmic infinite, differentiation is just as important for its crystalline life. At their outer limit all crystal-images merge into the single refrain of a cosmic inorganic life, but they retain a simultaneous particularity that is their present actuality. It is here and now that crystals express themselves, but unlike the movement-image's pre-existing conditions of appearance, the 'here and now' of crystal-images is entirely unpredictable and sponta-neous, and depends on a process of experimentation. This is the Bergsonian vitalism of a crystalline artistic process, it is the "bursting forth of life" (C2, 91/121). Does this mean art exists only in the crystal? In ontological terms this is true, although as we shall see and have seen, the crystal-image in this sense has many other names in Deleuze's work and in his work with Guattari. Indeed, it is the specificity of this vocabulary to the particular "artistic-machine" it de-scribes that focuses our cosmic and mystical enthusiasms on *this* world, a world with no "beyond" but the "to come" it creates. Each *this* will have to be de-scribed—it means created—in its singularity. In the cinema each modern direc-tor creates his or her own crystals through a unique diagram that at once constructs actual images as the passing present, and contains all of the past, the virtual dimension into which it plunges, like a sieve. Constructing this diagram is the action of cine-thought, the site (the sight) of the splitting of time, and the crystallisation of the universe. Deleuze examines a wide range of these diagrams, and the 'crystals' they produce, but a good example is that of Max Ophüls as it constructs his film *Earrings of Madame D . . .* (1953). Briefly, Ophüls' crystalline diagram operates at all levels of composition: in the film's specific images (crystal chandeliers, mirrors, the earrings of Madame D), in the famous camera movements and shots full of faceted reflections, and in the development of the story whose increasingly complex virtual dimension emerges in series of crystalline circulations and refractions from which there is no escape (this is true of other Ophüls' films as well, *Lola Montez* (1955) or *La Ronde* (1950) for example) As Deleuze states: "Ophüls's images are perfect crystals" (C2, 83/111). The crystal is diagrammatic, inasmuch as it creates an actual state-of-affairs at the same time as this actuality is itself creative, constructing a virtuality, a reality that is to come. The crystal-image is an image as the splitting of time, each image a present which enfolds and unfolds its past and future.

## IN FAVOUR OF THE FALSE AND ITS ARTISTIC POWER

This emphasis on the constructive powers of the crystal-image has important philosophical consequences for cinema. The crystal-image produces movements that are essentially "false," the false continuity and jump-cuts of Godard, or the merge of fantasy and reality in Fellini for example. Deleuze finds in these developments a Nietzschean inspiration, and marks the return, though not by its old name, of the simulacra, the "image without resemblance" (LS, 257/297).[40] The crystal-image is not a resemblance, not a description, nor is it a representation, because it has no extra dimension that would verify or deny its truth. This is the decisive Nietzschean intuition for Deleuze: "By raising the false to power, life freed itself of appearances as well as truth: neither true nor false, an undecidable alternative, but power of the false, decisive will" (C2, 145/189). Nietzsche is crucial at this point of Deleuze's account, for "it is Nietzsche, who, under the name of 'will to power,' substitutes the power of the false for the form of the true, and resolves the crises of truth, wanting to settle it once and for all, [ . . . ] in favor of the false and its artistic, creative power . . ." (C2, 131/172). In other words, the crystal-image enjoys the power of the false ontologically, for it is the vital power constructing and expressing an absolutely immanent and univocal duration, no longer a duration as the "outside" of time, but an "internal outside," a creative "will" of cine-thought emerging in a new cinematic aesthetics.

Deleuze provides an interesting discussion of documentary film to illustrate this point, focussing on the so-called "direct" cinema appearing at the beginning of the 1960s (C2, 150/196).[41] Don Pennebaker's film *Hier Strauss* (1965) for example, is a portrait of the governor of Munchen in this style. The camera follows Strauss in his day to day activities, telling the story without voice over or comment, seemingly "from within." The camera is so close it is "like being there," but this "like" is precisely the hallucinatory power of the crystal-image which no longer represents the truth, as something it "reports" or "documents," but constructs it. The camera is not dissolved in the "truth" it represents; rather the camera dissolves the true in finding its power of the false.[42] This has remarkable consequences, for what we see in *Hier Strauss* is not the "reality" of the central character, but the becoming with which he has merged. What Deleuze writes about Pierre Perrault's "cinema of the lived" applies equally to *Strauss,* "as he himself starts to 'make fiction,' when he enters into the 'flagrant offence of making up legends' and so contributing to the invention of his people" (C2, 150/196). Deleuze intends this comment literally, and the eponymous hero of *Hier Strauss* is seen promoting a new united Europe. He has a "vision" in which a "before" is inseparable from an "after," the film documenting Herr Strauss' tireless efforts on behalf of this world-to-come. This is how the film reveals the splitting of time, the continual appearance of new "befores" and "afters," in a crystal-image embodying, "the passage from one to the other" (C2, 150/196). In this way, Deleuze claims, the cinema of the time-image is "direct" cinema inasmuch as it destroys all models of the true in becoming the creator of truth. Direct cinema will not, he writes, "be a cinema of the truth, but the truth of cinema" (C2, 151/197). At this point we could well ask whether modern cinema finally travels under a Nietzschean banner rather than a Bergsonian one, or perhaps more generously, whether the artistic power of the false marks Deleuze's creation of the indiscerniblity of Bergson and Nietzsche,[43] a hyphenation giving the name to a Bergson beyond Bergson.[44]

With the introduction of Nietzsche the crystal-image becomes ethically as well as ontologically distinct from representation. Crystal-images are not judgements of life in the name of the higher authorities of the true and the good, they are immanent evaluations of the life they involve, are ethical images rather than moral representations (C2, 137/179–80). This is the Nietzschean-Bergsonian reality of a cinema of becoming rather than being, of time rather than movement. These images can express good or bad, but only in becoming good or bad, in other (Nietzschean) words, by transforming themselves in an affirmation of becoming or by negating themselves in representations of truth. In such a cinema of immanent evaluation we once again return to the onto-aesthetics we have already explored in relation to Spinoza and Nietzsche. Indeed, at this point in Deleuze's account he talks not of cinema, but of the "artistic will or 'virtue which gives,' [as] the creation of new possibilities, in the outpouring becoming" (C2, 141/185). This ontological definition of art will find its specificity in particular art forms, and in and as an ethics of the artist. But this is the artist not as subjective genius, but as Nietzsche put it as "pure mouthpiece," as a mystical seer or visionary who produces crystal-images as the expression and affirmation of the "artistic becoming" of—and here Deleuze's terminology becomes entirely Nietzschean—"the will to power" (C2, 142/185). Once again: "Only the creative artist takes the power of the false to a degree which is realized, not in form, but in transformation. [ . . . ] What the artist is, is *creator of truth,* because truth is not to be achieved, formed, or reproduced; it has to be created" (C2, 146/191). Behind all the film makers and all the painters, behind all artists, is Zarathustra, "the artist or outpouring life" (C2, 147/192). Once more we return to this mystical equivalence of the artist and life.

Nietzsche's appearance in the cinema books allows Deleuze to make a distinction between two concepts of duration. One duration, or whole, exists for the movement-image and one for the time-image, one for the organic regime and one for the crystalline. Quite simply the first assumes a pre-existing reality, the second does not. Becoming is at the heart of duration in both regimes, but they differ in the respective images each regime gives of duration. The organic sensory-motor assumes an open whole, and one which changes, but as an exterior "reality" its movements represent, the movement-image therefore is an "indirect or mediate representation" of time (duration) (C2, 277/361–62). The movement-image constitutes time in its "empirical form," in which "the movement-image gives rise to an image *of* time which is distinguished from it by excess or default, over or under the present as empirical progression: in this case, time is no longer measured by movement, but is itself the number or measure of movement (metaphysical representation)" (C2, 271/355). This number of time is either its minimum unity found in the interval (Joan's spiritual face as pure affect for example), or it is the maximum of movement in the universe (Vertov's materialist dialectic). But in either case, duration exists only in its indirect representation, as part of an organic whole (inside-outside, individual and Nature) in which the movements of duration are relative to the actions of the sensory-motor interval. This is the "general system of commensurability" required by the classical image (C2, 277/362).

That the crystal-image, or direct image of time will come from the disintegration of the sensory-motor and its spatio-temporal *a priori* is at least hinted at by Bergson. "Degrade the immutable ideas," he writes, "you obtain, by that alone, the perpetual flux of things" (CE, 317). Furthermore, if "we must accustom ourselves to think being directly, without making a detour," then we must, Bergson suggests, "install ourselves within it straight away" (CE, 298–9). But how do we do this, and how do we avoid simply "crossing over" and giving an image of duration as the sensory-motors outside? Such an image finally, would have the same problem Spinoza's univocity was found to have by Deleuze in

*Difference and Repetition*. Duration may contain all images, but as the outside of the sensory-motor it can only exist as the intense possibility or as a sublime impossibility of any expression. This would make the movement-image immanent to the whole, but the whole remains transcendent to the movement-image. Deleuze finds in the crystal-image a cinema adequate to Nietzsche's declaration that "*nothing exists apart from the whole!*" (TI, "The Four Great Errors," 8) and its famous consequences, "when we have abolished the real world: what world is left? The apparent world perhaps? . . . But no! *With the real world we have also abolished the apparent world*" (TI, "How the 'Real World' at last Became a Myth"). We have already seen Deleuze privilege Nietzsche's ontological equivalence of being and becoming as univocity's true formula, and in cinema this equivalence means the abolition of real and apparent worlds in the crystal regime. Here time is no longer subordinate to a movement which measures it and movement—now understood as the vibration of time splitting in the crystal—creates images adequate to it. These images express time in duration, but only by constructing or hallucinating its movements, only in other words, by thinking it according to a new image of thought. The eye has seen something new, but only by discovering a new way to think. As Deleuze and Guattari put it elsewhere (in relation to painting, but it is a condition of their aesthetics which also applies to cinema), "vision is through thought, and the eye thinks" (WP, 195/184). This new thought of the seer escapes the interval-brain and its sensory-motor in order to, following Bergson's advice, install itself directly in the real. We arrive at the plane of duration, and a time-image adequate to the plane's becoming, only when an image expresses the plane by constructing it. Duration, life in its entirety as time, does not pre-exist the vision-thought which grasps it, because this vision thinks and constructs it *in its* expression. Duration is seen and thought in an image that expresses it, an image that is inseparable from a genetic impulse that is always constructing duration anew. This is the vitalism of cinematic "vision," its indiscernibility from the expression/construction of duration itself. Deleuze returns this image-thought to its Bergsonian origin, but only by breaking with the sensory-motor as its interval. A new body-brain must emerge adequate to the modern image-thought, no longer a sensory-motor interval, but a direct nervous and cerebral shock: "It is only when movement becomes automatic," Deleuze writes, "hat the artistic essence of the image is realized: *producing a shock to thought, communicating vibrations to the cortex, touching the nervous and cerebral system directly*" (C2, 156/203). Here the image's power of the false is co-extensive with philosophy's power of thought. It is not surprising then, that the introduction of Nietzsche into Deleuze's account of cinema reintroduces the figure of the artist-philosopher. In relation to cinema this figure emerges from Deleuze's discussion of Antonin Artaud, and is called the "spiritual automaton," the seer whose visions exist "flush with the real," and whose automatic image-thought is the appearance of the moving matter of duration in a nervous-cerebral shock.[45] This thought is equivalent to a new vision, because it no longer travels through a sensory-motor that carries perceptions into action, but hallucinates pure optical and sound situations that construct a crystal of time.

A good example of the "spiritual automaton" appears in Michelangelo Antonioni's beautiful film, *Il Deserto Rosso* (1964). Here, Deleuze finds Antonioni's typically banal, deserted and everyday any-space-whatevers absorbing all characters and their actions (C2, 5/12). The empty and rotten industrial landscape of *Il Deserto Rosso* often appears out of focus, emphasising its abstract color compositions over its representational "reality," and lending it hallucinatory qualities that are doubly disturbing. First, because the space is detached from the character, inasmuch as Guiliano, a woman struggling with her mental health, can no longer act. Second, because these hallucinatory images appear as an indirect discourse, as visions *of* the character, in the sense in which this *of* seems at once subjective (are they point of view shots?) and objective (the abstract qualities of the landscape are not hallucinatory but real). These two aspects of abstraction and hallucination often work together, as when an out of focus shot picks out certain objects by color rather than form, making the image swim in an entirely non-representational manner. No doubt it is no longer the point whether what we see is the vision of a character or the camera, because the question is no longer one of delirium *or* description, but the way these come together in a modern vision as crystal image. The abstract color compositions of Antonioni's any-space-whatevers do not, therefore, act as metaphorical descriptions of Guiliano's mental state. They mark the dissolution of the sensory-motor interval into pure and "truly false" visual and auditory situations which are neither subjective nor objective. These images no longer appear in the interval-brain, because Guiliano's "visions," which are ours too, are not located in relation to any "outside" by which they could be judged. Indeed it is precisely the detachment of her visions from any encompassing structures (from their cause, which is only sketched, and from any narrative development—very little "happens" and the film begins and ends with almost identical images) that eliminates action as such, and makes distinguishing between images of subjective hallucination and objective description impossible, and in fact this distinction ceases to be important. As Deleuze writes of neo-realist film in general, but it applies very precisely to *Il Deserto Rosso*, "we no longer know what is imaginary or real, physical or mental, in the situation, not because they are confused, but because we do not have to know and there is no longer even a place from which to ask" (C2, 7/15). This unknown constitutes the position of Guiliano and the viewer, both are cast into a perceptual uncertainty which is not resolved but explored. Their vision is not other-worldly in any transcendental sense, nor does it attempt a higher order of truth (there is no romanticism in the woman's madness, nor any pity), it is simply a fact, the fact of a banal and everyday world stripped of its rational narratives and appearing in its pure visuality, beautiful but not extraordinary, sensual but not sensational.

Guiliano's struggle to integrate her experience of the "whole" into a social framework of expectations and roles leads to further hallucinatory passages and ek-stases.[46] But she fails. Sinking further into an emptiness where others cannot follow her, not her lover, nor her husband, who are all ill with action, with their meaningless lives, a point her lover acknowledges without knowing how to change it. Her vision of the young girl alone on a beautiful beach perfectly expresses Deleuze's words: "The world awaits its inhabitants who are still lost in neurosis" (C2, 205/267). Guiliano yearns for such a world, pure and sun drenched, where everything sings, but she is lost in sensory-motor banalities, a neurosis which represses her. This neurosis is a sensory-motor limit beyond which lies the psychosis of the "spiritual automaton," a schizo-sensation or vision of matter in its emergence, a sensation as participation, and Guiliano is continually shocked, overwhelmed, to the point of being a 'mouthpiece' of thoughts she cannot control but only react to. Her vision is a pure becoming in which she cannot maintain her identity, and which becomes increasingly abstract. Antonioni affirms both the beauty and the pain of this utterly modern vision, and the film registers both aspects in opening up spaces of virtual emergence, spaces on the one side unbearable and experienced as madness, on the other as abstract and tranquil spaces giving refuge from the active neurosis of the human interval.

In *Il Deserto Rosso* it is through Antonioni's use of color that a new world emerges, and it is in color that "the character or the viewer, and the two together, become visionaries" (C2, 19/30). Color is an abstract force encompassing viewer and image in the emergence of a new reality, a vision that is indiscernibly *of* being, and which *produces* being. This experience exceeds sensory-motor perception, both Guiliano's and our own, and the image and its abstract color compositions give a vision of a virtual infinity uncontained by any shared time, but nevertheless existing as a creative becoming, as the duration created by and expressed in *this* actual image. Guiliano becomes a visionary, a spiritual automaton who sees this unbearable excess of life, which is life, the virtual duration of actual events appearing in a time-image. This is a life that can barely be lived—and Guiliano barely lives—and appears in images which are often unbearable. This is life seen by the seer, Guiliano and us, those who "know how to extract from the event the part that cannot be reduced to

what happens: that part of inexhaustible possibility that constitutes the unbearable, the intolerable, the visionary's part" (C2, 19–20/31). This is, quite
precisely, the part Guiliano experiences. There is something terrible in reality," she exclaims, "and I don't know what it is." But she sees it, and Antonioni
shows it to us, not as a representation of madness, but in extraordinarily beautiful shots which envelop us, shots composed of abstract colors constituting a
world both fresh and frightening, a world in which the virtual and creative
powers of co-existence emerge for themselves. Once more, this is achieved
through Antonioni's colorism, which at its abstract limit tends, Deleuze
writes, to "efface" what it describes, and "carries space as far as the void" (C1,
119/168). This coloring void is not however, opposed to the genetic element,
but is its emergence in any-space-whatevers (of which Guiliano's life is full—
the red shack, the cream/purple hotel room, the half-painted empty rooms of
her shop, the noisy functionality of her husband's factory). In these spaces the
compositions of abstract color in the frame act as "the virtual conjunction of
all the objects it picks up" (C1, 119/167). It is color then, that is able to transform the space of action into a space of virtual construction, a space opening
out into a void of the sensory-motor indiscernible from the unthinkable plen-
itude of life. In *Il Deserto Rosso* the void of the any-space-whatever also has an
amorphous enveloping power, appearing in the white mists of Ravenna in
which the film's colors seem to swim, sinking below and rising to its surface.
Indeed, Deleuze describes Antonioni's voided space as "amorphous," having
"eliminated that which happened and acted in it. It is an extinction or a dis-
appearing, but one which is not opposed to the genetic element" (C1,
120/168). Guiliano's sensory-motor is overpowered by this any-space-whatever of color, effaced by the mist, by the room, by the shop, in a continual
fade. But in this void emerging around and in Guiliano a new life and vision
appears, one, Deleuze writes, "all the more charged with potential" (C1,
120/168).

Antonioni pushes his abstract colorism as far as possible in *Il Deserto Rosso*.
Guiliano's nervous and cerebral events, her visions, are both detached from any
pre-existing world—as pure optical situations—and are themselves creative hallucinations of an unbearably vital world at the heart of this one. But Guiliano's
wanderings never "cross the bridge" to the "other" side, whether this is imagined
as a spiritual "ascension" or a psychological "decent." In her confusion Guiliano
remains here and now and of this world. In one scene she drives to the end of a
pier, a dead end in the sea and not the bridge she thought, as if to deny her the
fatal allure of dissolution in a constantly moving ocean, an ocean she cannot
look at she says, because then she loses interest in what happens on land, but a
beyond she cannot reach because—as beyond—it does not exist. Color marks

the genetic explosion of the world, a "vision" abstract and real, an expression of the virtual in the actual (or an implosion of the actual in the virtual color conjunction), an explosion entirely cerebral and cinematic, nothing but (Guiliano's) schizo-sensation. The brain, Deleuze claims, becomes adequate to the modern world in this genetic encounter with color (e.g. in Antonioni's abstraction (C2, 317/266)). Deleuze's equation of Antonioni's color with modernism is consistant with Deleuze's discussion of painting, which will be our subject in the chapters to come. To construct a world with color will be Deleuze and Guattari's definition of artistic modernism, an art which will be anti-representational, and whose ontology will be shared equally by cinema and painting. For both, Deleuze writes, "Godard's formula, 'it's not blood, it's red' is *the* formula of colorism" (C1, 118/166). Antonioni is in full agreement with this when he comments: "People often say 'write a film,' why can't we arrive at the point of saying 'paint a film'?"[47] Such a colorism will require a new brain, a brain detached from the sensory-motor and operating as a "void" through which and as which thought emerges as the "virtual conjunction" of "vision" with an abstract, "truly false," but nevertheless actual hallucination.

## CINEMA CRACKS UP . . .

In this final intolerable vision of the life which exceeds her, and which she lives, Guiliano undergoes cinema's final metamorphosis, and becomes an Artaudian body, a Body without Organs (BwO). It may seem paradoxical to say the cinema can exist without organs, but Artaud's BwO is, as we shall see more fully in Chapter Six, without the organization of the organism rather than without organs. The BwO is not a spatio-temporal body, not a sensory-motor, but an inorganic or crystalline body, a crystal-image that creates as it expresses a perspectival and virtual whole of duration. In Artaud this body-image has a particular ontological status, it is the "innermost reality" of the cinema, but it can only be conceived of as "a fissure, a crack" (C2, 167/218). This crack is the nervous vibration which disrupts the organism, and gives the shock required to make the cinema think. The crystal-image is this crack, an image of time itself as the crack—and no longer the interval—of thought: Guiliano's visions, her crack up . . . For Artaud, cinema expresses the powerlessness of human thought, the impossibility of thinking the whole except as impossible. For Deleuze this is the power of the crystal, it gives an image of "the inexistence of a whole which could be thought" (C2, 168/218). Of course it had to happen, the whole has become a hole, and the crystal-image is a hole in thought.

"Any work of art," Deleuze has said, "points a way through for life, finds a way through the cracks."[48] Art in this sense gives an image to the disruptive force which cracks open our thought, but only as a "figure of nothingness," a

**Figure 3** Michelangelo Antonioni, *Deserto Rosso,* 1964, Austrian Film Museum.

"hole in appearances" (C2, 167/218). Artaud's crack, or (w)hole of thought, meets Nietzsche's power of the false to provide an abyssal cinema of crystal-images. Artaud's BwO, as the internal outside, as the (w)hole of thought which forces us to think, finds in Nietzsche's power of the false a revalued physiology, the modern body-brain of cinema and of art. Modern cinema constructs this new physiology in its visions, its pure optical and sound situations in which we are animated by an image which forces us to think, a "neuro-physiological" vibration as Artaud put it, an image which is both the (w)hole which could not be thought, and the crack through which this (internal) outside thinks. In *Il Deserto Rosso* it is constructed by what Antonioni calls his "psycho-physiology of color."[49] Here, Guiliano's increasingly nervous agitation and automation open onto a gap in her vision—her inability to see herself as whole—and she falls into this hole where things and people merge in an indeterminable mist. But what emerges in their place is a purely abstract vision, an inhuman convulsion of color as a living thing which attains a new determination beyond the sensory-motor. As a result, the climax of *Il Deserto Rosso*, the consummation of Guiliano's affair, offers no narrative closure, and culminates in her increasing distress in the throes of a hallucination turning the room purple. A vision of the (w)hole itself, a coloring void-vision. This image-thought can only be false, because it no longer has an outside which it represents, it is instead a crack in the world by which cinema goes beyond the true and the false to create the new. A cinema of conception/perception produces a vision, a BwO, a hole in/of the world, and requires the transformed regime of expression that emerges across the break between the two Cinema volumes. A modern cinema appears here that is not concerned with the movements of narrative, but with the duration that emerges through its cracks. As Deleuze has it: "We no longer believe in an association of images—even crossing voids; we believe in breaks which take on an absolute value and subordinate all association" (C2, 212/276). Montage takes on its modern meaning, no longer structuring the flow of time to give an indirect image of duration, but operating as a disjunctive conjunction, joining images in a break (breaking the movement-image) through which duration is expressed, constructing image-cracks or visions through which duration can emerge as what it is, the creative power of life.

Deleuze argues that when the crystal-image suspends the world with its aberrant movement, when it cracks open thought and appears as what was impossible to think, it produces an image of "what does not let itself be seen in vision" (C2, 168/219). As we shall see in the following chapter, this is also what Deleuze and Guattari will find in painting, a visionary power of inorganic life as the unthinkable that makes us think and see *something impossible to think and see*. An impossible thought and vision that requires a new body and brain, the BwO, as what sees (construction) and what is seen (expression). This (w)hole of duration is not totality, it is not a reassuring organic whole which is represented in our relations with the world, it is the (w)hole as break, this unthinkable crack, thought and seen as the being and becoming of thought itself. As ontological ground therefore, it is our very groundlessness. The whole is the virtual dimensionality to every actual thing, not pre-existing the thing, but continually re-constituting the thing according to the changing perspectives of its construction and comprehension in vision. The break or gap, in other words, is what is produced when we approach the reciprocity of virtual and actual in the image. This produces a break in our sensory-motor, as we have seen, but more than this our own image, the Bergsonian image we have never stopped being, finds its own "vision" in expressing duration through its constructive—and no longer *reductive*—break, a break which changes duration's nature. Now we can see how the Bergsonian definition of duration Deleuze gave as "*what differs from itself*"[50] must, in its modern form, be qualified by the definition given by Deleuze and Guattari: "Duration is in no way indivisible, but is that which cannot be divided without changing in nature at each division" (ATP, 483/604). At each division, a division made by the "section" or "perspective" of vision, the virtuality of duration is actualised and expressed, but only by making duration change in nature, an expression of becoming inseparable from its very construction. The "outside" of thought is not "out there," no matter how close this may be, it is the abyssal splitting of time itself *within the image,* the ontogenesis of duration. Not then the virtual *and* the actual, whole and part, but the actual image *in* its virtual vitality, the actual image as the expression and the construction of its virtual becoming, inseparable and indiscernible. "This is why thought," Deleuze writes, "as power which has not always existed, is born from an outside [duration] more distant than any external world, and, as power which does not yet exist, confronts an inside, an unthinkable or unthought, deeper than any internal world. [ . . . ] Thought outside itself and this un-thought within thought" (C2, 278/363).

## THE METHOD OF BETWEEN

In the organic regime, the whole was the open, expressed in a temporal interval that produced an image that was always indirect. In this way, classical cinema created an out-of-field as, "a changing whole which was expressed in the set of associated images" (C2, 179/233). But if the whole is neither outside nor inside, Deleuze points out, "the point is quite different" (C2, 179/234). The whole, duration as crack, or internal outside, is instead the "between" of the cinematic time-image, rather than an outside the movement-image expresses. This interstice of images however, should not be thought of as the between *of* images, because thoughts and images are themselves this "between." Indiscernibly virtual and actual, their actual individuation emerges from the virtual (w)hole (expression), which they simultaneously are, as the creation of a perspective on duration (once more we think of Bergson's famous cone) as the process of its infinite and virtual movement (construction). The whole is this constant creative vibration, the rhythmic beatings of crystal-life.

Cinema becomes in modern times "the method of BETWEEN, 'between two images,' which does away with all cinema of the One" (C2, 180/235). But perhaps this is simply the cine-aesthetic of the contemporary itself, the modernity of any and every age, a possibility we will come back to. This cinematic transformation parallels an ontological mutation of the whole that ceases being the One-Being, and becomes the constitutive "and" of things, the simultaneous construction and expression of a vital becoming. Deleuze's ontological aesthetic of the cinema therefore culminates in this univocity of becoming, and our route through Bergson arrives at the same point as those we took through Nietzsche and Spinoza. Art, cinematic or otherwise, is the creative force of life inasmuch as this expresses an immanent whole it constructs. Cinema is in this way an atheistic and mystical practice, the production of a crystal-image in which, as Deleuze writes of Stanley Kubrick's *2001, A Space Odyssey* (1968):

> The identity of world and brain, the automaton, does not form a whole, but rather a limit, a membrane which puts an outside and an inside in contact, makes them present to each other, confronts them or makes them clash. The inside is psychology, the past, involution, a whole psychology of depths which excavate the brain. The outside is the cosmology of galaxies, the future, evolution, a whole supernatural which makes the world explode. (C2, 206/268)

Chapter Four

# A Freedom for the End of the World: Painting and Absolute Deterritorialisation

Expression, like construction, signifies both an action and its result. [ . . . ] If the two meanings are separated the object is viewed in isolation from the operation which produced it, and therefore apart from vision, since the act proceeded from an individual live creature. Theories that seize upon "expression" as if it denoted simply the object, always insist to the uttermost that the object of art is purely representative of other objects already in existence. They ignore the contribution which makes the object something new.

—John Dewey, *Art as Experience.*[1]

## INTRODUCTION

The artwork, Deleuze and Guattari argue, is a productive machine that does not represent anything, is itself unrepresentable, and exists only as the conjunction of material flows and their traits of expression. Nevertheless, and consistent with what we have already seen in the last three chapters, art's affirmation gets captured in forms which negate it, which imagine it as something sad, and which subjectivise, organicise, and temporalise its inorganic consistency and emergent becomings. Painting too, like all the other arts. But, like all the other arts, painting also finds a way through the cracks, and operates as a critical practice that resists its formalization and departs on its thousand lines of flight.

Once again, painting resists this "capture" on two fronts. On the one hand, the aesthetics of creation presupposes no material or meaning, and is precisely what escapes such presuppositions in creating the new. In this sense the creative process, the "art" of absolute deterritorialisation as it will be developed in this chapter, is at work everywhere. On the other hand, this revolutionary force only appears within a specific milieu, in more or less concrete assemblages, in paintings as such. The point is not to set painting up in, or as, a dialectic between its specific representations or forms and their absolute deterritorialisation, but to

understand how paintings are *already* the immanence of an absolutely deterritorialised plane and its territorialised formalization. What is required, as Guattari
points out, is "a double enunciation: finite, territorialised and incorporeal, infinite" (Chaos, 55/82). Painting is, first of all, an articulation of its finite and infinite dimensions, an art of creation that in its finite processes of construction
absolutely deterritorialises the world (destratifies it Deleuze and Guattari will say)
and expresses its destratified and infinite "plane of consistency."

This chapter will therefore have two main objectives: First, a general account of the terminological and theoretical terrain on which this "double
enunciation" of painting takes place. Central to this account is an understanding of the concepts of deterritorialisation, both relative and absolute, and how
these articulate the relations between the strata and the plane of consistency.
This provides us with the components of a semiotics capable of revaluing the
"sign," a semiotic *practice* that Deleuze and Guattari call schizoanalysis. The
second aim of the chapter will be the exploration of the schizoanalysed sign
through the examples of Venetian Renaissance painting, and the work of
Jackson Pollock. The first will involve a discussion of art's "abstract machine,"
while the second will extend this discussion to its painterly components; the
abstract line, smooth space, and haptic experience. Thus, the two elements of
this chapter will provide us with a new image of abstraction, one that departs
from the work of Wilhelm Worringer, and challenges the classic modernist account of Pollock by Clement Greenberg and Michael Fried. This introduces
Deleuze and Guattari's concept of modernism, which will be taken up and developed in the next chapter.

## STRATIFIED

The material world, the Earth, is a plane of consistency, a genetic flux of unformed matter/energy existing at ontological ground zero. But, Deleuze and
Guattari argue, the Earth is constantly conglomerating and concretising according to various axiomatic relations of content and expression, a "double articulation" of the Earth emerging through what they call the "strata." The
strata impose limits on the autogenesis of the Earth as if from above, and as
such: "Every stratum is a judgment of God" (ATP, 44/58). It will come as no
surprise that one of the first signs of painting, when it is truly art, is an atheism that attacks these judgments.

The strata consist of various axiomatic relations of content and expression that determine things and their meanings. This double articulation of
the strata is doubled again by the distinction of form and substance, once for
expression and once for content. Content consists of a formed matter (the

"chosen" or territorialised matter being its substance—canvas and paint in painting for example—and the order it is chosen in, its coding, giving its form—*this* painting). On the other hand, the "choosing" of functional structures determines a substance of expression (the genre of a painting for example), which it combines into forms (once more, this expression, the meaning of *this* genre painting). In both cases, form is the code, and substance the territory formed. Meaning and things (the meaning *of* things) are therefore produced through the reciprocal presupposition of content and expression and their mobile relations within and between strata, (expression in one relation can be the content of another, as when an art historian writes about a painting). Strata are actualised by what Deleuze and Guattari call "machinic assemblages." These work in two directions, on one side they face towards the plane and employ "abstract machines" to "extract" a matter-function, and on the other the strata formalize this matter-function into "concrete assemblages," the actual things and statements which emerge through the strata's "pincers" of content and expression.

Deleuze and Guattari suggest three levels of strata, the geological or physiochemical, the organic, and the linguistic. Signs emerge in the organic and linguistic strata, where expression operates in a dimension separated from its content. This autonomy of expression means it can on the one hand reterritorialise a material form/substance as its content—constructing a sign—and on the other, it can itself be deterritorialised and re-formed as the content of another sign. At the organic level, the sign appears through the process of reproduction (life and death being the constant de- and re-territorialisation of content for new expressions), but the sign takes on its real meaning when this process is extended to language. Here the sign gains an autonomy from the "thing" it represents, things and signs being produced through different technical and linguistic regimes. The two regimes nevertheless operate in reciprocal presupposition, as the example of painting shows. A painting's content as "thing" consists of the substances it is formed from, and the technical operations that form them. The painting's expression, or what it represents, exists on another level and emerges through a formal organisation of functions or forms of expression.[2] Nevertheless, content and expression must be in reciprocal presupposition for a painting—as sign—to exist, but they remain distinct from each other as "meaning" and "thing." The contours of this relation are, however, dynamic and multifaceted. The technological axiomatic that produces a painting, its historical trajectory of material substances and processes of formation have undergone continual change, and the move from a cave painting to Antonioni's cinematic painting that we saw last chapter would describe only one possible history of painting's innovation of material and technique. Within the regime of expression there is also an extremely open process at work defining a painting's historical meaning (the form of expression), not to mention the history of the meaning of painting (expression's substance). For example, is the figure seated next to Christ in Leonardo's *Last Supper* a woman, as one recent theory has it? Similarly, the long debate around the relative merits of line over color marks only one possible "phylum" of the shifting meaning of painting. Nevertheless, some aspects of painting's expressive regime have remained stable, most notably a content-expression relation determined by what Deleuze and Guattari call the "imperialism of the signifier" in which "the semiotic of signs is necessarily linked to a semiology of the signifier" (ATP, 65/84–5). Here, where semiotics becomes semiology and structuralist linguistics becomes the dominant model, a representational relation is imposed on content and expression, an "oversimplified" model in which the painting as substantial "thing" is "subjugated" to the "increased despotism" of the regime of signification (ATP, 66/85–6). Painting's meaning now exists within linguistic assemblages of expressions (signifiers) and contents (signifieds), whose reciprocal presupposition with the techniques of formed substances ("things") remains, but this substance of painting is over coded by the meaning it represents as a sign. Painting's materiality and the processes that form it therefore find expression only through the constant circulation of signifiers, or "significance" as Deleuze and Guattari call it. Signifiance implies the autonomy of meaning from materiality in a seemingly free circulation of signifiers, but this freedom hides the face of another despot, that of the subject. The understanding of signs according to a signifier/signified relation implies for Deleuze and Guattari an individual subject who expresses it. In this way, *signifiance* and *subjectivation*[3] are the two facets of a representational economy that defines not only the meaning of painting (as what it means to paint), but also what it means to think.

In *Difference and Repetition* Deleuze explains the co-implication of signifiance and subjectivation in terms of a representational image of thought.[4] This "dogmatic" image of thought, as he calls it, assumes an "I think" which pre-exists and determines perception, and is therefore entirely relevant to a discussion of art. Here, Deleuze is critiquing the Kantian rationalist model where the faculties of conceiving, judgment, imagination and memory constitute a "common sense" shared by all, as the condition of possibility of any perception. Any perception presupposes this common sense, which in turn assumes a subjective identity—a "Self" as the unity and ground of common sense—and an objective identity in what the faculties sense and represent (DR, 226/291). A painting, in being experienced, becomes determined by "common sense" as a subjective sign representing a singular and self-same object, an object whose materiality is always already taken up in this representational economy of thought. As a result, painting appears in a perception that has already been determined as a representation of an object for a subject, a representation given meaning by the signifier which expresses it and which gives its content. As we shall see, when painting emerges in its materiality, or more precisely when the construction of its material becomes expressive, it will no longer be representative, and it will create a sensation that assumes a new way to think.

Deleuze and Guattari's understanding of a semiotics of content and expression rests on the work of Louis Hjelmslev, who sought an alternative to the signifier/signified of structuralist linguistics.[5] But structuralism is only the latest symptom of a representational image of thought which has dominated our thinking since Plato. It's "the same circle," and "we're still spreading the same canker" (*le même gangrène,* ATP, 65/85). Against the "signifier enthusiasts" (ATP, 66/86) Deleuze and Guattari posit the Hjelmslevian sign, whose content-expression relation has, "the advantage of breaking with the form-content duality" (ATP, 43/58). In this sign expression is kept in direct contact with its material dimension, and stands, Deleuze and Guattari claim, "in radical opposition to the scenario of the signifier" (ATP, 66/85). We are not signified, Deleuze and Guattari argue, we are stratified, and engaging with this process begins with a "semiotic of signs" opposed to a "semiology of the signifier" (ATP, 65/85). This revaluing of the sign however, is only the first step towards a revaluation of painting, and now we must take the necessary further steps towards its absolute deterritorialisation.

## ABSOLUTE DETERRITORIALISATION

Content and expression allow us to understand the way signs only appear in a "specific, variable assemblage" necessarily involving both meaning and things (ATP, 66/85). But this "concrete assemblage" emerges from a deeper "machinic assemblage" it actualises. The machinic assemblage operates the articulation of content and expression on its side facing the strata, but on its other side it faces the plane of consistency, where its "abstract" machine composes material flows into traits of content (degrees of intensity, resistance, conductivity, heat and speed) and traits of expression ("tensors" or functions operating as differentials, such as clear-obscure, line-color, or closed-open form). Signs do not, on this account, appear as signifiers or as representations, but as particular assemblages of material forces and functions stratified into relations of content and expression. This understanding of the sign is therefore ontological, because it puts the sign back into contact with the material and vital plane of consistency that constitutes it. In this sense Deleuze and Guattari propose a critical semiotics that will reveal the signs abstract machine, and in so doing free a sign's material becomings from the strata, allowing them to be sensed in themselves. The abstract machine, while immanent to the sign, is the "destratified" element that avoids any distinctions between content and expression. The abstract machine is the "pure Matter-Function" of a sign, operating on the plane of consistency where "it is no longer even possible to tell whether it is a particle or a sign" (ATP, 141/176). The task of semiotics will therefore be to interpret stratified signs in order to revalue (destratify) them, in order to make the operation of their abstract machines sensible.

Abstract machines are absolutely deterritorialised, and are the "primary" elements of any machinic assemblage, operating before its territorialisation and coding into signs. "This absolute deterritorialization," Deleuze and Guattari write, "becomes relative only after stratification occurs on that plane or body: It is the strata that are always residue, not the opposite" (ATP, 56/74). The semiotic problem is therefore how to approach signs in their absolutely deterritorialised state, as particles-signs. This problem has as its condition Deleuze and Guattari's assumption of the "perpetual immanence of absolute deterritorialization within relative deterritorialization" (ATP, 56/74).[6] Absolute deterritorialisation does not introduce an "excess or beyond" (ATP, 56/74) to the strata, but is the immanent operation of the abstract machine in stratification. Although the strata subjugate matter-function through processes of relative de- and re-territorialisation (relative that is to the axiomatic limits of the strata), the abstract machine is always seeking to conjugate these movements into an absolute deterritorialisation, a "destratification," as "the abstract machines absolute positive deterritorialization" (ATP, 142/177). This absolute deterritorialisation of the abstract machine has two important elements that are necessarily related. First, it appears within the strata as the absolute deterritorialisation of content and expression, as the crack through which something new emerges. But second, on the absolutely deterritorialised plane of consistency the abstract machine operates in a "piloting role," creating new possibilities for life, creating a real to come, "*a new type of reality*" (ATP, 142/177). As Deleuze and Guattari put it in an example that equally applies to painting: "Writing now functions on the same level as the real, and the real materially writes" (ATP, 141/177). We shall shortly see how Venetian Renaissance painting and the work of Jackson Pollock, each in its own way, achieves this.

The abstract machine appears according to two "complementary" movements, either within the strata which "harness" it and turn its deterritorialisations relative, or as the absolute deterritorialisation of the strata, in lines of flight on a "passage to the absolute" (ATP, 144/180). According to these two modes of effectuation we will either remain organicised, signified and subjectified in a stratified body and thought, or we will be absolutely deterritorialised, destratified in the creation of a new reality, emerging as a new I/eye adequate to its "properly diagrammatic experience" (ATP, 145/180–1). As a result our question becomes, "given a certain machinic assemblage, what is its relation of effectuation with the abstract machine?" (ATP, 71/91). In other words, how is the abstract machine stratified, and in what ways does the assemblage open onto destratification? This question is not easy to answer, because its answer must be constructed through a process of critique, through, as Deleuze and Guattari call it here, a "schizoanalysis." The immanence of the abstract machine implies that the new realities it creates do not exist apart from the strata, but only appear in the absolute deterritorialisation *of* the strata. Just what this appearance could be we shall now go on to see.

With the absolute deterritorialisation of signs, with their destratification, the possibility of signs no longer defined by distinctions between contents and expressions, or forms and substances is introduced. Once more this begs the question, and Deleuze and Guattari ask it, "how can one still identify and name things if they have lost the strata that qualified them, if they have gone into absolute deterritorialisation?" (ATP, 70/90). The answer has two parts. First, such a sign appears through the conjugation of deterritorialising movements in the strata, accelerating (or decelerating) deterritorialisations to an absolute speed, by which the sign appears *as* destratification. This process frees "variables" to "operate in the plane of consistency as its own functions" (ATP, 70/90). This brings us to the second part of our answer, that absolutely deterritorialised "variables" appear under their own, destratified conditions. Here the abstract machine constructs continuums of intensity which appear as *particles-signs,* as the non-representative "asignifying traits" (FB, 100/94) which constitute the plane. These signs appear when relations of content and expression no longer define the abstract machine, and it emerges "flush with the real, [as] it inscribes directly upon the plane of consistency" (ATP, 65/85). This second sense of an abstract machine "inscribing" "flush with real" implies that in destratifying signs the abstract machine does not simply "return" them to the plane of consistency, but that particles-signs construct the plane at the same time as they express it. How? Particles-signs, we know, are asignifying traits, but as their hyphenation suggests, they are composed from traits of content and traits of expression as the matter-function of the abstract machine. As we have seen, traits of content are absolutely deterritorialised contents (matter-flows), and traits of expression are "tensors" inseparable from matter and determining its tendency in relation to its immanent functions. The abstract machine conjugates certain traits of content to construct a material plane of consistency, and it is this plane that the abstract machine's functions express (in its traits of expression).

The question for painting is how its signs appear as particles-signs, how painting is sensible beyond the common sense of subjects, their objects, and

their representational image, or signifier. Particles-signs express a destratification, a radical break with, or line of flight from the strata that introduces
something new. But in another sense, they express an abstract machine as the
"diagram" of the plane, a force of construction by which the plane's vital ontogenesis is expressed in signs. Particles-signs will therefore appear in painting
both as its destratification, as what escapes the stratifying articulations of content and expression, and as a new reality they construct. No creation without
destruction. Destratification fractures our harmonious common sense to construct a new sensibility, a destratified, desubjectivised sensibility adequate to
the asignifying particles-signs it produces. A particle-sign will therefore require a new sensibility, because it "is not a sensible being but the being *of* the
sensible. It is not the given but that by which the given is given. It is therefore
in a certain sense the imperceptible. It is the imperceptible precisely from the
point of view of recognition" (DR, 140/182). A-subjective and a-signifying
particles-signs are released by the imperceptible and continuous variation of
matter-function, by which the abstract machine constructs and expresses the
plane of consistency. And if particles-signs are flush with the real, then so is
their sensation. They can only be sensed outside of the schema of subjects and
their objects, as the insanity of common sense, and the imperceptible of rational perception. They are mad rather than meaningful, and appear, Deleuze
and Guattari argue, in the asubjective sensations of the schizophrenic.
"Someone" Deleuze tells us, "who neither allows himself to be represented nor
wishes to represent anything" (DR, 130/177).

## SCHIZOANALYSIS IS LIKE THE ART OF THE NEW

Schizoanalysis will be, quite precisely, the analysis of stratified matter that liberates its deterritorialisations and turns them absolute. In this way, schizoanalysis will construct sensations as particles-signs. Consistent with its immanence
to the material it attempts to destratify, schizoanalysis is a process and not a
goal, a pragmatics, a continued experimentation. "The completion of the
process," Deleuze and Guattari state, "is not a promised and pre-existing land,
but a world created in the process of its tendency, its coming undone, its deterritorialisation" (AO, 322/384).[7] Schizoanalysis will be the continual process
of freeing matter from its determination by the strata, a never-ending process
of revolution that leaves "physical and semiotic systems in shreds," and produces from their ruin "asubjective affects, signs without significance" (ATP,
147/183). The schizoanalyst is a "mechanic" because "schizoanalysis is solely
functional" (AO, 322/385). He or she is a "handyman," one who destratifies
signs in order to create a new reality.[8] In this way, "the negative or destructive

task of schizoanalysis is in no way separable from its positive tasks—all these tasks are necessarily undertaken at the same time" (AO, 322/384–5). The mechanical nature of this process is important, because it suggests the way in which it is achieved through direct material interventions rather than through a psychoanalytic interpretation of symbols.[9] The "schizoanalysis" of particles-signs is a material process, an intervention rather than an interpretation. "For reading a text," Deleuze and Guattari write in a passage clearly also applying to painting, "is never a scholarly exercise in search of what is signified, still less a highly textual exercise in search of a signifier. Rather it is a productive use of the literary machine, a montage of desiring machines, a schizoid exercise that extracts from the text its revolutionary force" (AO, 106/125–6).

Schizoanalysis is an analysis of stratified signs, Deleuze and Guattari write, and is "the only way you will be able to dismantle them [strata] and draw your lines of flight" (ATP, 188/230). Schizoanalysis attempts to accelerate (or decelerate) the deterritorialising movements of the strata beyond their threshold of reproduction and towards an irrevocable "breakdown," a breakdown through which matter-functions "break through" the strata. But how does the artist achieve this, how does he or she construct the new? The artist and art-work begins by creating a "catastrophic" breakdown. "The artist," Deleuze and Guattari write, "stores up his treasures so as to create an immediate explosion" (AO, 32/39). Their example is Turner's late land and seascapes, and especially his last watercolors, which produce an "explosive line," a line without outline or contour (i.e. it is non-representational), that "makes the painting itself an unparalleled catastrophe (instead of illustrating the catastrophe romantically)" (FB, 105/98). This explosive quality (its anti-romantic quality will become important in the next chapter) of the line will be a constant feature of Deleuze and Guattari's painting diagram, one we will see them trace in Venetian painting, Gothic art, and the work of Jackson Pollock and Francis Bacon. Deleuze and Guattari devote a particularly beautiful passage to Turner's "breakthrough" paintings:

> the canvas turns in on itself, it is pierced by a hole, a lake, a flame, a tornado, an explosion. The themes of the preceding paintings are to be found again here, their meaning changed. The canvas is truly broken, sundered by what penetrates it. All that remains is a background of gold and fog, intense, intensive, traversed in depth by what has just sundered its breadth: the schiz. Everything becomes mixed and confused, and it is here that the breakthrough—not the breakdown—occurs." (AO, 132/157–8)[10]

There are a couple of important points to note here. The first is one I have already mentioned, that what appears in this work is precisely the "breakdown" of stratified signs by which the particles-signs of the plane appear *as* a "break-through": an absolute deterritorialisation necessarily immanent to the strata. But this break is productive, and the "schiz" appears as intense matters-functions at work on/in the plane. This means the "breakthrough" of the painting is not utopic in the sense in which it, with Jim Morrison, would break on through to the other side (although it does, perhaps, kiss the sky). The utopia of Turner's paintings is not another world, but is the appearance of *this* world in its reality, in its being as becoming, in its ontological emergence as a sensation. In this sense, schizoanalysis is a utopian pragmatics, for, as Deleuze and Guattari explain: "Utopia does not split off from infinite movement: etymologically it stands for absolute deterritorialisation but always at the critical point at which it is connected to the present relative milieu, and especially with the forces stifled by this milieu" (WP, 99–100/95–6).

The schizophrenic, in his or her "misery and glory" (AO, 18/25) experiences matter as destratified, as an atemporal and intense matter. "The schizophrenic," Deleuze and Guattari write, "is as close as possible to matter, to a burning, living centre of matter" (AO, 19/26). Schizoanalysis experiments with stratified signs in order to bring them as close as possible to the matter they already are, to the point where, as in Turner, the "artisan" paints flush with the real. The schizo-artisan in his or her glory is however, clearly distinguished from the misery of the schizophrenic clinically defined. The schizophrenic as patient escapes the strata of signifiance and subjectivation only at the price of his or her ability to produce signs. The schizophrenic steps into a silent and painful outside, a madness, living from 'the other side' an opposition between the strata and plane of consistency that the strata enforce.[11] The schizo-artisan on the other hand, "scales the schizophrenic wall" (AO, 69/81) and makes what they are escaping from escape itself. Their artistic creativity lies in being able to destratify an assemblage and through this process express its immanent material flows in particles-signs (AO, 341/407–8). We don't have to look far amongst artists to find examples of a schizoanalytic practice, and a schizoanalytic life. Henry Miller describes it beautifully as that moment when "the world ceases to revolve, time stops, the very nexus of my dreams is broken and dissolved and my guts spill out in a grand schizophrenic rush, an evacuation that leaves me face to face with the Absolute."[12]

As the passage from Miller implies, schizoanalysis is neither a psychotic breakdown, a terrifying and painful autism, nor a purely theoretical aphasia, but a practice, something we must accomplish for ourselves, in schizo-analysing our own lives. Not least the thinker, who's thought must not simply represent the schizo-production of others, but must take a little of their 'madness' in order to construct something new. Deleuze makes this point in a well-known passage from *The Logic of Sense.* Commenting on the alcoholism of Malcolm Lowry and F. Scott Fitzgerald, and on Artaud and Nietzsche's madness, Deleuze asks:

> Are we to become the professionals who give talks on these topics? Are we to wish only that those who have been struck down do not abuse themselves too much? Are we going to take up collections and create special journal issues? Or should we go a short way further to see for ourselves, be a little alcoholic, and a little crazy, a little suicidal, a little of a guerrilla—just enough to extend the crack, but not enough to deepen it irremediably? [ . . . ] How is this *politics,* this full *guerrilla warfare* to be attained? (LS, 157–8/184)

This politics of self-schizophrenization will emerge more fully in the next chapter, but it is also implicit in Deleuze and Guattari's suggestion—a suggestion I have tried to extend—of a schizoanalysis of Venetian painting.

## A THOUSAND LINES OF FLIGHT, THE CASE OF VENETIAN PAINTING

Deleuze and Guattari argue that the strata of signifiance and subjectification form a "sticky mixture," a mixture of a white wall (signifiance) and black holes (subjectivation) creating faces as recognizable forms of our generic humanity and individual identity (ATP, 138/172). As such, faciality is the means by which all faces may be compared through a sliding scale of similarity that determines their relative positions. But the face is not an expression of impartial or universal judgment, although it likes to appear as such, for the face is that of the White Man himself, Jesus Christ Superstar, the typical European. Quite simply, "you've been recognized," Deleuze and Guattari write, and faciality "has you inscribed in its overall grid." Faciality is ultimately a form of policing, a "deviance detector," which inscribes any attempt to escape its normative system within its boundaries, for all there is, is divergence from the white-man's face, without outside. "There are only people who should be like us and whose crime it is not to be" (ATP, 177–78/218). Their punishments include racism, poverty, confinement or death. Obviously: "The face is a politics" (ATP, 181/222), and in this political dimension it is easy to see how the ubiquitous production of faces within the arts is only one aspect, and not necessarily the worst, of its pernicious powers.

The face and its faciality machine have their correlate in the landscape. Landscapification codes the world, imposing physical and psychological hierarchies (determining my "place" in the world) that compliment the process of facialisation. In this sense, a sense both aesthetic and political: "The 'problem' within which painting is inscribed is that of the *face-landscape*" (ATP, 301/369).[13] Painting approaches this "problem" from two sides, on the one hand enabling its reproduction, but on the other creating deviations from its normative axiomatic. This latter process is painting's "brighter side" (ATP, 178/218) where, and here Deleuze and Guattari are beginning to talk about the Venetians: "Painting has taken the abstract white wall/black hole machine of faciality in all directions, using the face of Christ to produce every kind of facial unit and every degree of deviance" (ATP, 178/218–9). Painting becomes a deterritorialisation machine: "The aim of painting," Deleuze and Guattari rather generously argue, "has always been the deterritorialisation of faces and landscapes, either by a reactivation of corporeality, or by a liberation of lines and colors, or both at the same time" (ATP, 301/370).

Venetian painting of the Renaissance is a "reactivation of corporeality" and a "liberation of line and colour" that introduces material and iconographic innovations (new traits of content and expression) to painting, and does so in a way that attacks its representational regime, its face-landscape machine. This movement of deterritorialization emerges in painting with the shift in the Renaissance towards a theology of the incarnation. Debates about the meaning of the incarnation were explored in painting, which developed a new iconography centring on the passion story, and the Madonna and Child.[14] But more fundamentally, Deleuze argues, with this shift in theological focus God is no longer a pure transcendent essence, but has become its opposite, the event or "accident" of a man's death. This "accident," especially as it appears in painting, embodies Christianity's inherent atheism, an atheism that would liberate painting in a dramatic way: "Christianity contains a germ of tranquil atheism that will nurture painting;" Deleuze argues, "the painter can easily be indifferent to the religious subject he is asked to represent" (FB, 124/117). An atheist painting produced from within the church structure that nurtures it emerges when "the form begins to express the accident and no longer the essence" (FB, 125/117). It becomes a small step for the painter to use the accident of Christ on the cross to explore completely different concerns: a landscape, some drapery, or other more bizarre twists of the imagination. This is, Deleuze claims, the "radical break" in painting that occurs around 1450, in which "the flows of painting go insane."[15] At this time, Deleuze and Guattari write: "The most prodigious strokes of madness appear on canvas under the auspices of the Catholic code." They mention: "Christ-athlete at the fair, Christ-Mannerist queer, Christ-Negro" (ATP, 178/219). It is not the case however, that painting turns against the church, and starts to disbelieve.[16] Instead, painting discovers the atheism that is the creative part of Christianity, the descent of the divine into the flesh, and begins to experiment with this new corporeality, pushing it to extremes: "Christ's body is engineered on all sides and in all fashions, pulled in all directions, playing the role of a full body without organs [i.e. the plane of consistency], a locus of connection for all the machines of desire, a locus of sadomasochistic exercise where the artist's joy breaks free. Even homosexual Christs" (AO, 369/442–43). Although this last claim seems optimistic, it is certainly true that iconography at this time breaks with the rigid codes of Byzantine and Gothic art. What is crucial however is that these deterritorialisations of the expressive regime are conjugated to others taking place on the level of content, most importantly the introduction of new painting materials in Italy at this time. Although these deterritorialisations will be reterritorialised by the classical aesthetics dominant in central Italy, the Venetians will project the deterritorialisation of material into the absolute, their technique and use of color inventing a new painting machine. This will be the abstract machine of modern painting, where painting breaks with representation because "the *semiotic* components are inseparable from *material* components and are in exceptionally close contact with molecular levels" (ATP, 334/413). Here painting emerges in particles-signs, where the semiotic components (traits of expression) are inseparable from their material elements (traits of content). Painting will become, with the Venetians, a materialist experimentation inseparable from the vitalism of the plane, a materialist-vitalism no longer representational but real. Venetian art succeeds in making painting *live,* and this will be its value for Deleuze and Guattari. It is not a representation of the ideal and eternal, but a material vitality that finds expression in the construction of a new reality, a reality painting will not exhaust, to this very day (there is no "death of painting"). In this way, Venetian art fulfils one of Deleuze and Guattari's clearest affirmations of a vital art:

> art is never an end in itself; it is only a tool for blazing life lines, in other words all of those real becomings that are not produced only *in* art, and all those active escapes that do not consist in fleeing *into* art, taking refuge in art, and all of those positive deterritorializations that never reterritorialize on art, but instead sweep it away with them toward the realms of the asignifying, asubjective, and faceless. (ATP, 187/230)

At this point however, we must turn to a much more precise account of Venetian art to understand, exactly, how it achieves this. Venetian painting emerged in part from a Byzantine tradition of images especially present in Venice. Under Byzantine control early in its history, Venice, even once independent, maintained significant economic links to Constantinople and its empire. As Venice was without classical ruins, the great Byzantine church, San Marco, dominated the city physically and aesthetically, its lush decoration and spectacular mosaics being an important influence on Venetian painting.[17] These are some of the reasons why Venice, unlike central Italy, did not break with the Byzantine influence in painting, and in many ways continued its lines of research.[18] Beyond their aesthetic influence however, the function of Byzantine mosaics within the church was to provide a path by which the viewer could transcend their body and regain the divine realm of the spirit, and this spiritual path was one Venetian painting rejected. Nevertheless, Byzantine mosaics offered an alternative to the classical subordination of light to line that dominated the Italian Renaissance, an alternative the Venetian painters developed in their own direction.

Classical representation utilized the line as an expressive contour imposing an ideal and organic form on matter. The classical line was hylomorphic, and operated as a mould, this function being privileged over light and color, which merely provided the material elements of the picture. Representation was first of all the representation of the organic world, of man's world, and in the realm of art it was first of all the line that described this world. Byzantine art developed an alternative to this type of representation in abandoning the contour-line, and using instead the modulation of areas of light and shadow to construct form. This 'reversal' provided a means of composition Venetian art was to exploit against the classical emphasis on line favoured in the Renaissance of central Italy, a reversal the Venetians accelerated into the absolute deterritorialisation of color.[19] In the Byzantine mosaic, Deleuze writes: "Beings disintegrate into light," (FB, 129/121) and this was a deterritorialisation of both organic representation and the human essence it represented. This Byzantine deterritorialisation nevertheless introduced its own reterritorialisations, for the alternations of "black shores and white surfaces" (FB, 128/120) composing Byzantine figures involved an equally rigid system of faciality. Byzantine art was in fact typified by an extreme emphasis on the face of the "old despot," God the father and the son, who appeared in hieratic isolation in the upper reaches of the church. Venetian painting before 1450, Deleuze and Guattari write, "molds itself to the Byzantine code where even the colors and the lines are subordinated to a signifier that determines their hierarchy as a vertical order" (AO, 369/442). This vertical hierarchy works to lead us towards our essence—that to which we are compared and that to which we aspire—but this essence doesn't define our "natural" organism, but is the spiritual "grace" of a heavenly world appearing in the brilliance of the mosaic's divine light. To ascend into this divine light means transcending our organic form, and the church in this sense was a machine through which we could achieve this transfiguration.[20] But this ascension into pure light meant more than a break with the beautiful classical body and its representation; it meant the evaporation of all materiality into a spiritual void. In this sense, Byzantine art expresses the philosophical transition from Plato to Plotinus. Plotinian mysticism demanded a dematerialization of the soul that was also a radical negation of consciousness. This final step in retracing God's emanation into being travels up, into the light defining the spiritual and visual presence of God in San Marco, allowing our gaze to pass through the black holes of God's eyes in order to gaze upon the internal abyss from which Plotinus' God emanates his gift. Being must disintegrate in light, in order to discover the divine void. [21]

Venetian painting will borrow the Byzantine dissolution of classical line in the modulation of light, but it will do so through affirming rather than negating corporeality and the materiality of paint. In taking up the Byzantine modulation of light in its own ways (ways we shall have to elaborate) Venetian painting broke with the classical line, but more importantly it broke with this line as it was "re-born" in central Italy in the fifteenth century. For painters of central Italy line was the most important element in painting because it defined form, while light was only a secondary element that revealed it. This approach drew on the classical philosophical tradition articulated by Aristotle, who elevated form over matter and the intellectual over the sensuous. In his *Poetics* Aristotle privileged line over color because it had the clarity necessary to translate the intellectual act of invention, whereas color was merely a property of matter, both of the thing and of the medium used to represent it.[22] This was a more optimistic response to Plato's view of the material world as a dim and deceptive shadow of the transcendent realm of ideas and essences, and found in art the possibility of representing the essential and true. Line was the fundamental means by which art could approach the ideal, and light merely gave volume to the forms a line defined and revealed their color. As the most important element in the construction of form, line was the first step in a painting's composition, and by the middle of the fifteenth century was achieved by making a full scale cartoon, which was then transferred to the painting surface. The colors of each object had also been determined in advance, and these were applied following the linear contours. Color theory at this time also appealed to an Aristotelian metaphysics, and every effort was made to retain a color's purity as a supplement to the painting's linear clarity. An important element in this practice was the belief, once more inherited from Aristotle, that light was separate from color, and inasmuch as light and shadow created an objects volume these effects were gained through the mixture of the "non-colors" white and black with the color. The first account of such a method appeared around 1390 in

Cennino Cennini's *Libro dell'Arte,* which claimed to explain Giotto's painting technique. This involved the practice of "modelling up," where the pure color was placed in the shadowed areas of an object, and two lighter tones were then mixed by adding white, and were used to create plasticity. This method had mutated by the time of Leon Battista Alberti's *Della Pittura,* written in 1435–6, where the perspective system and the color theory of the Renaissance appeared in a systematized form. Alberti proposed a method whereby a space was defined by perspective, forms were drawn within this space, their color determined by drawing an imaginary line through their centre, and then modelled "up and down" through the addition of black and white according to the degree of illumination. The light source was fixed at a right angle to the picture plane, and gave the direction and strength of the shadows and highlights. The object's color was understood (once more following Aristotle) as being a "local tone" or true color belonging to the object itself apart from any visual factors such as light conditions or proximity to other colors. This "true" color was revealed but not produced by light, which was believed to have no color. In Cennini's system, colors had different value ranges depending on the intensity of their pigments, making consistent modelling a problem. Another difficulty from the point of view of naturalism was that the pure pigments placed in the shadowed areas tended to project forward because of their intensity, counteracting the painting's illusion of depth. Alberti's system solved both problems by placing the pure color in the middle, and so most projected part of the object, and standardized the tonal range of all colors by adjusting them both "up" and "own" through the addition of black and white.[23]

Although giving greater naturalism, Alberti's coding of color retains the classical emphasis on a true, ideal color consistent with its metaphysical commitments. Central Renaissance painting idealises color and light effects, because its color system ignores empirical experience, giving central Italian painting its timeless, eternal appearance. In empirical experience an object's color is inseparable from the quality of light illuminating it, and the colors of the objects surrounding it. The Venetians were the first to respond to these conditions, and this led them to revalue color's value. Starting with Giovanni Bellini, painters in Venice began to explore the empirical lighting effects of the time of day, or the weather conditions (a good example is Giorgione's *La Tempesta,* c.1509, Accademia, Venice[24]). They realized that light did not effect color through a simple binomial graduation of value, and began to experiment with other forms of mixing which lead to what Deleuze defines as a Modern colorism, where light and dark is achieved through the mixing of pure color. But before we analyse this change in the Venetian regime of expression we will have to turn to the various new materials being introduced at the time that made it possible.

The most significant of these factors was the introduction to Italy of a new medium—oil—in the 1460s. This development is usually attributed to the painter Antonello da Messina. Vasari claims Da Messina learnt the technique directly from Jan van Eyck, and although we now know this was impossible (van Eyck died before da Messina was born), recent research indicates he may have visited Flanders to learn the technique.[25] Additionally, some of van Eyck's works had come to Italy, and the painters Rogier van der Weyden and Petrus Christus had visited by this time. Oil as a medium dramatically effected Renaissance painting, giving a greater depth and vibrancy to color than that achieved by mixing the pigments with egg tempera. Most importantly it meant that the layering of glazes could create shadow, and black no longer needed to be mixed with a color, a practice often producing murky effects. Black was still used in the monochrome under painting that gave the lighting structure of a scene, but a color's value could now be controlled through the overlay of different amounts of similar pigments (for example, a series of reds and pinks achieved through the layering of different intensities of each). This practice did not however, contravene the classical demands of "pure" color and its condemnation of "corrupt" colors (those created through direct mixing) as in glazing each color retained its integrity, and only similar colors were overlaid. Oil began being used in Venice in the early 1470s, most notably by Giovanni Bellini, but da Messina's presence there in 1475–7, and the influence of the work he did there (especially the altarpiece for S. Cassiano, now in the Kunsthistorische Museum, Vienna) was an important factor in its quick adoption. The Venetians accelerated the possibilities of the oil medium beyond its use in central Italy in numerous ways. They began to overlay glazes of complementary colors to create shadows (the so-called "colored grey"), meaning the inseparability of light and color in nature could find its adequate expression in a painting technique. They also began to inflect an object's shadow with color from nearby objects, which gave a much more realistic light effect. Finally, they directly mixed colors together, adding "broken tones" to their palette. In these ways the Venetians absolutely deterritorialise the classical line to start painting with color-light. Deleuze and Guattari put it very succinctly: "what would appear to be another world opens up, an *other* art, where the lines are deterritorialized, the colors are decoded, and now only refer to the relations they entertain amongst themselves, and with one another" (AO, 369/442). As we shall see, Deleuze will claim that this liberation from the systematic addition of white and black to create a color's value will be the definition of colorism, and the condition of possibility of a painter being able to paint inorganic forces. This deterritorialisation of the Renaissance line-color value system did not emerge in isolation however, and was conjugated to other important "traits of expression" of the new oil medium. These were concentrated in technique, where oil's greater fluidity and slower drying time enabled the painter to work up the composition on the canvas, and to explore the affects of a much freer brushwork.

Venetian painters, starting with Giorgione, stopped working out their compositions in detail before beginning to paint. Drawing no longer prede-termined the composition, the composition was worked out through the process of painting.[26] This is another major break with central Renaissance methods, for, as Marcia Hall points out: "Color, rather than line, is the pri-mary means of constituting the image, [ . . . ] making the painting process the process of creation."[27] The picture's composition and color scheme were often reworked during painting, and this required a new technique. First of all faster, more intuitive and empirical, with the painter responding to problems and inspirations generated through the material process of painting. Painting no longer simply represented the idea of the painter, or his patron, but began to express its matter-force, its paint-painting machine. The central Renaissance painters had a three step practice, drawing the forms, applying a monochrome lighting scheme, and adding the color last. Giorgione, and Titian after him, begins with a very broad laying-in of light and dark areas within which colors are increasingly integrated.[28] "Titian," Deleuze and Guattari note, "began his paintings in black and white, not to make outlines to fill in, but as a matrix for each of the colors to come" (ATP, 173/212). Titian develops this technique to a point in the late paintings where there was no longer a clear distinction between the "under painting" and the applica-tion of color (Tintoretto also used this technique extensively). Light and color were applied together in the gradual working up of the forms, a process rely-ing less on a preconceived drawn plan, than a series of continual reworkings. In the late Titian opaque and translucent paint and dark and bright colors are applied simultaneously. Furthermore, some passages in the later work seem to have been applied with Titian's fingers. Truly an artist painting flush with the real![29]

In emphasising the importance of the Venetian deterritorialisation of the line in a painterly construction of color-light, we are not only following Deleuze and Guattari, but one of their major art-historical references on this point (and on others), the German art historian Heinrich Wölfflin. Wölfflin's *Principles of Art History* is a remarkable forerunner to what we could call a 'diagrammatic' understanding of art, and provides a taxonomy of five "tensors" or functions through which to understand art. Each function was bi-polar (linear-painterly, plane-recession, closed-open form, multiplicity-unity and clear-unclear) and an art work, Wölfflin argued, appeared in relation to these poles.[30] Wölfflin's prin-ciples are not outside history, but in Deleuze and Guattari's terms are "prior to" history (ATP, 142/177). This is the position of the abstract machine, and Wölfflin's principles are important examples of how traits of expression appear in the realm of art. The most important of Wölfflin's principles for our purposes are those of linear-painterly and clearness-unclearness.[31] Wölfflin explains how a "depreciation" of the line emerges in "the emancipation of the masses of light and shade till they pursue each other in independent interplay," producing what he calls "a painterly impression."[32] The art work no longer appears according to the linear determination of forms, each separate and distinct, but in an "all-over" affect in which "everything was enlivened by a mysterious movement," a movement in which an "interflow of form and light and color can take effect."[33] This new "interflow," along with the broken tones and loose brushwork we will shortly examine, breaks out of the eternal forms of Renaissance painting to directly involve us. We must reconstitute the painting through the active participation of our eye, and in this way the paintings appeal to our sensual rather than cerebral or religious instincts, enfolding us into the diagram of/as their real conditions. Like Byzantine art then, Venetian painting rejects the line for an expression that "has its roots only in the eye and appeals only to the eye."[34]

As Wölfflin's principle suggests, the Venetian renunciation of the line and their use of the new medium of oil led to an emphatic "handling" of the paint, and the force of the brushes movement became immediately visible in the work. This was partly a change in Venetian taste, and reflected the elevation of the artist above mere craftsman. But it was also a technique that Titian developed into an alternative to the layering of glazes. By juxtaposing and overlapping daubs of unbroken paint, he could modulate color-light in a faster and more calligraphic style, the activity of his brush adding drama to his scenes. Form now appears through the composition of colored patches punctuated by the terser passages of impasto.[35] Once more this innovation shows how traits of expression, here the expressivities of the brush, are directly connected to the new material traits of content liberated in the Venetian abstract machine

Titian conjugated this deterritorialisation of the brush stroke with another innovation on the level of content, the move from gessoed panels as support to canvas. The painters of central Italy preferred gessoed panels because they provided a very smooth surface that received the brush much like paper received chalk, and suited their emphasis of the line. Canvas however, had a weave that when pronounced remained visible, and disrupted the application of the paint. This disturbed the linear qualities of the stroke, and amplified the softer and more diffused modelling preferred by the Venetians. It also introduced a new possibility for producing broken tones, when colored under painting lying in the recessions of the weave showed through a color applied over it with a fast brush.

Tintoretto employed all of these material and expressive innovations in his work, but he pushed the Venetian reversal of the Renaissance separation of color and light to a new level. He did so through the practice of working on dark grounds, on which he laid on light areas with a rapid and often translucent stroke. In a remarkable affirmation of the new materiality of the Venetian abstract machine Tintoretto sometimes seems to have mixed his dark grounds simply by scraping together all the paint on his palette.[36] At this point, Deleuze claims, Venetian painting becomes "baroque" inasmuch as in it everything illuminated emerges from an infinity of shadows. Although it is not my intention to focus on Deleuze's work on the baroque here, it is worth noting as a broader abstract machine that functions within Venetian painting as well as philosophy and mathematics. The baroque emerges from the absolute deterritorialisation of the organic line of classical representation into folds, folds that give form by descending to and rising from a dark obscurity. The dark obscurity of matter itself, which in Venetian painting is folded by the brush into expressive and abstract patches of color-light to reveal form. In Venetian painting as "baroque" machine (Tintoretto is Deleuze's specific example):

> the painting is transformed. Things jump out of the background, colors spring from the common base that attests to their obscure nature, figures are defined by their covering more than their contour. Yet this is not in opposition to light; to the contrary, it is by virtue of the new regime of light. (TF, 31–2/44–5)

This new regime of light takes the luminism the Venetians inherited from Byzantine mosaics and deterritorialises it, before extending it into a new colorism where relations of light and dark are not added to, but constructed by, forces of color. Wölfflin anticipates Deleuze here, arguing that the baroque is a new regime of expression emerging within the tensor "clearness-unclearness." "For classic art," Wölfflin writes, "all beauty meant exhaustive revelation of the form; in baroque art, absolute clearness is obscured even where a perfect rendering of facts is aimed at. The pictorial appearance no longer coincides with the maximum of objective clearness, but evades it."[37] Deleuze will push this diagrammatic definition of the baroque even further however, claiming that it is "the inseparability of clarity from obscurity" which produces "the effacement of the contour" (TF, 32/45). It is the new visual clarity of color-light, and its hazy, flowing forms in Venetian painting that is inseparable from its dark material obscurity (Tintoretto's scraped palette). Semiotic and material dimensions are in absolute proximity. This is where the Venetian abstract machine constructs a new plane of consistency, invents a new materiality of painting, but not without unleashing new traits of expression, new ways to paint. Not least of these is

Figure 4 Titian, *The Death of Actaeon,* 1565-76, National Gallery, London.

the discovery of color-light, which will make Venetian painting adequate to the
material-vitalism, the inorganic life it expresses. Once more Wölfflin describes
this new living dimension of Venetian color in a beautiful passage that could be
Deleuze's: "We see that the emphasis lies no longer on being, but on becoming
and change. Thereby color has achieved quite a new life. It eludes definition and
is, at every point and at every moment, different."[38]

   Deleuze and Guattari give an account of the deterritorialisation of the
line by color that can easily be applied to Venetian painting. The representational line, they argue "proceeds by articulating segments" in order to delimit
form (in other words, like the Albertian value scale, the line works by over
coding matter). The deterritorialised matter-function of Venetian color-light
on the other hand, draws "a metastratum of the plane of consistency" (ATP,
56/74). This introduces new traits of expression that no longer function
through line, but through "the architecture of planes and the regime of color"
(WP, 179/170). This is not the abandoning of line, but its transfiguration, the

Venetian response to Deleuze and Guattari's cry: "Free the line" (ATP, 295/362). With the Venetians, the line loses "any function of outlining a form of any kind," and joins the absolutely deterritorialised traits of content, to emerge again in matter-flows of color animating the surface of the painting. "By this token," Deleuze and Guattari write, "the line has become abstract, truly abstract and mutant, a visual block, and under these conditions the point assumes creative functions again, as a color-point or line-point" (ATP, 298/366). The "living blocks" of Venetian color-light are no longer preformed by common sense into an object the subject represents, nor are they formed by semiological and technical stratifications of the plane. In the abstract machine of Venetian painting matter and function are co-extensive, and color and technique are the inseparable elements of its construction and expression of a new plane of consistency for painting. This finally defines Venetian particles-signs; they are no longer representational, for in them it is *the material that passes into sensation*" (WP, 193/183). This means the technical plane (the new traits of content and expression affecting the painting's construction) is inseparable from the sensation expressing the aesthetic plane of composition. In this sense, Deleuze and Guattari write, the technical plane "ascends into the aesthetic plane of composition and, [ . . . ] gives it a specific thickness independent of any perspective or depth. It is at this moment that the figures of art free themselves from an apparent transcendence or paradigmatic model and avow their innocent atheism, their paganism" (WP, 193–4/183).

Venetian painting is in this respect, Deleuze and Guattari argue, modern. Here, "art accedes to its authentic modernity which simply consists in liberating what was present in art from its beginnings, but was hidden under aims and objectives, even if aesthetic, and underneath recodings or axiomatics: the pure process that fulfils itself, and that never ceases to reach fulfilment as it proceeds—art as 'experimentation'" (AO, 370–1/445). What emerges in Venetian painting is a "pure" process of experimentation comprising the modern "phylum" of art, a phylum defined by its non-representational abstract machine, defined by in other words, its abstraction. Nevertheless, art's modernity—its abstraction—appears in concrete historical assemblages that are obviously very different. In fact, Deleuze identifies two general directions that modernist painting assemblages may take. One, taken by the Venetians, is to dissolve the representational line in the pure opticality of light-color. The other direction available to abstraction is what Deleuze and Guattari call the "Gothic" line, for which they offer another famous example, the painter Jackson Pollock. Pollock does not dissolve the line in light, but deforms it through a continual movement, a constant changing of direction in which it is either "splitting in breaking off from itself or turning back on itself in whirling movement" (FB,

129/121). This line is very different from that of the Venetians, but nevertheless performs a similar deterritorialisation, for it is "never the outline of anything" (FB, 130/122).

## ABSTRACTION—THE RETURN TO SMOOTH SPACE

Pollock's paintings are composed of "drips," swirling lines of paint sometimes coalescing into patches of color. But rather than dissolving the line into colorlight, as the Venetians did, Pollock frees the line from itself, by unleashing its abstract vitality. "With Pollock," Deleuze writes, "this line-trait and this colour patch will be pushed to their functional limit: no longer the transformation of the form but a decomposition of matter which abandons us to lineaments and granulations" (FB, 105/98–9). This is a succinct statement of the transition we will now make from Venetian painting to that of Pollock, from the transformation of form to the decomposition of matter. This transition will involve new materials and new techniques, and will require a new terminology to describe it. Pollock's abstract line is clearly both material and nonrepresentational, its thick skeins of paint weaving a "smooth" space without depth and in which relations are dynamic. "Smooth" and its antipode "striated" are terms for the ontological "space" of the plane of consistency and the strata respectively.[39] Lines and their trajectories appear within striated space according to their articulation of points. A line becomes a contour when it moves from one point to another, or when it is itself a sequence of points delimiting inside from outside. This line-point system establishes an extensive space of measures and properties through perspective, and populates it with signifiers and subjects. "Abstract lines" escape the "false problem" of perspective by no longer appearing within its striations, they do not represent things, but compose a moving visual block that returns striated space to smooth. Smooth space is traversed by the absolutely free line, a line that enjoys infinite movement and is, as Deleuze and Guattari will say, "an absolute that is one with becoming itself, with process. It is the absolute of passage" (ATP, 494/617). This free and abstract line traverses the plane of consistency in constructing its matter-flows and expressing its functions. The abstract line, Deleuze and Guattari write, and here we are once more approaching Pollock's paintings, is "without origin, since it always belongs off the painting, which only holds it by the middle; it is without coordinates, because it melds with a plane of consistency upon which it floats *and that it creates*; it is without localizable connection, because it has lost not only its representative function but any function of outlining a form of any kind—by this token, the line has become abstract, truly abstract" (ATP, 298/366, italics added).

The first matter-force, or trait of content of Pollock's abstract line is the "drip," both the paint and its various forces of fall and splatter, its gravity, speed and projection. The "drip" is important for two reasons. First, it implies the horizontality of the canvas, its famous descent onto the floor of Pollock's studio, which turns the "drip's" matter-force expressive in a new way (no sign in Pollock's painting of the 'vertical drip' and splash favoured by his contemporaries). Second, the removal of the painting from the wall deterritorialises Pollock's relation to it, allowing him to work 'within' it, from every side and even walking through it. Pollock thereby exemplifies Deleuze and Guattari's "law of the painting," that it be done at close range, without any optical distance.[40] This new physical relation to paint and canvas liberates the artist's hand from traditional signs of 'handling,' producing new asubjective traits. Furthermore, applied with sticks, sponges, and even icing syringes, Pollock's "drip" is the catastrophic breakdown of traditional techniques in a manual power that decomposes the paint material, freeing it from conscious control to release new traits of expression. This is Pollock's schizoanalytic diagram, an absolute deterritorialisation of painting's content into matter-forces (traits of content) inseparable from the absolute deterritorialisation of paintings expression onto new functions (traits of expression). No more representation, no more artist. Through this absolute deterritorialisation of painting something "abstract" appears, something Pollock called the unconscious, but which can only be understood in Deleuze and Guattari's terms as something real, "a non-figurative and nonsymbolic unconscious, a pure abstract figural dimension ('abstract' in the sense of abstract painting), flows-schizzes or real-desire apprehended below the minimum conditions of identity" (AO, 351/421). This abstract dimension emerges in Pollock's "drips" and their abstract lines, these *"traits of expression"* of his abstract machine, expressing the "plane of consistency upon which it floats and *which it creates."* In this way, a very different way from the Venetians, Pollock's abstract lines "assemble a new type of reality."

Although it is true that modernism and the abstraction that defines it have a long history for Deleuze, it is important to see how its abstract machine does not remain the same, and how its experiments have a definite history. Venetian painting constructed form through the modulation of color-light, which despite its radicality remained within an optical regime, and did not entirely abandon a representational function. The human face emerged from color-light, and although this process was abstract, the face was not significantly deformed by it, meaning the Venetian abstract machine retained a certain subjective dimension, a "homely atmosphere" as Deleuze calls it (using Francis Bacon's term), which "still conserves a menacing relation with a possible narration" (FB, 134/126). There seems little danger of narration appearing in Pollock's work of 1947–50 (the period of the "drip" paintings). On the one hand there is his non-representational line, and on the other his refusal to use value—the interplay of light and dark—to create form or depth. Clement Greenberg had already emphasized this aspect of Pollock's work, even though, as we shall see, he interprets it in a very different way from Deleuze. "In several of his 'sprinkled' canvases of 1950," Greenberg writes, "*One* and *Lavender Mist* as well as *Number One* (1948), he had literally pulverized value contrasts in a vaporous dust of interfused lights and darks in which every suggestion of a sculptural effect was obliterated."[41] Deleuze's difference with Greenberg is not over Pollock's "pulverising" of value-effects, but with Greenberg's argument that the results are entirely optical. For Deleuze there are two possible rejections of the representational line; one, and it is the one we have seen the Venetians take, is through light, and remains optical. The other is through the Gothic line, the line Pollock takes, which escapes the optical to become haptic. Painting, Deleuze writes, "can only move in one of the following two directions: *either towards the exposition of a purely optical space,* which is freed from its references to even a subordinated tactility [i.e. the colour-light of the Venetians . . . ] *or, on the contrary, toward the imposition of a violent manual space*" (FB, 127/119–20). In this manual, haptic space, it is the hand and not the eye that operates as an organ of touch and connection. Everything works here through continuity and conjunction, the hand is dis-organised, removed from the human body and its organic representation through a pure activity, "a speed, a violence, and a life the eye can barely follow" (FB, 129/121).[42] We can already feel that just such a hand, a hand that extends beyond the organism, executes Pollock's work.

Before going on to elaborate this Gothic line, and Pollock's use of it, two things need to be noted. First, Venetian painting clearly retains a degree of representation and narration, and develops them within the still subjective atmosphere of its color-light effects. This does not negate the absolute deterritorialisation Venetian painting achieves, but it is an aspect of their abstract machine that is deterritorialised in turn by a painting that is even more abstract. Second, this evaluation should not be seen to privilege Pollock over the Venetians (as we shall see Deleuze will point out other problems with Pollock's abstract machine in his book on Bacon), but rather, as with the classical and modern regimes of cinema, each have their own beauty and achievement which shouldn't be heirarchised in being identified as different.

## ABSTRACTION AND EMPATHY

Deleuze and Guattari's understanding of Pollock's abstraction, and more specifically their reading of his abstract line, draws heavily on the German art historian Willhelm Worringer. His book *Abstraction and Empathy* develops the opposition of classical and non-classical regimes of artistic expression as different types of aesthetic enjoyment, different types of "will to art."[43] Empathy is an "objectified self-enjoyment," [44] pleasure taken in an object as the affirmation and confirmation of human "volition in motion," a pleasure in other words, in our apperceptive activity and organic vitality. As Worringer puts it: "In the forms of the work of art we enjoy ourselves" (AE, 14). Empathy tends towards an aesthetics of organic naturalism, a subjective appreciation of the beauty of "nature." Here: "Man was at home in the world and felt himself at its centre" (AE, 102). The world of Poussin, not of Pollock. Empathy is, in classical terms, Apollonian, inasmuch as it overcomes the individuated perspectives of human consciousness by giving us an experience of our shared, harmonious, beautiful and "purely organic being" (AE, 33). Through empathy, Worringer writes, "chaos becomes cosmos."[45]

The "urge to abstraction," on the other hand, is "directly opposed to the empathy impulse" (AE, 14). As such, the aim of abstraction is "de-organicising the organic," (AE, 129) in order to become "part of an increasing order superior to all that is living" (FG, 17). Abstraction seeks these transcendent essences in order to express them through an "abstract eternalisation of existence in the crystalline body" (AE, 87). Abstraction therefore departs from mimetic naturalism and favours geometric designs, or positioning schematised figures on a flat plane that does not imitate space.[46] Abstraction rejects the organic and optical world of classical art in favour of a haptic sensation, a touch revealing the certainty of inorganic truths, as the "irrefragable necessity of [an object's] closed material individuality" (AE, 41). As a result in the haptic world of abstraction, Worringer writes: "Life as such is felt to be a disturbance of aesthetic enjoyment" (AE, 24). Worringer achieves for aesthetics a Nietzschean "revaluation of values" (which is how Worringer puts it (FG, 9)). Like Nietzsche, he finds the value of aesthetic value in the "will" (to art), understood in its onto-aesthetic antipodes of empathy and abstraction. This revaluing of aesthetics in ontological terms is clearly very important for Deleuze and Guattari, but nevertheless Worringer's duality of empathy and abstraction is not sufficient for them, because the abstract alternative to classical organic representation is a wholly transcendent one. Finally Deleuze and Guattari replace Worringer's opposition with their more "primordial duality" (ATP, 496/619) of the smooth and the striated.

To understand this "primordial duality" and its relation to the abstract line however, we must pass through Worringer's discussion of what he calls the "northern line," and Deleuze and Guattari's understanding of this as the defining feature of Gothic art. The northern line, Worringer argues, is an abstract line that is no longer 'crystalline' but has become mobile and expressive.

This abstract line is divorced from organic life but is, as Deleuze and Guattari put it, "all the more alive for being inorganic" (ATP, 498/623). The abstract line of Gothic art Worringer argues, expresses the "cloudy mysticism" of the German peoples of northern Europe (AE, 107). It's cloudy because it never achieves the clear necessity and regularity of a transcendental abstraction, it is forever searching for crystalline vision, a search inspiring an "ecstasy of movement" (FG, 41). This movement does not express an organic thing, or an ideal and transcendent "non-thing," but a hybrid "will" in which empathy turns away from the human to discover the "mechanical laws" of a "living" matter (AE, 113). These mechanical laws determine the "living movement of forces," (AE, 117) an inorganic life constructing, to use a phrase from Worringer which Deleuze and Guattari take as their own, the "vitalized geometry" (FG, 41) of Gothic art. Gothic art carries us into the infinite in an "extravagant ecstasy" (AE, 117) but this infinity is constructed by the mechanical forces of an immanent inorganic life. The infinity of the abstract line, in other words, is none other than our own, once "we lose the feeling of our earthly bonds; [and] we merge into an infinite movement which annihilates all finite consciousness" (FG, 108). In the Gothic abstract line, Worringer writes (and it is a line Deleuze will also echo), northern man "finds himself only by losing himself, by going out beyond himself" (FG, 115).[47]

The man or woman who loses their self in going beyond themselves is, for Deleuze and Guattari, the nomad, who in expressing this movement creates nomad art. The Nomad shares some features with Worringer's northerner, first of all what Deleuze and Guattari call a "vagabond monotheism" whose abstract line constructs a smooth space, or what they here call a "*local absolute*" (ATP, 382/474). Unlike the mystics of medieval times however, nomadic monotheism is, Deleuze and Guattari claim, "singularly atheistic" (ATP, 383/475). This marks the beginning of Deleuze and Guattari's deviation from Worringer, as they peel the abstract line away from the necessary connection it retains for him with religious worship.[48] Indeed at this point they "take some risks ourselves, making free use of these notions" (ATP, 493/615).

This "free use" begins with Deleuze and Guattari's understanding of inorganic life as a vital materialism. It is nomad art ("and its successors," Deleuze and Guattari note, "barbarian, Gothic, and modern" (ATP, 492/614)), which expresses this vital materialism through the "science" (but it is equally an aesthetics) of "metallurgy." Metallurgy acts as an expressive "will" of matter itself, and as such is a schizoanalytic work, flush with the real. We can understand Deleuze and Guattari's point, and its deviation from Worringer, through their respective discussions of the Gothic cathedral. Worringer argues that Gothic architecture is inorganic because the mechanical energies of the stone that it releases are not material but mystical. Gothic architecture expresses these abstract and spiritual forces of transcendence despite the stone, by negating stone's material properties (FG, 106). Deleuze and Guattari on the other hand argue that Gothic cathedrals were constructed according to a "nomad science" that rather than using off-site and on-paper plans which provided a hylomorphic form and required a uniformly prepared matter, these schizo-scientists—metallurgists—constructed their cathedrals through on-the-ground projections which took into account the singular properties and forces of each material element. This required cutting stones according to their particular position in relation to all the others, and was achieved by a technique of "squaring" rather than with a template. The building is no longer a form that defines a space, nor the expression of immaterial and ideal forces, but a construction of abstract lines expressing the continual variations of the stones matter-force. In this way, Deleuze and Guattari write: "It is as if Gothic conquered a smooth space" (ATP, 364/451). Gothic construction was not achieved through a transcendent plan, and this, perhaps, makes it "atheist."

Deleuze and Guattari's abstract line is neither abstract nor Gothic in Worringer's sense, because its inorganic vitality is immanent to its material, rather than that which attempts to transcend it. For Deleuze and Guattari, the "prodigious idea of *Nonorganic Life*" that Worringer considered the invention of the Barbarians, was in fact "the intuition of metallurgy" (ATP, 411/512). The metallurgist—a nomad schizoanalyst—produces art in which a "dynamic connection between support and ornament replaces the matter-form dialectic. [ . . . ] Nomad art *follows* the connections between singularities of matter and traits of expression, and lodges on the level of these connections, whether they be natural or forced" (ATP, 369/457). Rather than *search* for the transcendent, as Worringer's Gothic line does, the nomadic abstract line *follows* a vital matter, and in so doing expresses its construction of smooth space.

The abstract line, "this vital force specific to Abstraction is what draws smooth space" (ATP, 499/623). The abstract line draws a smooth space in which one senses this force (and has a haptic sensation), "only by touching it with one's mind, but without the mind becoming a finger, not even by way of the eye" (ATP, 494/616).[49] The mind participates in what it sees, beyond subject or object (and beyond signifiance and subjectivation), in a sensation inseparable from the action of a force. The haptic, for Deleuze and Guattari, is the tactile function of the eye, a "grabbing" or "touching" specific to a "connective function" of the gaze. Smooth space therefore emerges through this material participation of the eye—its "touch"—which constructs "visual-blocks" by following the matter-force on the inorganic plane. The haptic eye produces a metallurgical vision, a participatory modulation of the plane of consistency as an open ended "work in progress." As Deleuze and Guattari describe it: "In striated space, one closes off a surface and 'allocates' it according to intervals, assigned breaks; in the smooth, one 'distributes' oneself in an open space, according to frequencies and in the course of ones crossings" (ATP, 481/600).

If the abstract line is the vital force specific to Abstraction, how should we understand it in relation to art, and more specifically painting? As Deleuze and Guattari ask: "What then should be termed abstract in modern art?" Their answer follows directly: "A line of variable direction that describes no contour and delimits no form . . ." (ATP, 499/624). This abstract line is immediately referenced to Michael Fried's definition of the line in "certain works by Pollock" (ATP, 575/624), the works, obviously enough, of 1947–50. In these works the line has been set free and attains its Gothic dimension, an absolutely unrepresentational line both mystical and atheist in its expression/construction of inorganic life. Pollock's abstract line and the smooth space it draws produces a mystical modernity, one whose description is now somewhat familiar, in Pollock's work "the absolute is local, precisely because place is not delimited" (ATP, 494/617).

## CERTAIN WORKS BY POLLOCK. . . .

The definition of Pollock's line by Michael Fried to which Deleuze and Guattari refer is one Fried shares with his contemporary, the great modernist critic Clement Greenberg. Greenberg saw Pollock as a crucial moment in painting's move towards its constitutive essence, its material flatness,[50] and its production of "sensations, the irreducible elements of experience."[51] For Greenberg "pure" (i.e. modernist) painting rejects both the representational line, and value contrasts in creating a new kind of space:

> The picture has now become an entity belonging to the same order of space as our bodies; it is no longer the vehicle of an imagined equivalent of that order. Pictorial space has lost its "inside" and become all "outside." The spectator can no longer escape into it from the space in which he stands. If it deceives his eye at all, it is by optical rather than pictorial means: by relations of color and shape largely divorced from descriptive connotations, and often by manipulations in which top and bottom, as well as foreground and background, become interchangeable.[52]

It is interesting to note the seeming similarity to Deleuze and Guattari's account, inasmuch as in both the painting exists in a corporeal space, and produces an asubjective affect. "You become," according to Greenberg, "all attention, which means that you become, for the moment, selfless and in a sense entirely identified with the object of your attention."[53] But it is precisely at this point of seeming similarity that we can begin to map their divergence. Greenberg was also sensitive to the importance of the Byzantine break with classical representation, and also located it in the 'quasi-abstract' use Byzantine mosaics made of light and shade. This dissolved the sculptural illusion of volume, Greenberg argued, in favour of affirming the flatness of pictorial space.[54] Pollock achieved this Byzantine effect in his "middle period" (1947–50) where the aluminium paint and "interlaced threads of light and dark pigment" of the paintings come forward "to fill the space between itself and the spectator with its radiance."[55] Despite this affect being achieved through the materiality of Pollock's paintings, finally for Greenberg it "uses the most self-evidently corporeal means to deny its own corporeality."[56] Greenberg argues that Pollock's paintings "deceive the eye" into leaving the body for a pure opticality. This opticality is essential to modernism as such, Greenberg argues, because it enables painting's "spiritualizing escape" towards its "fundamental language."[57] If Byzantine art dematerialised reality by invoking a transcendental one, then modernism does something similar through its paradoxical invocation of the material against itself. Modernism's purity of material and flatness of surface can finally only be seen, and in becoming purely optical it is dematerialised, and reaches an essence that escapes representation by being addressed to eyesight alone. For Greenberg, Byzantine and modernist art, the "radically transcendental and the radically positivist" extremes of art, meet in a "counter-illusionist art."[58] "For the cultivated eye," he claims, "the picture repeats its instantaneous unity like a mouth repeating a single word."[59] Modernist abstraction therefore achieves an optical mysticism in which painting is able to transcend its representational function, but only by leaving the body to arrive at its spiritual "beyond." Our merge with the painting is achieved only in our disembodiment, and its truth is ideal rather than haptic. Once more, we're back to Plato, and Greenberg's still spreading the same canker. Where Greenberg sees Pollock as a Byzantine, he is, according to Deleuze and Guattari, Gothic.[60] The aluminium patches of Pollock's work (*Cathedral*, 1947, Dallas Museum of Fine Arts) do not reveal the glowing light of the transcendent, but rather the pouring of a metallurgist.

Deleuze and Guattari part ways with Michael Fried at a similar point, that at which he starts talking about the "disembodied energy"[61] and the "negation of materiality" in Pollock's paintings. [62] Fried writes that Pollock's line "is a kind of space-filling curve of immense complexity, responsive to the slightest impulse of the painter and responsive as well, one almost feels, to one's own act of looking."[63] Thus, perception begins to approach participation, but for Fried, as for Greenberg, this optical participation transcends the body. Pollock's line, Fried

Figure 5 Jackson Pollock, *Cathedral*, 1947, Dallas Museum of Art. © 2004 Pollock-Krasner Foundation / Artists Rights Society (ARS), New York

writes, "addresses itself to eyesight alone. The materiality of his pigment is rendered sheerly visual, and the result is a new kind of space—if it still makes sense to call it space—in which conditions of seeing prevail rather than one in which objects exist, flat shapes are juxtaposed or physical events transpire."[64] We have left a perspectivised space for a pure material flatness, but as soon as we have done so this materiality evaporates in a disembodied "opticality" existing as the "conditions of seeing." Pollock's "purity," his pure "opticality" transcends all theatricality (representation) in Fried's account, but only in an apotheosis arriving at its transcendental conditions of possibility, the ideal conditions of sight itself.[65] This "visual plenum" transcending subject and object and uniting eye and painting in Pollock's work forms, Fried and Greenberg argue, a 'continuum' in which the viewer is in indissoluble connection with eternity, but it is an unchanging eternal, making the painting curiously monosyllabic, the mysterious repetition of, as Greenberg put it, a single word.[66] Ummmmmmmmmm.[67] We have arrived at a space far away from that created by Pollock's writhing and cacophonic surface of lines.

Pollock's abstract line is "visionary" in the sense we have seen Deleuze define it in relation to modern cinema. The "vision" of the abstract line is achieved through and in the body, a body whose affectual capacities are no longer organised and subjectivised—a vision that is no longer optical. Painting's task has always been to render forces visible, but the haptic eye constructed by Pollock's paintings and the visions they produce, are very different from the purely optical perception Greenberg cannot get beyond (because, precisely, it *is* the ideal beyond). Pollock's visions are, on Deleuze and Guattari's account, irreducibly physical, and their expression of movement cannot be separated from the continual variation of their material plane. Rather than a disembodied and disinterested eye, Deleuze and Guattari see Pollock's work as producing (and being produced by) a schizo-eye/I, an eye *in* matter. "Where there is close vision," they write, "space is not visual, or rather the eye itself has a haptic, nonoptical function" (ATP, 494/616).

Pollock's line is, as Deleuze and Guattari write, a "local integration moving from point to point and constituting smooth space in an infinite succession of linkages and changes in direction" (ATP, 494/617). Pollock's abstract line constructs a haptic space in which the distinction between what is material and what visual, between subject and object, breaks down in a "pictorial vitalism,"[68] in a sensation of the painting that is a way of being (in) the painting, a way of becoming with it. The abstract line constructs a haptic sensation, and creates an eye freed from any optical function conditioned by a transcendental common sense. As a result, Deleuze and Guattari take Fried's definition of Pollock's abstract line and understand it in entirely different ontological terms: the ontological terms of the abstract machine. Here the abstract line is the matter-function of the Pollock machine, on the one side conjugating matters-forces into new traits of content (the "drip"), and on the other releasing the traits of expression of a new type of abstraction, an "abstract expressionism" of the vitality of its inorganic life. The paint is alive. This new painting machine deterritorialises the subjective and objective poles of vision absolutely, creating a smooth space in which we are always (in) the middle. It would only be in this sense that we could understand Fried's observation: "There is no inside or outside to Pollock's line or to the space through which it moves."[69] Pollock's paintings have a depth that is not spatial but intense; their smooth space does not contradict their visual flatness, but connects this surface to an immanent, infinite, and genetic processuality appearing in a molecularised matter, as particles-signs of sensation. Not a divine faciality, but an atheistic and mystical interface. Deleuze and Guattari are explicit on this point: "That is why it is so wrong to define sensation in modern painting by the assumption of a pure visual flatness: the error is due perhaps to the fact that thickness does not need to be pronounced or deep" (WP, 194/183). The materialism of Pollock's paintings is not, in this sense, simply defined by their materiality, but by their material vitalism, by the expression of the abstract and inorganic forces from which they are constructed. It is this vital element that turns the celebrated thickness of Pollock's paintings haptic, a transformation that has as its condition our implication in the paintings' abstract machine, our part in its ongoing process. Pollock's paintings express this merge at the same time as they construct it, through a sinuous, ropy line "that is constantly changing direction, a mutant line which is without outside or inside, form or background, beginning or end and that is as alive as a constant variation—such a line is truly an abstract line, and describes a smooth space" (ATP, 498/621).

Willem de Kooning said, "Every so often, a painter has to destroy painting. Cézanne did it. Picasso did it with Cubism. Then Pollock did it. He busted our idea of a picture all to hell. Then there could be *new* paintings again."[70] It was Pollock's break with those definitions of painting which had acted as its criteria, most importantly those of verticality, figuration, representation, and a striated depth, which make his work so important in the history of modernism. But this history, as it is written by Greenberg and Fried, and as Deleuze and Guattari write it, is not the same, and in their respective accounts, Pollock is not the same painter. Greenberg and Fried figure Pollock as a radical deterritorialisation of painting, but one that makes him simply one of "the key staging posts" of "the modernist-formalist genealogies of *visual* abstraction."[71] Pollock is consequently reterritorialised as the modernist representative of an optical idealism.

Deleuze and Guattari on the other hand, see Pollock's paintings as particles-signs composed by schizoanalytic abstract lines. Pollock's "abstract expressionism" is defined by the inorganic and material traits of expression it discovers, and the new abstract machine of matter-function it constructs with them (ATP, 499/623). In Pollock's paintings then, we see, Deleuze and Guattari write: "Traits of expression describing a smooth space and connecting with a matter-flow" (ATP, 498/622). This creates, in a beautiful description of a Pollock painting, a "stationary whirlwind" (ATP, 499/623), both expressive and abstract. Pollock seems to have sensed the vital-materialism of his paintings, of course. "The painting has a life of its own," he said, 'I try to let it come through. It is only when I lose contact with the painting that the result is a mess. Otherwise there is pure harmony, an easy give and take, and the painting comes out well." Pollock the mechanic; an artisan of immanence. When he is in contact with the painting, when he does not take a step back from it, when he participates in it, then he is one with the life that creates the painting, which is the inorganic life expressed in constructing the painting. "When I am *in* my painting," he says, "I don't know what I am doing. It is only after a sort of get acquainted period that I see what I have been about. I have no fears about making changes, destroying the image, etc., because the painting has a life of its own."[72]

Chapter Five

# Songs of Molecules: The Chaosmosis of Sensation

I hear the violincello or man's heart complaint,
And hear the keyed cornet or else the echo of sunset.

I hear the chorus. . . . it is a grand opera. . . . this indeed is music!

A tenor large and fresh as the creation fills me,
The orbic flex of his mouth is pouring and filling me full.

I hear the trained soprano. . . . she convulses me like the climax of my
    love-grip;
The orchestra whirls me wider than Uranus flies,
It wrenches unnameable ardors from my breast,
It throbs me to gulps of the farthest down horror,
It sails me. . . . I dab with bare feet. . . . they are licked by the indolent
    waves,
I am exposed. . . . cut by bitter and poisoned hail,
Steeped amid honeyed morphine. . . . my windpipe squeezed in the fakes
    of death,
Let up again to feel the puzzle of puzzles,
And that we call Being.

—Walt Whitman, "Song of Myself"[1]

## INTRODUCTION

In *What Is Philosophy?* Deleuze and Guattari give a concise definition of art: "Art wants to create the finite that restores the infinite" (WP, 197/186). We saw in the previous chapter how the absolutely deterritorialised particle-sign emerges in painting as the expression and construction of a plane of consistency having simultaneously finite and infinite dimensions. This chapter will continue to explore art's (in)finitude, this time beginning from the "chaosmosis" of Guattari's "aesthetic paradigm," and following its production of the affect, the refrain and

sensation. Where the previous chapter was primarily concerned with art's material and technical aspects, this one will focus on what can provisionally be called
art's "subjective" processes. How in other words, is the onto-aesthetic dimension
active in the experience of the work of art? We have already encountered an important element of our answer; art experiences are real, and are determined by
their real and immanent conditions. But how are these experiences produced,
how do they work, and what makes them aesthetic? After replying to these questions we shall look at Guattari's "detachment" of the readymade from Marcel
Duchamp as a case study of a revalued aesthetic experience. Then we will have
to show how, despite surface similarities—not least in the quote from *What is
Philosophy?* with which we began the chapter—Deleuze and Guattari reject
Romanticism as an aesthetic model, and propose in its place their own concept
of "modernism," a modernism that is on the one hand inseparable from actual
practices (creating the finite), and on the other from ontological processes both
cosmic and chaotic (restoring the infinite). "Modernism" as Deleuze and
Guattari describe it will therefore require distinction from its usual understanding in the realm of art, as this was suggested by Clement Greenberg. This finally
will involve an understanding of sensation, especially as Deleuze and Guattari
give it in their last book.

## AFFECT

We begin from the perception in which any work of art first appears. Guattari
claims it is the combination of a "sensory affect," the simple empirical perception (the views I have from the window as I work at my desk), and a "problematic affect," the network of associations and feelings evoked by this particular
sensory event (the sunset as a planetary event, planes landing make me miss absent friends, my mind drifts towards the distant hills. . . . etc.). In the problematic affect connections are made beyond my immediate sensual experience,
introducing all sorts of temporal and emotional flows. These deterritorialising
affects, Guattari suggests, make experience the nexus of series of affectual connections, "a multi-headed enunciative lay-out [*àgencement*]," as he puts it, of
which "I" am merely the "fluctuating intersection" (REA, 160/255). Perception
is, Guattari argues, this fluid process of "individualised subjectivising" (REA,
160/255) taking place in and through an in-principle (and in-effect) infinite
network of affects. This means that not only do I pass from sensory to problematic affect continuously and without noticing, but that the art work, as affect,
"sticks just as well to the subjectivity of the one who is its utterer as it does to
the one who is its addressee" (REA, 158/251). The affect is in this sense a "pre-
personal category" (REA, 158/251) without discursive limits, and lives beyond

these limits. Together the sensory and problematic aspects of the affect constitute what Guattari calls a "polyphonic and heterogenetic comprehension of subjectivity" (Chaos, 6/17). This process is *"subjectivation,"*[2] the continual emergence of new affectual individuations that are not produced by an "I" as their subjective reference point, but produce it as part of a wider ontological process of creation constituting what Guattari calls the ethico-aesthetic paradigm. This new paradigm is ethical as well as aesthetic because it implies, as Guattari puts it, "a crucial ethical choice: either we objectify, we reify, we 'scientifize' subjectivity, or else we attempt to seize it in its dimension of processual creativity."[3]

In this ethico-aesthetic dimension, subjectivation is the ongoing emergence of new affective connections opening onto the outside of a subjective "I." In its aleatory affectual events subjectivation is always coming-into-being, assembling itself, or, to use a term which is by now familiar, becoming. To understand the art work in terms of this becoming means transvaluing the subject and object co-ordinates given by traditional aesthetics into "vectors of partial subjectivity," and deterritorialising the fixed subject onto the plane of subjectivation (Chaos, 22/39). This plane, Guattari argues, does not issue "from ready-made [*"déjà là"*] dimensions of subjectivity crystallised into structural complexes, but from a creation which itself indicates a kind of aesthetic paradigm" (Chaos, 7/19). This aesthetic paradigm constitutes the fundamental ontological condition of art, as it does for any creation, and at this level, Guattari writes: "One creates new modalities of subjectivity in the same way that an artist creates new forms from the palette" (Chaos, 7/19). Subjectivation is a creative process of self-organisation (the self organisation of the affect beyond the "self") composing a continuous variation of affects, and is the fundamental aesthetic process constituting (the experience of) a work of art.

The shift to the aesthetic paradigm, Guattari argues, deterritorialises the assumptions of science (intended in its widest sense—the human sciences—and so including aesthetic philosophy), because within it affects precede subjects, and problematic affects precede sensory ones. This means that aesthetics for Guattari, as it is with Deleuze, is more than a phenomenology (we will see precisely why next chapter). It is in the associative and creative power of affect rather than in subjects or objects, or their perceptual relation, that we shall discover the process through which subjectivation attains an existential consistency. An asubjective consistency for, as Guattari puts it: "Affect is a process of existential appropriation through the continual creation of heterogeneous durations of being" (REA, 159/252). In the aesthetic paradigm affects are only nominally unified under a subject, and once freed from their subjective over-coding find a self-organising consistency as a refrain [*ritournelle*]. We will come back to this refrain and consider it fully a little later, but for now it is our first glimpse of art as a finite creation (a subjectivation), whose processuality *restores* the infinite (its affectual aesthetic dimension). When we understand affects as non-subjective but nevertheless consistent and communicating networks, Guattari writes, "the complex ceases to be propped upon the elementary (as in the conception that prevails in scientific paradigms) and organises, at the whim of its own economy, synchronic distributions and diachronic becomings" (REA, 161/255). Subjectivation, in other words, is an autonomous self-organising process that gives consistency to a multiplicity of different virtual elements and expresses their cohesion in a process of becoming. In this sense, subjectivation is, and once more this is a term we shall return to, the creation of '*an existential territory.*'[4]

## EVERYTHING IS A MACHINE

The problematising affect operates, Guattari writes, as a "virtual fractalisation," (REA, 161/255) of the subject, through which an infinite connectivity emerges as the intense and virtual dimension expressed in actual experience (sensory affects).[5] This infinite virtual dimension does not exist outside of its actualisation in the processes of subjectivation, meaning the virtual cannot be experienced in itself, or, perhaps better, its "in-itself" only exists as experienced. Consequently, we cannot talk about a virtuality separate from its actual emergence, making any question as to the virtual's existence entirely fractal.[6] Such a question always involves a multiplicity of others, as Brian Massumi has suggested: "Which virtual? Under which mode of accompaniment? How appearing? How fully does the virtual range of variations actualize in any given appearing? How fully does the virtual range of variations actualize in any given object or substance?"[7] The careful critique required to answer these questions introduces on the one hand a movement of deterritorialisation that frees the virtual from its subjective and semiotic determinations, and on the other affirms the virtual in its proper place, as the active ontological element expressed in the actual. This critical mode of production emerges without an intentional subject as an "autopoiesis," and is, Deleuze and Guattari argue, "self-positing." "What depends on a free creative activity,' they write, 'is also that which, independently and necessarily, posits itself in itself: the most subjective will be the most objective" (WP, 11/16). Affectual autopoiesis is the "free creative activity" proper to the aesthetic paradigm, neither subjective nor objective, but, as Guattari puts it, "machinic."[8]

Autopoiesis is the machinic *in*folding of the affects' virtual dimensions in the *un*folding of its new actualities. Subjectivation is such an autopoietic and machinic process, creating new "existential universes" rather than simply reproducing a "self."[9] This process emerges from the fundamental ontological state of the aesthetic paradigm—*chaosmosis*. Chaosmosis is, according to Guattari, a "chaosmic see-sawing" (Chaos, 96/133) between chaos and complexity, a coming-into-being which (re)creates the affect's finite existence "to finally give back some infinity to a world which threatened to smother it" (Chaos, 96/134). Chaosmosis is the virtual and infinite genetic plane on and through which the actual world appears and becomes. In this sense, chaosmosis is not chaos itself, but the autopoiesis of chaos into an expressive matter, what Deleuze and Guattari call the raw aesthetic "moment"(ATP, 322–3/395–6). Chaosmosis is, then, the ontological ground zero of the aesthetic paradigm. Chaosmosis, once more, is not chaos, but is the energetic and material plane in its ontogenetic process of subjectivation. Chaosmosis is the emergence of the "directional components" of chaos, as chaos's own "ecstasies" (ATP, 313/384).[10] In this sense: "Art is not chaos," Deleuze and Guattari argue, "but a composition of chaos that yields the vision or sensation, so that it constitutes, as Joyce says, a chaosmos, a composed chaos—neither foreseen nor foretold" (WP, 204/192).[11] On this chaosmic plane of composition a new world emerges (the world is continually *emergent*), a world of autopoietic living machines. Chaosmosis is living composition, but it is an inorganic life, as present in machines as it is in man, for in terms of its creative powers, as Samuel Butler wrote: "The difference between the life of a man and that of a machine is one rather of degree than of kind."[12] Life is machinic (i.e. inorganic) because it is the chaosmic composition of a plane of virtual and actual—infinite and finite—consistency into living abstract machines "which," Guattari argues, "never cease producing new, artistic as well as scientific and technical possibilities."[13]

To understand art in terms of this new aesthetic paradigm will mean changing terminology, methodology, and most importantly, and as I have already repeatedly argued, ontology. The embodiment of chaosmosis in an art work, as the immanence of virtual and actual, of infinite and finite dimensions, implies new questions: not "what is it?" but "what does it do?" or "what does it become?" not "what thing or idea does it represent?" but "what virtual universe does it embody or express?" We can understand this change in interrogatory mode by considering Deleuze and Guattari's brief analysis of artists who paint machines. Artists like Leger and Picabia did not represent machines, but introduced machinic processes into art that allowed their work to explore new modes of subjectivation. This is what makes these "machinic paintings" interesting, Deleuze and Guattari argue, they "show how humans are a component part of the machine, or combine with something else to constitute a machine."[14] These art works do not represent machines, but *are* machines operating at the interface of the actual and the virtual. "Leger," Deleuze and Guattari write, "demonstrated convincingly that the machine did not represent anything, itself least of all, because it was itself the production of organised intensive states."[15] Understanding art in the aesthetic paradigm is no longer a matter of asking about painters as subjects, or paintings as objects, but of understanding, as Deleuze puts it: "The painting machine of an artist-mechanic."[16]

Art machines operate in the aesthetic paradigm under "molecular conditions." Here matter is not formed by a hylomorphic code, as if from the "outside," but is autopoietic and expressive. "Hylomorphic" is a term composed of *hyle* meaning matter, and *morphic* meaning form, and describes the operation of a pre-existing mould imposing form on matter. Deleuze and Guattari reject this Aristotelian distinction of matter and form because, as the figure of the mould suggests, "form will never inspire anything but conformities" (DR, 134/166). Deleuze's rejection of hylomorphism rests on the "profoundly original theory" of Georges Simondon.[17] Simondon argues that matter can no longer be thought of as a simple or homogeneous substance receiving its form from an exterior model. Matter, he argues, is made up of immanent intensive and energetic traits or forces ("singularities") whose differential relations both determine form, and maintain the inherent dynamism of form, through an immanent process of "modulation." Modulation, Deleuze says, is "moulding in a continuous and variable manner. A modulator is a mould which constantly changes the measuring grid that it imposes, with the result that there is a continuous variation of matter across equilibrium states."[18] Matter is chaosmic, and finds consistency (expressive equilibrium states) in refrains that both resolve the "problem" posed by pre-individual being, and keep this problem active in a continual modulation producing the living emergence of individuation.[19] The individuation of matter, no longer understood hylomorphically, but as autopoietic, changes ontological registers. This ontology of individuation is in fact one we are already familiar with, as Simondon's vocabulary tells us: "Individuation must be grasped as the becoming of the being and not as a model of the being which would exhaust its signification."[20] The finite individual is therefore only the most limited aspect of the process of individuation, and can only be properly understood according to the immanent "pre-individual" (intense and differential) singularities it expresses. This is the understanding Deleuze and Guattari develop in relation to art as a "refrain."

## COMPOSITIONAL REFRAINS

In art it is modulation that composes the affectual assemblages constituting a subjectivation, and it is in the process of subjectivation that a machinic and autopoietic art practice becomes indiscernible from the art-work it produces.

Deleuze and Guattari call this compositional process a "refrain," which begins, Guattari writes, with "the detachment of an existential "motif" (or leitmotiv) which installs itself like an "attractor" within a sensible and significational chaos. The different components conserve their heterogeneity, but are nevertheless captured by a refrain which couples them to the existential Territory of my self" (Chaos, 17/33). To detach a motif is already to create, or to change, a world. We are always in the middle of this process of de- and reterritorialisation, because any "motif" is detached from another refrain that composes it. Nevertheless the creative process of the refrain begins with deterritorialisation, and therefore requires, Guattari argues, "a blind trust in the movement of deterritorialization at work."[21] The artist detaches some material, frees the motif so that it can attract and compose new sensations and senses—new affects—according to a new refrain. Art is composed through this continual process of deterritorialisation.

The same refrain emerges in *A Thousand Plateaus* in an account of common experience. In the face of a threatening and dangerous chaos we attempt to shelter in a moment of calmness and stability. It's only natural. Not however, in a calm centre we recognise and which pre-exists us, but a calm we create with the comforting rhythms of a song, a motif that enacts a processual conversion of chaos into a spatio-temporal territory in which we can exist. The refrain constructs an existential territory or "home" out of "landmarks and marks of all kinds" (ATP, 311/382), through rhythmical processes of selection, elimination and extraction. This home protects and extends the germinal forces of the territory, acting as a filter or sieve through which it extracts what it needs to transform and resist chaos. All we want is a little consistency. Finally the home opens, a window or door leads us not into chaos, "but [to] another region, one created by the circle itself" (ATP, 311/383). As if, Deleuze and Guattari suggest, the circle "tended on its own to open onto a future, as a function of the working forces it shelters" (ATP, 311/383). Through doors and windows opening onto the future the territory extends lines of improvisation or experiment (a "prospection" of virtual universes as Guattari puts it), further deterritorialisations creating the becomings of our world. Creation here means inorganic life, a multiplicity of sonorous, gestural and motor forces which bud into "lines of drift" producing new complexities in the initial refrain. This ethico-aesthetic paradigm is therefore a new ontology of art, one which will radically change our understanding of art's experience through its "immense complexification of subjectivity" and its production "of new and unprecedented existential harmonies, polyphonies, rhythms and orchestrations."[22]

Despite the refrain being a musical term, as an autopoietic machine operating in the aesthetic paradigm it is applicable to all art forms, including the

visual arts. "The image," Deleuze writes, "is a little ritornello" (ECC, 159).[23]
An image is composed of, it composes, lines, volumes and colours—its "land-marks or marks"—into a "rough sketch" (ATP, 311/382). This sketch is elab-orated in various affectual rhythms that both express and compose a refrains virtual infinity, a singular assemblage of affects that is in continual variation.
It lives. "The image is not an object," Deleuze writes, "but a 'process'" (ECC, 159). [24] This means that producing an art-work—as refrain—is not the exclu-sive realm of the human artist, because the "artist" is simply the inhuman and asubjective process of subjectivation. Similarly, the refrain is not contained by an objectively defined "art work" existing apart from this process in which it is continually recreated. In the aesthetic paradigm "we are not," Guattari writes, "in the presence of a passively representative image, but of a vector of subjectivation" (Chaos, 25/44).

The refrain then, is the machinic "interface," or "umbilical point" (Chaos, 80/113) between virtual and actual dimensions, and is the compositional prin-ciple of a work of art. The refrain assumes a chaosmic cosmos, "a deterministic chaos" (Chaos, 59/86) from which it emerges as a "chaosmic folding" (Chaos, 111/154) or "nucleus of chaosmosis" (Chaos, 80/113). As such, the refrain has a double function. On the one hand it acts as a "vacuole of decompression" (Chaos, 80/113), destratifying subject-object distinctions and the schemas of space and time they assume, molecularising them, and reopening contact with their virtual infinity. On the other hand this process produces an autopoietic node or "motif" through which virtual universes compose themselves, gaining consistency to the point of expression in a subjectivation. The refrain is this two-fold and simultaneous operation of "unclasping" [*décrochages*] (ATP, 326/402) or "unframing" [*décradage*] (Chaos, 131/181) actual coordinates from their stratified systems, in order to "grasp" (compose) new virtual universes in an on-going and actual becoming. There is a deterritorialisation of actual things into a chaotic virtuality, and a reterritorialisation of this virtual chaos into an au-topoietic actuality (an "existential territory"). And both together, as Guattari ex-plains: "Formations of sense and states of things are thus chaotised in the very movement of the bringing into existence of their complexity" (Chaos, 80–1/114). This two-step dance is the onto-aesthetic process of art, Guattari writes, where "every aesthetic decentring of points of view [ . . . ] passes through a preliminary deconstruction of the structures and codes in use and a chaosmic plunge into the materials of sensation. Out of them a recomposition becomes possible: a recreation, an enrichment of the world [ . . . ] a proliferation not just of the forms but of the modalities of being" (Chaos, 90/126).

Art begins with this refrain: "different questions." Questions leading us beyond the answers we know, and beyond the artworks and artists we love. But only to return them again, differently, no longer as artists or artworks, but as the work of art, as refrains of chaosmosis, as the lines of our own becoming. "Viewed from the angle of this existential function," Guattari writes, "— namely, in rupture with signification and denotation—ordinary aesthetic categorisations lose a large part of their relevance. Reference to 'free figuration,' 'abstraction,' or 'conceptualism' hardly matters! What is important is to know if a work leads effectively to a mutant production of enunciation. The focus of artistic activity always remains a surplus-value of subjectivity" (Chaos, 131/181). In the aesthetic paradigm questions about an art-work's "meaning" must be rethought in the light of their "intolerable nucleus of ontological creationism" (Chaos, 83/117). Here, Guattari argues, meaning no longer emerges according to the pre-existing poles of artist and viewer, but through the expressive and autopoietic functions (refrains) of their chaosmic material-affects. In art properly so-called, and as all of our examples have repeatedly shown, "the expressive material becomes formally creative" (Chaos, 14/29). Guattari however, gives an example of his own, one very different from that of painting.

## THE BOTTLE RACK CHANGES DIRECTION . . .

Guattari's example is Marcel Duchamp's *Bottle Rack* ["*Egouttoi,*'" or "*Le porte-bouteilles*"], one of the first readymades from 1913. This work, Guattari writes "functions as the trigger for a constellation of referential universes engaging both intimate reminiscences (the cellar of the house, a certain winter, the rays of light upon spider webs, adolescent solitude) and connotations of a cultural and economic order—the time when bottles were still washed with the aid of a bottle brush . . ." (REA, 164/259–60). As we saw with Warhol's paintings, Duchamp's bottle-rack seems to answer to Deleuze's imperative to insert art into life (DR, 293/375). The readymade's affectual heterogeneity means its individuating instance can no longer be identified with an object or a subject, but only as their mutual becoming. How is this reading different from more traditional understandings of the readymades? The readymade has often been interpreted as producing an infinite range of affects, as an in-principle open field of associative possibilities. But it is another claim to argue that this multiplicity of affect individuates in a way undefined by, and counter to, subjective and objective discursive forms. To make this claim one must radicalise the readymade, and argue that it removes these forms, or at least makes them subsequent to the chaosmic emergence they embody. This is precisely what Guattari does, first by claiming that the affect is in itself "pre-personal," but further by arguing that the readymade in particular exemplifies the aesthetic process of the refrain's "ontological creationism." As such, the readymade is an example of an art work in which artists "not only create [affects] in their work, they give them to us and make us become with them, they draw us into the compound" (WP, 175/166). Elsewhere Guattari has coupled Duchamp with Bakhtin to make the argument that this process of subjectivisation is a "transfer" between the creator and "onlooker" of a work of art.[25] The readymade restores infinity to the creative process, and installs it in the art work's actuality, as the continual affectual variation the work in fact is. This is what would make Duchamp the archetypal artist, and the readymade the fundamental work of art. As Guattari suggests: "With art the finitude of the sensible material becomes a support for the production of affects and percepts which tend to become more and more eccentred with respect to preformed structures and coordinates. Marcel Duchamp declared: 'art is the road which leads towards regions which are not governed by time and space'" (Chaos, 100–1/140–1). These regions are those of existential emergence, continually re-opening new temporalisations and smooth spaces. In this sense we could say Guattari uses Duchamp in much the same way as he argues the readymade as subjectivation works itself. It is an extraction or detachment of an object from its discursive field in order to open it up to new mutations, new virtual universes. Although I will go on to argue that in many ways this is a problematic use of Duchamp, it is, to be fair, no less than what Guattari calls on others to do with him: "[W]e invite our readers,' he generously writes, 'to freely take and leave the concepts we advance. The important thing is not the final result but the fact that the cartographic method co-exists with the process of subjectivation and that a reappropriation, an autopoiesis of the means of production of subjectivity are made possible."[26]

Guattari's detachment of Duchamp's *Bottle Rack* would follow Duchamp's own statement, that "it's a bottle rack that has changed direction." This "change in direction" would be the crucial definition of an aesthetic practice of creative subjectivation, one that Deleuze affirms in his philosophical, but no less Duchampian terms. "One imagines a *philosophically* bearded Hegel," he writes in the preface to *Difference and Repetition,* "a *philosophically* clean-shaven Marx, in the same way as a moustached Mona-Lisa" (DR, xxi/4). But one can also imagine that shaving Marx would be considerably more work than changing the bottle rack's direction. By this I mean that the success of Deleuze's "ventriloquism" of his philosophical interlocutors, the way it produces a new Nietzsche or Spinoza, to take two of our examples, depends on their "change in direction" being articulated by the philosophers themselves, revealing a creative life immanent to their own concepts and systems. The problem with Guattari's reading of Duchamp is that in changing the direction of the *Bottle Rack* he seems to ignore Duchamp's own direction, and thus determines its meaning according to his own, very different rules. This would

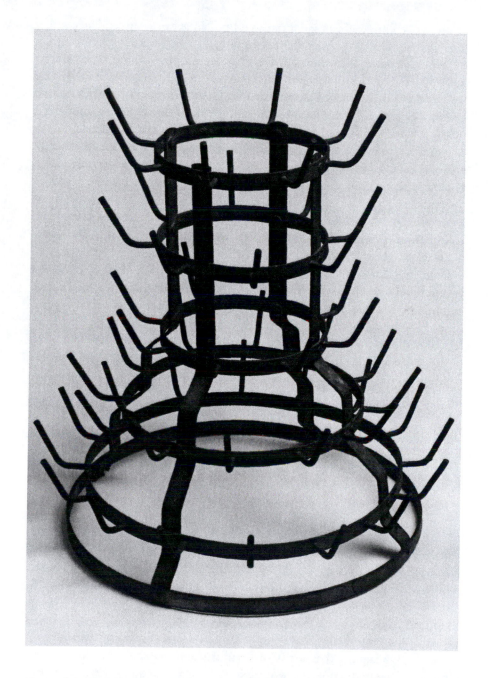

**Figure 6** Marcel Duchamp, *Bottle Rack,* 1913, Philadelphia Museum of Art. © 2004 Artists Rights Society (ARS), New York / ADAGP, Paris / Succession Marcel Duchamp

be an over-coding rather than a trans-coding, an act of transcendence rather than transversality. We remember one of Deleuze and Guattari's definitions of the schizo as being able to make what they are escaping from escape from itself (AO, 69/81–2), and this is the dynamic of the aesthetic paradigm we have seen Guattari developing. But in the case of Guattari's references to Duchamp and the readymade this is not the case, and the best that could be said of it is that it is a provocative, and perhaps playful, quotation out of context.

In fact, the work of Guattari and Duchamp seem to move in opposite directions. Guattari wishes to escape the overdetermination of the subject in a signifying system through a material expression of chaosmosis (a subjectivation) inseparable from an actual creation. Duchamp on the other hand, wishes to escape materiality by embracing a symbolic system in which art appears only on condition of its semiotic nomination. This would be the direction the readymade takes towards conceptual art, a trajectory developing the practice of art as a "language game." Where Guattari seeks a democratisation of art by removing its condition of human subjectivity, Duchamp seeks a democratisation through a nomination depending entirely on an inherently subjective power of signification. The readymade in Duchamp's sense is not primarily a proliferation of affect, but the shifting of art's definition onto a purely conceptual act.[27] The readymade is nothing but the question "is this art?" and the insistence that art's condition is the discursive act—"this is art." Deleuze and Guattari explicitly reject this direction for art, arguing that with it art "depends on the simple 'opinion' of a spectator who determines whether or not to 'materialize' the sensation, that is to say, decides whether or not it is art. This is a lot of effort to find ordinary perceptions and affections in the infinite and to reduce the concept to a *doxa* of the social body or great American metropolis" (WP, 198/187). In other words, the readymade does not operate as the machinic composition of problematic affects into refrains and subjectivations, because it establishes its own condition in a nomination that depends on the subjective act of signification.

Guattari attempts to consolidate his appropriation of the readymade through Duchamp's famous affirmation of the artist's indifference towards any aesthetic qualities in the object. It is this indifference, Duchamp argues, which is the readymade's condition of possibility.[28] Guattari claims that this "indifference" detaches the work from the discursive field of art, and opens it to a "mutant desire," one that "consummates" its "disinterestedness."[29] But it is precisely this moment of consummation that seems most problematic in relation to Duchamp, that artist of onanism and "celibate machines." For clearly Duchamp did not see the rejection of art achieved in the readymade as expressing the "mutant desire" of a genetic material plane of composition. Rather, the readymade abstracts art from vital processes by reducing it to an infinite chain of signifiers, to the celebration of "language games." Éric Alliez has gone the farthest in this critique of Duchamp, arguing that his reduction of art to the infinite play of signifiers enacts the Lacanian cut between the Symbolic and the Real.[30] The readymade in this sense would be the denial of an asubjective aesthetic paradigm of expressive materiality, in favour of an immaterial process of linguistic construction, one that could do nothing but represent subjects for other signifiers. In this sense, Alliez argues, Duchamp's readymade is "de-ontological," and must be placed in opposition to Deleuze and Guattari's ontology of the aesthetic paradigm.

Deleuze and Guattari's use of the term "readymade" in *A Thousand Plateaus* and *What is Philosophy?* is therefore non-Duchampian, not only in its ontological commitments, but also in describing an animal process of art constructing a territory. This process, they argue, is already art because it is the construction of an affectual assemblage in which matter becomes expressive. "Territorial marks are readymades. [*Les marques territoriales sont des* readymade]" Deleuze and Guattari write, "[they are . . . ] merely this constitution, this freeing of matters of expression in the movement of territoriality: the base or ground of art" (ATP, 316/389). For Deleuze and Guattari then, and this is a point we shall return to, art escapes human subjectivity to become-animal, and animal constructions of a territory through the "unclasping" of pre-existing material, as in the behaviour of the stage-maker bird, is "nearly the birth of art." "Take everything and make it a matter of expression." Deleuze and Guattari tell us: "The stagemaker bird practices *art brut*. Artists are stagemakers" (ATP, 316/389). The artist-animal uses readymade colors, lines and sound to construct an existential territory—a subjectivisation—as an expression of the vital forces of an inorganic life. (Art is a natural expression, but Nature has been "denatured," an important point we will come back to in our discussion of Kant and Romanticism.) Indeed, Deleuze and Guattari claim "art begins with the animal, at least with the animal that carves out a territory" (WP, 183/174). We can immediately see that this definition of art is travelling in a very different direction to Duchamp's. A conclusion confirmed by Duchamp himself in the 1955 interview he made with James Johnson Sweeney, and from which Guattari quoted. "I believe," Duchamp said, "that art is the only kind of activity in which man, as man, shows himself to be a true individual capable of going beyond the animal phase. Art is an opening toward regions which are not ruled by space and time."[31] Art, in other words, opens onto the realm of the signifier, a realm that transcends the animal and guarantees art's immaterial reality by grounding it within human thought.

Finally then, Guattari's use of the *Bottle Rack* as an example of subjectivation is not convincing. It does not succeed—in Guattari's own terms—in co-implicating the detachment of art from its discursive structures with a "chaosmic plunge into the materials of sensation" (Chaos, 90/126). Rather than simply disqualifying Guattari's argument, however, his attempt at appropriating Duchamp's readymade casts in greater relief both the difficulty and the radicality of what he is proposing. Similarly, it also serves to emphasise from a methodological point of view that a 'blind trust' in deterritorialisation must nevertheless, and in its Nietzschean modality, be a critical practice of selection and affirmation, a careful construction capable of expressing chaosmic forces. Guattari's privileging of art and artists in this process remains crucial, not least for the way it points beyond Duchamp's conceptualism and towards art's renewed political engagement. As Guattari suggests: "Perhaps artists today constitute the final lines along which primordial existential questions are folded. How are the new fields of the possible going to be fitted out? How are sounds and forms going to be arranged so that the subjectivity adjacent to them remains in movement, and really alive?" (Chaos, 133/184). These questions take us beyond Duchamp to an interrogation of the aesthetic paradigm in terms of its "ethico-political implications" (Chaos, 107/149), implications that shall now be examined.

## THE POLITICS OF CHAOS

The subjectivation emerging in the refrain is an ontological force of resistance—a permanent revolution—acting against systematic controls of creative becoming.[32] The ontology of the aesthetic paradigm is therefore inherently political, because through it we escape our stratified image of thought—and its representational politics—to restore an infinite freedom to the finite world. The ready-made, once more understood by Deleuze and Guattari in a completely different way to Duchamp, creates a subjectivation always in excess of any limited identity (of a political subject as much as an artistic one). This excess operates, in a Nietzschean sense, as the eternal return of the ready-made, as its inorganic life *as* a repetition of creative differences.[33] This keeps the ready-made in a constant process of "unclasping," in excess of all representational systems and any metaphysical determinations. This "unclasping" is accompanied by the refrains positive political moment, its self-organisation in an aesthetic composition of the chaosmic plane; the readymade as an anarchist politics; the readymade as an ontological revaluation/revolution of everyday life. "But most importantly," as Deleuze said in 1968, "all this corresponds to something happening in the contemporary world. [ . . . ] You see, the forces of repression always need a Self that can be assigned, they need determinate individuals on which to exercise their power. When we become the least bit fluid, when we slip away from the assignable Self, when there is no longer a person on whom God can exercise his power or by whom He can be replaced, the police lose it."[34]

Freed from its Duchampian definition, the readymade embodies the politics of the aesthetic paradigm as an autopoietic subjectivation expressing its inorganic Life. In this sense then, the aesthetic paradigm of the readymade is not the impossibility of defining art, (Duchamp called the readymade "a form of denying the possibility of defining art"[35]) but its redefinition as a living, creative expression/construction in permanent revolution with any preconceptions. As a result, to understand this creative expression/construction requires our own 'unclasping,' our own redefinition as subjectivation, our own embrace of a political aesthetics capable of creating a people yet to come. At this point the problems of politics are aesthetic, and in fact Guattari uses almost identical terms to describe them. Communism today, he writes with Antonio Negri, "allows an 'ungluing' of the dominant realities and significations by creating conditions which permit people to 'make their territory,' to conquer their individual and collective destiny within the most deterritorialized flows."[36] A communist politics is therefore inseparable from aesthetic processes of creation, and extends "political art" to include any act that is truly creative. Political art—it means an onto-aesthetics. "When I 'consume' a work," Guattari argues, "—a term which ought to be changed because it can just as easily be absence of work—I carry out a complex ontological crystallisation, an alterification of beings-there. I summon being to exist differently and I extort new intensities from it" (Chaos, 96/134). In other words, this onto-political definition of art collapses old distinctions between creation and consumption onto a single plane of production. A plane completely unrestricted to art, and traversing all sorts of fields not usually considered "artistic." Guattari uses the same paradigm when discussing the innovative practices at La Borde clinic, for example (Chaos, 69–71/99–102). This extension of art into the everyday is precisely the mark of its political power and necessity. Indeed, Guattari argues that "aesthetic machines" are "the most advanced models" for effective resistance to capitalistic subjectivity, because they directly confront capital's "deafness to true alterity" (Chaos, 91/127). Art-political practice works in both dimensions of the aesthetic paradigm, on the one hand it resists actual political forms of oppression, creating alternative subjectivities (relative deterritorialisations), but in so doing it also brings us to a new chaosmic paradigm of being, in which we are freed to express our inhuman material becomings. The politics of birds. As a result, art, according to Guattari, "has become the paradigm for every possible liberation" (Chaos, 91/127).

But beyond being simply another name for a vitalist ontology, art also has a privileged connection to the aesthetic paradigm as a realm of experimentation in which new ways of understanding and living in the world are constantly appearing. "Patently," Guattari writes, "art does not have a monopoly on creation, but it takes its capacity to invent mutant coordinates to extremes: it engenders unprecedented, unforeseen and unthinkable qualities of being" (Chaos, 106/147). Consequently, Guattari sees art's production of affects as being an especially important process of political resistance. "The aesthetic power of feeling," he writes, "although equal in principle with the other powers of thinking philosophically, knowing scientifically, acting politically, seems on the verge of occupying a privileged position within the collective Assemblages of our era" (Chaos, 101/141). No doubt this privilege would have to be analysed in detail to understand art's political possibilities. No doubt contemporary art has been generally unable to do this, not least because of its insistent retreat into a postmodern "conceptualism." But nevertheless, because "aesthetic machines" already operate as refrains, they "offer us the most advanced models—relatively speaking—for these blocks of sensation capable of extracting full meaning from all the empty signal systems that invest us from every side" (Chaos, 90/126). This is not to claim artists are the new revolutionary heroes—God forbid—but to affirm art's (precisely, art *against* the all too human artist) revolutionary power.

"Revolutionary art" is hardly a slogan to conjure with. But for Deleuze and Guattari it takes a new meaning, that art and politics share the same ontological and ethical imperative: to create! The same imperative to face the same problem. "We lack creation," Deleuze and Guattari claim, "*We lack resistance to the present*" (WP, 108/104). Aesthetic resistance breaks with our received understandings and perceptions—our "opinions"—the clichéd feelings and expressions which define our present. Opinions are the correspondence of perceived qualities and subjective affections, such that these correspondences constitute an orthodoxy operating in the realm of the lived. In this way, Deleuze and Guattari write, "all opinion is already political" (WP, 145/138). When I express an opinion I not only express the orthodoxy I believe in, or which I wish to impose, but also express all the constitutive and stratified opinions which make such expressions possible; that I am a subject, that I think, what thought is. . . . etc. As a result, for Deleuze and Guattari "the misfortune of the people comes from opinion" (WP, 206/194). This task of resisting the opinions of the present gives the first co-ordinate of art's indiscernibility from politics: materialism. As Deleuze and Guattari put it: "By means of the material, the aim of art is to wrest the percept from perceptions of objects and the states of a perceiving subject, to wrest the affect from affections as the transition from one state to another: to extract a bloc of sensations, a pure being of sensations" (WP, 167/158). Art, like politics, begins from this absolute, or perhaps we could say ontological, deterritorialisation of the object and the subject as sensation's conditions of possibility. What is required is, as the poet Pessoa put it: "An apprenticeship in unlearning."[37] The aesthetic process of subjectivation is just such an apprenticeship for in it the artist "has forgotten the world," as Nietzsche said, not to mention him- or herself, not in order to leave the world, but in order to re-enter it, to re-create it, in its at once aesthetic and political dimension.[38]

It is not simply a matter of picking sides, us the artists against them. As if such group identifications were enough to produce an effective politics. Just the opposite. Aesthetic singularity and its creative lines of flight always await to be produced, and must be, for only a permanent revolution can resist the incessant reappropriation of art in the spectacle of commodified "poses" and fashionable accessories. But art has one advantage, the aesthetic paradigm animates a material realm it shares with opinion, but which it retains a prior relationship with. The question is not which is "right," but what is the right war machine? It is always a question of means and not ends. What then, must be done? The political artist's first task is to clear his or her material of all the clichés by which opinion predetermines its possibilities. This is the destruction which must precede any true creation, and which frees the material to express its chaosmic machinery in constructing sensations. "Because the picture starts out covered with clichés," Deleuze and Guattari write, "the painter must confront the chaos and hasten the destructions so as to produce a sensation that defies every opinion and cliché (how many times?)" (WP, 204/192). How many times? Every time the finite is created which restores the infinite. Each time, again.

The first liberation will be from ourselves—the first cliché—even, or especially, from ourselves as artists. No longer subjective, aesthetic creation implies an ongoing and autopoietic subjectivisation that composes affects into mystical expressions. The "pre-personal voices" of the refrain, Guattari writes, induce "an aesthetic ecstasy, a mystical effusion" (REA, 165/262). The politics of such a mysticism imply an atheist heresy that refuses a subjectivity conforming to God's image, and itself aspires to God's vision. "I am God" is a mystical and atheist statement we have already seen Guattari make, and is indiscernible from saying "I am a political artist." The political art work on this account leads a double life, at once finite, and as infinite becoming: "Fabricated in the socius," Guattari writes, "art is only sustained by itself. This is because each work produced possesses a double finality: to insert itself into a social network which will either appropriate or reject it, and to celebrate, once again, the Universe of art as such, precisely because it is always in danger of collapsing" (Chaos, 130/180). But art's double life confronts it with a double danger, on the one hand, of being appropriated "after the fact" by the fine-arts system, spectacularised according to all the clichés which make it "art," and, on the other, of collapsing into a chaos which cannot be actualised in a composition, a deterritorialisation ending in a black hole annihilating its own expression. This is the double danger, Deleuze and Guattari write, "either leading us back to the opinion from which we wanted to escape or precipitating us into the chaos that we wanted to confront" (WP, 199/188). These dangers are really the same one, for both reinscribe art into a system in which it exists either as inside or out, as finite *or* infinite. Art must fight these dangers with its own dual action, as resistance to the controlling forces of the inside (relative deterritorialisation), and as expressive refrains unleashing the forces of chaosmosis (absolute deterritorialisation).

This double life of art is, of course, one life, and this articulation is crucial for our understanding of art's political power and function. As Deleuze and Guattari put it: "There is always a way in which absolute deterritorialisation takes over from a relative deterritorialisation in a given field" (WP, 88/85).[39] This would justify, one presumes, Guattari's "blind trust" in deterritorialisation. As we saw last chapter, an absolutely deterritorialised chaosmic matter is prior to, and has priority over, all metaphysical attempts at its reterritorialisation. This priority means that the relative deterritorialisations of an experimental art always materialise (subjectivise) this ontological dimension, even if it is immediately reterritorialised. The political question therefore, is not to simply strive for the absolute deterritorialisation of the refrain in the cosmos (as we shall see, too romantic), but rather to realise this movement as precisely what gives the (our) subjectivation its consistency, what makes the actual autopoietic. How, in other words, can art—here and now—speak the voice of chaosmosis, and do we have the strength to believe it? Our problem of course, our problem as artists, is not simply to "hear" this voice—too easy, too metaphysical—but to sing with this voice, to embody our own refrains, and "rejoin the songs of the Molecules" (ATP, 327/403). With this last quotation we have, perhaps, begun to hear a certain romantic tone to Deleuze and Guattari's aesthetics, a tone already echoing in the various ecstasies and mystic moments we have attributed to art. Now has come the time to interrogate this possible Romanticism, an interrogation Deleuze and Guattari undertake themselves in relation to their most musical concept, the "refrain."

## ROMANTICISM

Deleuze and Guattari distinguish three "ages" of art, Classicism, Romanticism and Modernism. All three arise within certain historical conditions, but are not determined by them, each referring instead to the diagrammatic features of different abstract machines, found today as much as at other times (ATP,

346/428). The classical artist confronts chaos as a raw untamed matter upon which he or she imposes form. This process proceeds with a "one-two," the binary differentiation of form, and the articulation of these forms in series. This is the classical form of form, as it were, acting as the precondition to any creation. To recall our discussions of last chapter, the classical artist represents the formed substances of this world through a hylomorphic line, an act of creation reproducing an organic milieu that is the same both inside and outside the frame. Art functions to subject a chaotic and unclean matter to the pure beauty of an ideal form.

Deleuze and Guattari are obviously not classicists. Their relation to Romanticism however, is not so clear, and as we have seen their formulations regarding art often have a romantic ring to them. The immanence of an infinite Nature to its expression in life is one example that we will return to, but another is the intolerable, unbearable aspect of this creative and cosmic infinity (chaosmosis), as it assaults and overpowers our perception. Indeed, Deleuze points out this affinity with Romanticism in *Cinema 2*. The purely optical and sound image of modern cinema, we recall, "outstrips our sensory-motor capacities." Deleuze gives the example of Rossellini's *Stromboli* (1950), where Ingrid Bergman's Karin is finally overwhelmed by the beauty and power of the volcano and seeks divine consolation. Modern cinema, Deleuze argues, finds something too strong for the human sensory-motor, something that shatters it, and is revealed in a "vision." "Romanticism," Deleuze writes, "had already set out this aim for itself: grasping the intolerable or the unbearable, the empire of poverty, and thereby becoming visionary, to produce a means of knowledge and action out of pure vision" (C2, 18/29). Although this connection to Romanticism remains purely gestural in *Cinema 2*, Deleuze seems to be claiming for modern cinema a new aesthetics of the sublime. What this might be and how Deleuze and Guattari 'unclasp' it from Kant's famous use of the term can be understood through their discussion of Romanticism in *A Thousand Plateaus*. There they clearly reject Romanticism as a diagram for artistic practice, and posit instead a new definition of "modernism."[40]

The romantic artist, Deleuze and Guattari argue, abandons the classical project of imposing universal forms on the chaos of matter, and instead creates territorial assemblages which express the Earth as their intense and infinite essence. The Earth as "Nature" contains all the forces of the universe, and constitutes the deepest level of reality. But this depth transcends our ability to comprehend it, and is projected outside any attempt to express it. Nature, for the romantic, is a subterranean, intense, groundlessness operating as a lost or hidden foundation which the artist-hero sets out to find. This search for the immanent forces of Nature as our true reality will lead the romantic artist back to the transcendental. This path is laid out in the "profoundly romantic" (ECC, 33/47) philosophy of Kant, a path Deleuze will partially follow, before making it change direction entirely. Experience, for Kant, is determined by various transcendental and *a priori* forms and processes. Perception emerges from the faculty of the imagination, through the syntheses of apprehension and reproduction on a sensible manifold (given by intuition) and within the *a priori* forms of space and time. The perceptual syntheses produced by apprehension and reproduction nevertheless remain to be recognized as an object, and this is only possible Kant argues, because perception presupposes an object form (object=x) as the necessary correlate of the *cogito* ("I think"). In assigning predicates to perceptions according to the *a priori* categories of the understanding, the final synthesis of recognition produces a concept of the object or what Kant calls a synthetic judgment.[41] The synthetic judgement producing a concept of an object is 'metrical' because it applies categories to our perceptions that are in all cases the same, making it Deleuze and Guattari say, "dogmatic" (ATP, 313/385). We have already seen how Deleuze wants to be done with judgment, and Deleuze will read Kant (a Kant, we could say, without his sock garters) as wanting the same thing. To do so Deleuze develops Kant's exploration of "aesthetic comprehension" in the *Critique of Judgement*. There Kant discovers that the syntheses of imagination in perception presuppose a unit of measure. This unit is not given *a priori*, but is subjectively determined on a case by case basis and is, as a result, in constant variation. Aesthetic comprehension, Deleuze argues, produces a refrain that expresses our comprehension of a chaotic Nature in a rhythm. A rhythm is undetermined by a concept, and is in this sense contrasted to metrical dogmatism. But rhythm is constantly changing and as a result Deleuze says, ventriloquising Kant: "The rhythm is something which comes out of chaos, and the rhythm is indeed something which can indeed perhaps return to chaos."[42] Rhythms are composed from chaos by aesthetic comprehension, before being used as variable units of measure in judgments. But, and here Deleuze is still following Kant, rhythm dissolves into chaos when something exceeds our subjective ability of comprehension. This, Kant argues, happens in front of certain "sublime" natural phenomena whose "intuition convey the idea of their infinity."[43] At this moment the rhythms of aesthetic comprehension that form the basis for perceptions and judgments are "drowned in chaos." "My whole structure of perception," Deleuze says, "is in the process of exploding."[44] This explosion is caused by either an extensive infinity (the mathematical sublime), or an intensive infinity (the dynamic sublime). The latter is a material force filling time and space ("Nature"), but that cannot be comprehended and coded by the faculties. The dynamic sublime is therefore "pure" Nature, both the ground of our experience, but also its groundlessness. As such, the sublime is the limit of our possible perception and understanding of Nature, and the appearance of an excess, an "outside" to the human organism and its dogmatic judgements. It is this sublime excess that modern cinema discovers in the breakdown of the sensory-motor, and Deleuze and Guattari will extend this positive function of the sublime (although without using this term) to art in general in *What Is Philosophy?* Nevertheless, and despite its sublime appearance, we can understand this breakthrough proper to art only by indicating the ways it deviates from Kant's account, even if these begin from it.

Three points need to be made here.

First, in the Third Critique Kant will discover another faculty "saving" us from chaos, and this is the faculty of Ideas, or Reason. Kant claims that the experience of the sublime actually propels us out of our senses, as it were, to comprehend the transcendental realm of Ideas, the truth of the supersensible as understood by our "pure intellectual judgment," or "reason."[45] "The sublime in nature is only negative," Kant writes, "it is a feeling of imagination by its own act depriving itself of its freedom by receiving a final determination in accordance with a law other than that of its empirical enjoyment."[46] The sublime "awakens" the faculty of reason, which is able to comprehend the supersensible "substratum" of infinity, and return the sublime to the imagination as the presentation of the unpresentable.[47] This "emancipation of dissonance" (ECC, 35/49) as Deleuze puts it, creates "a new type of accord" (DR, 321/187) between the faculties, a "discordant accord" (ECC, 35/49). Thus the sublime, in overpowering imagination opens onto reason; "the faculty concerned with the independence of the absolute totality."[48] As Kant writes:

> the feeling of the unattainability of the idea by means of the imagination [i.e. by the sublime], is itself a presentation of the subjective finality of the imagination in the interests of the mind's supersensible province, and compels us subjectively to think nature itself in its totality as a presentation of something supersensible, without our being able to effectuate this presentation objectively.[49]

The breakdown induced by the sublime allows the breakthrough to the transcendental, or as Deleuze wryly notes: "When something doesn't work [for Kant], he invents something which doesn't exist."[50] Here then is the point at which Deleuze and Guattari *change directions,* where, as Deleuze puts it: "Kant held fast to the point of view of conditioning without attaining that of genesis" (DR, 170/221), Deleuze and Guattari will seek in Nature not the transcendental conditions of life, but its genesis.

Second, for Deleuze and Guattari the Ideas are in fact the forces expressed by a chaotic Nature, those abstract rhythms which emerge from chaos

as its genetic movements, its chaosmosis. These forces are precisely what cannot be thought or sensed by our all too human common sense and rational
representations, but which nevertheless are the genetic movements of our
thoughts and sensations. These "sublime" forces, Deleuze will argue, will require a "superior empiricism" (DR, 143/186) adequate to their intolerable
and inhuman experience, adequate, as we shall see, to the percepts and affects
making up a sensation. As a result, chaotic nature is not, as it was for Kant
and the romantics, what both overpowers us and restores us to the divine, but
is a destruction that transforms the human, mutating our metrical concepts
into the rhythms of an immanent and infinite inorganic life. If, for Kant and
for Deleuze and Guattari, Nature is chaos or chaosmosis, they understand its
affects in completely different ways. For Kant chaos marks the limits of our
humanity, but the beginning of our transcendental essence, for Deleuze and
Guattari chaotic Nature is the genetic impulse of Life (chaosmosis), from
which rhythmical refrains emerge to construct existential spatio-temporal ter-
ritories—subjectivations—that express the living dynamism from which they
were born. This means that although Deleuze and Guattari, like Kant, posit
'Nature' as life's immanent field of forces, these are not reified into a transcendental plane determining our subjectivity, but form instead and in a
Spinozian manner, our plane of composition—our becoming—our inhuman
life. Thus, for Deleuze and Guattari "the plane of Nature" is not "a product
of the imagination" (ATP, 258/375).

Third, there is for Deleuze and Guattari, as for Kant, "something intolerable and unbearable" in life, but unlike Kant this is not a source of terror,[51] and
does not reveal our transcendental Ideas, but projects us beyond them. So although Deleuze and Guattari take Kant's concept of "aesthetic comprehension"
as the rhythmical expression of Nature, and his idea that it introduces a sublime
and intolerable element into sensibility, they are no romantics because they do
not seek life's redemption in the sublime's "supersensible destination" of a "transcendental origin."[52] For Deleuze and Guattari the intolerable is precisely what
is already expressed in the natural rhythms of life, as what composes those
rhythms, or refrains. Of course reconnecting with these forces is not easy, and
requires the inventions of great art—inhuman percepts and affects (mutant subjectivations) emerging from the difficult task of overcoming the human. The
artist must venture into this catastrophe-chaos in order to bring something out
of it, to construct something of it, a process that will involve pain, not least, as
Nietzsche said, that of childbirth. Finally then this is what distinguishes Deleuze
and Guattari from Kant, they regard chaos as the genetic and immanent plane
of life (Nature), present, but not as the unpresentable, in the refrains of an artistic life. Nature's expressivity is, therefore, that of the stagemaker bird, a pure

constructivism. This means that if art creates the finite that restores the infinite, it doesn't do so in the romantic sense of the sublime. Art doesn't function to overwhelm our finitude in the infinity of Nature, nor does it seek to restore the infinite to us as supersensible and transcendental Ideas. Rather art seeks to create the finite sensation through which the infinite is restored, not as a "beyond," but as the finite's immanent and genetic infinity, not "Nature" but *this* Nature, as it is being expressed and constructed right here and right now. Art in this sense is no longer romantic for Deleuze and Guattari, but modern.

For Deleuze, Kant is the "hinge" between Classicism and Romanticism, because the *Critique of Judgment* is "the great book which all the Romantics will refer to. They had all read it, it will be determining for the whole of German Romanticism."[53] Indeed, when he writes of the sublime, Kant could be describing not only the iconography, but the clichéd affects of generic Romantic scenes:

> Bold, overhanging, and, as it were, threatening rock, thunderclouds piled up to the vault of heaven, born along with flashes and peals, volcanoes in all their violence of destruction, hurricanes leaving desolation in their track, the boundless ocean rising with rebellious force, the high waterfall of some mighty river. [ . . . ] The astonishment amounting almost to terror, the awe and thrill of devout feeling that takes hold of one when gazing upon the prospect of mountains ascending to heaven, deep ravines and torrents raging there, deep shadowed solitudes that invite to brooding melancholy.[54]

This Kantian iconography of Romanticism is inseparable from its affects of subjective desolation and dislocation. Romantic art, like Kant, finds in the sublime the expression of a personal longing [*Sehnsucht*] for what is forever beyond the artist, the infinity of nature and its dynamic chaos that he or she can never comprehend except as disjunction.[55] The best a romantic artist can achieve through this disjunction is a transcendence by which we can contemplate Nature from above, as it were, as in Casper David Friedrich's *Der Wanderer über dem Nebelmeer* (c.1815, Hamburger Kunsthalle, Hamburg), or a dissolution, a death by which we may enter the mysteries of the spirit of the world.

The Romantics took this dissonance as their thematic, meditating endlessly on "the pull of the ground," on the sublime formlessness paradoxically founding our accordance with Nature. This makes the romantic refrain dissonant and despairing, a mournful cry expressing a subjectivity of exile, the trajectory of the wayfarer, an always deterritorialised soul (ATP, 340/418–9). This was, Deleuze argues, the distinctive feature of the romantic *Lied,* "to set out

from the territory at the call or wind of the earth" (ECC, 104/132), knowing
that: "The signpost now only indicates the road of no return" (ATP, 340/419).
As the sad voice in Mahler's *Ruckert Lieder* sings,

> I have lost touch with the world
> where I once wasted too much of my time.
> Nothing has been heard of me for so long
> that they may well think me dead.
> Neither can I deny it,
> for I am truly dead to the world
> and repose in tranquil realms.
> I live alone in my heaven,
> in my devotion, in my song.[56]

The territory is swept away in the chaos of Nature, and the artist sings with
longing of its impossible presence and sublime glory. From these melancholic
depths, Deleuze argues, Romanticism reveals its dialectical logic, seeking "a
reconciliation of Nature and Spirit, of Spirit as it is alienated in Nature, and
of Spirit as it reconquers itself in itself. This conception was implied as the dialectical development of a totality which was still organic" (C1, 54/80). This
attempt to reconcile an infinite Nature with man's infinite spirit in a dialectical negation of human finitude, *through art,* is the Hegelian destiny of
Romantic art, and is entirely different from Deleuze and Guattari's proposal
for restoring infinity through art: "Modernism."

## MODERNISM

Modernism, Deleuze and Guattari announce, is the age of the cosmic.
Modernism will overcome the romantic groundless/ground dialectic, and assume a chaosmos in which molecularised matter directly "harnesses" and expresses cosmic forces in a "continuum" [*consistant*], in an immanent plane of
composition (ATP, 343/423). Once more this is a two-stage process: first, the
molecularisation of matter, and then the harnessing of cosmic forces. This immediately removes us from a sublime and romantic Nature, and places us in the
modernist machine. The machinery of modernist art produces a molecularised
material and captures and renders sensible its chaosmic forces, like Jackson
Pollock. This implies a move beyond Romanticism as a pure expressionism, to
an art capable of constructing the universe, and a transformation of "Nature"
into a "mechanosphere" (ATP, 343/423). "The forces to be captured," Deleuze
and Guattari write, "are no longer those of the earth, which still constitutes a
great expressive Form, but the forces of an immanent, nonformal, and energetic

Cosmos" (ATP, 342–3/422–3). Modernism, Deleuze and Guattari argue, is an art—an abstract Machine—whose matter-function no longer obeys a romantic or classical form, but constructs a material expression adequate to the c(ha)osmic forces it has released—no longer expression through disjunction, but expression through construction.

This modernist machine needs to be distinguished from the canonical, and still Kantian, definition of modernism given by Clement Greenberg. Greenberg argued that modernism is the "intensification" of western civilisation's "self-critical tendency."[57] Modernism is art's self-critical impulse, it is what renders an art '"pure," and in its "purity" finds the guarantee of its standards of quality as well as of its independence.'[58] In painting, this "self-purification"[59] initially served to free it from the theatrical representations of literature, which painting had been trying to imitate since the seventeenth century, and subsequently from the equally pernicious state of kitsch, into which, Greenberg thought, painting was sinking. Greenberg conceived of Kant "as the first real Modernist"[60] inasmuch as Modernism is an elaboration in the realm of art of Kant's critical philosophy, and finds in the specificity of each art's medium the *a priori* conditions of an objective and absolute aesthetic judgement. Modernist painting finds its "essence" by abandoning representation for abstraction (Greenberg's famous "flatness"). Modernist abstraction was thus, for Greenberg, materialist, and he set it directly against "the dogmatism and intransigence of the 'non-objective' or 'abstract' purists of painting today who support their positions with metaphysical pretensions."[61] Abstract painting therefore explored in a self-critical way its *a priori* material conditions; on the one hand the painting's flatness and color, and on the other the expression of "sensations, the irreducible elements of experience."[62] Modernist abstract painting revealed its *a priori* essence in the production of matter-sensations. This, and here the echo with Deleuze and Guattari is uncanny, revealed the eye "as a machine unaided by the mind," and capable of what Greenberg called, following Kant, "disinterested contemplation."[63] This disembodied and disinterested machine-eye was capable of making a universal aesthetic judgment, it was capable, Greenberg thought, of identifying "good" art as that which exceeded its historical and representational tradition in giving a sensation of its *a priori* truth or essence.

Paintings self-critical "unclasping" from its literary and kitsch traditions is imagined by Greenberg as an immanent and dialectical process that finds its teleological accomplishment (its "absolute opticality") in "American-type" abstraction.[64] The teleological trajectory of Greenbergian Modernism in life (Pollock crowned) was in fact a reflection of its teleological transcendence *of* life in discovering its own transcendent truth. In this way, and despite his "modern" vocabulary, Greenberg remains Romantic, not simply as a Kantian, but also as a Hegelian dialectician on the path to "Absolute Sensation." Deleuze and Guattari's conception of Modernism is therefore clearly opposed to Greenberg's. For Deleuze and Guattari Modernism is neither chrono- nor teleo-logically determined, nor is its *a priori* essence revealed in a disinterested judgement. Indeed, the two aspects of Greenberg's account that would seem at first glance to intersect with Deleuze and Guattari's account, his empiricism and his materialism, evaporate into a prior—and indeed *a priori*—optical-ideality. Deleuze and Guattari's Modernism is both more materialist and more empirical than Greenberg's. Deleuze and Guattari assume a molecular and chaotic matter, whose forces emerge and are expressed through the refrain that composes and expresses them. The modernist problem is therefore, "how to consolidate the material, make it consistent, so that it can [ . . . ] capture the mute and unthinkable forces of the Cosmos" (ATP, 343/423).[65] This process doesn't begin with the purification of art, but with the molecularisation of matter (its absolute deterritorialisation) allowing the immanent forces of the chaosmos to be "harnessed" in consistent and autopoietic blocs of sensation. The modernist aesthetic paradigm assumes a Nature of "*material-forces*" (ATP, 342/422) and begins from the romantic problem of the sublime: their expression. But Modernism avoids the romantic reconstitution of a transcendental expressionism (as the imagination's break down and redemption in a sublime beyond), by composing finite sensations (refrains or subjectivations) that express (that express *by* constructing) matter-forces on a cosmic plane of chaosmosis. In a sensation molecular matter is constructed by, and so expresses—"renders visible" (as the painter Paul Klee put it)—the immanent forces of inorganic life. Modernism therefore, is not a representation of the unrepresentable, but the creation of a sensation inseparable from its infinite plane of composition. The sensation is the modernist condition of art because art is created, as Deleuze and Guattari write, when "the plane of the material ascends irresistibly and invades the plane of composition of the sensations themselves to the point of being part of them or indiscernible from them. [ . . . ] All the material becomes expressive. [ . . . Indeed] it is difficult to say where in fact the material ends and sensation begins" (WP, 166,167/157).[66] It is only by means immanent to a molecularised (i.e. a chaosmic) material that it is possible to create a block of sensations, a pure being/becoming of sensations (WP, 167/157). The crucial term here is "create," because it indicates how the relation of finite art works to the infinity of chaos(mosis) (Nature) is not premised on a destruction of subjective experience that restores a transcendental truth. Rather, the catastrophe rendered by confronting chaos (absolute deterritorialisation) is the necessary condition of any true creation, of any sensation. Art is, then, a "*passage*" from finite to infinite

(WP, 180/171) and back again. But it is a return through which everything changes direction, not least life itself, and puts on the artist—the subjective artist—"the quiet mark of death" (WP, 172/163). The death of man will be the necessary condition for the emergence of a sensation.[67] This "mark of death" is nothing but the condition for the artist reaching the "sacred source" (WP, 172/163), life in its capitalized form, the inorganic Life of chaosmosis.

Materialism and empiricism are the two conditions of modern art's construction in and expression of this "molecular pantheistic Cosmos" (ATP, 327/403). The modernist artist cannot harness the cosmic forces of chaosmosis without both molecularising the matter he or she works with, (a catastrophic materialism extending to their own humanity) and becoming a "visionary" capable of giving a sensation of this process (their "superior empiricism"). Artist and art-work become indiscernible in this cosmic matter-vision, as an inhuman subjectivation of the vital matter of the universe. Matter captures, in the hands of the modern artist, the forces of an energetic cosmos, and as Guattari, the mystical modern artist exclaims: "No more than to the cosmos do I recognise any limit to myself" (REA, 168/265).

Modern art therefore creates the finite which restores the infinite, by creating a finite refrain which is forever restoring the processual infinity of its own becoming. As such the refrain creates itself as it unfolds, it is an actual expression of the constant construction of its virtual and chaosmic plane of composition. Art creates a finite work, of course, but only as the actual expression of chaosmic emergence, a cosmic locality. As Deleuze and Guattari put it: 'From depopulation, make a cosmic people; from deterritorialisation, a cosmic earth—that is the wish of the artisan-artist, here, there, locally" (ATP, 346/427).[68] From relative deterritorialisations, attain the absolute! This means the romantic clichés of the child, the lunatic, "still less the artist" (ATP, 345/426), must be overcome, and in their place we must become the truly modern figure of "the cosmic artisan: a homemade atom bomb" (ATP, 345/426). The "cosmic-artisan"—it begs Deleuze and Guattari's question: "why so enormous a word, Cosmos, to discuss an operation that must be precise?" (ATP, 337/416). Once more, in answering, we are back to the beginning of the chapter, and Guattari's definition of the affect. I look out my window, a banal act, perhaps, but in it a problematic universe of virtual affects opens in which "I" am dissolved on lines of flight, becomings the artisan makes visible, becomings the artist puts into affects. "How can we convey how easy it is, and the extent to which we do it every day?" (ATP, 159–60/198). The artisan begins simply, by looking around him or herself, "but does so," Deleuze and Guattari write, following Klee once more, "in order to grasp the trace of creation in the created," in order to grasp the movements of chaosmosis, the most microscopic and the most cosmic. And why? Simply to make a work (ATP, 337/416). To create the finite that restores the infinite. In this sense modernism is a mysticism, and the modernist artist is an atheist-mystic creating a local-absolute. Modernist art restores a mystical Absolute, a cosmic infinity, by constructing a finite local work, the expression of the former being inseparable from the construction of the latter, because the Absolute of chaosmosis is never given, and always remains to be created. How? As we have seen in our discussion of Guattari, modern art begins as an art of destratification, by which artists go beyond the perceptual and affective states of the lived in order to see, "the mutual embrace of life with something that threatens it" (WP, 171/161). The sublime, chaos, something unbearable. But the artist does not discover the transcendental truth of life through this threat (like Kant), but embraces the danger as the necessity of transforming life into something that is truly living, the life of a people yet to come. Perhaps no more than a few strokes of the pen are required; the lightest touch can contain a new world of infinite movement. "One is then like grass, one has made the world, everybody/everything, into a becoming" (ATP, 280/343). Artists and their works are "Leaves of Grass," like Walt Whitman, that "caresser of life wherever moving," "Walt Whitman, one of the roughs, a kosmos." Walt Whitman, nothing but the question, "Who need be afraid of the merge."[69]

## SENSATION

How can we understand this mystical modernism in relation to actual art works, and to the way art actually works? In *What Is Philosophy?* Deleuze and Guattari give a variety of answers that all circle around the sensation, their explanation of this concept building on what we have already developed, inasmuch as the refrain is a sensation (WP, 184/175). The sensation is the specific realm of arts appearance: "Whether through words, colors, sounds, or stone, art is the language of sensations" (WP, 176/166). Sensations, as we shall see, are the being and the becoming, the "percept" and "affect" of a modern art.

An art work, Deleuze and Guattari state, is "a bloc of sensations, that is to say, a compound of percepts and affects" (WP, 164/154). Percepts and affects are first of all the absolute deterritorialisation of our human perceptions and affections, the "unclasping" of vision and experience from our human sensibility. Once more, Deleuze and Guattari's discussion of art begins from a revalued physiology of art. Perception is a subjective state induced by an object, and affections are the subjective increases or decreases of power ("feelings") a perception induces. Perceptions and affections are therefore subjective responses to objects, and represent a stratified state of affairs. "No art and no sensation," Deleuze and Guattari write, "have ever been represen-tational"(WP, 193/182). Percepts are not perceptions of an object, because they do not exist in reference to another thing, and an affect is not an affec-tion because it is not the state of a perceiving subject.[70] Percepts and affects are not found "in" an artist or a viewer, nor are they art works or the mean-ings these works may contain. A sensation emerges in the deterritorialisation of the perceptual co-ordinates of the subject-object through a catastrophe, the confrontation with chaos every artist must pass through in order to compose something from the matter molecularised in this passage. Each artist does it in their own way, and we shall see next chapter how one, the painter Francis Bacon, uses precise techniques to achieve it. This is why an artwork must "stand up for itself"—because it must find a way to get to its feet once it has abandoned the support of the subject or object. Sensations, Deleuze and Guattari write, "are beings whose validity lies in themselves and exceeds any lived. They could be said to exist in the absence of man because man, as he is caught in stone, on the canvas, or by words, is himself a compound of per-cepts and affects. The work of art is a being of sensation and nothing else: it exists in itself" (WP, 164/155).

In having a sensation we pass outside the subject and object, and be-come inhuman. For Deleuze and Guattari: "*Affects are precisely these nonhu-man becomings of man, just as percepts [ . . . ] are nonhuman landscapes of nature*" (WP, 169/160).[71] An affect is a rise or fall of power within a machinic assemblage. As such, the affect is the becoming-other of the assemblage, a cor-poreal (re)composition expressing the cosmic plane of Nature in a Spinozian sense. The affect, Deleuze and Guattari write, is a sensory becoming, and "sensory becoming is otherness caught in a matter of expression. The monu-ment [the art work] does not actualize the virtual event but incorporates or embodies it: it gives it a body, a life, a universe" (WP, 177/168). Becoming is the affect of passage between, or as Deleuze and Guattari also like to say, of a zone of indiscernibility immediately preceding, a "natural" differentiation of places or things. The affect is nonhuman then, because it exceeds the bounds of the "living" in being a sensation of the creative movement of inorganic life.

This is why the affect is inseparable from a percept, because its becom-ing is only the expression of its real conditions, of the percept or "nonhuman landscape" in which it emerges. The affect we could say, is a material change, the percept the empirical experience implied by this becoming. The percept is what Deleuze called in relation to cinema a "hallucination" or "vision," and in *What Is Philosophy?* Deleuze and Guattari call it a "creative fabulation" (WP, 171/161). The conditions of vision therefore, are not given (contra Kant) and it is vision—a percept—that constructs the non-human landscapes of nature.

Once more, these visions will be expressed in the art-work, but in themselves are cosmicizations of force, a rendering visible of "the imperceptible forces that populate the world, that affect us, make us become" (WP, 182/172). "Visions" are percepts of the mobile, heaving, and "cubist" (WP, 171/162)[72] landscape where "becomings unfold."[73] A percept is in this sense a perspective, "a kind of superior *viewpoint*," as Deleuze writes in his book on Proust, "an irreducible viewpoint which signifies at once the birth of the world and the original character of a world, but also forms a specific world absolutely different from the others, and envelops a landscape or immaterial site quite distinct from the site where we have grasped it."[74] This viewpoint or percept is not subjective, and rather than originating in an individual, it is itself a "principle of individuation."[75] The "superior viewpoint" of the percept creates a world, but this creation is inseparable from its expression in affects, or becomings. The percept is a perspective that constructs a world, and we become with this world—as the world giving birth to itself. "We are not in the world," Deleuze and Guattari write in a mystical formulation, "we become with the world; we become by contemplating it. Everything is vision, becoming. We become universes" (WP, 169/160).

The affect and percept can be seen as consistent with our previous discussions of art. The affect emerges from a molecularisation of matter in a non-human becoming, a release of new traits of content for arts modern machine. The percept is a cosmicization of forces releasing new traits of expression, new artistic visions. But of course they must be brought together, or rather, to understand the sensation we must understand how they necessarily appear together. We have seen the abstract machine fulfil this function, but here Deleuze and Guattari coin a new term, "aesthetic composition," as the machinic process specific to art. Guattari gives a good explanation; "a block of percept and affect, by way of *aesthetic composition,* agglomerates in the same transversal flash the subject and the object, the self and other, the material and incorporeal, the before and after . . ." (Chaos, 93/130 italics added).

The percept and affect form the two "pincers" of aesthetic composition: "The clinch of forces as percepts and becomings as affects." As such, percept and affect are "completely complementary" (WP, 182/173). The percept constructs the virtual, chaosmic plane of forces, "expanded to infinity" (WP, 188/179), as the real conditions of the affect, the actual becoming expressing this plane. The percept gives the plane of consistency in which forces compose matter, while the affect simultaneously actualises this plane in a subjectivation, a material becoming. In sensation everything happens at once, "the principle of composition itself must be perceived, cannot but be perceived at the same time as that which it composes or renders" (ATP, 281/345).

Composition is the real condition of sensation then, not as an abstract and transcendental condition of all sensation, but as the condition of *this* sensation. The plane of composition, Deleuze and Guattari write, "is not abstractly preconceived but *constructed* as the work progresses" (WP, 188/178 italics added). Composition is the action of the percept and affect, it is the construction of a sensation in which the infinity of the Chaosmos (percept) is immanent to the finite material which expresses it (affect). As Deleuze and Guattari write, "composition is the sole definition of art. Composition is aesthetic, and what is not composed is not a work of art" (WP, 191/181). But through this aesthetic composition we are returned to an ontological plane inseparable from art. If with Nietzsche the high point of the meditation is that being is becoming, then here, art takes on its modern Spinozian modality, where "everything in Nature is just composition" (EPS, 237/216).

How then do we create a sensation, how do we become artists and compose art works? Deleuze and Guattari take advice from Virginia Woolf: "Saturate every atom," she advises, eliminate all waste, deadness, and superfluity, in order to "put everything into it" (WP, 172/163 and also ATP, 280/343). It's a process of critique, an affirmation, a selection that involves necessary destruction. Eliminate everything of our current and lived perceptions in order to have a vision, a vision of the infinity we are: "Present at the dawn of the world" (ATP, 280/343). Only such an absolute deterritorialisation will enable us to walk into everything, to create a world, everyone/everything, as a becoming which expresses the immanent chaosmos as our infinite plane of composition.[76] This is Mrs Dalloway's reality, who

> felt herself everywhere; not "here, here, here"; and she tapped the back of the seat; but everywhere. She waved her hand, going up Shaftesbury Avenue. She was all that. So that to know her, or any one, one must seek out the people who completed them; even the places. Odd affinities she had with people she had never spoken to, some woman in the street, some man behind a counter—even trees, or barns.[77]

Art composes sensations as the expressive movements of all that is, while never ceasing to be singular and precise actual individuated expressions. As Mrs. Dalloway suggests, life and art become coextensive in the aesthetic paradigm, and arts creative fabulation, its "odd affinities" are life's absolute deterritorialisation in art, as art creates the world. Living, that is inorganic life, is this process of creation, and art embodies it in sensations. "Life alone creates such zones where living beings whirl around, and only art," Deleuze and Guattari write, "can reach and penetrate them in its enterprise of co-creation" (WP, 173/169). As if, when art creates a sensation it is nothing less than life, inorganic life, a subjectivation. Such a creation, such a work of art has no formal or material preconditions to its modernity; nothing is given, except what is created. "The artist," Deleuze and Guattari write, "must create the syntactical or plastic methods and materials necessary for such a great undertaking, which re-creates everywhere the primitive swamps of life" (WP, 173–4/169).

Art's ontological status as creation, its ontological creationism, is precisely what makes it appear and exist only as a *particular* sensation. Art is always *this* sensation. *This* sensation makes it impossible for us to be lost in the romantic and mystical mist of an ecstatic transcendence. Art cannot exist apart from its actual singularity, its now-here, which is precisely what restores its infinite and cosmic plane of composition, its no where. Erewhon, as Samuel Butler discovered it, is the land of such great reversals. But Virginia Woolf has her own version, of course, Mrs. Dalloway-Shaftesbury Avenue-Everybody/everything, all together in an immanent mysticism. Each particular and artistic creation, each work of art, or sensation, is therefore the creation of creation as such (how many times? just One, One eternally returning). In creating a finite that restores the infinite art embodies an ongoing and infinite creationism. Sensation is, as Guattari puts it, "a permanent 'work in progress'" (REA, 167/264).

This final, mystical evaporation of a distinction between art and its creative chaosmic Life, reinscribes art as a political force. Art first of all acts against art as it is traditionally understood, to open a realm of aesthetic freedom, a realm where we regain the real, to gain the freedom to live. Art, in the sense of "fine arts," Deleuze and Guattari bluntly state, "is a false concept, a solely nominal concept" (ATP, 300–1/369). Fine art isolated from life avoids and obscures the vital processes of its aesthetic paradigm, and this is its repressive politics. Deleuze refuses such an art, writing in relation to Beckett: "We will not invent an entity that would be Art, capable of making the [representative] image endure" (ECC, 161).[78] The absolute deterritorialisation of art as a nominal concept is inherently political, because it refuses the given; all the opinions, perceptions and affections which tell us who we are and that prevent us from creating—from truly living. In this sense, Deleuze argues, "there is a fundamental affinity between the work of art and the act of resistance."[79] This "resistance" begins by rejecting nominal concepts of art, and proceeds through the radicalisation of certain movements of deterritorialisation in expressing their absolute ontological conditions (as we saw with Venetian painting and Pollock in the last chapter). The absolute deterritorialisation achieved by art in the sensation is finally a process of permanent revolution in the name of the future, in the name of life, in the name of all things yet to come. When art is creative its ontology is political, because "promoting a new aesthetic paradigm," Guattari writes, "involves overthrowing current forms of art as much as those of social life. I hold out my hand to the future" (Chaos, 134/185).

This future unfolds in a Cosmic genetic experiment, the becoming-animal of the world. Art is a bio-aesthetics: "Not only does art not wait for human beings to begin," Deleuze and Guattari write, "but we may ask if art ever appears among human beings, except under artificial and belated conditions" (ATP, 320/394). Art is the becoming-animal of the world, it creates new forms of life outside our stratifications, our comfortable organicism, and opinionated thoughts. Art seethes in the "primitive swamps of life" currently confined to the edges of our biological maps, but appearing in sensations that overflow human perceptions and affections to take us somewhere else. According to Deleuze and Guattari's map:

> It is within our civilisation's temperate surroundings that equatorial or glacial zones, which avoid the differentiation of genus, sex, orders, and kingdoms, currently function and prosper. It is a question only of ourselves, here and now; but what is animal, vegetable, mineral, or human in us is now indistinct—even though we ourselves will especially acquire distinction. The maximum of determination comes from this bloc of neighbourhood like a flash (WP, 174/164–5).[80]

This flash of individuation appears as a sign, a sign of things to come, our becoming-animal, our sensations of a promiscuous and humid heterogenesis in which art and life are indiscernible. The readymade returns—against Duchamp—in the song of a bird. Art is "haunted" by the animal, and art works are "ritual monuments of an animal mass that celebrates qualities before extracting new causalities and finalities from them. This emergence of pure sensory qualities is already art" (WP, 184/174). Art works emerge as the intemperate politics of a life which cannot be lived, but which lives in art and its mutational molecular matter of subjectivating sensation. Art and politics as an animal line of flight; mount the witches broom for the tropics!

## Chapter Six
# The Agitations of a Convulsive Life: Painting the Flesh

And I join my slime, my excrement, my madness, my ecstasy to the great circuit which flows through the subterranean vaults of the flesh. All this unbidden, unwanted, drunken vomit will flow on endlessly through the minds of those to come in the inexhaustible vessel that contains the history of the race. Side by side with the human race there runs another race of beings, the inhuman ones, the race of artists who, goaded by unknown impulses, take the lifeless mass of humanity and by the fever and ferment with which they imbue it turn this soggy dough into bread and the bread into wine and the wine into song. Out of the dead compost and inert slag they breed a song that contaminates.

—Henry Miller, *Tropic of Cancer*.

## INTRODUCTION

Deleuze develops a "logic of sensation" through his encounter with the work of Francis Bacon, a logic that is both explicitly Bacon's, and stands as Deleuze's most developed statement of his thinking about painting. Deleuze's logic therefore, is on the one hand a critical practice, the elaboration of an onto-aesthetic methodology via a detailed discussion of Bacon and his oeuvre, and on the other a broader discussion of the history and function of painting in relation to its crucial term, sensation. Of course, this double register of Deleuze's work on art, its at once "micro" and "macro" operation is the very process we have been following throughout this book, the process of "Art as abstract machine." This machine is explored here through what Deleuze calls Bacon's "diagram," the way he, and by extension any painter, composes chaosmic forces and expresses them in sensations.[1] Examining this process will therefore involve us directly in Bacon's work, as well as allowing a final and full statement of art's ontological implications.

To immediately give an example, one which will be occupying us at length here, Deleuze advances the term "flesh" [*chair*] as both an entirely appropriate description of Bacon's figures, flayed open or otherwise disarranged like so much meat, and a philosophical concept for a new corporeality of experience achieved by painting a sensation. Furthermore, the figure of the "flesh" is important for phenomenology, and we will spend some time clarifying Deleuze's relationship to this other notable philosophical engagement with painting. Bacon's diagram will also intersect with many of the themes we have already discussed, including a new configuration of an "Egyptian" line and the "colourism" of Cézanne and the post-impressionists. Also important are Deleuze's explorations of the wider philosophical connotations of Bacon's diagram in terms of Alois Riegl's concept of "haptic" space, and Goethe's theory of color. Through these various investigations we will see how the "logic of sensation" operates on an indiscernibly ontological and aesthetic surface, the surface of flesh, which once again will open onto an immanent, mystical and "spiritual dimension."

The immanence of aesthetics and ontology in Deleuze, as we have repeatedly seen, is the necessary result of the ontological ground of his philosophical system being becoming, the continual construction of new actual forms expressing their immanent and productive chaosmic dimension of matter-force. But the cosmic genesis of art is no reason to abandon its careful analysis in favour of abstract metaphysical speculations. Just the opposite in fact, because it will only be through a detailed analysis of Bacon's paintings and statements that Deleuze will arrive at the chaosmic forces that animate them. The "logic of sensation" Deleuze finds in Bacon's work is therefore systematic in both an abstract and particular sense, but it is first of all articulated by the artist and his paintings. Consequently, in understanding it we will have to overcome a common problem: "We do not listen enough to what painters have to say" (FB, 99/93). "We" are no doubt philosophers, who have of course, only rarely listened to artists, let alone seriously considered their work. In his book on Bacon Deleuze seeks to rectify this problem by giving Bacon's paintings as much philosophical weight as that given to any of the individual philosophers he has written about. Bacon's "logic of sensation" is for Deleuze, entirely philosophical, and Bacon's paintings function as, and give rise to, thought. That a "logic of sensation" could be a form of thought is an assertion that rests on their shared genesis in an encounter of forces. "All begins with sensibility" (DR, 144/188) Deleuze writes, because a sensation of ontogenetic force can give rise to a painting or a concept, and on this level both share the same "logic."[2] We will come back to this point repeatedly, as it is crucial to my argument that a "logic of sensation" not only describes a thinking painting, but is also a mode of thought.

Deleuze addresses the ontological, art historical and painterly aspects of Bacon's "logic of sensation" through the concept of the "diagram," the abstract machine that composes matter and force into a painting. With the diagram we are immediately within the Deleuzian double dimension of aesthetics, for the diagram creates a finite work that simultaneously restores to it an infinite ontological dimension. This restoration will begin with a destruction, one in which, as Deleuze dramatically puts it, "it is as if the two halves of the head were split open by an ocean" (FB, 100/94).

## THE DIAGRAM

We begin our discussion of Bacon's paintings, appropriately, with a fundamental violence; a splitting of the head through which we see "the emergence of another world" (FB, 100/94). This other world can be oceanic as well as a "Sahara," (*Jet of Water*, 1979, private collection, *Sand dune*, 1981, Foundation Beyeler, Basel) having the ambiguous geography of art's plane of consistency, the infinite emergence of its matters-forces. Bacon's diagram begins with a catastrophe by which chaos appears on the canvas, and proceeds by composing this chaos into a sensation. As Deleuze puts it: "The diagram is indeed a chaos, a catastrophe, but it is also a germ of order or rhythm" (FB, 102/95). Bacon's diagram is therefore "modern" in the sense we developed last chapter, it molecularises matter and cosmicizes forces through a catastrophe, and then composes these matters-forces into sensations. Nevertheless, Bacon's diagram is his own, and like all great artists he finds his own way to embrace chaos and assemble a pictorial order from it.

This suggests a "diagrammatic" art history in which we can trace differences and similarities between diagrams, rather than rehearse the biographies of the artists who provide their names. Deleuze is not interested in writing a *Lives of the Artists,* although his diagrammatic art history is just as precise as any other. "Not only can we differentiate among diagrams," Deleuze writes, "but we can also date the diagram of the painter" (FB, 102/95).[3] Dating the diagram gives it a historical specificity that is potentially misleading. The diagram is neither a transcendental determination of a historical event, nor is it simply reducible to a historical event. Rather the diagram operates a fold between chaos and history by which the actual gains a new power of expression coextensive with the new virtual plane of composition the diagram draws. Each diagram therefore confronts chaos, dives into it, but only in order to create "a new type of reality." As a result, Deleuze and Guattari write, "it does not stand outside history but is instead always "prior to" history" (ATP, 142/177). This "priority" is ontological rather than temporal, and like the priority of sensation to thought, the diagram acts as history's immanent condition, but does not exist apart from the history that actualises it. That's why it can be dated. Perhaps we could say that the diagram begins and ends in history, but somewhere in the middle it leaves it. "History today," Deleuze and Guattari write, "still designates only the set of conditions, however recent they may be, from which one turns away in order to become, that is to say, in order to create something new" (WP, 96/92).

The diagram is a way to understand art history as the emergence of new artistic realities according to "prior," but nevertheless immanent ontological conditions. This is a significant reconfiguration of our understanding of art history, focussing on the ontological work of painting, its mechanisms of self-creation. In doing so, Deleuze transforms subjective questions of artistic intention or influence, and formal questions of technique or iconography, into questions about painting's ontological machine. Obviously Deleuze is not the first to do this, and he draws freely on Alois Riegl's concept of a "will to art" [*Kunstwollen*] here, both theoretically and in its quite specific "historical" formulations (FB, 122/115).[4] Furthermore, painting diagrams—as abstract machines—create sensations that put us "flush with the real," drawing us into their process to both experience and participate in the ongoing chaosmosis immanent to a paintings actual historical appearance. As we have repeatedly seen, this is going to require a new form of vision, what Deleuze will here call a "haptic eye." The artistic diagram is therefore both "visionary" in constructing an artwork from chaos, and is expressed in a "vision" (the haptic vision of the art work) that renders it visible.

An abstract machine's date, Guattari writes, is "not synchronic but heterochronic" (Chaos, 40/62).[5] In other words, a new diagram is not simply the simultaneous appearance of various other art styles according to a new combination, and as part of an art historical reality that pre-exists and determines this emergence. The diagram creates a new reality out of heterogeneous realities, not just for the time to come, but also for the time that has been, for the history which has supposedly led up to it. It is in this sense that Bacon's diagram recapitulates the history of painting in his own way. Bacon's diagram creates a new reality for painting, and in doing so recapitulates (perhaps we could say revitalizes) art history by constructing a new genealogy, one beginning with the Egyptians and encompassing a rather dizzying trajectory through Byzantine, Venetian, Gothic and abstract art. This "creative" art history obviously shares a method with Deleuze's history of philosophy, which similarly "discovers" (a discovery inseparable from an invention) a materialist-vitalist tradition opposed to the representational and organ-isational image of thought. The point is that both Deleuze and Bacon undertake an ontological "reinvention" of history, rather than a historical revisionism, and both move through a series of "stopping places" that they compose into a new diagram,

and the new reality it creates. This is finally the meaning of the "heterochronic" diagram, that while it composes its own tradition, this tradition is
itself composed of creative breaks that both constitute it and have created it
anew each time. This heterochronic tradition is therefore fractal rather than
historical, each one of its breaks reanimating the others, and making them
creative once more.[6] Indeed, Deleuze's reading of Bacon's "recapitulation" of
art history is itself a recapitulation, given that Deleuze barely mentions
Picasso and Velázquez, two very important figures for Bacon, and does not
mention another—Ingres—at all.[7] This should not be taken as a weakness of
Deleuze's reading however, but as a symptom of its creative energy: "There is
no act of creation," Deleuze and Guattari write, "that is not transhistorical
and does not come up from behind or proceed by way of a liberated line"
(ATP, 296/363). We will see this line in action more precisely when we turn
to Bacon"s use of the Egyptian contour.

Deleuze places great importance on art's materiality, both its actual matter and the material processes that form it. Each art form is determined by
these material conditions, and Deleuze mentions line and color for painting,
sound for music, and moving light for the cinema.[8] Although line and color
give the conditions shared by all paintings as such, just as obviously painting
employs very different compositional practices, very different diagrams, in relation to them. These diagrams are not simply "artistic" however, but are also
ontological. On the one hand, each diagram determines a different set of material and formal relations, and thereby creates a new reality, and on the other,
each diagram embodies a different "will to art." Deleuze does not give an exhaustive account of these "wills" here, but we saw three possibilities emerge in
the last chapter with the Classical, the Romantic and the Modern. Deleuze is
more interested in Bacon's precise process of painting, and focuses on those
diagrams Bacon recapitulates in constructing his own. It is to these abstract
ontological and particular aesthetic processes of Bacon's diagram that we shall
now turn.

To begin, all diagrams share certain features, and the first is found in
Nietzsche's famous pronouncement that there is no creation without destruction. The "preparatory work that belongs to painting fully" (FB, 99/93),
Deleuze argues, is introducing a catastrophe onto the canvas that destroys the
representational qualities of figuration. This is necessary because, as Deleuze
and Guattari put it in *What Is Philosophy?*: "The painter does not paint on an
empty canvas, [because the] canvas is already so covered with preexisting,
preestablished clichés that it is first necessary to erase, to clean, to flatten, even
to shred, so as to let in a breath of air from the chaos . . ." (WP, 204/192). The
"catastrophe" cleans the painting of cliché in the obvious sense of removing

**Figure 7** Francis Bacon, *Portrait of Isabel Rawthorne,* 1965, Tate Gallery, London. ©
2004 Estate of Francis Bacon / Artists Rights Society (ARS), New York / DACS, London

predictable and received meanings, but in a more dramatic sense it breaks with its representational function. All this will be necessary in order for a sensation to render the diagram's plane of composition visible. Let's return to the splitting of the head with which we began our account of the diagram to see how this works. Split heads are ubiquitous in Bacon's work, dissecting the face vertically (*Study for a self-portrait*, 1982, private collection, New York), horizontally (*Painting*, 1946, MOMA, New York), or more commonly, as a "mashing" of the face occurring without an axis (*Three studies for the portrait of Isabel Rawthorne*, 1965, University of East Anglia, Norwich). This split is a catastrophe that deterritorialises the representational aspects of the face, in order for other forces to appear. Bacon achieves this catastrophe by making random marks (Deleuze calls these lines-traits), and wiping the canvas to produce "clearings" on it (Deleuze calls these color-patches). These traits and patches are destratified lines and colors acting as both the destruction of representational form and their clichés, and as the pictorial diagram, the basic "sieve" through which chaos can be composed. As a result, the diagram "has no form of its own" (ATP, 141/176), because it is instead a catastrophe in which "form collapses" (FB, 135/127).

Bacon's "insubordinate color-patches and traits" (FB, 156/146) are purely manual (marks and wipes), and introduce the catastrophe into the eye and its optical space, beginning, as we shall go on to see, our own dissolution. These traits and patches produce, Deleuze writes, "a frenetic zone in which the hand is no longer guided by the eye and is forced upon sight like another will, which appears as chance, accident, automatism, or the involuntary" (FB, 137/129). These "accidental" movements of the hand introduce chaos into the process of creation; they are Bacon's hand throwing the dice Deleuze writes, using another Nietzschean figure, a throw that eternally returns in the act of painting. It is worth listening to Bacon's own account to get a sense of his method:

> You know in my case all painting [ . . . ] is accident. So I foresee it in my mind, I foresee it, and yet I hardly ever carry it out as I foresee it. It transforms itself by the actual paint. I use very large brushes, and in the way I work I don't in fact know very often what the paint will do, and it does many things which are very much better than I could make it do. Is that an accident? Perhaps one could say it's not an accident, because it becomes a selective process which part of this accident one chooses to preserve. One is attempting, of course, to keep the vitality of the accident, and yet preserve a continuity.[9]

This is a wonderful description of the catastrophic aspect of Bacon's diagram, which employs material and manual rather than mental or optical compositional process. The "accidental" traits and patches of paint are pure matter-force dislocated from both a represented object and an expressive subjectivity (Bacon is simply the manual component of his diagram). Paint is molecularised in the accident, Deleuze suggests, giving a world of infinite smallness and infinite largeness, "as if the units of measure were changed, and micrometric, or even cosmic, units were substituted for the figurative unit. A Sahara, a rhinoceros skin: such is the suddenly out-stretched diagram" (FB, 100/94). The canvas has become a space undecidably microscopic or cosmic, breathing the air of chaos and infolding its infinite distances.

But despite this chaotic landscape, or rather because of it, something is going to happen: "The essential thing about the diagram is that it is made in order for something to emerge from it, and if nothing emerges from it, it fails" (FB, 159/149). This means the diagram "must remain operative and controlled" (FB, 110/103), in order for the emergence of what Deleuze, quoting Bacon, calls "possibilities of fact" (FB, 101/95). These "possibilities of fact" are the other side of Bacon's catastrophic marks and wipes, they are the liberation of "lines for the armature and colours for modulation" (FB, 121/113), (we will examine both a little later) and are the beginning of a compositional process which will culminate in the "fact" of a sensation. The diagram therefore has a dual operation, it "is a violent chaos in relation to the figurative givens, but it is a germ of rhythm in relation to the new order of the painting" (FB, 102/95–6). Creation emerges from destruction—Chaosmosis. We have repeatedly encountered this formula because on the ontological level all aesthetic expressions share the same problem, composing the forces of chaos into a sensation, according to the same proviso, "no art is figurative" (FB, 56/57).[10] Bacon's diagram escapes figuration in order to compose the rhythms of chaos into new sensations, the sensations of Figures.

## THE FIGURE

We have already encountered Deleuze's argument that in the "entire" history of Western art the destruction of classical organic representation has taken one of either two paths, that towards "*a purely optical space,*" or towards "*a violent manual space*" (FB, 127/119–20). In the first, the contour described by a line (figuration) is submerged by a "purely optical play of light and shadows" in which the tactile elements are "annulled" and which produces the form "through an inner relationship that is specifically optical" (FB, 128/120). The optical pole utilises manual techniques to create the appearance of depth, contour, relief, etc., but the purely optical effects it creates subordinate the hand. At the other pole there is a free-action of the hand creating a "manual" space that subordinates the eye. Here there is movement without rest, a "pure activity" and "*nonorganic* vitality" (FB, 129/121) within which the eye cannot distinguish forms. These two poles find their modern expression in geometrical abstraction and abstract expressionism.[11] Even a perfunctory view of Bacon's paintings shows that he does not conform to either approach, although elements of both appear in the flat colored grounds and random gestural marks which are the constant features of his work. Bacon, Deleuze argues, explores a "third way" which avoids both these poles.

This "third way" breaks with the figuration of organic representation to produce a "Figure," a production whose condition of possibility is the heterochronic assemblage of Bacon's diagram, his own recapitulation of the history of painting. But Deleuze will not trace the development of Bacon's diagram in terms of historical influence, because a diagram is always composed of active re-inventions. Instead Deleuze isolates the basic "assemblages" that act as Bacon"s "stopping points and passages" (FB, 135/127). Bacon's reinvention of the "Egyptian assemblage" exemplifies this "passage" and as such it is the first stopping point of his diagram. Deleuze follows Riegl in defining Egyptian art according to the space of bas-relief, in which form and ground appear on the same plane, both separated and united by a contour operating as their common limit. The contour thereby creates a shallow space in which neither optical nor manual functions dominate, but unite in a "haptic function" of the eye that "discovers in itself a specific function of touch that is uniquely its own, distinct from its optical function" (FB, 155/146). Deleuze and Guattari call this the eye's "cutaneous Vision" (ATP, 151/187), a vision that emerges between the optical and manual poles of painting, and which undergoes in Bacon's "Egyptian" contour an ongoing series of "logical reversals and [ . . . ] substitutions" (FB, 154/145).

Bacon's contour characteristically marks an armature demarcating a shallow space from a flat colored ground, within which the Figure appears. In the Egyptian assemblage however, the contour was used to isolate an essential form, so while the haptic space it produces deterritorialises an organic representational schema, it simultaneously reterritorialises the images onto a "formal and linear presence that dominates the flux of existence and representation." In this way form and ground are re-solidified and their reversal controlled (FB, 123/115).[12] Bacon's selective recapitulation of the Egyptian assemblage is "scrambled" (FB, 124/116) because only partial. He takes the haptic space of bas-relief, but deterritorialises the Egyptian line's figurative, essentializing and unitary functions, so that "a new Egypt rises up" (FB, 134/126). How? Bacon's contour draws a "place" in which exchanges occur between the "material field" of color and what appears in the armature.

These exchanges occur according to two formulas of what Deleuze calls a "derisory athletics" of the Figure (FB, 12/21). In the first: "The material structure curls around the contour in order to imprison the Figure" (FB, 14/22). This produces a "violent comedy" (FB, 15/23) of confinement in which the contour becomes an apparatus for the Figure's gymnastic leaps into the field of color (*Triptych,* 1970, National Gallery of Australia, Canberra). The second formula, operating in the other direction, begins with a spasm internal to the body "in which," Deleuze writes, "the body attempts to escape from itself *through* one of its organs in order to rejoin the field or material structure" (FB, 16/24) (*Figure standing at a washbasin,* 1976, Museo de Arte Contemporaneo, Caracas). In the first formula the field confines the body, which in attempting to escape is projected into a Figure, while in the second the body's escape passes through itself, producing a Figure in attempting to dissipate into the field. In this way the contour establishes a series of necessary reversals between the field and the body (in this it is "Egyptian") which "makes deformation a destiny" (FB, 18/25). Nevertheless, Bacon's Figures are not deformed in the same way as those of Egyptian art, and here he breaks with the Egyptian diagram to introduce new forces, those of contraction-dilation, which are combined with other matters-forces to create a new Figure and a new sensation.[13]

The contour deforms the human organism, but only in order for something to emerge. This "something" can be seen in Bacon's paintings of the face. Bacon's diagram of random marks and wiped zones wrecks the face, breaks with faciality, and what crawls from the wreckage are "completely anti-illustrational" (FB, 176/31) *animal traits,* as the "common fact" emerging between man and animal (FB, 21/28).[14] This common fact is what Deleuze calls their "flesh or meat" (*chair ou viande,* FB, 22/28), a common molecular matter traversed by intense forces producing in the Figure an animal athleticism, convulsive contractions and dilations into the field. The becoming-animal of the Figure is not a represented transformation, but an embodied deformation; it is an expression of the meat's escape from organic form into the "cutaneous Vision" of the painting's flesh.

Bacon's diagram operates another deformation, which is implied by the first. The creation of a haptic space deforms the eye which sees it, liberating the eye from its role in the organism as the apex of optical space. Haptic space implies a new vision and a new visibility, "a haptic vision of the eye"(FB, 161/151), coextensive with the sensation. The deformation of the Figure only becomes a sensation through a deformation of the eye, a deformation necessary for the eye to become capable of this "vision." This is the remarkable consequence of Bacon's diagram, its deformations and reinventions cannot be limited to the painting, but also encompass the act of vision. The "flesh" of Bacon's paintings emerges from this double-deformation, flowing between the poles of subject and object, the flesh of the Figure includes the seer and the seen. This vocabulary of the "flesh" as both seer and the seen immediately suggests the phenomenological project of Maurice Merleau-Ponty. But Deleuze is not a phenomenologist, and we must now disentangle Deleuze's account from its phenomenological formulations, in order to flesh it out more precisely.

## DELEUZE AND PHENOMENOLOGY

Phenomenology is a remarkable instance of philosophy taking painting seriously.[15] As such it is an important forerunner to Deleuze's work on Bacon, one Deleuze directly acknowledges and engages with.[16] As Deleuze points out, phenomenology regards Cézanne as the painter par excellence (FB, 178/39) because he makes visible a pre-rational world of sensations in which subject and object are not clearly differentiated. This is, for the phenomenologists, the ontological insight of Cézanne, nothing less than a vision of the world as a sensation of "being-in-the-world." Deleuze seems happy to adopt this phenomenological vocabulary, writing,

> sensation has one face turned towards the subject (the nervous system, the vital movement, "instinct," "temperament"—a whole vocabulary common to both Naturalism and Cézanne), and one face turned toward the object (the "fact," the place, the event). Or rather, it has no face at all, it is both things indissolubly, it is Being-in-the-World, as the phenomenologists say: at one and the same time I *become* in the sensation and something *happens* through the sensation, one through the other, one in the other. And at the limit, it is the same body which being both subject and object, gives and receives the sensation. As a spectator, I experience the sensation only by entering the painting, by reaching the unity of the sensing and the sensed." (FB, 34–5/39–40)

On the face of it then, Deleuze seems to share not only the phenomenologists' vocabulary, but also their understanding of Cézanne's sensations. But in fact Deleuze understands sensation, and in particular the "unity" of sensing and sensed it implies, very differently, and his use of this vocabulary will take on a very different sense.

To understand this break we must understand a little of Merleau-Ponty's philosophy of painting. Merleau-Ponty sees in Cézanne's landscapes nothing less than the ontogenesis of the visible. Cézanne's paintings are a perception of the invisible genetic world in the visible and actual one, a vision, Merleau-Ponty argues, which involves perception in the genetic emergence of the visible. "The painter," he writes, "recaptures and converts into visible objects [ . . . ] the vibration of appearances which is the cradle of things."[17] Painting then, expresses the phenomenological reality of the world, it expresses the "texture of the real" as Merleau-Ponty calls it, which "is in my body as a *diagram* of the life of the actual" (EM, 126 italics added). Once again Deleuze and Merleau-Ponty's projects seem to converge on the body, which in both accounts expresses an immanent, living, and genetic diagram. But it is in their concepts of this bodily "diagram," and its relation to the "flesh," that Deleuze and Merleau-Ponty's differences become fully visible.

The "flesh," for Merleau-Ponty, incarnates a "reversibility," an "intertwining" or "chiasm" between the visible and invisible world, between vision and its invisible ontogenesis. Merleau-Ponty, in the famous fourth chapter of *The Visible and the Invisible* describes this intertwining or chiasm in terms of the color red. Red, he argues, emerges from virtual and differential relations between red things, implying a certain "redness" which is in itself invisible but which is the condition for the appearance of red things. In our sensation of a color, invisible and visible being are intertwined, meaning red, as Merleau-Ponty writes, is "less a color or a thing, therefore, than a difference between things and colors, a momentary crystallization of colored being or of visibility. Between the alleged colors and visibles, we would find anew the tissue that lines them, sustains them, nourishes them and which for its part is not a thing, but a possibility, a latency, and a *flesh* of things" (VI, 132–3). The flesh is therefore the condition of possibility of the visible, it is the medium in which things become visible, in which a virtual "redness" becomes a "red" thing in the "carnal formula" of the "lived body" (EM, 126). The flesh is the condition of both seer and seen and as such is "the formative medium of the object and the subject" (VI, 147). As Merleau-Ponty puts it, "the thickness of flesh between the seer and the thing is constitutive for the thing of its visibility as for the seer of his corporeity; it is not an obstacle between them, it is their means of communication" (VI, 135). The "lived body" Merleau-Ponty argues, encompasses subject and object in its vision of flesh, and is the "element," the "incarnate principle," of "an anonymous visibility," or "vision in general" (VI, 142).[18] The flesh is therefore incarnated in a lived body, but it depends on an abstract but nevertheless immanent principle that Merleau-Ponty calls the "Sensible in general."

The "Sensible in general" enables, Merleau-Ponty argues, "the return of the visible upon itself" (VI, 142). This is a crucial formulation, for it implies that vision involves a process of reflection by which it is able to "see" its constituent element, the flesh of the world. The flesh of things therefore appears in a "carnal adherence of the sentient to the sensed and of the sensed to the sentient" (VI, 142). In other words, the flesh appears in the vision of a "lived body," but this appearance requires both a sensibility which "sees" and a sentience which recognises it. In this way the flesh is the "overlapping and fission, identity and difference" (VI, 142) of a Sentience and a Sensible in general. Nevertheless, Sentience in general comes "before" (VI, 142) the Sensible in general, and "brings to birth a ray of natural light which illuminates all flesh and not just my own" (VI, 142). The flesh is therefore illuminated by a "Sentience" which renders it sensible, in and as a lived body. What then is "Sentience"? Despite its priority it cannot be clearly separated from sensibility, and together they form what Merleau-Ponty calls, once more anticipating Deleuze's vocabulary while producing a very different meaning, a "fold" (VI, 146). The flesh, he argues, is "folded" around a "central cavity" (VI, 146), which is "not an ontological void, a non-being" (VI, 148), but is the inseparability of sentience and sensibility around which the flesh is folded and the body and the world "adhere to one another" (VI, 148).

A sensation emerges from this fold as an ungraspable moment of reversibility between sentience and sensibility. This moment of "hiatus" (VI, 148), as Merleau-Ponty calls it, is illustrated by his famous example of a hand touching a hand which touches. The point is that I cannot touch touch itself, and it is this impossibility which reveals the inevitable chiasm between sensibility and its sentience. "My left hand is always on the verge of touching my right hand touching the things," Merleau-Ponty writes, "but I never reach coincidence; the coincidence eclipses at the moment of realization, and one of two things always occurs: either my right hand really passes over to the rank of touched, but then its hold on the world is interrupted; or it retains its hold on the world, but then I do not really touch *it*—my right hand touching" (VI, 147–8). Sentience and sensibility never come together, except as a chiasmic reversibility which coheres in and folds the flesh, but is never fully present itself. The reversibility of seer and seen in the flesh therefore revolves around this central ungraspable cavity forever "making itself the outside of its inside, and the inside of its outside" (VI, 144). It is this interminable pulse of identity and difference which constitutes the flesh and its "paradox of expression" (VI, 144).

These formulations carry all the Heideggerian implications of Merleau-Ponty's flesh, and serve to distinguish it from Deleuze's. For Merleau-Ponty the flesh is folded around an "interior armature which it conceals and reveals" (VI, 149), an armature of "lines of force and dimensions" (VI, 148) casting an ideal light into the flesh as the invisible condition of its visibility. As

Merleau-Ponty writes, "the experiences of the visible world are [ . . . ] the exploration of an invisible and the disclosure of a world of ideas" (VI, 149). Flesh acts as a "screen" (VI, 150) which simultaneously reveals and conceals these invisible ideas, which, as the example of the touching hands showed, "retreat in the measure we approach" (VI, 150). The ideas are what the sentient-sensible flesh forever circles, they are the invisibility the flesh embodies, and finally they are "the Being of this being" (VI, 151). Merleau-Ponty's flesh therefore incarnates a metaphysical ideal, a Being that casts its light on the flesh in which I am one with what I sense, but this being-in-the-world is a presence-absence, a chiasmic intertwining, a veiling/unveiling of an invisible Being in vision. As a result, "Seeing," for Merleau-Ponty, "is not a certain mode of thought or presence to self, it is the means given me for being absent from myself, for being present from within at the fission of Being only at the end of which do I close up into myself" (EM, 146). Painting expresses this "fission" inasmuch as it reveals the "coming-to-itself of the visible" (EM, 141). A visibility of "a certain absence, a negativity that is not nothing, [ . . . ] the invisible *of* this world, that which inhabits this world, and renders it visible" (VI, 151).

Painting then, is being-in-the-world, because it gives a sensation of the flesh's "duplicity of feeling" (EM, 126). This "duplicity of feeling" occurs in flesh according to its "strict ideality" (VI, 152), and creates a pathic space in which flesh "feels" its paradoxical foundation/fission as the visibility of an invisible Being. In Merleau-Ponty the eye becomes a hand, but in its pathic rather than haptic space it can only actualise a virtual idea it cannot touch or see. The eye is in the flesh, but remains determined by the transcendental ontological dimension it enfolds but never reaches, the invisible diagram of ideas. Immanence is only ever expressed in an incarnation of its genetic absence.[19] To return to color, colored being is the actualisation of an idea ("redness") in flesh, and this virtual color "imposes my vision upon me as a continuation of *its own sovereign existence*" (VI, 131 italics added). The diagram, for Merleau-Ponty, constitutes the immanent conditions of "natural perception" in the "lived body," but it remains in itself sovereign, as a pure ideality that can never be actualised. As Deleuze points out, phenomenology, in giving this "natural light" to vision, returns us to a classical philosophy where the light of spirit illuminates the darkness of matter (C1, 60/89).

Merleau-Ponty posits the ideas as immanent to the flesh, but this doesn't get us very far because, as Deleuze and Guattari put it: "They are not successive contents of the flow of immanence but acts of transcendence that traverse it." Ideas are "trajectories of truth," and as such constitute an "Urdoxa" of "*original opinions as propositions*" (WP, 142/135). As a result,

Merleau-Ponty remains determined by Husserl's famous phenomenological formula, "all consciousness is consciousness of something," and the "flesh" remains a subjective category. [20] The natural perception of the lived body assumes the common sense of a sentience-sensible in general, constituting a "consciousness" which is transcendentally determined, and operates a passive synthesis. Sentience, Deleuze and Guattari argue, re-introduces a "proto-consciousness" to the "lived-body" which is determined by the "a priori materials" which transcend the lived (WP, 178/168) and remain its "meaning of meanings" (WP, 210/197). As a result, the "lived body" can only ever express its conditions of possible experience, and fails to experience its real genetic conditions, which remain invisible. This dooms phenomenology's account of the flesh to a countless retelling of what Deleuze and Guattari call "the mystery of the incarnation" (WP, 178/169). This produces a poetic "mixture of sensuality and religion," but is nevertheless too "pious" (WP, 178/169). Deleuze clearly marks his break with phenomenology here: "The phenomenological hypothesis," he writes, "is perhaps insufficient because it merely invokes the lived body. But the lived body is still a paltry thing in comparison with a more profound and almost unlivable Power" (FB, 44/47). This unlivable power of life, Deleuze argues, is not an idea incarnated in the flesh of the lived body, but is the vital force emerging from chaos to be experienced in a sensation. It is sensation then, which animates the "flesh" of Bacon's Figures. For Deleuze the genetic conditions of flesh exist according to a "logic of sensation" different to that of the phenomenologists, a logic by which the diagram both constructs these conditions while remaining entirely immanent in the sensation. The diagram creates the finite that restores the infinite. This is why phenomenological "flesh" is finally "too tender," its diagram transcends it and it is merely a "thermometer" (WP, 179/169) or "developer" of this diagram (WP, 183/173). Phenomenology remains Romantic then, in being a pure expressionism, whereas Deleuze posits the complete immanence of the diagram and flesh, an immanence which enables painting to construct its genetic conditions (the eternal return of the catastrophe), each time they are expressed in sensations.

Deleuze and Guattari argue that for this to be possible the flesh requires a "second element," a "house" or "framework" in which the flesh can "blossom" (WP, 179/169). This takes us back to Bacon's diagram and its "Egyptian" contour, which constructs an armature, a "house" in which the flesh of his Figures is convulsed. But this convulsion expresses forces that come from the field, or more exactly *become* through the relation of field and Figure as they are articulated in and by the contour. The house, in other words, is a diagrammatic opening onto an intense chaosmos, through which forces are composed into a "compound" of sensation, on one side the sections of color making up the house (percepts), and on the other the non-human becomings embodied in the intense movements of the Figures (affects). "Art begins," Deleuze and Guattari write, "not with flesh but with the house" (WP, 186/177). Meaning that art begins with a diagram, in Bacon's case the contour, which builds a house from the chaos it unleashes, composes chaos, and expresses its forces in the convulsed flesh of the Figures which inhabit it. Bacon's paintings are "agitations of a convulsive life" (LS, 82/101). It is the diagram which constructs the cosmos-chaos into a house, and through which its forces are expressed in flesh. The phenomenological flesh is "too tender" for such a construction and in order for the sensation to stand up on its own it needs the armature of a diagram.[21] A diagram that neither transcends the chaos it constructs nor the flesh in which it is expressed, but marks the immanence of their planes in the painting. "The difficult part," Deleuze and Guattari wryly comment, "is not to join hands but to join planes" (WP, 179/170).

Although momentarily on the edges of our discussion, color nevertheless remains central to this debate. For "it is through and in color," Deleuze and Guattari write, "that the architecture will be found" (WP, 192/182). Color will be the material of sensation for Deleuze, and the modulation of color will construct the architecture of its expression. Deleuze develops this architectural colorism in relation to the painter Cézanne, and this both emphasises his difference from phenomenology, and introduces another important "stopping place" for Bacon's diagram.[22] Cézanne constructs form through the modulation of color, producing a landscape or an apple that, in one of Cézanne's formulations often repeated by Deleuze, gives the world before man but completely in man, because it gives the genetic conditions of the world *as this* world, as forces composed into sensation. Cézanne's paintings do not simply make visible an invisible cavity which determines and transcends them, but construct a house through which the flesh of the world becomes a world, restoring the infinite to sensation. As Éric Alliez has put it, painting forces is no longer a matter of expressing the flesh in color, but of constructing the universe by color.[23]

## THE HAPTIC EYE AND THE MODULATION OF COLOR

The two signs of genius in great painters, Deleuze and Guattari say, are their use of color, and the care with which they use it to join up planes to create the pictures depth (WP, 179/170). Cézanne's diagram employs just this kind of colorism: "Planes in color, planes!" Deleuze and Guattari quote Cézanne, for the painting exists at "The colored place where the heart of the planes is fused" (WP, 179–80/170). Cézanne's diagram composes chaos through constructing colored planes, and by connecting them expresses these chaosmic forces of the world on the canvas. Cézanne's colorism (and Deleuze suggests this is the formula for any colorism, FB, 139/130) involves replacing contrasts of value with contrasts of tone, creating and joining planes through the modulation of color rather than through a modelling achieved by adding black and white. Constructing value through the addition of black and white is, as we have seen, a "digital" overcoding of a color's tone, and assumes a light that transcends it.[24] Against this long tradition of painting Cézanne recapitulates an "analog" colorism, and constructs form by modulating the differential relations between "cold" and "hot" planes. Deleuze finds the conditions for this modulation of color in Goethe, who argued that there were two fundamental colors, yellow and blue (hot and cold), whose differential relations produce all the others.[25] This implies, for Deleuze, a colorism that not only modulates the relations between colors, but assumes that color itself is nothing but a variable differential relation "on which everything else depends" (FB, 139/130).[26]

The differential composition of color can be understood in terms of Deleuze's description of the sensible in *Difference and Repetition*. There he argues: "Every phenomena refers to an inequality by which it is conditioned" (DR, 222/286). This inequality or difference is the colors "intensity," its differential equation, "in so far as this is the reason of the sensible" (DR, 222/287). Every color appears as the differential equation of two colors which are themselves differentials, each color being constituted by a heterogeneous series of differences, an "infinitely doubled difference which resonates to infinity" (DR, 222/287). This is a Goethean theory of color in which we see "the aspiration of each color to totality by appealing to its complimentary color" (FB, 139/130). This mystical colorism encompasses the viewer as much as the painter, for as Goethe puts it, "when the eye sees a colour it is immediately excited, and it is its nature, spontaneously and of necessity, at once to produce another which with the original colour comprehends the whole chromatic scale. A single colour excites, by a specific sensation, the tendency to universality."[27] The eye does not see color, it constructs the universe by color, because a color is nothing but a vision of all the differential relations which make up a cosmos. As Deleuze writes, "if you push color to its pure internal relations (hot-cold, expansion-contraction), then you have everything" (FB, 139/130). The modulation of pure color is the "properly *haptic* function" (FB, 133/124) of painting, because it replaces an optical space defined by a perceiving eye/I and produced through the representational code of light and dark values, with a tonal surface agitated by differential color-forces (hot-cold, attraction-repulsion, action-negation etc.), requiring our involvement in a "close-vision" (FB, 133/124). This close-vision marks our indiscernibility from the painting *in* sensation, and implies a "haptic function of the eye" (FB, 133/125). Objects no longer appear in optical space, but are "in" the eye, constructed from colors that exist "within sight itself" (FB, 133/125). Colorism then, is the visionary part of painting, and, Deleuze writes, "merely claims to give this haptic sense back to sight" (FB, 140/131). Color creates a haptic space where color is within the eye, and vision is coextensive with the construction of Nature by color-forces, as this is expressed in a sensation.

"Differential calculus," Deleuze claims, "is the psychic mechanism of perception, the automatism that at once and inseparably plunges into obscurity and determines clarity" (TF, 90/119). Vision is automatic because it is not outside what it "sees," it neither "reflects" a pre-existing object, nor its transcendental conditions of possibility, but is instead the necessary immanence of sensation and the differential relations it embodies. Cézanne's modulated colors do not represent Nature, they are the necessary and analogical sensations which render visible the infinite and obscure (and not "invisible" in the phenomenological sense) forces of Nature's becoming. For Cézanne, both painting and Nature emerge in the same way, they pass through a catastrophe in order for their "geologic lines" to appear as a "stubborn geometry" or "frame." This "frame" passes through the catastrophe to give rise to color-light, and in this way, as Deleuze quotes Cézanne, "the earth to rise towards the sun" (FB, 111/105).[28] This poetic image of ascension is the process by which the stubborn geometry of the frame as the "possibility of facts" become sensations, become "facts." Cézanne's diagram is analogical in this sense, through the same process as that of Nature itself, it connects natural forces and planes of color, constructing sensations of *Montagne Saint-Victoire,* of some apples, or of the landscape of Provence (ATP, 343/423). Cézanne doesn't represent Nature, he constructs with color sensations, as Nature and in Nature; a pictorial naturalism. The autonomism of vision is determined by the differential calculus of Nature, independent of the organism, but nevertheless within a haptic eye, operating as an analogical synthesiser forever creating a vision, vision as being-in the world.[29] Rather than representing Nature then, Cézanne's diagram constructs a sensation of Nature (*Natura naturata*) as Nature expressing itself (*Natura naturans*).[30] As Cézanne said, "*art is a harmony parallel to nature.*"[31]

"Painting," Deleuze argues, "is the analogical art par excellence. It is even the form through which analogy becomes a language, or finds its own language: by passing through a diagram" (FB, 117/110). We might say that the painting diagram then, is a way "the real materially writes" (ATP, 141/177). Painting writes with the analogical language of a differential colorism, and in this sense Bacon is entirely Cézannean.[32] But Bacon also departs from Cézanne. Cézanne constructs a "strong depth" (FB, 119/112) where his planes join, whereas Bacon's paintings form a shallow space. As a result they produce a different deformation by unleashing different forces; Cézanne deforms the landscape and the still life to deterritorialise perspective, whereas Bacon's forces will deform the body. Similarly, Cézanne's colorism modulates color following the order of the spectrum. This, Deleuze argues, runs the risk of "reconstituting a code" (FB, 140/132), as does the fixed size of Cézanne's "patches," which tends to homogenize the forms they create. The solutions to these problems are found in Van Gogh and Gauguin. First, they erect flat fields of color that provide an armature within which specific forms can appear. Second, they introduce a further set of differentials to painting's diagram, the "very fine differences of saturation" in the bright tones of the field, as well as the differential mixtures of complementary colors in the "broken tones" that define the figures (FB, 141/132–3). Finally, there is the difference between the differentials constituting the flat fields and the broken tones, through which the whole painting is put into circulation. Bacon's diagram therefore changes direction from that of Cézanne to arrive at this new post-impressionist "stopping point," where the modulation of colors "takes on a completely new meaning and function, distinct from Cézannean modulation" (FB, 141/132). With Van Gogh and Gauguin's modulation of the differentials of the flat fields and the broken tones of the Figure, Bacon finds the solution to the two problems Cézanne's diagram posed; "how, on the one hand, to preserve the homogeneity, or unity of ground as though it were a perpendicular armature for chromatic progression, while on the other to also preserve the specificity or singularity of a form in perpetual variation" (FB, xii-xiii).[33] Clearly however, Bacon's paintings also differ from the post-impressionists, even if he specifically addresses Van Gogh during his "malerisch" phase (*Study for Portrait of Van Gogh IV,* 1957, Arts Council collection, London). Indeed, Bacon will depart from Van Gogh's homogeneous surface of brushstrokes in the articulation of his three basic elements of armature, contour and Figure. Similarly, Bacon's colors differ from Gauguin's inasmuch as his catastrophe frees them from the outline, and "we find ourselves before flows of color" (FB, 149/141). Bacon's diagram will therefore set off from Gauguin's and Van Gogh's solutions, and recapitulate them in his own way.

The unique solution Bacon's diagram offers for the Cézannean problem emerges, Deleuze writes, when its three distinct elements, the armature, Figure and contour, *"converge on color, in color"* (FB, 144–5/137). This convergence means that modulation composes the unity of the painting, both the distribution of each element and the way these act on each other. As we have

seen, the field of color approaches a differential infinity not through differences of value, but in its "very fine differences of saturation" (FB, 142/133).
This constructs a "color contour" that articulates the Figures relation to the
field, and acts as "a colored pressure that ensures the Figure's balance, and
makes one regime of color pass into another" (FB, 152/143). The contour, in
other words, emerges from the fields of color, and in doing so gives the "place"
for the Figure to arise in its "broken tones," and to express a perpetual variation of contraction/dilation in relation to the field. This perpetual variation is
expressed through three differential relations, broken-complete tone, broken-
flat field, and poly-mono chrome. Bacon's diagram is therefore composed of
its three "basic" elements working in reciprocal presupposition, but nevertheless according to their own distinct differential economies, all of which converge in the modulation of color. This produces the "flow" of color in Bacon's
paintings, and sets them apart from Cézanne and the post-impressionists. It
is in this color-flow that "*color-structure* gives way to *color-force*," and Bacon's
diagram creates a new colorism, where color renders visible the exercise of a
force on a zone of the body or head (FB, 150/141–2). This making visible of
defiguration will be the "primary function" [*la fonction primordiale*] of the
Figure, and is, Deleuze writes, "one of the most marvellous responses in the
history of painting to the question, How can one make invisible forces visible?" (FB, 58/58). We will turn to this question, and Bacon's answer, a little
later.

## COSMIC RECAPITULATION

Despite these differences between Cézanne's, Van Gogh's, Gauguin's and
Bacon's diagrams (and, we could add, between these and the Venetian's and
Pollock's), all express the inorganic life of the world by composing it into analogical sensations, and all create new diagrams for doing so through their respective use of color. By switching our attention at this point from their
differences to their shared "ontological creationism" we can understand in
more detail how creation is always the function of colorism in painting.[34]
Deleuze writes: "Universal variation, universal interaction (*modulation*) is
what Cézanne had already called the world before man, 'dawn of ourselves,'
'iridescent chaos,' 'virginity of the world.' It is not surprising that we have to
construct it since it is given only to the eye we do not have" (C1, 81/117). In
other words, we must construct this ontogenetic world in color, but we will
do so only by constructing an eye capable of seeing it. This will be where seer
and seen come together for Deleuze, in the "pure vision" of a non-human eye,
a haptic-eye whose visions construct matter at the same time as perceiving it.

At this point, Deleuze writes: "One might say that painters paint with their eyes, but only insofar as they touch with their eyes" (FB, 155/146). Vision is not "pure" in any optical or ideal sense, but purely material and entirely in things. It is "pure" in the sense of having no outside, existing as the simultaneous construction of the world by the eye, and of the eye by the world. The painter's "haptic vision" is of and in color, constructing its differential relations into analogical expressions. Together these are visions as "colouring sensations." "'Colorism,'" Deleuze writes, "seems to us to be irreducibly haptic" (FB, 192/125). Coloring sensations are therefore the "summit" of a logic of sensation (FB, ix), because in them the immanent and ontogenetic universe is rendered visible, through the visions of an eye we do not have, the haptic eye whose sensations both construct and express the inorganic vitality of the world.

The painter's haptic eye and its modulation of color in sensation are abstract in the sense we have already seen. Modulation, Deleuze writes, has "nothing to do with resemblance" (C2, 27/41–2), neither the resemblance of an image to its object (e.g. Bacon's portraits), nor the self identical subject (the painter) such a resemblance implies (modulation works through the diagram). Aesthetics is never a question of representation, but of invention, a question of how to escape formula and cliché, how to create something new. And this problem is not confined to the artist or to his or her work, it is the ontological problem of how to re-create the world. Nevertheless, painting has an immediate access to this new world through its ability to construct a sensation. The modulation of color constructs a coloring sensation in which the eye both has *and is* this sensation, and this haptic vision means that the eye is not just in the world, but that the sensation it is constructs the world. The birth of the world before man . . ."We are not in the world," Deleuze and Guattari write, once more distinguishing themselves from phenomenology, "we become with the world; we become by contemplating it. Everything is vision, becoming. We become universes" (WP, 169/160). We can understand these ecstatic lines better by returning to my suggestion at the beginning of the chapter that sensation was painting's way of thinking. Sensation, we could say, is a haptic thought.[35] This rather odd statement can be explained in terms of Deleuze and Guattari's account of the brain. The brain, they argue, is where the sensation emerges, each sensation, as we have seen with the example of color, expressing its infinite differential conditions only by constructing them anew in its haptic vision. In the brain each sensation involves, Deleuze and Guattari argue, "trajectories constituted within a field of forces" this "vision" operating as *a survey of the entire field*" (WP, 209/197). The brain is on one side "an absolute consistent form that surveys *itself* independently of any supplementary dimensions," a "self" extending to the Cosmos inasmuch as it is inhabited by an infinity of differential relations as "so many *inseparable variations*" (WP, 210/198). On the other side it is an actual sensation, the contraction of all these vibrating variations (differentials) into an expression or "contemplation" (WP, 213/201) of color. This "contemplation" is the irreducibly sensual movement of thought, which in being inseparable from the construction of the universe it expresses, returns the plane to itself as something new, as the becoming of being. The coloring sensation of one of Bacon's paintings is just such a contemplation, an expression of its immanent differential universe achieved in the percepts (visions) and affects (becomings) it constructs. Contemplation therefore, does not take place in a dimension apart from a chaosmic matter-force, because the brain as a nervous system is immersed in matter, and a color is a direct action upon it. (FB, 52/53) The aesthetics of painting is in this sense both a materialism and an empiricism, as Deleuze and Guattari put it: "Sensation itself vibrates because it contracts vibrations" (WP, 211/199). The coloring sensation is a haptic thought in which our brain's nervous system (the body-brain, or BwO) constructs a new differential universe (a "vision" or percept) in a "contemplation" that is expressed in an affect. The coloring sensation is this at once cosmic and quite particular becoming, and as such, as Cézanne said: *Color is the place where our brain and the universe join up.*"[36] This is a Deleuzian "eye-brain" as opposed to a phenomenological "Eye and Mind." [37] The "contemplation" of the eye-brain is a close and cutaneous vision folding the flesh, an affectual flesh enfolding the seer and the seen, sensing and sensation, the eye and the world. "Colouring sensations" are therefore the analogical expressions of the continuous variation of matter-force "within sight itself" (FB, 133/125). Once more, sensibility is contemplation, the movement of a nervous thought constructing the universe, and expressing it in a sensation. A sensation therefore, is irreducibly haptic: "It is color," Deleuze writes, "and the relations between colors that form this haptic world and haptic sense" (FB, 138/129). There is no inside and outside, no Being and being, only the mutual infolding and unfolding of an eye-brain in matter. Coloring sensation is the ongoing birth of the world, the world as *spatium*, as Deleuze puts it, "neither an inside nor an outside, but only a continuous creation of space, the spatializing energy of color" (FB, 134/126).[38]

Bacon's "Figures" now expand to embody a vital flesh (a body-brain) in which seer and seen and painting and viewer become indiscernible. How? Bacon's paintings, as we have seen, employ a colorism inseparable from sensation. Sensation however, implies a new sensibility, a new physiology in Nietzsche's terms, constructed in the contemplative visions and compulsive affects of the eye-brain. It is sensation therefore, that articulates an expression of matter-forces with the construction of a haptic eye necessary for its real experience. This haptic eye, as a visual sense of touch, must be in the painting, one with its flesh, not so much to sense the forces the painting expresses (it is not a thermometer), but as the condition of possibility of it being a sensation at all. As Deleuze writes, and the importance of this passage justifies its repetition, "at the limit, it is the same body which, being both subject and object, gives and receives the sensation. As a spectator, I experience the sensation only by entering the painting, by reaching the unity of the sensing and the sensed" (FB, 35/39–40). What emerges in Bacon's paintings then, is not narration, nor representation, but a set of *completely different relations*" (FB, 157/147), differential relations whose cosmic and particular vibrations compose the absolute locality of *this* Figure, of this becoming. The passage to the haptic eye, therefore, "is the great moment of the act of painting," (FB, 160/150) because it is the culmination of the logic of sensation in the expression/construction of "the fact itself" (FB, 160/150). The "fact" is sensation as being-in-the-world, as the "single continuous flow," as Deleuze writes of Michelangelo, which gathers together all the elements of the painting (including us) in an image that "no longer represents anything but its own movements" (FB, 160/150). This, finally, will be painting's great moment, its continuous movement, its vibration of vibrations.

We have, up to this point, examined the visions of the body-brain and its haptic eye, its coloring sensations, and now we must enter their flesh to better experience its physical becomings, its convulsions. This takes us beyond the too "tender" phenomenological flesh, and into that of the Body without Organs, whose flesh is strong enough to express its immanent becoming, its eternal and infinite movements of construction.

## PAINTINGS HYSTERICAL FLESH, THE BODY WITHOUT ORGANS

Antonin Artaud has been a frequently visited "stopping place" for our recapitulation of Deleuze, and he appears once more in Deleuze's discussion of Bacon's flesh. For Artaud the organs are organised into an organism by God's judgement, and as such are the structure of our servitude and of our suffering. The body is a result, to appropriate Milton's wonderful phrase, of "the tyranny of heaven."[39] This oppressed organism is the reason for Artaud's ferocious attack on God, for as Artaud famously pronounces, "there is nothing more useless than an organ. / When you will have made him a body without organs, / then you will have delivered him from all his automatic reactions and restored him to his true freedom."[40] The body without organs, Artaud argues, emerges from the "pressing urgency of a need" to abolish the "idea" of God and replace it with the "explosive necessity," or "assertion" of the body.[41] This is the body as a "physical system," a "nervous matter," before or beyond God. The body "escapes judgement," Deleuze writes, "all the more inasmuch as it is not an "organism," and is deprived of this organisation of the organs through which one judges and is judged" (ECC, 130–1/164). To be done with judgment then, means dismantling the organic body, and the BwO, "is what remains when you take everything away" (ATP, 151/188). What remains is living matter, its chaosmic vibrations and the sensations which express it. It is the living matter of the BwO which is constructed by Bacon's diagram, first by taking everything away in the catastrophe, and second by producing the "colouring sensations" in the flesh of his Figures, now expanding (or contracting) beyond the painting's surface and as far as the cosmos in a truly mystical "fact."

Artaud's organs are a battle ground, the site of a cosmic combat over the body's construction rights—over its "spiritual" dimension as Deleuze calls it—between the immanent ontogenetic forces of "a powerful and nonorganic life" (FB, 46/48) and God's transcendental judgement. This is also the fight waged by Bacon's diagram, a corporeal crusade which, Deleuze writes, "attests to a high *spirituality,* since what leads it to seek the elementary forces beyond the organic is a spiritual will. But this spirituality is a spirituality of the body; the spirit is the body itself, the body without organs. . . ." (FB, 46–7/49). We have seen how Bacon's diagram constructs Figures convulsed by forces. These convulsions, the ecstasies of chaos itself, are the "facts" which emerge in and as a haptic sensation/eye, and free a new kind of mystical perception. A baroque vision where, Deleuze writes: "The task of perception entails pulverising the world, but also one of spiritualizing its dust" (TF, 87/116). Bacon's diagram opens the body to forces that deform it, which produce breaks and disjunctions in its normal organic functioning. In this way Bacon reveals the immanent spiritual dimension of the BwO, the atheistic divinity created by the paintings' catastrophic disjunction, their breakthrough into the living immanence—the construction/expression—of the flesh. Deleuze and Guattari write: "The body without organs is not God, quite the contrary. But the energy that sweeps through it is divine, when it attracts to itself the entire process of production and serves as its miraculate, enchanted surface, inscribing it in each and every one of its disjunctions" (AO, 13/19).

The BwO is, as Deleuze stresses, "opposed less to the organs than to the organization of the organs we call the organism" (FB, 44/47). The BwO is a dis-organisation that takes us to "the limit of the lived body" (FB, 44/47).

Indeed, the BwO is more a trajectory than a thing, because "you can't reach it," Deleuze and Guattari say, "you are forever attaining it" (ATP, 150/186). The BwO is the limit of the lived inasmuch as it is the point of emergence of the lived, it is the point at which the rhythmical ontological conditions of chaosmosis are expressed as they construct sensations. Unsurprisingly then, the BwO is the destruction of organic representation: "Nothing here is representative," Deleuze and Guattari write, "rather, it is all life and lived experience" (AO, 19/26). The BwO, they write, "is the body without an image" (AO, 8/14).

The flesh of the living BwO will be inseparable from its perception, or better its "contemplation." "There is a mind in the flesh," Artaud writes, and the sensations which arise when forces meet the flesh are, as Artaud puts it, "neuro-physiological vibrations."[42] For Artaud then, "whoever says flesh also says sensibility,"[43] and, as Deleuze adds in his discussion of cinema, whoever says sensation also says thought, because on the BwO both are analogical vibrations emerging from the direct action of forces.[44] Thought, whether in painting or elsewhere, exists in a flesh that embodies life's confrontation with the unthought, with as Artaud puts it: "These unformulated forces which besiege me." And in thinking this unthought force, or in having a sensation, we truly live, because we have created something new, something previously unthought or unsensed. "This is what I mean by Flesh." Artaud writes, "I do not separate my thought from my life."[45] The life of flesh, the convulsions of a living BwO, express these unthinkable forces in sensations. To think—convulsed with life—does not mean for Artaud "I am," but that the BwO becomes.

Sensation expresses the action of a force on a BwO. This gives rise to a strange double dimension in Bacon's paintings, on the one hand forces convulse the Figure, and on the other it is the Figure which produces sensations within us. We can only understand this double dimension of the Figure through the BwO, which encompasses painting and viewer in its flesh. The Figure in this sense, and as Deleuze writes, is "the sensible form related to sensation; it acts immediately upon the nervous system, which is of the flesh" (FB, 34/39). The Figure is a BwO, and the BwO both gives and receives the sensation (FB, 35/39–40). A force traverses the painted Figure, but this becomes a sensation only in the flesh that encompasses it, in the haptic eye capable of such a vision. What is painted *is* a body, a living BwO that emerges in a haptic eye, and which is "experienced as sustaining *this* sensation" (FB, 41/45). *This* sensation is a contemplation, and as such "surveys" its spiritual dimension in its act of appearance, constructing an infinite virtual body as the immanent condition of its particularity. *This* sensation is therefore a spasm or vibration of the flesh at once in the painting and in the spectator, a convulsion or sensation, arising from "*the action of invisible forces on the body*" (FB, 41/45). So what are these "invisible forces" expressed in the Figures "affective athleticism"? They are not *the* invisible as such, but they are not visible accept in their affects. As such, they are the "obscure" forces, convulsions "in direct contact with a vital power," or, as Deleuze finally puts it, "Rhythm" (FB, 42/46). Rhythm, as we saw last chapter, is the ontogenetic power of life itself, and is what both constructs the BwO and is expressed in the sensation. "Paint the sensation," Deleuze writes, "which is essentially rhythm. . . ." (FB, 72/71). In a sensation, in its rhythmical flesh the chaosmos destroys me, and constructs me anew as a BwO, and in and through it I become with the world, I become-universe, but only as the universe creating itself. (FB, 42–3/46)

The BwO embodies rhythm, that "profound and almost unlivable Power" (FB, 45/47), that is experienced as *this* sensation. This requires Bacon's diagram, which both constructs sensations' genetic conditions (through the catastrophe of the BwO) and allows something to emerge from them (the figure, or figural whole). How? The diagram's dual operation of construction and expression forms the two phases of the BwO. As Deleuze and Guattari explain it: "One phase is for the fabrication of the BwO, the other to make something circulate on it or pass across it" (ATP, 152/188). The BwO is fabricated by the ontogenetic rhythm of inorganic life, of chaosmos, at that point "where rhythm itself plunges into chaos" (FB, 44/47). Bacon's diagram is just such a plunge, but it brings something back, it expresses this unlivable power in the convulsion of the Figure. The BwO is therefore both the genetic condition for sensation (its "fabrication" or construction through the catastrophe as the "possibility of fact"), and the sensation itself (what happens, the "fact itself").

Deleuze explains the BwO of Bacon's diagram precisely and in detail. The BwO is drawn by a wave that "traces levels or thresholds in the body according to the variations of its amplitude" (FB, 44–5/47). This "wave" is at once the catastrophe, bursting the body's organic co-ordinates, and what emerges from it according to the series of thresholds and levels it leaves behind as "possibilities of fact." We have already encountered the BwO then, in Bacon's accidents. But these accidents are inseparable from the rhythms they release, the lines and colors they liberate in sensations. The BwO is both produced and producer, because its thresholds are continually coming into contact with new forces, which provoke new vibrations, new sensations or "facts." "Sensation is vibration" (FB, 45/47) Deleuze writes, which would be the materialist definition of Bacon's paintings, as they synthesize the vibrations of the universe into an analogical sensation, into a becoming taking place on the level of its conditions. In this sense the BwO is the great analogical machine, for its vibrations are not visible signs *for* an invisible level, because it has no other level than that on which forces become visible. The BwO is the mechanism of the Deleuzian definition of abstraction: "making the invisible forces visible *in themselves*" (WP, 182/172 italics added). When a sensation expresses a BwO it raises itself to its own conditions (FB, 57/57). By doing so, sensation gives an analogical expression of the BwOs intense movements, not represented but real (FB, 51–2/53). In the sensations of the BwO Bacon's diagram meets Artaud's theatre of cruelty (FB, 45/48), both are a theatre that "is in reality the *genesis* of creation."[46] A theatre of life, a "theatre of metamorphosis" (DR, 240/310), a theatre of the inorganic and vital life of chaosmosis.[47]

But there seems to be an immediate problem, aren't Bacon's paintings full of organs? Escaping their eviscerated bodies, or undergoing facial spasms perhaps, but nonetheless organs are popping out everywhere. The BwO however, does not mean the absence of organs, and is in fact defined by, Deleuze writes, "the *temporary and provisional presence* of determinate organs" (FB, 48/50). These organs appear exactly at the point where the wave flowing through the BwO crosses a threshold or changes gradient and encounters external forces (FB, 47/49, see also ATP, 153/189). This accounts not just for the appearance of organs in Bacon's work, but also for the violent movements by which one organ seems to move into another (the eye-mouth, or nose-ear of *Four studies for a self-portrait,* 1967, Brera Museum, Milan). Organs, in this sense, and like haptic eyes, are defined by "a presence acting directly on the nervous system" (FB, 51/53). This "hysterical" presence, as Deleuze calls it, gives rise to the organ as a sensation, for each sensation has its own organ or haptic eye. The BwO is the immanent genetic condition for each of its organ-sensations, but each sensation expresses these invisible conditions by constructing a new organ adequate to its particular vision.

Hysteria enjoys a special relation with painting because, Deleuze writes: "With painting, hysteria becomes art" (FB, 52/53). Painting is hysterical because it is the attempt to release "presences" which lie beneath representation, to express them in a colored sensation, in a vision and its affect. Painting is the privileged medium for hysterical art because "color is a direct action on the nervous system" (FB, 52/53). Painting, in modulating color, vibrates with forces, makes them visible *in themselves* through its construction of provisional and temporary organs, its haptic eyes adequate to these sensations. As a result, and once more, there is a full reciprocity and simultaneity of arts double dimension, as Deleuze puts it,

> the eye becomes virtually the polyvalent indeterminate organ that sees the body without organs (the Figure) as pure presence. Painting gives us

eyes all over. [ . . . ] This is the double definition of painting: subjectively, it invents the eye, which ceases to be organic in order to become a poly-valent and transitory organ; objectively, it brings before us the reality of a body, of lines and colours freed from organic representation. And each is produced by the other: the pure presence of the body becomes visible at the same time that the eye becomes the destined organ of this presence. (FB, 52/54)

In hysteria the eye as undetermined (inorganic) organ is immanent to the sensation it has and is, and by which the BwO becomes-visible.

## THE COMPLEXITY OF BACON'S DIAGRAM

Returning to the specificity of Bacon's diagram, Deleuze makes an "empirical list" of the forces Bacon "detects and captures [ . . . ] like a detective" (FB, 63/62). As we have already seen, Bacon captures forces of isolation by wrapping the field around the contour to produce the Figure. Through this force of isolation deforming forces emerge in the spasms gripping the body or head of the Figure, and forces of dissipation become visible when the Figure escapes into the field. In these simple "active" sensations rhythm appears in the Figure as a physical vibration (the vomiting and defecating Figures in *Triptych May-June 1973,* private collection, Switzerland). But other, more complex deformations and dissipations become visible when Figures undergo a coupling within the painting and rhythm is liberated into the diverse levels of different sensations. Coupling is not a merge of two Figures, but a rendering indiscernible (in this sense Deleuze calls it "passive") in which a single "fact" common to the two figures emerges, a single Figure which expresses the force of coupling itself, its "combat of energies" (FB, 68/67) (*Three Studies of Figures on Beds,* 1972, private collection, Switzerland). The coupling of energies does not depend on two figures however, and can be disembodied. It exists wherever there is a "resonance" of forces as the condition of sensation. Nevertheless, coupling does not explain the triptych, for there the Figures and couples remain separated and are connected by something other than resonance. This means the triptychs have a different "common fact," and a different type of rhythm that is able to produce it. This new rhythm is what Deleuze will call the "rhythm-attendant" [*rythme témoin*], and through it, "it is the rhythm *itself* that becomes sensation, it is rhythm that becomes Figures" (FB, 73/71 italics added). To discover how this happens Deleuze asks a simple question: "What is a Triptych?" The only possible response to this question, he argues, emerges from their very precise "empirical study" (FB, 74/73).

**Figure 8** Francis Bacon, *Triptych, August 1972*, 1972, Tate Gallery, London. © 2004 Estate of Francis Bacon / Artists Rights Society (ARS), New York / DACS, London

The triptychs are composed of the three rhythms, an active and passive rhythm related to the actions and couplings of the Figures, as well as an additional rhythm given in the "attendent-function" [*fonction témoin*] that observes these couplings. These "explicit" attendants can be found throughout the triptychs, but Deleuze quickly discards them as being too "superficial," too figurative. What he is interested in is the way these witnesses transform into a "more profound attendant," no longer a figurative element of the painting but a "figural-attendant" [*témoin figural*] or "rhythm-attendant" [*rythme témoin*] (FB, 75/73–4). The figural-attendant is defined by "its horizontality, its almost constant level" (FB, 75/74), a kind of ground-zero, or "constant value" by which the other two rhythms can be evaluated (*Triptych, August, 1972*, Tate Gallery, London). Thus the "figural-attendant" is an "attendant-witness" [*témoin suivant*], the becoming-visible of the other rhythms, such that rhythm "has itself become a character" (FB, 76/74–5).[48]

The active and passive rhythms are visible in various differential distributions of force (resonances), which Deleuze lists in relation to their empirical appearances in the triptychs; descending-rising, diastolic-systolic, the naked and the clothed, and augmentation-diminution. (FB, 77–9/76–7) For our purposes what is important about these differential oppositions is not so much their precise operations, which Deleuze describes in detail, but the fact that these always appear in relation to the attendant function acting as the paintings rhythmical condition. Furthermore, a precise empirical list of the differential forces of a triptych constructs a "perspective" of (we could say it "witnesses") the "combinatorial freedom" of the painting, a combinatorial freedom which means, "no list can ever be complete" (FB, 79–80/77). In other words, the combinatorial freedom of a Bacon painting is in principle infinite, because it is—as a BwO—continually coming into contact with new forces, with new eyes, it is constantly being recomposed in new visions or perspectives. This takes us back to the argument of chapter one regarding Deleuze's conception of Nietzschean critique: "Everything," Deleuze writes, "can coexist, and the opposition can vary or even be reversed depending on the viewpoint one adopts, that is, depending on the value one considers" (FB, 80/77). This means the empirical analysis of a triptych's differential forces operates through the "witness-function" to construct a perspective, a perspective-rhythm which simultaneously gives the painting its specific empirical form, its specific sensation, and constructs the BwO this form expresses.

This perspectival reality of the triptych however, is not, according to Deleuze, sufficient to explain how its differential relations in their inherent variability appear as such. To explain this we must look to the condition of the perspective—the witness-function—and understand more precisely how it works. Deleuze's argument calls on Kant at this point, who defined the principle of intensity as an instantaneously apprehended magnitude appearing only in relation to negation=0 (FB, 81/78). If intensity is defined in this way then the differential relations of forces appear as sensations through their relation to the witness-rhythm=0. We recall that the BwO was what appeared when everything was taken away, the "matrix of intensity," as Deleuze and Guattari put it, "intensity = 0" (ATP, 153/189). But equally the BwO is defined by what happens on it, the differential relations our perspective embodies, which emerge only in relation to this ground zero. The BwO is, as producer and produced, the double dimension in which Bacon's paintings exist as and through their sensations. The BwO: "*Production* of the real as the intensive magnitude starting at zero" (ATP, 153/189–90 italics added). This "real" emerges, according to the specific character of Bacon's diagram, in the primacy he gives to descent. The differential forces of a sensation are experienced in Bacon's paintings as a fall. This gives a seemingly paradoxical formula to Bacon's diagram, in which *"The active is the fall"* (FB, 80/78). This means that when forces appear as sensations they embody a change in state that is understood in relation to the intensity=0 of the witness-function as a fall ("everything that develops is a fall" FB, 82/79). As a result, Deleuze writes: "The fall is what is most alive in the sensation, that through which the sensation is experienced as living. [ . . . ] The fall is precisely the active rhythm" (FB, 82/79), and is the rhythm which emerges as specific to each triptych, or at least to each of its perspectives.

Finally, the law of the triptychs involves all of the rhythms so far delineated, the three "rhythm figures," active, passive and witness, the witness rhythm=0, and the active fall. This means the law of the triptych "can only be a movement of movements, or a state of complex forces" (FB, 83/80). In other words, the triptychs are composed directly by rhythm, which appears in itself, and are entirely hysterical. But the "highpoint of the meditation" seems at this point a little hollow, for doesn't it simply reiterate what we have known from the beginning? Doesn't it simply repeat the catastrophe of Bacon's diagram and the resonance of forces that emerge from it to create a sensation? Despite its complexity the "law" of the triptychs seems to return us to this fundamental operation of the diagram that was in place from the beginning, and merely reiterates the ontology of sensation that we by now know by heart. Indeed, Deleuze seems to confirm this, writing: "These laws have nothing to do with a conscious formula that would simply need to be applied; they are a part of this irrational logic, or this logic of sensation, that constitutes painting" (FB, 83/79). The empirical taxonomy of the triptychs' forces therefore leads us back to a point, even before Bacon, of the logic of ontogenetic emergence as such, to the immanence of aesthetics and ontology which has been our topic throughout. Could it be possible that Deleuze's painstaking "empirical" analysis of the triptychs discovered nothing that wasn't, perhaps in the form of a "secret" first principle, already in place?

If this is true the logic of sensation Deleuze finds in Bacon's paintings would be on one side an elegant and precise analysis of one painter's work, and on the other already entirely explained by the most abstract formulations of Deleuze's onto-aesthetics. This is clearly seen in the work done by Deleuze's concept of the fall, which on one side is described as the specific mechanism of Bacon's triptychs, and on the other appears as a concept necessarily connected to the degree 0 of intensity, and already widely used in the conceptual definition of the BwO.[49] This leads to the question as to exactly what in Deleuze's account of the triptychs is specific to Bacon's diagram, and what is simply the application of a more generalised account of the BwO. This problem is critical inasmuch as Deleuze will finally claim that all Bacon's paintings operate according to the triptychs' logic, for "there are nothing but triptychs in Bacon, even the isolated paintings are, more or less visibly, composed like triptychs" (FB, 85/81). It seems as if all of Deleuze's painstaking empirical work has finally evaporated into an ontological structure which was in place from the start, and that empirical appearances are entirely determined by a higher spiritual, or at least conceptual, reality they simply express.

Deleuze and Guattari suggest a rather elegant riposte to this problem in *A Thousand Plateaus*. There they ask whether there is a BwO of all BwOs, a higher One in which all its attributes (presumably including Bacon's diagram) can be comprehended. This means, is there a single ontological entity (THE BwO) which would finally comprehend and encompass all its instances, all the BwOs constructed as its expressions? (ATP, 154/190–1). Deleuze and Guattari turn this question on its head, arguing that it is not in fact a question of the One *or* the multiple, the abstract *or* the specific, as if they were opposed terms. Our question then, was badly posed, because it is not a matter of understanding the ground zero of the BwO—chaos, difference, duration, etc.—as an ontological unity which the variety of BwOs would all in their way express. Bacon's diagram shares a certain abstract machinic consistency with other painting diagrams, a necessity by which painting begins with the construction of a BwO. This leads to other common principles, for example, Deleuze argues: "Most artists [ . . . ] seem to have encountered the same response; the difference in intensity is experienced as a fall" (FB, 81/78). But everything falls differently. Each fall is different because the fall is simply the activity of difference itself. If difference is the ontological ground of Deleuze's system, a likely enough claim, then it does not appear in relation to, or as an expression of anything but itself. THE BwO is therefore indistinguishable from the infinity of BwOs which constitute it. As a result, the ground zero these BwOs share is not an ontological Substance prior to their activity, and which their activity expresses, but the real condition for the construction of this Substance, as a real sensation, in the inorganic life of Bacon's Figures. The ontological conditions of Bacon's paintings do not pre-exist them, as what they would simply express, but are constructed in his diagram, in their own way and according to their own laws. Bacon's diagram and all the other constructions of the BwO do not come together in a single unity, except, as Deleuze and Guattari say, as "a fusional multiplicity that effectively goes beyond any opposition between the one and the multitude" (ATP, 154/191). This means that although all the BwOs form an "ontological unity of substance" (ATP, 154/191), these BwOs construct this substance differently in their expressions, that is, in the expression of an always mobile constructive difference. The point is not what "is" the BwO, but how is it constructed by *this* diagram, in *this* perspective, and as *this* sensation? This is finally the fractal logic not just of Bacon's paintings, but of Deleuze and Guattari's ontological system; differenciation means infinity at every level, because becoming is the immanence of singularity and unity in life. What Deleuze writes of the laws of Bacon's triptychs could therefore equally apply to Deleuze's ontological structure as a whole, with no loss of specificity: "The constants they imply change depending on the case at hand. They govern extremely variable terms, from the viewpoint both of their nature and their relations. There are so many movements in Bacon's paintings that the law of the triptychs can only be a movement of movements, or a state of complex forces, inasmuch as movement is always derived from the forces exerted upon the body" (FB, 83/80). One more time, *this* body, *this* painting, *this* sensation.

Finally then, we can say that it is precisely at its most abstract dimension that Deleuze's account of Bacon's paintings attains its greatest specificity. The moment the BwO as ground 0 emerges in Bacon's paintings in terms no longer their own is also the moment Deleuze has produced the most empirical construction of their expressive forces. This paradoxical confluence is not by chance, as it is in fact the necessary result of Deleuze's ontological assumptions. Bacon's paintings express the affects of forces on a BwO (as ground 0) in sensations, these sensations simultaneously construct a perspective in which something happens, in which the BwO lives. The "monochromatic eternity" (FB, 85/81) of the BwO, its "spiritual dimension" exists, and can only exist in its construction, in and as the sensations of Bacon's painting. The ontological ground zero of Deleuze's system, the One-All of Substance, is a fusional multiplicity that only exists as Being-in-the-World, that is, in sensations which construct and express our living flesh.

Conclusion
# A Break, a Becoming, and a Belief . . .

flirters, deserters, wimps and pimps, speeding like bullets, grinning like chimps, above the heads of TV watchers, lovers under the overpasses, movies at malls letting out, bright gas station oases in pure fluorescent spill, canopied beneath the palm trees, soon wrapped, down the corridors of the surface streets, in nocturnal smog, the adobe air, the smell of distant fireworks, the spilled, the broken world.

—Thomas Pynchon, *Vineland.*[1]

## THE BROKEN WORLD

The spilled, the broken world. Deleuze and Guattari's world as much as Pynchon's, a world of creative breaks through which chaos spills. Fireworks. And the break also composes chaos, it's a disjunctive conjunction, an eternally returning 'and . . .' Chaos spills into life—chaosmosis. But how to break and how to compose? These are the questions of art. How to break with the human, all too human, with its clichés, its self-obsessed egoism, its organic thought? How to break through these limitations on life in order to extend our compositions as far as the infinite, to succeed in a becoming-universe? It requires a mystical art capable of constructing and expressing a universe in a sensation, a world from and in *this* sensation as a sensation of *this* world. Art then, is as atheist as it is mystic, because the infinity it restores to sensation is nothing but its own living process: a life. Art is the construction of a living world of sensation; a world that never stops becoming something else, never stops breaking and composing, never stops emerging as something new. "Any work of art," Deleuze writes, "points a way through for life, finds a way through the cracks."[2]

Art is a guidance device, a machine that finds in the cracks a means of escape and discovery. Because "Art as abstract machine" both breaks and creates, it creates by breaking. This has been a constant refrain for us: no creation without destruction. And it means, each time, again. This is the first condition of art, to break with the ontological and aesthetic assumptions that negate its life. In doing so art emerges as a compositional process creating new realities, constructing a work that expresses the world, and expressing in a work the unending construction of the universe. This is the definition of art as an active immanence, a creative power always operating on the principle of *to come*. In the face of this *to come,* the artistic element of the present—the contemporary itself—is in a permanent process of cracking open: "Works are developed," Deleuze writes, "around or on the basis of a fracture they can never succeed in filling" (DR, 195/252).

We saw this in the Nietzschean artist-philosopher and his or her art of critique. Critique as affirmation breaks with man's nihilism, and overcomes his negation of living will to power. This affirmation gives us a new physiology, a new way of feeling. First break: the Overman. This affirmation produces a new image, an image adequate to becoming, to its powers of the false, to its creative eternal return. Second break: the simulacra. This affirmation produces a new image of art and artist, as the *work* of art, the vital process by which the will to power is expressed, and in which the will to power is forever constructed anew. Third break: an art of immanence. Art as affirmation gives a real experience of its real conditions, beyond the Kantian double definition of aesthetics, beyond any pre-given conditions of possibility. Art operates as a libratory innovation, opening up a future that is unknown.

In Spinoza, the same problem: How can we break through man's inadequate understanding of the world? It means, how can we understand what is beyond man and yet entirely within man, how can we understand the infinity of God as we construct and express it in Nature, how in other words, is essence existence? Once more, it is a question of new feelings, or as Spinoza puts it, of affects. Affects no longer understood according to the subjects that have them and the objects that cause them, but according to the common notions they create. Through understanding common notions another world appears, a world in the process of being composed, a vision of God/Nature in which I see how I am God, without God either abandoning infinity, or leaving this world as his plane of composition. Spinoza's art of beatitude emerges as this "atheist mysticism," a radical break with a transcendent God, in a vision of God/Nature as the continual construction of the world. Beatitude begins with the common notion, an epistemology of the *here and now* that leaves behind man's sad imaginations to actively pursue a joy adequate to an infinitely creative God *as* Nature. To express this God/Nature is nothing but understanding how our joy, our love, is the very force constructing God's pantheistic becoming, Nature's creative difference from itself. Art is nothing without joy.

Deleuze's cinema books are also constituted around a break, or rather a series of breaks. That which determines the movement-image, the break between the sensory-motor and a duration it gives an indirect image of, a break that at its limit appears as the sublime. And then another break, a break*down* of the sensory-motor, through which visions emerge, images as pure optical and sound situations. This is the direct image of time in "modern" post-war cinema, and it emerges through the "crack" constituting a new brain, the cine-brain of a "neuro-physiological automaton," an automatism capable of expressing duration as it is constructed, capable of thinking the splitting of time. And the break between these breaks, the ontological break between the movement-image and the time-image, their differing durations, and the different cine-brains they imply. With cinema images begin to create time, not only producing images that express their ontological conditions, but constructing images as ontological machines. Modernity emerges here as an art form experimenting on its own immanent and real conditions, and art opens onto a "to come" that becomes the definition of its true contemporaneity.

Painting also appeared according to this logic. First of all the artist achieves a breakthrough, one determined by breaking down the strata of signifiance and subjectivation, and the preconditions on perception they impose. This is a break with representation as an image of thought in which painting acts as a signifier, and where its material movements are subordinated to a regime of "meaning" overcoding it. Venetian Renaissance painting exemplifies painting's power of breakthrough, a critical or "schizoanalytic" process by which onto-aesthetics finds its specific co-ordinates in an abstract machine. The abstract machine frees material forces (traits of content) to compose new signs (traits of expression), particles-signs expressing a new corporeality, a corporeality of paint. This new corporeality and the powers of composition it unleashes usher in a new modernity for painting, one in which color and line break with their representational functions to become abstract. Abstraction, as an onto-aesthetic definition of art and not simply a formal one, implies a new type of perception as much as a new style, a perception capable of breaking down a subject's distance from the canvas, and breaking through a subjective optics, to construct a smooth and haptic space of sensation. This is the abstraction of both Jackson Pollock and Francis Bacon, who push it in their own directions.

This non-optical space is where affect breaks free from its subjective co-ordinates to construct a subjectivation, an art-work as a mobile affectual assemblage that is both autopoietic and machinic. This is a break with both the artist as intentional agent of creation, and with the art work as pure expression. Once more we find a new onto-aesthetic dimension; an "aesthetic paradigm" in which the creative processes of chaosmosis are seen at work "flush with the real." Here, the art-work finds a new life, a vitality in which its construction is a direct expression of its ontological conditions. As such, an art work is an affectual subjectivation that expresses a percept, a vision of the universe embodying the constructive powers of chaosmosis. This implies a further break, as the Aristotelian concept of a hylomorphically formed matter is replaced by a molecularised matter. A matter freed to embody the chaosmic forces of the world, as they construct the world. This is also art's break with Romanticism, by which it expresses a new constructivist Nature, a modern nature or "Mechanosphere" in which the art-work is composed through the cosmic forces it embodies in an inhuman and animal sensation.

Our major example of this revalued art practice was the work of Francis Bacon, whose paintings operate a catastrophic "diagram" that breaks with the clichés occupying the canvas by introducing a chaos that wipes them away. But this chaos is itself 'artistic,' it contains the creative forces that are expressed in being composed by Bacon's diagram. Bacon composes these forces through his fractal art history, a series of engagements with historical art styles by which he takes less than their whole, but more also, as each 'recapitulation' is a reinvention. Bacon's break with an historical style is entirely affirmative, inasmuch as it takes each style's break, its creation of a new ontological space for painting, in order to utilise this power in its own way, and so break with it again. Bacon's creative breaks compose a new body, a Body without Organs, an embodiment of painting beyond its objective or subjective conditions. The BwO is a painting-body operating as an Artaudian "nerve-meter," expressing its chaosmic conditions through a strict constructivism no less rigorous for being hysterical. Bacon's abstract machine is on one side entirely actual, a formal diagram of unerring precision, and on the other utterly cosmic, plunging into chaos to bring back something new. Bacon arrives in his work at the "fact" of a body becoming, not just those of Bacon's figures but our own, a merge made visible in the construction of a "haptic eye," and its visions of a transversal "flesh."

And each of these breaks is itself produced by another, that of Deleuze and Guattari's machine. Deleuze breaks with Nietzsche's eternal return of the same, to make the same that which returns difference. Deleuze breaks with Spinoza to make the attributes the mechanism by which modal existence expresses a differential essence, an essence constructed by an actuality giving joy. Through the attributes immanence becomes a univocal reality in which expression=construction, an atheistic onto-aesthetics *against* any transcendent or emanative onto-theology. Deleuze's cinema will break with Bergson, by discovering a crack in the sensory motor through which a crystal-image emerges to express and construct duration. Just as Deleuze and Guattari will break with Peirce and Hjelmslev, moving beyond their semiotic theories in putting them to work in their own way. The list goes on. A break with Worringer to free the Gothic line, a break with the romantic sublime, a break with modernist art-theory to produce a modern painting no longer optical but haptic. A break with phenomenology to find Bacon's painting as being-in-the-world. No creation without destruction, and Deleuze and Guattari are forever setting machines in motion which break with their previous determinates in order to create something new. This is the destruction-creation of the aesthetic paradigm, and defines the conditions for any work of art, the break that allows it to create the spilled and broken world.

## THE SPILL

The spilled and broken world. Perhaps we should reverse Pynchon's phrase, because it is through the break which something will emerge, spill into being if you like, something will be created. But of course, and as we have repeatedly seen, these two things happen together, and together they define the parameters of Deleuze and Guattari's materialist-vitalist ontology: a break releasing vital matters-forces, the forces constructing a becoming-world. What is constructed is a point of view, a perspective—in other words: a life. Art does not live in the world, nor in us, it constructs a world while simultaneously expressing it, it lives as this immanent plane of composition. This plane of composition is a differential plane of forces, expressed in the construction of sensations, and constructed by sensation's living refrains of colors and abstract lines, an irreducible doubled dimension, expressed in a life, as life, in art and as art. Art is this process of creation, at once cosmic and molecular, the internal-outside of pure immanence. "We will say of pure immanence," Deleuze writes, "that it is A LIFE, and nothing else. It is not immanence to life, but the immanent that is in nothing is itself a life. A life is the immanence of immanence: it is complete power, complete bliss."[3]

Pure immanence is ontology as the theory and practice of a creative life, because we cannot think this ontological power "in itself"; it has no "in itself" and only exists as the becoming-new in things, in art. This makes Deleuze and Guattari's ontology inseparable from aesthetics, inasmuch as pure immanence is what appears, as what appears—what appears when essence is existence. What appears is sensation. Sensation is the being of sensation—difference—but this differential essence only exists as affects (becomings) and visions (percepts), in other words it only exists *in and as experience:* a life. Sensation must be constructed in experience, in and as art, for its infinite and ontogenetic plane of matters-forces, its differential field, only exists as such. *Nothing is given.* Inasmuch as art creates a sensation then, art creates the finite that re-stores the infinite. I have suggested that this double dimension of sensation, of art, implies a Deleuzeo-Guattarian onto-aesthetics as the always doubled interrogation of art; what is it, and how does it appear? Inseparable questions. Sensation is at once *this* sensation, this work of art, and its cosmic conditions, art is an expression that constructs the world. "We are not in the world," Deleuze and Guattari write, "we become with the world; we become by con-templating it. Everything is vision, becoming. We become universes" (WP, 169). Finite and infinite; the artist, the mystical atheist, the visionary, the life.

We have seen this visionary art emerge in each of the chapters of this book. In Nietzsche Deleuze finds the ontological conditions for appearance in the will to power, but will to power is never outside of its expressions in the world, its simulacra. Artists are those strong enough to affirm will to power, and art's expression of life's genetic conditions is nothing but the re-creation of these conditions. As a result, the simulacral art work embodies the eternal return of will to power as difference, as becoming. In Spinoza Deleuze finds a univocal ontology of God/Nature, and an expressionism in the modes and through the attributes. The constant variation of the modes, God's constant becoming, expresses the affect's essence, an essence which is itself determined only by the differential relations it maintains with the infinite essences consti-tuting God. Through a vision of affectual essence then, through an art of common notions, it is possible to know God as God knows himself: beati-tude. Deleuze uses Bergson's term for a creative and univocal being in the cin-ema books, duration. Duration as the past, not previous to the present but coexisting with it, producing the image as it is forever splitting into past and present. Duration emerges in this absolutely contemporary moment consti-tuting the fracture of time. Modern cinema's visionarys or seers produce im-ages of this split, images which construct time's bifurcations as an expression of its virtual infinity. Similarly, in the sensation a finite work produces an ex-perience restoring it to its infinite and immanent plane of composition. Finally, in the abstract lines of Pollock and the complex diagram of Bacon a new vision of painting emerges, a "haptic" vision in which the eye "touches" the painting. Vision is no longer the passive reception of a separate I/eye, but a corporeal convulsion encompassing a becoming indiscernibly in the work and of the world. Painting has become the 'making visible' of sensation, a sen-sation which constructs and expresses the world.

If we can say, or have said, that Deleuze and Guattari offer an ontology which cannot be thought apart from its creative processes, apart that is from the production of feelings or sensations that both express and construct the material and energetic world, then we must say, as precisely as possible, how art does this. This is to understand the other (artistic) side of Deleuze and Guattari's abstract machine.

## ART AS ABSTRACT MACHINE

The abstract machine on the one hand composes the matter and force making up a plane of consistency, and on the other expresses it in an actual assemblage. It is on the one hand a general term for the onto-aesthetics of creation, and on the other the particular event of construction, the construction of an infinite plane expressed in a work of art. Art as abstract machine therefore means autopoiesis, the autopoiesis of the chaosmos. The autopoietic abstract machine appears as a refrain or sensation, a composition of a virtual plane of immanence expressed in an affectual assemblage that is entirely actual. The refrain or sensation is the creation of art, art as the construction of affectual bodies or subjectivations expressing an infinite virtuality they actualise, and a counter-actualisation that constructs the virtual and infinite world anew.

Art as Abstract Machine operates specifically in sensation, which nevertheless has a double sense in relation to art. On the one side, it means a transformation of sensibility, a break with human perceptions and meanings in order for the being of sensation to appear directly as sensation. Again, this has various fields of resonance within Deleuze and Guattari's work. We have already mentioned its relevance to our discussion of Nietzsche, Spinoza, and Bergson. In the later chapters, this revalued or transformed sensibility emerged in a haptic, smooth space co-extensive with the operation of a haptic eye. Haptic space and the eye that is its productive condition appear together in an affective assemblage or subjectivation, an animal vitality or "flesh" of the BwO. The BwO embodies a new sensibility defining art's bio-aesthetic dimension, a dimension in which art is no longer simply the realm of human expression, but sings a song of molecules.

Along with the revalued sensibility involved in having a sensation, is a revalued artistic technique capable of producing it. This is the 'practical' side of the abstract machine, inasmuch as any machine involves a "practice." We looked at various examples, all of which shared a basic necessity; they broke with representation. Each art form does so according to its particular material modality. Painting's materiality involves line and color, and it is by using line and color against its representational functions that painting expresses the immanence of inorganic life directly in a sensation. This involves freeing color from its overcoding by the line so that form emerges through the modulation of color as a set of differential relations, and freeing the line from its

representational function so as to give it a non-striated movement. In both
cases, what is involved is a "molecularisation" of matter, by which its materiality is able to become expressive, and able to "clasp" chaosmic forces in a sensation. "Paintings eternal object is this": Deleuze and Guattari write, "to paint
forces" (WP, 182/172). For painting, this means composing a coloring sensation, and we looked closely at the way both the Venetian painters of the
Renaissance, and Francis Bacon, each in their own way, do this. In both cases
this process involves an absolute deterritorialisation of painting's material elements, both its matter, and its processes of composition. These, in escaping
the overcoding of a classical line in the Venetian case, and through the catastrophe with which Bacon's diagram begins, allow for new mechanisms of construction and expression to emerge, defining a new reality of painting.
Obviously, this reality is not the same for the Venetians and for Bacon, but
each in their own way approach an abstraction in which color is able to render the forces of the plane of composition visible. This means that in both
cases an abstract machine is in operation through which art becomes adequate
to its real conditions, and art produces a sensation. Here sensation is gained
through colorism, a use of color's differential relations that opens painting
onto infinity, while composing a world. In a sensation, a painting's color-
forces emerge in movement, and our perceptual participation in color's differential quantities enables a becoming to take place both on and in front of the
painting's surface. Nevertheless, colorism emerges in painting according to
specific historical conditions, and we saw how the Venetian break with the
painting diagrams that preceded and accompanied it expressed both the dynamisms of new materials, and older traditions such as Byzantine art, to
which this materiality was conjugated.

In certain of Jackson Pollock's paintings it is the line that is freed from
any descriptive function. Pollock achieves this breakthrough by inventing a
new compositional machine, one that unleashes new abstract and vital forces
in paint. Pollock's paintings not only create a new type of abstraction, but carry
abstraction to its limit, beyond any optical perception (beyond that is, the
"pure opticality" of Greenberg's modernist reading) in a haptic smooth space
where the viewer-painting relation is replaced by the vital movements of abstract lines that traverse it. Finally, in cinema we saw a different materiality, that
of duration, where the universe exists as moving images of light. This materiality of cinema is nevertheless what its images both construct and express and
Deleuze offers an intricate and precise taxonomy of the ways cinema achieves
this. With time-images cinema discovers the way to move beyond its
Bergsonian conditions to directly express duration—as whole and as part, as
multiple in Bergson's terms—in a vision of and as the becoming of time.

What is common to all of these examples is the necessarily double dimension of their abstract machines. Nevertheless, and as Deleuze and Guattari often stress, the abstract machine is not a "thing," it is a process, and its most important moment is no doubt its creation, which must be undertaken each time, anew, and *for real.* This is once more the imperative of this books title, because "Art as Abstract Machine" means nothing unless we do it. This returns us to the necessity of affirmation, ours first of all, because it is only by experimenting, by attempting this operation of invention, of making a leap of faith into the unknown that we will have a sensation, and that we can aspire to the title of artist (or of art as abstract machine). Affirmation is the engine of Deleuze and Guattari's constructivism, the mechanics of their philosophical creations (even when what is constructed is not altogether convincing, as in the case of Guattari's image of Duchamp), and must be the starting point for any approach to their system made in good faith. But what is the meaning of this seemingly banal pre-requisite of Deleuze and Guattari's philosophy—affirmation? What is affirmed in each case—Nietzsche, Spinoza and Bergson, as well as the variety of artistic examples we have discussed—is a creative immanence, a vital materialism both expressed and constructed by the work of art. And more than just a simple declaration of faith in a divine creation, it is precisely this affirmation that is the way that immanence works, that God *is* Nature, or the will to power returns. Affirmation is the break necessary for something to happen: "Hence the sole thing that is divine is the nature of an energy of disjunctions, when it attracts to itself the entire process of production and serves as its miraculate, enchanted surface, inscribing it in each and every one of its disjunctions" (AO, 13/19). To believe in the break, to affirm a disjunction in which product and production are in absolute immanence, to affirm finally, a plane of abstract machines, is the very condition of art's possibility, the very condition of its *actuality.* Affirmation would be, then, Guattari's "blind trust in the movement of deterritorialization at work."[4]

## THE LEAP OF FAITH

It seems paradoxical that Deleuze and Guattari's philosophy, so avowedly atheist, so utterly materialist, and so ecstatically inhuman, should bring us back to that most human quality, trust or belief. Why then is belief necessary? Because belief in this world is the atheist, materialist, and inhuman condition of its sensation. Because in the end we cannot think this inhuman world, it is precisely what cannot be thought, and cannot be represented, and yet it is that which our deranged senses are forever feeling. To return to *Cinema 2,* and one of Deleuze's most beautiful passages, he describes the spiritual automaton, (but it is equally Nietzsche's Dionysus, Spinoza's man of beatitude, or the painter him or herself—Pollock "in" his painting) the one who has received a shock, and has seen a vision of the world in its infinite becoming. What to do in the face of such an image? Of course we react, we feel and we see, but no longer with eyes which can represent, or a mind which can explain. "The spiritual automaton is in the psychic situation of the seer," Deleuze writes, "who sees better and further than he can react, that is, think. Which, then, is the subtle way out? To believe, not in a different world, but in a link between man and the world, in love or life, to believe in this as in the impossible, the unthinkable, which none the less cannot but be thought" (C2, 170/221). The visionary sees more than his or her humanity can bear, the inhuman univocity of the reciprocal construction/expression of the seer and the world. Here all organic complementarities between man and world are broken, and must be replaced with something else, with belief. There is, and Deleuze is at his most affirmative here, "the erasure of the unity of man and the world, in favour of a break which now leaves us with only a belief in this world" (C2, 188/245). Any construction, any expression of this world, of the world as new, requires belief, and belief becomes the complete bliss of pure immanence. We discover in a sensation, in art as it is understood by Deleuze and Guattari, the necessity for a mystical and yet atheistic belief in man *and* the world, in their irreducible and incomprehensible link, nothing less than the belief in "the identity of thought and life" (C2, 170/221). Of course, this is a certain sort of thought, and a certain sort of life, the particular expression and most cosmic construction of a mystical aesthetics, the atheism of art. But art in these terms is precisely what cannot be thought or lived; it exceeds our human life and thoughts and must be believed in. Belief as inorganic thought, chaosmic thought, is what comes after man's organic relation to the world is broken. Our connection to the world has changed ontological co-ordinates, and is now "the impossible which can only be restored within a faith. [ . . . ] Only belief in the world can reconnect man to what he sees and hears" (C2, 172/223). It is the belief of Dionysus, who alone has, according to Nietzsche, "the *faith* that only what is separate and individual may be rejected, that in the totality everything *is* redeemed and affirmed—*he no longer denies.* . . . " (TI, "Expeditions of an Untimely Man," 49). This is the faith of the truly intoxicated, an atheistic belief in this world as a being-in-the-world, a mystic materialism without any transcendental dimension. This is the belief that our sensation encompasses man and the world in a cosmic co-creation, and is, finally, our belief in art, the belief necessary to art. An art that fulfils Deleuze and Guattari's fundamental ontological, aesthetic and ethical condition—to create. But believing in art in this post-modern world is not so easy. As

Deleuze and Guattari warn us: "It may be that believing in this world, in this life, becomes our most difficult task, or the task of a mode of existence still to be discovered on our plane of existence today" (WP, 75/72). The art of belief waits to be created. Again.

So perhaps this book has been nothing but a statement of belief. Could there be a more perverse ending to a book of philosophy than a statement of belief? No doubt this is not the first. But as the expression of a life, sometimes painful, often uplifting, it exists, if as nothing else, then at least as an expression of belief.

# Notes

## NOTES TO THE INTRODUCTION

1. Gilles Deleuze, "Cold and Heat," *Photogenic Painting, Gerard Fromanger,* p. 64.
2. I use "Deleuze and Guattari" here, as I do in the book's title, to refer to the work done by Deleuze alone, by Guattari alone, and by the two together. Where I am discussing the work Deleuze or Guattari have done separately this will be indicated in the text, as will any divergences between their oeuvres, or across them, when they are relevant to our discussion.
3. We need only think of Professor Challenger from *A Thousand Plateaus:* "Disarticulated, deterritorialized, Challenger muttered that he was taking the earth with him, that he was leaving for the mysterious world, his poison garden" (ATP, 73/93).
4. Gilles Deleuze, "Mysticism and Masochism," *Desert Islands and Other Texts, 1953—1974,* p. 134. ("Mystique et masochisme," *L'île Déserte et Autres Textes, textes et entretiens, 1953—1974,* p. 186)
5. This formulation comes from Éric Alliez who has explored its implications from his earliest work in *La Signature du monde: Ou qu'est-ce que la philosophie de Deleuze et Guattari?* (a translation is forthcoming from Continuum) where it is stated at the end of the first appendix, to his latest, *L'Oeil-cerveau. De la peinture moderne* (with Jean-Clet Martin) and *La Pensée-Matisse* (with Jean-Claude Bonne) (both are forthcoming from Seuil and Gallimard respectively) where he develops its implications in terms of a new genealogy of modern art. I was fortunate enough to attend Éric Alliez's seminar at the Akademie der bildenden Künste Wien from 2000—2003, and my understanding of this point, and many others concerning Deleuze and Guattari's philosophy of art, pays an immeasurable debt to his work.
6. Michel de Certeau, "Mysticism," *Diacritics,* 22.2, summer 1992, p. 12. See also *The Mystic Fable, Volume I, The Sixteenth and Seventeenth Centuries.* De Certeau's work retrieves mystical expressions from their scientific objectification, and considers them instead as "formalities" (i.e. abstract machines) existing across a wide range of discourses and practices. It provided an initial

inspiration for my project here. De Certeau also rejects any separation of the ontological elements of mystical discourse from their expressions, suggesting a constructivist understanding of mysticism that I have also tried to pursue. De Certeau argues: "The Other that organizes the text is not an outside of the text. It is not an imaginary object that one might distinguish from the movement by which it is sketched. To locate it apart, to isolate it from the texts that exhaust themselves trying to express it, would be tantamount to exorcising it by providing it with its own place and name" (*The Mystic Fable*, p. 15). This is a precise definition of mysticism in terms of the expressionism=constructivism equation.

7.  John Rajchman for example, has written: "It is a shame to present him [Deleuze] as a metaphysician and nature mystic." ("Introduction," Gilles Deleuze, *Pure Immanence, Essays on A Life*, p. 7) Similarly, if less categorically, Ronald Bogue writes: "Though this blending of bodies and sensations, of people, art-works, and cosmos, may sound like sheer mysticism, it is based on a coherent theory of nature as creation" (*Deleuze on Music, Painting, and the Arts*, p. 170).

8.  This is part of the rather hilarious interview "Faces and Surfaces," *Desert Islands and Other Texts, 1953–1974*, p. 281. ("Faces et Surfaces," *L'île déserte et autres texts, textes et entretiens 1953–1974*, p. 392)

9.  Gilles Deleuze, "Mysticism and Masochism," *Desert Islands and Other Texts, 1953–1974*, p. 134. ("Mystique et masochisme," *L'île déserte et autres texts, textes et entretiens 1953–1974*, p. 186)

## NOTES TO CHAPTER ONE

1.  Friedrich Nietzsche, *Thus Spake Zarathustra*, "Of the Bestowing of Virtue," 3. All reference to this book now found in the text following the abbreviation "Z."

2.  Gilles Deleuze, "Nomad Thought," *The New Nietzsche*, p. 145. ("Pensée Nomade," *L'île Déserte et Autres Textes, textes et entretiens, 1953—1974*, p. 357)

3.  Friedrich Nietzsche, *The Gay Science*, 290. All references to this book now found in the text following the abbreviation "GS."

4.  Friedrich Nietzsche, *The Will to Power*, 795. All references to this book now found in the text following the abbreviation "WtP."

5.  Friedrich Nietzsche, *Twilight of the Idols*, "Expeditions of an Untimely Man," 33. All references to this book now found in the text following the abbreviation "TI."

6.  Friedrich Nietzsche, *On the Genealogy of Morals*, I, 6. All references to this book now found in the text following the abbreviation "GM."

7.  Gilles Deleuze, "Coldness and Cruelty," *Masochism*, p. 14. Similarly, Deleuze has written that "symptomatology is located almost outside medicine, at a

neutral point, a zero point, where artists and philosophers and doctors and patients can come together." "Mysticism and Masochism" *Desert Islands and Other Textes, 1953—1974*, p. 134. ("Mystique et masochisme," *L'île Déserte et Autres Textes, textes et entretiens, 1953—1974*, p. 186) It would be as an art of symptomatology that we can understand Deleuze's table of types and qualities in his book on Nietzsche. (NP, 146/166) Similarly, his discussion of the "clinical essence" of each art is also a symptomatology (FB,54/55). As he writes elsewhere: "There is always a great deal of art involved in the grouping of symptoms, in the organisation of a *table* where a particular symptom is dissociated from another, juxtaposed to a third, and forms the new figure of a disorder or illness. Clinicians who are able to renew a symptomatological table produce a work of art; conversely, artists are clinicians, [ . . . ] they are clinicians of civilisation" (LS, 237/276). This introduces the necessity of a taxonomy of symptoms, a *critical and clinical* taxonomy, which I shall examine in chapters 3 and 6.

8. The passage these quotations come from acts as a succinct Deleuzian gloss to the lines from *Twilight of the Idols* cited above: "According to physicists," Deleuze writes, "noble energy is the kind capable of transforming itself, while the base kind can no longer do so. There is will to power on both sides, but the latter is nothing more than will-to-dominate in the exhausted becoming of life, while the former is artistic will or 'virtue which gives,' the creation of new possibilities, in the outpouring becoming" (C2, 141/185).

9. Hence Nietzsche's famous line: "*Beyond Good and Evil*—At least this does *not* mean 'Beyond Good and Bad'" (GM, I, 17). Beyond the weak man's "bad" morality of good and evil, the strength of the eagle is good.

10. The Nietzschean art of creative critique will remain a condition of Deleuze's project till the end, and is affirmed in the last book he wrote with Guattari: "Criticism implies new concepts (of the thing criticised) just as much as the most positive creation" (WP, 83/80).

11. Gilles Deleuze, "Nietzsche," *Pure Immanence, Essays on A Life*, p. 73. (*Nietzsche*, p. 24)

12. Gilles Deleuze, "Nietzsche," *Pure Immanence, Essays on A Life*, p. 74. (*Nietzsche*, p. 25)

13. "To interpret," Deleuze writes, "is to determine the force which gives sense to a thing. To evaluate is to determine the will to power which gives value to a thing. We can no more abstract values from the standpoint from which they draw value than we can abstract meaning from the standpoint from which it draws its signification. The will to power as genealogical element is that from which senses derive their significance and values their values" (NP, 54/61).

14. As Deleuze writes: "Nietzsche replaced the ideal of knowledge, the discovery of the true, with *interpretation and evaluation*." Gilles Deleuze, "Nietzsche," *Pure Immanence, Essays on A Life*, p. 65. (*Nietzsche*, p. 17)

15. As Nietzsche puts it: "For assuming that one is a person, one necessarily also has the philosophy that belongs to that person; but there is a big difference. In some it is their deprivations that philosophise; in others, their riches and strengths" (GS, preface, 2). Similarly, Nietzsche writes: "It has gradually become clear to me what every great philosophy has hitherto been: a confession on the part of its author and a kind of involuntary and unconscious memoir; moreover, that the moral (or immoral) intentions in every philosophy have every time constituted the real germ of life out of which the entire plant has grown. To explain how a philosopher's most remote metaphysical assertions have actually been arrived at, it is always well (and wise) to ask oneself first: what morality does this (does he-) aim at?" (*Beyond Good and Evil*, 6) This means, as Deleuze is fond of pointing out, we always get the thoughts and feeling we deserve. See; NP, 104/119, DR, 159/206–7, and "How Do We Recognise Structuralism?" C.S. Stivale, *The Two-Fold Thought of Deleuze and Guattari: Intersections and Animations,* p. 270. ("A quoi reconnaît-on le structuralisme?," *L'île Déserte et Autres Textes, textes et entretiens, 1953—1974,* p. 254)

16. Henry Miller, *The World of Sex,* p. 94, New York: Grove Press, 1965.

17. This passage clearly marks the differences between Deleuze and Martin Heidegger's well-known interpretation of Nietzsche. For Deleuze the immanence of being and becoming is central to his univocal ontology, not just in relation to Nietzsche, but throughout his oeuvre. For Heidegger, interpreting Nietzsche as the "last metaphysician," this passage "suggests that Becoming only is if it is grounded in Being as Being." This implies, Heidegger argues, that "for Nietzsche will as will to power designates the essence of Being." Because art is the way will to power, or Being, becomes "genuinely visible," it will be possible to "grasp will to power itself in its essence, and thereby being as a whole with regard to its basic character" in art. As we shall see, for Deleuze will to power has no basic character and is not a metaphysical category because it is always under construction, always creating the perspectives constituting its becoming. The Heidegger quotations are from *Nietzsche vol.1, Will to Power as Art,* p. 19, 39, 72, and 92.

18. T. S. Eliot, "Preludes," *The Wasteland and other poems,* p. 10, London: Faber and Faber, 1972.

19. One of Deleuze's most important arguments, his anti-Hegelian affirmation of difference, is therefore entirely Nietzschean. Deleuze writes: "Difference is not the negative; on the contrary, non-being is difference [ . . . ]. This (non)-being is the differential element in which affirmation, as multiple affirmation, finds the principle of its genesis. As for negation, this is only a shadow of the highest principle, the shadow of difference alongside the affirmation produced. Once we confuse (non)-being with the negative, contradiction is inevitably carried into being; but contradiction is only the appearance or the epiphenomenon, the illusion projected by the problem, the shadow of a

question which remains open and of a being which corresponds as such to that question (before it has been given a response)" (DR, 64/89).

20. Friedrich Nietzsche, *Human, All Too Human*, 51. All references to this book now found in the text following the abbreviation "HH."

21. Friedrich Nietzsche, Letter, 2 December 1887, *Unpublished Letters*, p. 125.

22. In this sense, Nietzsche writes, anti-art gives witness to "a specific anti-artisticality of instinct—a mode of being which impoverishes and attenuates things and makes them consumptive. And history is in fact rich in such anti-artists, in such starvelings of life, who necessarily have to take things to themselves, impoverish them, make them leaner" (TI, "Expeditions of an Untimely Man," 9).

23. Friedrich Nietzsche, *The Antichrist*, 14. All references to this book now found in the text following the abbreviation "A."

24. Affirmation in itself, Deleuze argues, is becoming, or will to power. But as the object of another affirmation, of an interpretation, will to power takes on being: "It is primary affirmation (becoming) which is being, but only as the object of the second affirmation" (NP, 186/214). The song of the artist-philosopher: "*Eternal affirmation of being, eternally I am your affirmation*" (Nietzsche, quoted, NP, 187/215).

25. These words are spoken by Birkin, who is considered a self-portrait of Lawrence. *Women in Love*, p. 48, London: Penguin, 1985.

26. Gilles Deleuze, "Nietzsche," *Pure Immanence, Essays on A Life*, p. 85. (*Nietzsche*, p. 34)

27. Deleuze and Guattari suggest a kind of intoxicated sobriety, quoting Henry Miller: "To succeed in getting drunk, but on pure water" (ATP, 286/350). Intoxication is not the same as inebriation, as Nietzsche often stressed. See *Daybreak*, 50, 188, 269.

28. Nietzsche introduces the concept of the Dionysian in his first book, *The Birth of Tragedy*, where the indiscernibility of art-work and artist in intoxication is already present. Nietzsche writes of the Dionysian artist: "No longer *artist*, he has himself become a *work of art*, the productive power of the whole universe is now manifest in his transport, to the glorious satisfaction of the primordial One" (*The Birth of Tragedy*, p. 24). In *The Birth of Tragedy* the Dionysian is opposed to an Apollonian art of representational forms, an opposition Nietzsche tries to sublate in the Greek art of tragedy: "Tragedy is an Apollonian embodiment of Dionysiac insights and powers" (*The Birth of Tragedy*, p. 8). This sublation will mean that *The Birth of Tragedy* "smells offensively Hegelian" to Nietzsche by the end of his working life. (*Ecce Homo*, "Birth of Tragedy," 1. References to this book now found in the text following the abbreviation "EH.") Nietzsche progressively distances himself from this early oppositional formulation and its Romantic influences and gestures (especially in the second Preface, the "Attempt At A Self Criticism" of 1886),

and replaces it with a concept of the Dionysian as the critical animal artistic
state necessary to will to power's transvaluation.

29. Jacques Derrida, *Spurs,* p. 77. It must be pointed out however, that Derrida's
interpretation of Nietzsche differs markedly from Deleuze's. For Derrida will
to power is a Heideggerean Being, whose productive presence is forever
veiled/unveiled in an artists work. Art, on this account, is a mechanism of
deference that "writes" will to power's presence/absence in a work. In this
sense, an artists "style," Derrida writes, "uses its spur as a means of protection
against the terrifying, blinding, mortal threat (of that) which *presents* itself,
which obstinately thrusts itself into view. And style thereby protects the presence, the content, the thing itself, meaning, truth—on the condition at least
that it should not *already* be that gaping chasm which has been deflowered
in the unveiling of difference. *Already,* such is the name for what has been effaced or subtracted beforehand, but which has nevertheless left behind a
mark, a signature which is retracted in that very thing from which it is with-
drawn" (*Spurs,* p. 39). Style, for Derrida, unveils the difference between that
which presents itself and its presentation, and is the signature of the formers
withdrawal from the latter. For Deleuze, style is the expression of the immanence of will to power and form, its intoxicating presence in the self-overcoming—the becoming—of forms.

30. Similarly, Deleuze writes, "man is in the image and likeness of God, but
through sin we have lost the likeness while remaining in the image . . . simulacra are precisely demonic images, stripped of resemblance" (DR,
127/167).

31. Deleuze is ever the generous adversary however, and in the concept of the
simulacra Deleuze will find Plato escaping himself. By affirming the simulacrum, Deleuze writes, he is "demonstrating the anti-Platonism at the heart
of Platonism" (DR, 128/167).

32. Alain Badiou, in a fascinating attack on Deleuze, attempts a "reversal" of
Deleuzianism on the site of the simulacra, by reinserting the distinction
between essence and appearance (idea and copy) into the heart of Deleuze's
account of univocal being. Badiou writes, "if one classes—as one should—
every difference without a real status, every multiplicity whose ontological
status is that of the One, as simulacrum, then the world of beings is the
theatre of the simulacrum of Being.

   Strangely, the consequence has a Platonic, or even Neoplatonic, air to it.
It is as though the paradoxical or super-eminent One immanently engenders
a procession of beings whose univocal sense it distributes, while they refer to
its power and have only a semblance of being. But in this case, what meaning is to be given to the Nietzschean program Deleuze constantly validates:
the overturning of Platonism? [ . . . ] Deleuzianism is fundamentally a
Platonism with a different accentuation. [ . . . ] it is necessary to affirm the
rights of simulacra *as so many equivocal cases of univocity* that joyously attest

to the univocal power of Being"(*Deleuze: The Clamour of Being*, p.26–7). Badiou's "reversal" of Deleuze is ironically Deleuzian, inasmuch as he attempts to produce a "mutant child" through this ventriloquism. Badiou's key suggestion is that simulacra are merely equivocal cases of univocity, ("simulacrum *of* Being") and so conform to a Neoplatonic metaphysics of expression in which the univocal One remains transcendent. This is the crucial point, and where Badiou broadens his critique to suggest Deleuze must sacrifice a real multiplicity in order to maintain a Univocal Being. As I shall argue however, for Deleuze the simulacrum is not *of* Being, but is being in its becoming. This implies, as we have already shown, that it is only in being constructed by will to power that "this" world expresses will to power. In other words, there is no Being apart from becoming, and there is no supplementary dimension to the plane of immanence (will to power) on which the One and the many, being and becoming are continually constructed and expressed. This expressive/constructive power of univocity Deleuze finds in Nietzsche is nothing but the power of the eternal return, where "Returning is being but only the being of becoming." (DR, 41/59) Éric Alliez has attempted his own "reversal" of Badiou's rejection of Deleuze's work with Guattari. Alliez argues: "Badiou erects an image of Deleuze as a metaphysician of the One, whose essential *monotony—in itself indifferent to differences,* subtracted as it is from the 'inexhaustible variety of the concrete' and from the anarchic confusion of the world—can and must cause us to dismiss the works co-authored with Félix Guattari, beginning with the *Anti-Oedipus.*" "The Politics of the *Anti-Oedipus*—Thirty Years On," in *Radical Philosophy,* no.124, march-april 2004. Alliez on the other hand, argues that Deleuzian philosophy becomes truly alive, becomes a "bio-politics" that overcomes his earlier "bio-philosophy," *after* Deleuze begins to work with Guattari. See "The BwO Condition or, The Politics of Sensation," in *Biographien des organlosen Körpers*.

33. "Overturning Platonism," Deleuze writes, "means denying the privacy of original over copy, of model over image; glorifying the reign of simulacra and reflections" (DR, 66/92).

34. Pierre Klossowski, *Nietzsche and the Vicious Circle*, p. 132. Klossowski goes on to say, "every authentic artist is conscious of producing something that is *false,* namely a *simulacrum.*" p. 223. Klossowski's book was very influential for Deleuze.

35. This is the problem with philosophers as opposed to artists, they don't know how to lie. As Nietzsche says about philosophers: "They know what they have to prove, they are practical in that—they recognise one another by their agreement over 'truths.'—'Thou shalt not lie'—in plain words: take care, philosopher, not to tell the truth . . ." (TI, "Expeditions of an Untimely Man," 42).

36. Of course, it is not only philosophers who become artists in these terms, as artists have often understood their work as simulacra. Van Gogh, for example,

who wrote: "I long most of all to learn how to produce those very aberrations, reworkings, transformations of reality, as may turn into, well—a lie if you like—but truer than the literal truth" (Vincent van Gogh, Letter to Theo, July 1885, *The Letters of Vincent van Gogh,* p. 307, translated by A. Pomerans, London: Penguin, 1996). Van Gogh's paintings are no doubt a good example of simulacrum, inasmuch as their agitated colors and brush strokes, their writhing lines and vibrant colors embody in an immediate materiality the vital life they affirm. Indeed van Gogh often seems to echo Nietzsche in his letters, affirming at one point the necessary connection of a vital art to a vital life. He writes to his sister Wils, "remember that what people demand in art nowadays is something very much alive, with strong colour and great intensity. So intensify your own health and strength and life, that's the best study" (letter, summer or autumn 1887, in *The Letters of Vincent van Gogh,* p. 337). Van Gogh's paintings are not representational but processual, a vital sensation appears in which crows, the sky, the shimmering golden wheat field are nothing but matter in movement, forces vibrating the world, a material world of which I am a part, and whose life appears only in the inhuman affirmation which interprets it. Jean-Clet Martin has discussed van Gogh's work in these terms: "The wall that Vincent dreamed of passing through, of patiently eroding, this was finally the limit separating inside from outside, the surface of the painting that turned its back on things. Now this border is over with, since the brain is becoming world even as life enters painting. The membrane separating the seen from the seer has opened up, absorbing things into the heart of the eye that contemplates them." "Of Images and Worlds: Towards a Geology of the Cinema," in *The Brain is a Screen: Gilles Deleuze and the Philosophy of Cinema,* p. 75.

37. Aesthetics becomes an "apodictic" discipline, Deleuze writes, "only when we apprehend directly in the sensible that which can only be sensed, the very being of the sensible: difference, potential difference and difference in intensity as the reason behind qualitative diversity. It is in difference that movement is produced as an 'effect,' that phenomena flash their meaning like signs" (DR, 56–7/79–80).

38. Deleuze's gloss on this passage is helpful, and also gives his rather ingenious interpretation of the Nietzschean eternal return *of the same.* "We misinterpret the expression 'eternal return' if we understand it as 'return of the same.' It is not being that returns but rather returning itself that constitutes being insofar as it is affirmed of becoming and of that which passes. It is not some one thing that returns but rather returning itself is the one thing that is affirmed of diversity or multiplicity. In other words, identity in the eternal return does not describe the nature of that which returns but, on the contrary, the fact of returning for that which differs" (NP, 48/55).

39. Nietzsche writes something similar; "it is always well to divorce an artist from his work, and to take him less seriously than *it.* He is, after all, only a condition of the work, the soil from which it grows, perhaps only the manure of

that soil. Thus he is, in most cases, something that must be forgotten if one wants to enter the full enjoyment of the work" (GM, III, 4).

40. This is the meaning of Nietzsche's affirmation of selection: "What does all art do? Does it not praise? Does it not highlight? By doing all of this it *strengthens* or *weakens* certain valuations. . . . Is this no more than incidental? An accident? Something in which the instinct of the artist has no part whatever? Or is it not the prerequisite for the artist being an artist at all . . . is his basic instinct directed towards the meaning of art, which is *life*? Towards *a desideratum of life*? Art is the great stimulus to life: how could it be thought purposeless, aimless, *l'art pour l'art*?" (TI, "Expeditions of an Untimely Man," 24). The artist selects, and in selecting makes things more beautiful. The problem is that with the artist, Nietzsche writes, "this subtle power usually comes to an end where art ends and life begins" (GS, 299). Thus, the problem of "art" is the selection of forces that overcome the artist as human, for as Nietzsche argues, "man becomes the transfigurer of existence when he learns to transfigure himself" (WtP, 820).

41. These paintings, almost always produced in series, begin with the *Marilyn* paintings (started in the month of her suicide), and continue with series of Liz Taylor (painted while she was critically ill), Jackie Kennedy, Elvis, car crashes, food poisoning (*Tunafish Disaster*), suicides (most famously the young woman lying on a car after jumping to her death from the Empire State building) and the first series of *Electric Chair* works, among others.

42. Paul Patton, for example, finds this unlikely, writing: "To the extent that Warhol's work still plays with the idea of representation, it is not the most appropriate aesthetic correlate to Deleuze's non-representational conception of thought" ("Anti-Platonism and Art," in *Gilles Deleuze and the Theatre of Philosophy*, p. 155).

43. Gilles Deleuze, "Cold and Heat," *Photogenic Painting, Gerard Fromanger*, p. 65.

44. On the intricate repetitions of the various *Elvis* paintings, see Raiji Kuroda, "Collapsing/Collapsed Discourse on Warhol, Regarding Two *Elvis* Series," *Andy Warhol 1956–86: Mirror of His Time*.

45. It is well known that most of these works were actually executed by Warhol's assistant at this time, Gerard Malanga. More to the point is Warhol's own affirmation of this process as "like a Factory would do it." Gretchen Berg, "'Nothing to Loose,' an interview with Andy Warhol." 1967, *Andy Warhol: A Factory*, unpaginated.

46. Andy Warhol, "Interview with Gene Swanson," *Art in Theory, 1900—1990, An Anthology of Changing Ideas*, p. 731, edited by C. Harrison and P. Wood, Oxford: Blackwell, 1992.

47. Interestingly enough, the exact number of the *Elvis* series is not known. See, Raiji Kuroda, "Collapsing/Collapsed Discourse on Warhol, Regarding Two *Elvis* Series," *Andy Warhol 1956–86: Mirror of His Time*.

48. A good example of this reading is Hal Foster, *The Return of the Real, The Avant-garde at the End of the Century.* Foster understands Warhol's simulacral series as a play of signifiers over an unsignifiable and traumatic Real.

49. As Warhol famously suggested: "If you want to know anything about Andy Warhol just look at the surface of my paintings and films and me, and there I am. There's nothing behind it." Gretchen Berg, "'Nothing to Loose,' an interview with Andy Warhol" (1967, *Andy Warhol. A Factory,* unpaginated).

50. Gretchen Berg, "'Nothing to Loose,' an interview with Andy Warhol."

51. See for example Thomas Crow's influential reading of these works as a humanist intervention by Warhol "in which the mass-produced image as the bearer of desires was exposed in its inadequacy by the reality of suffering and death." Deleuze, on the contrary, is arguing that mechanical repetition is entirely adequate to the eternal return as death. Thomas Crow, "Saturday Disasters: Trace and Reference in Early Warhol," *Reconstructing Modernism: Art in New York, Paris, and Montreal 1945–1964,* p. 318.

52. Although Elvis was obviously alive when the series bearing his name was created, the image itself is redolent with death. The film it advertises, *Flaming Star,* tells the story of a half Indian (Elvis) whose mother and father are killed in the course of conflict between Indians and whites. The title refers to the Indian belief that the "flaming star of death" is seen just before one dies, and in the film both Elvis and his mother utter the words: "I can see the flaming star of death." See Raiji Kuroda, "Collapsing/Collapsed Discourse on Warhol, Regarding Two *Elvis* Series," *Andy Warhol 1956–86: Mirror of His Time.* For a fascinating glimpse into the continued "life" of the simulacrum Elvis, after his "death," where "the shade of Elvis is now an anarchy of possibilities, a stain of freedom less clear, but no less suggestive than the man himself." see Griel Marcus, *Dead Elvis, A Chronicle of a Cultural Obsession,* p. xviii, New York: Doubleday, 1991.

53. Despite being published eighteen years later, Deleuze's description of Warhol's films in *Cinema 2* seems to echo *Difference and Repetition.* Deleuze discusses Warhol's films in terms of an "everyday theatricalization of the body," (C2, 192/249) or in the terms of *Difference and Repetition* "a veritable *theatre* of metamorphoses and permutations" (DR, 56/79). This does, perhaps, also suggest some continuities in Deleuze's approach in relation to our discussion here. Certainly, the appearance of Nietzsche in *Cinema 2,* in relation to cinema's "powers of the false" does echo many of the concerns of this chapter, and will be dealt with more fully in Chapter Three. It is interesting to note that while the term "simulacra" does fall out of Deleuze's vocabulary, he mentions the time-image's "*simulation*" in relation to cinema's power of the false, which carries a similar meaning (C2,148/194).

54. "[I]t is the masked," Deleuze writes, "the disguised or the costumed which turns out to be the truth of the uncovered" (DR, 24/37).

55. A "sign," Deleuze argues, expresses difference on one side, but on the other "tends to cancel it" (DR, 20/31). This two-sided aspect of the sign is developed by Deleuze, both in *Difference and Repetition* and in the article "How do we Recognise Structuralism?" in terms of "structure" and "structuralism." Deleuze argues that the differenciating element, which like death is what causes differences to repeat but is not itself given in the repetition, is the unimaginable element "object=x." This "object" "has no identity except in order to be displaced in relation to all places. As a result, for each order of structure the object=x is the empty or perforated site that permits this order to be articulated with the others, in a space that entails as many directions as orders. The orders of the structure do not communicate in a common site, but they all communicate through their empty place or respective object=x" (DR, 278/264). For Deleuze the meaning of structuralism and its series is found in this term without place animating any structure. This term is what lies "beneath" structuralism—namely nothing—because all structures are the repetition of the object=x in series. In this sense, a sense which has a good deal of historical precision, Pop art would be type of structuralism. But in *Anti-Oedipus*, Deleuze turns on structuralism and on one of its major figures, Jacques Lacan, and rejects both its negative ontology (as the expression of a real but *empty* place), its understanding of becoming in terms of serial structures, and its retention of a paradigm of signification.

56. Éric Alliez has explored this tension in Deleuze's work between that done before Guattari and that after—in terms of the concept of the BwO—in "The BwO Condition or, The Politics of Sensation," *Biographien des organlosen Körpers*.

57. This would also be one way to understand the move from Nietzsche to Spinoza as Deleuze's crucial philosophical reference. The question becomes less how to overcome man, than how man can become the God he *already is*. "A freeman thinks about nothing less than death," Spinoza writes, "and his knowledge is a meditation on life, not death" (*Ethics*, IV, p67).

58. "Cold and Heat," *Photogenic Painting, Gerhard Fromanger*, p. 65.

## NOTE TO CHAPTER TWO

1. Benedict de Spinoza, *The Ethics*, in *A Spinoza Reader*. All references to this book now found in the text according to the standard form. For example, the above quote is Ethics, V, P24. That is, *The Ethics*, book V, proposition 24. Definitions (D), demonstrations (d), colloquiums (c), scholia (s), appendix (App.), Lemma (L), and Preface (Pref.) also appear as abbreviations after quotations cited in the text.

2. Félix Guattari, "I Am God Most Of The Time," *Chaosophy*, p.51.

3. Walt Whitman, "Starting from Paumanok," *Selected Poems*, p.4. Toronto: Dover, 1991.

4.  The distinction between Substance, attributes and modes can be understood according to a scholastic distinction Spinoza sometimes employs. God expresses itself in itself as *natura naturans,* while expressing itself in its modes (produced within itself), as *natura naturata.* It is the attributes however, which articulate the absolute immanence of God's univocity, because the attributes as essence constitute the *natura naturans,* as well as being what is expressed by modes as *natura naturata.*

5.  Gilles Deleuze, *Seminar Session On Scholasticism and Spinoza,* 14 January 1974. Deleuze is often vehement in his opinion of Hegel: "What I detested more than anything else was Hegelianism and the Dialectic." quoted by Brian Massumi, "Translators Introduction" (ATP, 517).

6.  For a discussion of Hegel's reading of Spinoza in these terms, see, W. Montag, "Preface" to *The New Spinoza.* Also, Pierre Macherey, "The Problem of the Attributes," *The New Spinoza,* p.72–3. Alberto Toscano discusses "the compulsive ritual of exorcism which German philosophy had submitted itself to with regard to Spinozism." in "Fanaticism and Production: On Schelling's Philosophy of Indifference" in *Pli,* 8, 1999, p.47.

7.  Gilles Deleuze, *Seminar Session On Scholasticism and Spinoza,* 14 January 1974.

8.  Antonio Negri, in his important book *The Savage Anomaly* understands Spinoza's ontology in a similar way, writing: "There is no dialectic. Being is being, nonbeing is nothing. Nothing: phantasm, superstition, shadow. It is opposition. It is an obstacle of the constructive project" (p. 220). The mutual admiration of Negri and Deleuze, especially in relation to their respective work on Spinoza, is well known. Nevertheless differences and tensions between their readings exist, some of which will be the subject of further footnotes.

9.  Plato's metaphysics were revived in a neo-Platonism which emerged in the middle of the third century, and which dominated the ancient world till the beginning of the sixth. Its most important figure was Plotinus, whose lectures and notes were edited by Porphyry, and appeared as the *Enneads.* This tradition passed into Christianity through numerous thinkers, the most important being St. Augustine. Augustine's book *City of God* codified in Christian terms the rejection of the body and the embrace of the spirit he found in neo-Platonic mysticism. For an account of Augustine's relation to neo-Platonism see John D. O'Meara, *Studies in Augustine and Eringena.*

10.  Quoted in Phillip Goodchild, "Why is Philosophy so compromised with God?" *Deleuze and Religion,* p.165.

11.  As Deleuze explains Plotinus, "the One does not come out of itself in order to produce Being, because if it came out of itself it would become Two, but Being comes out of the One. This is the very formula of the *emanative* cause." *Seminar on Spinoza,* 25 November 1980. Deleuze also gives a brief account of neo-Platonism in LS, 255/294. It would be over the question of Spinoza's immanent/emanative Substance that Negri and Deleuze would

first part ways. Deleuze cannot allow for an emanative interpretation of Spinoza's Substance as this would lead to a pure expressionism, without the modal construction of Nature. Negri however, sees Spinoza's ontology as emanative, inasmuch as it remains within a pantheistic realm in which God is in Nature, but our mystical comprehension of God is limited to retracing his emanations. This implies a static divine rather than a God/Nature under construction, and is precisely what Deleuze seeks to avoid. "Spinozism," Negri writes, "resorted to mysticism, and through mysticism there re-emerged the old and always repeated pantheistic illusion of the immobility of being." *Time for Revolution*, p.214. Deleuze's reading of Spinoza's expressionism is directly oppossed to Negri's on this point. For Deleuze, expressionism would "free univocal Being from a state of indifference or neutrality, to make it the object of a pure affirmation, which is actually realized in an expressive pantheism or immanence" (EPS, 333/309).

12. Plotinus, quoted by Deleuze (EPS, 172/156).

13. The question of Deleuze-Spinoza's relation to Plotinus revolves around the relation of an emanative to an univocal ontology, and the structure of expressionism each involves. According to Deleuze, this relation is not always clear, for: "Expressive immanence is grafted onto the theme of emanation, which in part encourages it, and in part represses it" (EPS, 178/162, see also EPS, 171–2/155–6). Finally, however, Deleuze argues that emanation represses expressionism because it cannot do without a "minimal transcendence" (EPS, 180/163). Deleuze therefore distinguishes an emanative ontology/theology from a univocal and immanent one, and this is the distinction I will pursue in relation to Spinoza's "mysticism." As an interesting alternative account, Éric Alliez explores the confluences of Deleuze and Plotinus in *Capital Times: Tales from the Conquest of Time*, p.34–38.

14. Quoted in Jeremy R. Carrette, *Foucault and Religion, Spiritual Corporeality and Political Spirituality*, p.100. London: Routledge, 2000.

15. Quoted in Ray L. Hart, "God and Creature in the Eternity and Time of Nonbeing (or Nothing): Afterthinking Meister Eckhart," *The Otherness of God*, p.44. Eckhart's God is similar to Plotinus' One in this respect, that the One cannot be signified because it is "in truth beyond all statement" (*Enneads*, V, 5, 13). Quoted in Olivier Davies, "Thinking Difference, a comparative study of Gilles Deleuze, Plotinus and Meister Eckhart," *Deleuze and Religion*, p.77.

16. Michael Hardt has suggested a provocative atheist version of incarnation in these terms. "Incarnation," he writes, "is first of all a metaphysical thesis that the essence and the existence of being are one and the same. There is no ontological essence that resides beyond the world. None of being or God or Nature remains outside existence, but rather all is fully realized, fully expressed, without remainder, in the flesh." in "Exposure, Pasolini in the flesh," *A Shock to Thought, Expressionism after Deleuze and Guattari*, p.70. I shall return to this spiritual flesh in Chapter Six.

17. Gilles Deleuze, *Seminar Session on Spinoza,* 24 January 1978.
18. Fernando Pessoa, "The Keeper of Sheep," *The Poems of Fernando Pessoa,* p. 20. Translated and edited by E. Honig and S. Brown, San Fransisco: City Light Books, 1998. For Deleuze and Guattari on Pessoa's work see WP, 167/158. For a short account of Pessoa's relation to Deleuze and Guattari see Brian Massumi, "Deleuze and Guattari and the Philosophy of Expression," *Canadian Review of Comparative Literature,* p. 756–7.
19. For the story of Spinoza's relationship to the Jewish church, and the significance of his background as a Marrano Jew, see Yirmiyahu Yovel, *Spinoza and Other Heretics vol.2 The Adventures of Immanence.*
20. Gilles Deleuze, *Seminar Session on Spinoza,* 25 November 1980.
21. Negri, while acknowledging that atheism is the creative moment in Spinoza, nevertheless warns that it does not avoid "in a definitive manner" that point in the Judeo-Christian tradition where all experience is brought back to unity. "To expropriate God of its creativity is not decisive," he argues, "if we allow creativity to be defined still by the unity of the creative project. By doing so we make the divinity worldly but do not eliminate it." Spinoza's atheism would in this way remain within the Christian tradition in retaining "the ultimate defining characteristic of the religious concept of creativity." *Insurgencies, Constituent Power and the Modern State,* p. 308. This would not seem a problem for Deleuze, who does not claim Spinoza's creative atheism is not religious, but that creativity as such is the atheism proper to religion. Similarly, creativity does not remain unified in God, on Deleuze's account, because God's unity exists only in the necessary multiplicity of its creative movements. In terms of Negri's political concept of constituent power, the creativity of Spinoza's multitude is restricted by its retention of an ideal unity in and as God. For Deleuze however, and as we shall see, this is not a restriction because God's ideal unity is nothing but the immanence of God in the multiplicity of modes. In other words, it is not a question of unity but of immanence. It is God's immanence that is articulated through creativity, understood as the genetic process in which God is constructed (becoming), as it is expressed (being). The creative project would be *both* unified and multiple on this account.
22. Gilles Deleuze, *Seminar Session on Spinoza,* 25 November, 1980. Deleuze and Guattari will extend this idea to philosophy, writing that: "Perhaps Christianity does not produce concepts except through its atheism" (WP, 92/88).
23. Art as creation therefore defines both Nietzsche and Spinoza's atheism, just as it defines their mysticism. I did not develop an argument for Nietzsche's atheistic mysticism in the previous chapter, although I believe it lies implicit in much that I wrote there. It seems to me that the critical expression/ construction of will to power, and the power of the false it implies and embodies in the simulacra, involves an atheistic mysticism which culminates in, and finds its proper name as, art. As Nietzsche wrote, this is: "An art so divine, so

infernally divine. . . ." (*The Antichrist*, 61). Of course, this common project of Nietzsche and Spinoza is marked by highly divergent means, and it hardly needs pointing out that Nietzsche's atheism will involve the death of God, while Spinoza's involves his true understanding, as what we already are.

24. Deleuze's formulation of Spinoza's immanent and expressive God, or Deity, finds explicit echoes in Alfred North Whitehead's "process" philosophy. For an interesting comparison of Deleuze and Whitehead framed in terms of the emanative/immanent relation I have already discussed, see Arnaud Villani, "Deleuze et Whitehead," in *Revue de Metaphysique et de Morale*, No.2, 1996. For Deleuze on Whitehead see TF, 76–82/103–12.

25. In *A Thousand Plateaus* Deleuze and Guattari offer a similar reading of Spinoza, this time through the intercession of Antonin Artaud. They argue that the BwO is an unformed matter with an "intensity = 0" (ATP, 153/189) and thus conforms to the "qualitative identity of the absolute" (EPS, 197/180) Deleuze finds in Spinoza's Substance. The BwO is modified in quantitative individuations measured as intensities, and expressed in actual bodies and ideas (we will see that Deleuze reads Spinoza in precisely these terms). This implies a single plane of immanence, the BwO, as a univocal being which is continually becoming in its intensive individuations. "The body without organs," Deleuze and Guattari write, "is the immanent substance, in the most Spinozist sense of the word; and the partial objects are like its ultimate attributes" (AO, 327/390). The BwO therefore seems to specifically reply to Deleuze's initial objection about Spinoza's ontology, inasmuch as it, "effectively goes beyond any opposition between the one and the multiple. [ . . . ] There is a continuum of all the attributes or genus's of intensity under a single substance, and a continuum of the intensities of a certain genus under a single type or attribute. A continuum of all substances in intensity and of all intensities in substance. The uninterrupted continuum of the BwO. BwO, immanence, immanent limit"(ATP, 154/191).

26. Gilles Deleuze, *Negotiations, 1972–1990*. This "identity" is elaborated in Deleuze's discussions of Nietzsche and Spinoza's shared devaluation of consciousness and morality, and their shared atheism. See SPP, chapter 2, NP, 39/44–5, and in Deleuze's discussion of the affect as an immanent evaluation in C2, 141/184–5.

27. Thomas Bernhard, *Extinction*, p. 188, translated by D. McLintock, London: Penguin, 1996.

28. Artaud and Spinoza seem on the face of it an unlikely combination, but for Deleuze they both reconstruct the body outside of God's judgement. "The *judgement of God*," Deleuze and Guattari write, "the system of the judgement of God, the theological system, is precisely the operation of He who makes an organism, an organisation of organs called the organism, because He cannot bear the BwO" (ATP, 158–9/196–7). Artaud's BwO is Spinoza's God/Nature, Spinoza's *Ethics* being, they say, "the great book of the BwO"

(ATP, 153/190). The ethical question for both is the same, "How Do You Make Yourself A Body Without Organs?" We will pick up this question again in Chapter Six.

29.  This Spinozian body of affect is developed by Deleuze and Guattari in *A Thousand Plateaus*. "A body," they write, "is not defined by the form that determines it nor as a determinate substance or subject nor by the organs it possesses or the functions it fulfils. On the plane of consistency, *a body is defined only by a longitude and a latitude:* in other words the sum total of the material elements belonging to it under given relations of movement and rest, speed and slowness (longitude); the sum total of the intensive affects it is capable of at a given power or degree of potential (latitude). Nothing but affects and local movements, differential speeds. The credit goes to Spinoza for calling attention to these two dimensions of the Body, and for having defined the plane of Nature as pure longitude and latitude. Latitude and longitude are the two elements of a cartography" (ATP, 260–1/318). Bodies are material flows distinguished by their movement and speed, and to which corresponds a degree of power that determines bodies' power to act. The body is always in movement, not just in material and intense transformations, but also on a plane which is itself alive with the vital movements of nonorganic life. Longitude and latitude give us a cartography to understand the becoming of affect, and the essential affectual capacities available to a given material assemblage. This capacity or power gives a "mode of individuation" (ATP, 261/318) very different from a person, subject, thing or substance. Deleuze and Guattari call this mode of individuation a "haecceity," which "consists entirely of relations of movement and rest between molecules or particles, capacities to affect and be affected" (ATP, 261/318).

30.  Deleuze argues that an idea's formal reality, its reality as an idea in itself is "the thing the idea is or the degree of reality or perfection it possesses in itself, [and] is its intrinsic character." In other words this is its essence and expresses God. Gilles Deleuze, *Seminar Session of Spinoza,* 24 January 1978.

31.  Gilles Deleuze, *Session on Spinoza,* 13 January 1981.

32.  Gilles Deleuze, *Seminar Session of Spinoza,* 24 January 1978.

33.  Gilles Deleuze and Claire Parnet, *Dialogues,* p.11. (*Dialogues,* p.18)

34.  See Gilles Deleuze, *Seminar Session of Spinoza,* 24 January 1978.

35.  Spinoza's attack on representation implied by his concept of univocity is also a direct attack upon orthodox theological models. These assumed 1) an equivocal model of being, where God is unrepresentable and yet more real than his earthly representations, and so assumes a different sort of being, or 2) an analogical model where God's being is different from ours, but is understood through a process of analogy, for example God being to man as man is to an art. Theologies of equivocity and analogy both require representation as their theoretical mechanism, although analogy became the orthodox Christian position, as formulated by Thomas Aquinas, because it assured a

common measure and hence a comprehensibility to the otherness of God. In being anti-representational a Spinozian theory of art will break with these orthodox theologies, to become atheist in the terms we have already discussed.

36. For Deleuze's account of the role of analogy in representation, see DR, 137–8/179–80.

37. Gilles Deleuze, *Session on Spinoza,* 13 January 1981.

38. Gilles Deleuze, *Session on Spinoza,* 13 January 1981. "The opposition of expressions and signs is one of the fundamental principles of Spinozism" (EPS, 181–2/165).

39. Gilles Deleuze, *Seminar Session On Scholasticism and Spinoza,* 14 January 1974, italics added.

40. Pierre Macherey, "The Problem of the Attributes," *The New Spinoza,* p.89.

41. Gilles Deleuze, *Seminar on Spinoza,* 13 January 1981.

42. Antonio Negri regards this final moment of Spinoza's *Ethics* as the point where his "asceticism" imposes on univocity a separation of the divine from life that denies a total immanence of being and becoming. Spinoza's asceticism, Negri argues, "forms an image of beatitude that, in separating itself from the production of desire touches upon the notion of beatitude without appropriating it" (*Time for Revolution,* p.187). This argument takes us back to Deleuze's "correction" of Spinoza through Nietzsche in *Difference and Repetition.* Indeed, one could imagine the difference between Deleuze and Negri on this point in the same terms as the difference between *Difference and Repetition* and Deleuze's later work. Accordingly, Negri's appeal to the "void" in *Time for Revolution* as being that with which being confronts itself in its processes of becoming echoes Deleuze's use of "death" and the "object=x" in *Difference and Repetition* as the genetic element in the repetition of difference. As we have seen, however, Deleuze abandons these terms in turning Spinoza away from the problem of the separation of Substance from the modes, and towards the entirely productive plane of immanence where the construction of Substance is immanent with its expression. Obviously a full discussion of the relation of Negri's work to Deleuze's, and visa versa, is outside the scope of this book. For a first approach to this question however, see Kenneth Surin, "Reinventing a Physiology of Collective Liberation," Going 'beyond Marx' in the Marxism(s) of Negri, Guattari, and Deleuze." *Rethinking Marxism,* 7 (1994).

43. There is of course, a strong tradition of love-mysticism which constitutes a transversal line finding religious, philosophical and literary expression. To gesture at Spinoza's connection to it is all that can be done here, although it would be a fascinating line for further research. For example, Hadewijch of Antwerp writes of the feminine and loving God: "If they love her (love) with the vigour of love, they will soon be one with love in love" (Hadewijch of Antwerp, *Strophic Poems*) To continue this gesture forward, it also speaks in Henry Miller's words: "Everything stands in a certain way in a certain place,

as our minds stands in relation to God. The world, in its visible, tangible
Substance, is a map of our love. Not God but life is love. Love, love, love"
(Henry Miller, *The Tropic of Capricorn*, p.222–3, London: BCA, 1982). Love
is also the culminating state of vital mysticism for Bergson, which he coun-
terposed to the religion of the church. He writes of the mystic that, "the love
which consumes him is no longer simply the love of man for God, it is the
love of God for all men. Through God, in the strength of God, he loves all
mankind with divine love" (Henri Bergson, *The Two Sources of Religion and
Morality*, p.199). Finally, we might add Deleuze himself to this abstract line
of love mysticism, who in the third kind of knowledge finds, "the love of a
God who is himself joyful, who loves himself and loves us with the same love
by which we love him" (EPS, 309/288).
44.  Michael Hardt, *Gilles Deleuze: An Apprenticeship in Philosophy*, p.108.

## NOTES TO CHAPTER THREE

1.  Henri Bergson, *Matter and Memory*, references to this book now found in the
    text following the abbreviation "MM."
2.  The philosophical implications of this universal variation are, at least as
    Deleuze explains them, by now familiar to us: "What in effect is duration?"
    Deleuze asks, "Everything that Bergson says about duration always comes
    back to this: *duration is what differs from itself*." "Bergson's conception of dif-
    ference," *The New Bergson*, p. 48. ("La conception de la différence chez
    Bergson," *L'île Déserte et Autres Textes 1953–1974*, p. 51)
3.  Deleuze's ontological valorisation of cinema, while being entirely
    Bergsonian, runs contra to Bergson's own theory of the "cinematographical
    mechanism." Bergson argued that cinematic images operate in the same way
    as conscious perception. Consciousness, he claimed, converts the movement
    of duration into a "series of snapshots," and throws them on a screen "so that
    they replace each other very rapidly" (*Creative Evolution*, p. 305, all refer-
    ences to this book now found in the text following the abbreviation "CE").
    As an example of natural perception Bergson thought the cinema could only
    give an image of movement which was a fast succession of frozen attitudes.
    "Whether we would think becoming, or express it, or even perceive it,"
    Bergson argues, "we hardly do anything else than set going a kind of cine-
    matograph inside us. We may therefore sum up what we have been saying in
    the conclusion that the *mechanism of our ordinary knowledge is of a cinemato-
    graphical kind*" (CE, 306). Deleuze reverses Bergson's view, arguing that
    movement belongs to cinema's image directly, not added from "above" as the
    general conditions of natural perception. Cinema, according to Deleuze,
    "immediately gives us a movement-image. It does give us a section, but a sec-
    tion which is mobile, not an immobile section + abstract movement" (C1,
    2/11). Deleuze finds Bergson's ontology so thoroughly cinematic that he

claims: "Even in his critique of the cinema Bergson was in agreement with it" (C1, 58/85). This rather odd statement is justified, Deleuze argues, by the fact that Bergson's critique is premised on his philosophy of the movement-image found "in the brilliant first chapter of *Matter and Memory*" (C1, 58/85). Deleuze insists on *Matter and Memory* as an initial affirmation of cinema counteracting Bergson's later rejection of it. Deleuze's insistence on the early Bergson is both an implicit critique of Bergson's retreat from the possibility of perceiving duration and his re-emphasis of a stable perceptual mechanism in *Creative Evolution*. For a discussion of Bergson's relation to cinema see Paul Douglas, "Bergson and Cinema: Friends or Foes?," *The New Bergson*. On the Deleuze-Bergson relation in the cinema books see, Gregory Flaxman, "Cinema Year Zero," *The Brain is the Screen, Deleuze and the Philosophy of Cinema*.

4. The reference is, of course, to Guy Debord's *Society of the Spectacle*. (Translated by D. Nicholson-Smith, New York: Zone Books, 1995). Debord also proposes an aesthetic of temporal contestation: "The point is to take effective possession of the community of dialogue, and the playful relationship to time, which the works of the poets and artists have heretofore merely *represented*" (section 187). Like Deleuze, Debord affirms the political necessity of re-inserting art into the everyday, placing creation back into the midst of life. Debord however, understands this reinsertion through the operation of the Hegelian dialectic. "Culture," he writes, "is the locus of the search for lost unity. In the course of this search culture as a separate sphere is obliged to negate itself" (section 180). For Deleuze, as we shall see, the separation of art and life has always been produced through false assumptions. In Bergson Deleuze finds an ontology of cinema capable of affirming its coexistence with life itself.

5. The phrase is Bergon's (CE, 319).

6. Zeno's paradoxes show how our rational concept of movement is inadequate because it conflates duration and extention, which are in fact different in kind (See B, 22/12). Bergson discusses Zeno's paradoxes in CE, 308–313.

7. "*Intuition* is the method of Bergsonism" (B, 13/1), Deleuze argues, and is the conceptual method adequate to time because it presupposes duration, "it consists in thinking in terms of duration" (B, 31/22). Deleuze develops the methodology of intuition at length in *Bergsonism*.

8. Gilles Deleuze, "Bergson's conception of difference," *The New Bergson*, p. 46. ("La conception de la différence chez Bergson," *L'île Déserte et Autres Textes 1953–1974*, p. 49)

9. The ontological status of this open "whole" of duration is another of the stakes in Alain Badiou's dispute with Deleuze. Deleuze explicitly distinguishes the "whole" from sets, writing: "The whole and the 'wholes' must not be confused with *sets*. Sets are closed, and everything which is closed is artificially closed. [ . . . ] The whole is not a closed set, but on the contrary that

by virtue of which the set is never absolutely closed, never completely shel-
tered, that which keeps it open by the finest thread which attaches it to the
rest of the universe" (C1, 10/21). Following his quotation of the latter part
of the above passage Badiou succinctly presents one of his major objections
to Deleuze. For him there is a problem with "this providential marking as to
the theory of the two—the virtual and the actual—parts of the object: it
sorely puts univocity to the test, by directly assigning the chance of thought
to a discernible *division* of its objects. It would seem that it is not very easy
to definitively abandon the presuppositions of the dialectic" (*Deleuze: The
Clamour of Being*, p. 85). Badiou sees the Deleuzian whole (duration) as transcending the actual, and as with his reading of Deleuze's simulacra, as rein-
stating a type of Platonism. This is precisely, as I hope to show, what Deleuze
attempts to avoid in his reading of Bergson. Badiou, in contrast to Deleuze,
understands the multiple (duration in Deleuze's Bergsonian terms) as a multiplicity of actual or closed sets whose becoming is generated not by their
opening onto each other in the "open" universe of duration, but by opening
onto the void. The creative properties of the event are therefore generated by
the disjunctive and genetic power of the void's radical exteriority. For Badiou,
"immanence excluded the All and the only possible end point of the multiple, which is always the multiple of multiples (and never the multiple of
Ones), was the multiple of nothing: the empty set" (*Deleuze: The Clamour of
Being*, p. 46). Finally, Badiou presents his opposition to Deleuze as, "for me,
multiplicities 'were' sets, for him, they 'were not'" (*Deleuze: The Clamour of
Being*, p. 48) Badiou elaborates his argument with Deleuze over the ontology
of set theory in, "Gilles Deleuze: The Fold: Leibniz and the Baroque," *Gilles
Deleuze and the Theatre of Philosophy*, and in 'One, Multiple, Multiplicities,'
*Theoretical Writings*.

10.  This is a phrase of Deleuze's, "The Brain is the Screen: an interview with
     Gilles Deleuze," *The Brain is the Screen, Deleuze and the Philosophy of
     Cinema*, p. 366.

11.  Or as Bergson has it: "Our sun radiates heat and light beyond the farthest
     planet. And, on the other hand, it moves in a certain fixed direction, draw-
     ing with it the planets and their satellites. The thread attaching it to the rest
     of the universe is doubtless very tenuous. Nevertheless it is along this thread
     that is transmitted down to the smallest particle of the world in which we live
     the duration immanent to the whole of the universe"(CE, 11).

12.  Against realism and idealism, Bergson argues, "it is a mistake to reduce mat-
     ter to the perception which we have of it, a mistake also to make of it a thing
     able to produce in us perceptions, but in itself is of another nature than they.
     Matter, in our view, is an aggregate of 'images.' And by 'image' we mean a
     certain existence which is more than that which the idealist calls a *represen-
     tation,* but less than that which the realist calls a *thing*—an existence placed
     halfway between the 'thing' and the 'representation.' This conception of

matter is simply that of common sense. [ . . . ] For common sense, then, the object exists in itself, and, on the other hand, the object is, in itself, pictorial, as we perceive it: image it is, but a self-existing image" (MM, 9–10). Further on, Bergson argues that perceptions of things-images in the eye are "vibrations of light." This means, "there is no essential difference" between "light and movements" (MM, 41).

13. This ontological movement is also found in images produced by other art forms. Indeed, Deleuze argues, around the same time as cinema's birth the other arts, "even painting, were abandoning figures and poses to release values which were not posed, not measured, and which related movement to the any-instant-whatever" (C1, 6–7/16). Painting explored the movement of matter through its experimentations with color, especially the work of Robert Delauney which drew on contemporary scientific theories of color as a radiant energy. This energetic-materialist theory of color rejected painting's representational function for an exploration of the vibrations produced by the simultaneous contrast of colors. Building on the scientific work done by Eugene Chevreuil, Delauney, Deleuze writes, discovered the different movements of sun and moon light, "one constituting a circular, continuous movement of complementary colors, the other a faster and uneven movement of jarring, iridescent colors, the two together making up and projecting an eternal mirage on to the earth" (C2, 11/20, see also 282–3/20). Delauney then, like cinema, constructs images in which light is movement. This has implications for painting similar to those Deleuze finds for cinema. Color is stripped of any representational function (as Godard so famously stated, "it's not blood it's red") and revalues the action of the eye, which now constructs a material vibratory thread enveloping brain and world. (Delauney explicitly claims this for his work in "On the Construction of Reality in Pure Painting" *Art in Theory 1900–1990, An Anthology of Changing Ideas*.) Guillaume Appollinaire explains the materialist aesthetics of Delauney rather well, writing in 1913: "Color is saturated with energy and its outmost points are prolonged in space. Here it is the medium which is the reality. Color no longer depends on the three known dimensions; it is color which creates them" (*The Cubist Painters: Aesthetic Meditations,* p. 45., translated by L. Abel, New York: Wittenborn Schultz Inc., 1945). In its materialism Delauney's painting shares an ontological ground with cinema, and his exploration of simultaneous contrasts was influential, Deleuze claims, on the pre-war French school of film-makers, which "owes much to Delauney's colorism" (C1 ,45/72). As do the films of Jacques Rivette (C2, 11/20). Painting and cinema therefore both develop a movement-image, each in their own medium. This shared ontology nevertheless admits, and indeed requires, distinctions between the arts according to their modalities of expression—cinema at this time was not concerned with color for example. As a result, each art form will require a taxonomy specific to it. This is entirely consistent with Deleuze's Bergsonian

understanding of duration as a multiplicity, which is neither indivisible nor immeasurable, but whose division implies a change in nature, each division in turn implying a change in the metrical principle of its measure (B, 40/31–2, and ATP, 483/604).

14. For Bergson, perception "limits itself to the objects which actually influence our organs and prepare our movements" (MM, 179).

15. As we shall see, Deleuze uses this initial "strength" of Peirce, while also pointing out the ways in which Peirce himself departs from it. Indeed, Deleuze says: "Peirce can sometimes find himself as much a linguist as the semiologists" (C2, 31/46). In fact, Deleuze will argue that Peirce finally makes of the sign something linguistic, because no "material that cannot be reduced to an utterance survives, and hence [Peirce] reintroduces a subordination of semiotics to a language system" (C2, 31/46). As a result, Deleuze (and Guattari) will, as they say, "borrow his terms, even while changing their connotations" (ATP, 531/177).

16. Charles S. Peirce, *76 Definitions of the Sign,* 5 (Collected Papers 7–356).

17. Charles S. Peirce, *76 Definitions of the Sign,* 16 (MS-599).

18. Charles S. Peirce, *76 Definitions of the Sign,* 4 (MS-380).

19. Peirce describes it as "a state of mind in which something is present, without compulsion and without reason; it is called *Feeling.*" "What is a Sign?," *The Essential Peirce, Selected Philosophical Writings, Vol. 2 (1893–1913),* p. 4.

20. Charles S. Peirce, "What is a Sign?," *The Essential Peirce, Selected Philosophical Writings, Vol. 2 (1893–1913),* p. 5.

21. Deleuze extends Peirce's model in applying it to the cinema, by adding transitional images moving from affection to action (the impulse-image) and from action to relation (the reflection-image). Thus Deleuze identifies six types of images, each of which are organised in an opposition reflecting the two sides of the sensory-motor interval, but which also have a genetic aspect reflecting their genesis in the "ground zero" of the perception image. The six types of visible movement images and their compositional and genetic signs are listed by Deleuze "in partial conformity with Pierce" (C1, 142/198), as the Perception-image (Dicisign, Reume, Gramme), Affection-image (Icon of power, Icon of quality, Qualisign), the Impulse-image (Fetish, Idol, Symptom), Action-image SAS (Synsign, Binomial, Imprint), and ASA (Index of lack, Index of equivocity, Vector), Reflection-image (Figures of attraction, Figures of inversion, Discursive sign), Relation-image (Mark, Demark, Symbol) (See also C2, 32/48). The nature of this "partial conformity" can be seen in comparing the distinctions of Deleuze's schema with those Peirce makes in "Sundry Logical Conceptions," and "Nomenclature and Divisions of Triadic Relations," *The Essential Peirce, Selected Philosophical Writings, Vol. 2 (1893–1913).*

22. Deleuze is here referring to his earlier discussion of the relation of the "open whole" of duration as plane of consistency to the artificial closure of sets (see note 9). We will see in what ways classical cinema was able to open its montaged sets, and reattach a thread connecting them to the universe.

23. Both techniques appear in *Man with a Movie Camera.*
24. Jonathan Bellor has developed Deleuze's reading of Vertov in interesting ways, especially his suggestion that Vertov's material consciousness is a cinematic answer to the soviet problem of 'self-conscious democracy' (p. 165). "Dziga Vertov and the Film of Money," *Boundary 2,* 26.3, 1999.
25. This is an echo of Peirce, who describes it as a "Feeling." Charles S. Peirce, "What Is a Sign?" *The Essential Peirce, Selected Philosophical Writings, Vol. 2 (1893–1913),* p. 4.
26. Charles S. Peirce, "Sundry Logical Conceptions," *The Essential Peirce, Selected Philosophical Writings, Vol. 2 (1893–1913),* p. 268–9.
27. We should note here a change in Deleuze's terminology. In relation to Spinoza, and in *A Thousand Plateaus,* as we have seen, "affection" (*affectio*) is a state of the body as it is affected by another body, and an "affect" (*affectus*) is the passage from one state to another as this indicates the increase or decrease of a bodies power. In the Cinema books "affection" and "affect" are known as "perception-image" and "affection-image," while "affect" refers to qualities or powers extracted from affections and treated as pure, autonomous, "possibles."
28. Charles S. Peirce, "What Is a Sign?," *The Essential Peirce, Selected Philosophical Writings, Vol. 2 (1893–1913),* p. 5.
29. Once again Deleuze focuses on montage as the creative mechanism of Dreyer's affectual film. Dreyer, Deleuze notes, avoids the shot-reverse shot constructions which tend to establish subjective relations, in favour of the "virtual conjunction" of "flowing close-ups" (C1, 107/152). This enables him to focus on the intensive affects of the face as the real "subjects" of the film.
30. The reasons for this breakdown, Deleuze argues, were "the war and its consequences, the unsteadiness of the 'American Dream' in all its aspects, the new consciousness of minorities, the rise and inflation of images both in the external world and in people's minds, the influence on the cinema of the new modes of narrative with which literature had experimented, the crises of Hollywood and its old genres. . . ." (C1, 206/278). We may wonder at the telegraphic nature of this sentence, which contains almost the entirety of Deleuze's historical contextualisation of cinema's production of time-images. But Deleuze's purpose is not to provide a historical reading of the time-image, but a symptomatic one. Deleuze, in other words, is not so much interested in showing how the world affects cinema, but to show how cinema remakes the world.
31. As Michael Goddard has pointed out, "while mysticism is not referred to explicitly by Deleuze in his works on cinema, the centrality of the crystalline regime, and its operation of opening to a direct image of time and of the virtual, is a parallel process to the mystical metamorphosis of subjectivity identified by Bergson." "The scattering of time crystals: Deleuze, mysticism, and cinema," *Deleuze and Religion,* p. 62.

32.  Henri Bergson, *The Two Sources of Morality and Religion*, p. 201.

33.  Henri Bergson, *The Two Sources of Morality and Religion*, p. 188. This cre-
     ative life is what Bergson calls in *Creative Evolution* life's "intention." "This
     intention," Bergson argues, "is just what the artist tries to regain, in placing
     himself back with the object by a kind of sympathy, in breaking down, by an
     effort of intuition, the barrier that space puts up between him and his model.
     It is true that this aesthetic intuition, like external perception, only attains
     the individual. But we can conceive an inquiry turned in the same direction
     as art, which would take life *in general* for its object."

34.  Henri Bergson, *The Two Sources of Morality and Religion*, p. 217.

35.  Henri Matisse, *Matisse on Art*, p. 217. J. Flam ed., Berkeley: University of
     California Press, 1995. For Matisse's Bergsonian approach to painting see,
     "Notes of a Painter" (1908) in the same volume.

36.  This introduces a theme which often appears in Deleuze's discussions of art,
     a new tactility of the image. This tactile image marks the transition from an
     "optical," or sensory-motor regime of signs, to "haptic" signs, from the ab-
     straction of representation to the reality of sensation. As we have seen, this
     materialism is a necessary part of Deleuze's aesthetics. Deleuze takes the dis-
     tinction of optic and haptic from the art historian Alois Riegl, and we will
     return to it in chapters 4 and 6. The haptic "flesh" of the time-image is briefly
     explored in *Cinema 2* in terms Deleuze also employs in other contexts, "it is
     the tactile which can constitute a pure sensory image," he writes, "on condi-
     tion that the hand relinquishes its prehensile and motor functions to content
     itself with a pure touching. [ . . . ] The hand then, takes on a role in the image
     which goes infinitely beyond the sensory-motor demands of the action,
     which takes the place of the face itself for the purpose of the affects, and
     which in the area of perception, becomes the mode of construction of a space
     which is adequate to the decisions of spirit. [ . . . ] The hand doubles its pre-
     hensile function (of object) by a connective function (of space); but, from
     that moment, it is the whole eye which doubles its optical function by a
     specifically 'grabbing' [*haptique*] one, if we follow Riegl's formula for indicat-
     ing a touching which is specific to the gaze" (C2, 12–13/22). The haptic, in
     other words, defines a space of sensation in which the sensory-motor distinc-
     tion does not operate, and the question is not so much that of perception by
     the eye, but of a construction of space by the hand, a "touching" in which
     subject and object merge. This question will be taken up and discussed at
     length in Chapter Six.

37.  Here Deleuze closely follows the work of Andre Bazin, whose name appears
     in the first sentence of *Cinema 2*. Deleuze takes from Bazin what he de-
     scribes as the "fundamental requirement of formal aesthetic criteria" in
     order to define the ontological break in cinema initiated by Italian neo-re-
     alism (although Bazin understands this in phenomenological rather than
     Bergsonian terms). Deleuze follows these criteria and expands them beyond

a strict definition of neo-realism to later Italian directors, and further to European cinema after the war, in defining an aesthetics of time-images.

38.  It is at this point that Deleuze refers to Bergson's famous "cone" diagram (MM, 162). There Bergson writes of the "double current" which goes from actual image to the 'thousand individual images' which are its virtual equivalent in memory, and which are 'always ready to *crystallize* into uttered words" (MM, 162, italics added). For Deleuze's more detailed discussion of this diagram see B, 57–62/53–7.

39.  "Perhaps," Deleuze suggests, "when we read a book, watch a show, or look at a painting, and especially when we are ourselves the author, an analogous process can be triggered [ . . . to] extract non-chronological time. [ . . . ] it is possible for the work of art to succeed in inventing these paradoxical hypnotic and hallucinatory sheets whose property is to be at once a past and always to come" (C2, 123/161–2).

40.  We see here that although Deleuze abandons the concept of the "simulacra," its disappearance is only nominal, and it is still in operation in *Cinema 2* as cinema's "power of the false."

41.  Deleuze conflates direct cinema with *cinema verite* at this point, discussing them, or at least their representative directors Don Pennebaker and Jean Rouch separately, but arguing they both achieve a cinematic constructivism in which distinctions between truth and falsity are dissolved in the process of constructing images, to the point of including the construction of the film itself. Construction becomes the "subject" of the film. For a more traditional reading, which attempts to make a rigorous distinction between "direct" cinema and *cinema verite*, see Bill Nichols, *Representing Reality, Issues and Concepts in Documentary*, p. 32–75, Bloomington: Indiana University Press, 1991.

42.  The proof of this is that the least convincing scene of *Hier Strauss* (at least as far as its "reality" is concerned) is that in which we find Strauss at home, reading the paper, the static nature of both action and camera ironically re-establishing our exteriority at exactly the moment when the "true" Strauss supposedly emerges.

43.  Deleuze suggests this when he writes, "the power of the false cannot be separated from an irreducible multiplicity" (C2, 133/174).

44.  This formulation comes from Éric Alliez, who has suggested that Deleuze finds in the Cinema books, a "*Bergsonism beyond Bergson* [ . . . ] a Bergsonism projected beyond the caesura between the metaphysical intuition of life and the philosophy of the concept, cleansed of any spiritualism of presence." "Midday, Midnight: The Emergence of Cine-Thinking," *The Brain is a Screen: Gilles Deleuze and the Philosophy of Cinema*, p. 295 and 297. Deleuze himself suggests such a projection of Bergson when he claims his "return to Bergson" is "a renewal or an extension of his project today" (B, 115, afterword to the English translation).

45. I have developed Deleuze's figure of the "spiritual automaton" in relation to Artaud and the films of Carl Theodor Dreyer in "Believing in the BwO: Artaud-Deleuze-Dreyer," *Biographien des organlosen Körpers,* edited by E. Samsanow and E. Alliez, Vienna: Turia+Kant, 2003.

46. At one point she explains that her doctor told her she must love her husband, her son, her job or her dog, but not husband-son-job-dog. To anticipate the next chapter, Giuliano's schizophrenia is a form of visionary mysticism.

47. Quoted in Peter Bondanella, *Italian Cinema, From Neorealism to the Present,* p. 219, London and New York: Continuum, 2002.

48. Gilles Deleuze, *Negotiations 1972–1990,* p. 145.

49. Quoted in Bondanello, *Italian Cinema,* p. 220.

50. Gilles Deleuze, 'Bergson's conception of difference,' *The New Bergson,* p. 48. ('La conception de la différence chez Bergson,' *L'île Déserte et Autres Textes 1953–1974,* p. 51)

## NOTES TO CHAPTER FOUR

1. The first part of the title comes from DR, 293/375. The epitaph is from John Dewey, *Art as Experience,* p. 82.

2. For a good account of Deleuze and Guattari's theory of the content-expression relation, see Brian Massumi, *A User's Guide to Capitalism and Schizophrenia, Deviations from Deleuze and Guattari,* chapter 2 "Force."

3. Brian Massumi leaves both terms untranslated in *A Thousand Plateaus.*

4. As Guattari puts it: "The signifying machine was based on the system of representation." "The Place of the Signifier in the Institution," *The Guattari Reader,* p. 151.

5. Deleuze and Guattari write that Hjelmslev was "the only linguist to have actually broken with the signifier and signified" (ATP, 523/85). Guattari in particular has worked extensively on Hjelmslev. See, Félix Guattari, "Semiological Subjection, Semiotic Enslavement," and "The Place of the Signifier in the Institution," *The Guattari Reader.*

6. Deleuze and Guattari draw heavily on the work of Michel Foucault in their account of abstract machines and their diagrammatic operation. Foucault, they say, showed the way for a diagrammatic analysis of history, inasmuch as he gave a "machinic" understanding of power that encompassed both its "minitiarized mechanisms, or molecular focuses" (ATP, 537/265), and their composition in "assemblages of power, or micropowers" (ATP, 531/175). These actual assemblages were singularities of an abstract 'diagram' or "a 'biopolitics of population' as an abstract machine" (ATP, 531/175). Although Deleuze and Guattari give a favourable account of Foucault's method they also point out their differences from it by emphasising the way the diagram functions to create a new reality. Foucault's analysis, in assuming the priority of power relegates creative forces to reactions to power, and

so makes creation relative to the power of the strata. "Our only points of dis-agreement with Foucault are the following," they write, "(1) to us the assemblages seem fundamentally to be assemblages not of power but of desire (desire is always assembled), and power seems to be a stratified dimension of the assemblage; (2) the diagram and abstract machine have lines of flight that are primary, which are not phenomena of resistance or counterattack in an assemblage, but cutting edges of creation and deterritorialisation" (ATP, 531/176). This is, in fact, a fundamental re-orientation of the Foucauldian model, one which assumes the power of absolute deterritorialisation as immanent to every relative deterritorialisation, and therefore makes creation "prior to" power, and operating as its condition. As Deleuze writes elsewhere, "desire is but one with a given assemblage, a co-functioning" ("Désir et Plaisar," *Deux Régimes de Fous, textes et entretiens 1975–1995*, p. 114). Furthermore, absolute deterritorialisation is present in the strata as the revolutionary practice which acts as the condition of their possible operation. See also, Gilles Deleuze, "Sur les principaux concepts de Michel Foucault," *Deux Régimes de Fous, textes et entretiens 1975–1995*, and Gilles Deleuze, *Foucault*.

7. Deleuze and Guattari give a diagram of pragmatics in which its processual creation of destratifying signs appears as a circle with four stages. It begins with an analysis of regimes of signs in terms of their expressive forms, and the content they determine. The second stage is the analysis of how regimes of signs transform (de- and re-territorialise) each other. The third "diagrammatic" component extracts particles-signs from the regimes by constructing "abstract-real machines" which absolutely deterritorialise the strata. The final "machinic" component returns us to the actual world, in order to show how it appears through, and is conditioned by, the destratifying break pragmatics has instituted. "To show," Deleuze and Guattari write, "how abstract machines are effectuated in concrete assemblages" (ATP, 146/182). This final stage, while appearing to return us to the circles starting point, has in fact fractured it by constructing a new reality. Pragmatics, or schizoanalysis is this critical process of eternal return. Deleuze and Guattari provide a useful diagram, ATP, 146/182.

8. In line with this suggestion, Deleuze and Guattari claim that "artisan" is a better term than "artist" for the schizoanalyst of art. The artisan, they write, "is determined in such a way as to follow a flow of matter, a *machinic phylum*" (ATP, 409/509), in freeing "a life proper to matter, a vital state of matter as such, a material vitalism that doubtless exists everywhere but is ordinarily hidden or covered, rendered unrecognisable" (ATP, 411/512). Guattari directly opposes this "cosmic artisan" (ATP, 345/426) to the "schizo-analyst technician." "There could never be a schizo-analyst technician," he says, "this would be a contradiction in terms. If schizo-analysis must exist, it is because it already exists everywhere; and not just among schizophrenics, but in the schizes, the lines of escape, the processual ruptures

which are facilitated by a cartographic auto-orientation. Its goal? One could say that it doesn.t have any, because it is not so much the end that matters but the "middle" itself." "Institutional Schizo-Analysis," *Soft Subversions,* p. 276. For an account of Deleuze's "stark blend" of materialism and vitalism, see John Mallurky, "Deleuze and Materialism: One or Several Matters?," *South Atlantic Quarterly,* 96, 3, 1997.

9.   In this regard, "schizoanalysis" is a war machine against psychoanalysis. As Guattari writes: "The Lacanian Signifier homogenises the various semiotics, it loses the multi-dimensional character of many of them. Its fundamental linearity, inherited from Saussurian structuralism, does not allow it to apprehend the pathic, non discursive, autopoietic character of the partial nuclei of enunciation" (Chaos, 72/103).

10.  For an extended account of Deleuze and Guattari's understanding of these paintings by Turner see, James Williams, "Deleuze on J. M. W. Turner, Catastrophism in philosophy?" *Deleuze and Philosophy: The Difference Engineer.*

11.  Deleuze and Guattari have received a lot of criticism over their supposed glamorisation of a tragic psychic condition, and have vigorously defended their use of the term "schizophrenia" against this charge. Both Deleuze and Guattari repeatedly emphasise the difference between schizophrenia as a clinical condition, and schizoanalysis or "schizophrenization" as an "ethical-aesthetic paradigm." As Deleuze writes: "It is not a question of opposing to the dogmatic image of thought another image borrowed, for example, from schizophrenia, but rather of remembering that schizophrenia is not only a human fact but also a possibility for thought—one, moreover, which can only be revealed as such through the abolition of that image" (DR, 148/192). The relationship between schizophrenia as a clinical condition and as a critical practice is more complex in Guattari's work. He was involved in the institution of La Borde that attempted to treat schizophrenia along anti-psychiatry lines. This involved experimenting with the distinctions between a clinical schizophrenic and a schizoanalytic health worker in order to elaborate a "schizo" unconscious emerging beyond institutional distinctions of doctor and patient. So although Guattari states: "Schizoanalysis obviously does not consist in miming schizophrenia" (Chaos, 68/98), he nevertheless accepts that schizophrenia as a clinical condition is the ground of an effective schizoanalysis. "The complexions of the psychotic real," he writes, "in their clinical emergence constitute a privileged exploratory path for other ontological modes of production in that they disclose aspects of excess and limit experiences. [ . . . ] Here a sense of being-in-itself is established before any discursive scheme, uniquely positioned across an intensive continuum whose discursive traits are not perceptible by an apparatus of representation but by a pathic, existential absorption, a pre-egoic, pre-identificatory agglomeration" (Chaos, 79/111). For Guattari schizophrenia can, in certain specific ways, be seen as exemplary of an ethical-aesthetics of ex-

pression: "Just as the schizo has broken moorings with subjective individuation, the analysis of the Unconscious should be recentred on the non-human
processes of subjectivation that I call machinic, but which are more than
human—superhuman in a Nietzschean sense' (Chaos, 71–2/102–3). This
privileging of schizophrenia is however, significantly qualified: "The problem
of schizophrenization as a cure consists in this," Deleuze and Guattari write,
"how can schizophrenia be disengaged as *a power of humanity and of Nature*
without a schizophrenic thereby being produced?" "La synthese disjonctive,"
*L'Arc* 43. For Guattari on La Borde see "La Borde: A Clinic Unlike Any Other,"
*Chaosophy.*

12. Henry Miller, *Tropic of Cancer,* p. 250, London: BCA, 1982.
13. For a detailed explanation of painting's face-landscape problem, see Ronald
Bogue, *Deleuze on Music, Painting, and the Arts,* chapter four.
14. For a fascinating account of some of the more surprising results—ithyphallic Christ Childs, ithyphallic crucified Christs, masturbating Christs, and
more, see Leo Steinberg, *The Sexuality of Christ in Renaissance Art and in
Modern Oblivion,* Chicago: University of Chicago Press, 1996.
15. Gilles Deleuze, *The Nature of Flows,* seminar 14th December 1971.
16. Steinberg's major argument in *The Sexuality of Christ in Renaissance Art and
in Modern Oblivion* is that no matter how bizarre we might find paintings of
the Christ child with an erection, for example, these were accepted by the
church as valid theological statements of Christ's incarnation. Deleuze however, wants to make a more radical claim, arguing that it is the church that
supplies "nothing but the conditions of his [the artist's] radical emancipation." Gilles Deleuze, *Seminar Session on Spinoza,* 25th November 1980.
17. In fact, as well as the extensive decoration of the church being Byzantine in
style, much of its material wealth, including the four horses on its roof, and the
enamels of the *Pala d'Oro,* the altarpiece of San Marco, were brought directly
from Constantinople after its sack and looting by the Crusaders in 1204.
18. In central Italy, as we shall see, the introduction of classical approaches to
drawing and modelling appeared in the early fourteenth century with Giotto
and Cimabue.
19. Peter Hills notes: "Such interchange between obscurity and brilliance became [ . . . ] vital to the colouring of sixteenth-century Venetian painting."
*Venetian Colour: Marble, Mosaic Painting and Glass 1250—1550,* p. 47.
20. In his description of the eleventh century church in the monastery of
Hosious Loukas, M. Chadzdakis writes, "the high mosaics with their gold
grounds shine: *such light, such beauty illumines the church.* The light, element
of victory and triumph, permanent symbol of Christ in ecclesiastical phrase-
ology, dominates throughout, clarifies all the forms and in its diurnal course,
vivifies the flowing surfaces and transmutes the material into precious spiritual substance." *Byzantine Monuments in Attica and Boeotia,* p. 12–3.

21. For the Plotinian aspects of Byzantine art see Éric Alliez, *Capital Times: Tales from the Conquest of Time,* pp. 57–64. For a detailed account of Deleuze's understanding of Byzantine art, and especially the importance of the work of Henri Maldinay in this regard, see Ronald Bogue, *Deleuze on Music, Painting and the Arts,* p. 143–4.

22. Vasari notes that drawing is the necessary first stage in the painting process. "The idea which the artist has in his mind must be translated into what the eyes can see, and only then, with the assistance of his eyes, can the artist form a sound judgement concerning the interventions he has conceived." *Lives of the Artists, Volume 1,* p. 443–4.

23. Light and shadow nevertheless retained their ideal value despite the greater naturalism afforded by Alberti's value system, because shadow and light were created only by mixing black or white with the local color. This gave, as Leonardo put it, a "true" shadow.

24. Vasari writes of Giorgione, "he fell so deeply in love with the beauties of nature that he would represent in his works only what he copied directly from life." *Lives of the Artists, Volume 1,* p. 272.

25. Marcia Hall, *Color and Meaning, Practice and Theory in Renaissance Painting,* p. 71.

26. This process has been made visible by the twentieth century techniques of the x-radiograph and the infrared reflectograph, which allow us to see the reworkings of the painting lying beneath its surface. The most radical example in Giorgione's work is the replacement in *La Tempesta* of a bathing woman by the young man in the lower left corner of the picture.

27. Marcia Hall, *Color and Meaning, Practice and Theory in Renaissance Painting,* p. 210.

28. Titian's assistant and well-known painter in his own right, Palma Giovane, captures the drama of this process. Giovane wrote of Titian's method: "He blocked in his pictures with a mass of colors that served as the ground . . . upon which he would then build. I myself have seen such under painting, vigorously applied with a loaded brush of pure red ochre, which would serve as the middle ground, then with a stroke of white lead, with the same brush then dipped in red, black or yellow, he created the light and dark areas that give the effect of relief. And in this way with four strokes of the brush he was able to suggest a magnificent form." Quoted in Emmachia Gustina Ruscelli, *An Examination of late Venetian Painting Techniques.*

29. A fine example of all these aspects of Titian's late style is *The Death of Actaeon* (1565–76, National Gallery, London). For a discussion of the techniques used in this work see Jill Dunkerton, "Titian's Painting Techniques," in *Titian,* p. 59.

30. Deleuze favoured this kind of art historical symptomotology of functions and also draws on the haptic-optic tensor of Alois Riegl, and Wilhelm Worringer's organic-abstract.

31. Deleuze points out their importance for him, FB, 190/119. Deleuze also draws on Wölfflin's *Renaissance and Baroque* in TF.
32. Heinrich Wölfflin, *Principles of Art History*, p. 19.
33. Heinrich Wölfflin, *Principles of Art History*, p. 19.20.
34. Heinrich Wölfflin, *Principles of Art History*, p. 21.
35. Vasari notes how Titian's last works "are executed with bold, sweeping strokes, and in patches of colour," that "makes pictures seem alive." *Lives of the Artists, Volume 1*, p. 458. This development has an obvious echo in Deleuze's discussion of Bacon's "patches," which we shall turn to in Chapter Six.
36. Marcia Hall, *Color and Meaning, Practice and Theory in Renaissance Painting*, p. 233.
37. Heinrich Wölfflin, *Principles of Art History*, p. 196.
38. Heinrich Wölfflin, *Principles of Art History*, p. 52.
39. Consistent with our earlier discussion of the relation of the plane and the strata in relative and absolute deterritorialisation, "smooth space is constantly being translated, transversed into a striated space; striated space is constantly being reversed, returned to a smooth space" (ATP, 474/593). Deleuze and Guattari's descriptive topology tends to lay out these poles in their pure state, but this is only in order to operate a symptomatology (a schizo-analysis) that returns striated spaces to smoothness. That is, in striated space we see things in terms of objects and their representations, in terms of cause and effect, in terms finally, of an *a priori* space and time that condition these relations. In smooth space however, perception changes, and becomes "based on symptoms and evaluations rather than measures and properties" (ATP, 479/598). Smooth space is a space of evaluative connection whereas striated space imposes distinctions and limits. Nevertheless, Deleuze and Guattari suggest that the extension of a striated representational space gives smooth space a milieu of propagation and renewal, without which its consistency might remain unexpressed. Striated space here becomes "a mask without which it [smooth space] could neither breathe nor find a general form of expression" (ATP, 486/607). And indeed, more than just a life support, striated space offers a "richness and necessity of translations, which include as many opportunities for openings as risks of closure or stoppage" (ATP, 486/607). In other words, striated space is where relative deterritorialisations occur, and it is only through these that a destratified smooth space will appear. The necessity of affirmative evaluation however, remains, and although the abstract line requires striated space in which to operate, "It is less easy," Deleuze and Guattari note, "to evaluate the creative potentialities of striated space and how it can simultaneously emerge from the smooth and give everything a whole new impetus" (ATP, 494/616). Striated space is never in itself creative, and is always attempting to restratify things in its various "apparatus of capture." Only when the abstract line draws or "abstracts" a vital mat-

ter from its representational signs is an absolutely deterritorialised smooth
space created, and an artwork appears which is truly "abstract."

40.  Although it seems that Pollock did view his paintings on the wall, before low-
ering them again for reworking. See Timothy J. Clark, "Jackson Pollock's
Abstraction," *Reconstructing Modernism: Art in New York, Paris and Montreal
1945—1964.*

41.  Clement Greenberg, "Abstract, Representational, and so forth," *Art and
Culture, Critical Essays,* p. 228.

42.  Deleuze and Guattari take the concept of the "haptic" from Alois Riegl's *Late
Roman Art Industry,* p. 32–3.

43.  This concept of the "will to art" [*Kunstwollen*] also comes from Riegl. Riegl
regarded art works as symptoms of a historical people's experience of space,
time and matter. "The character of this volition [*Wollen*]," Riegl wrote, "is
always determined by what may be termed the conception of the world
[*Weltanschauung*] at a given time" (*Late Roman Art Industry,* p. 231). Art expresses the "artistic will" of a culture, its abstract machine, and could only be
interpreted by disregarding the more obvious representational or symbolic
intentions of the work, and by suspending judgements of value. "The mis-
sion of our discipline," Riegl thought, "is not simply to find the things in the
art of the past that appeal to modern taste, but to delve into the artistic volition [*Kunstwollen*] behind works of art and to discover why they are the way
they are, and why they could not have been otherwise" (*The Group
Portraiture of Holland,* p.63). *Kunstwollen* is therefore a symptommatological
taxonomic tool, and shorn of its ethnographic pretensions provides a way in
which a rigorous analysis of formal qualities could move beyond the art object and towards its ontological mechanisms. See also, Alois Riegl, "The
Place of the Vapheio Cups in the History of Art," in *The Vienna School
Reader, Politics and Art Historical Method in the 1930s,* p. 35.

44.  The phrase is from the founder of the *Einfühlung* tradition of German aesthetics, Theodor Lipps, and that Worringer quotes in *Abstraction and
Empathy, A Contribution to the Psychology of Style,* p. 14. (References now
found in the text following the abbreviation 'AE') Lipps argued that art expressed its inner and psychological conditions, conditions that were not simply confined to the subjective interiority of the artist, but were shared with
the viewer of the work as well. Art, according to Lipps, expressed emotional
or physiological truths that we recognize by finding them in ourselves,
through empathy. Aesthetics thereby becomes the study of art's ontological
conditions, as they are found in the viewers "empathy" or "participation" in
the work. What is significant about this approach is that it did not understand empathy as determined by subjective factors in the viewer, but by a
transcendental vital energy that Lipps believed was that of organic life. On
Lipps see Moshe Barusch, *Theories of Art 3, From Impressionism to Kandinsky,*
p. 111–12.

45. Wilhelm Worringer, *Form in Gothic,* p. 21. References to this book now found in the text following the abbreviation "FG."

46. Deleuze and Guattari criticise Worringer for this crystallisation of the abstract line into 'the most rectilinear forms possible' (ATP, 496/619). Worringer believed these forms appear in the earliest art forms and so are the source of art. Deleuze and Guattari part ways with Worringer on this point, writing, "we do not understand the aesthetic motivation of the abstract line in the same way, or its identity with the beginning of art" (ATP, 496/620). Deleuze and Guattari also reject Worringer's rather negative understanding of abstraction as the product of anxiety, in which fear is the impulse for erecting monuments to "the eternity of an In-Itself." I shall return to some of these points in connection to Francis Bacon's use of Egyptian art, in Chapter Six.

47. We have already heard the echo in *Cinema 1:* "How can we rid ourselves of ourselves, and demolish ourselves?" (C1, 66/97).

48. "Where the abstract line is the exponent of the will to form," Worringer writes, "art is transcendental, is conditioned by the need for deliverance" (FG, 67).

49. This is a significant reinterpretation of Riegl's terms. For Riegl the haptic was associated with tactile sensation, the optic with visual sensation. Consistent with his assumption of an organic sensibility Riegl saw thought as subsequent to either experience.

50. Greenberg writes: "Because flatness was the only condition painting shared with no other art, Modernist painting oriented itself to flatness as it did to nothing else." "Modernist Painting," *The Collected Essays and Criticism, Vol. 1, Perceptions and Judgements 1939–44,* p. 87. I shall examine the immanent critical process by which Greenberg defines modernist art in the next chapter.

51. Clement Greenberg, "Towards a New Laocoon," *The Collected Essays and Criticism, Vol. 1, Perceptions and Judgements 1939–44,* p. 30.

52. Clement Greenberg, "Abstract, Representational, and so forth," *Art and Culture, Critical Essays,* p. 136–7.

53. Clement Greenberg, "The Case for Abstract Art," *The Collected Essays and Criticism, Volume 4 Modernism with a Vengeance,* p. 81.

54. Clement Greenberg, "Byzantine Parallels," *Art and Culture,* p. 167–8.

55. Clement Greenberg, "Byzantine Parallels," *Art and Culture,* p. 169.

56. Clement Greenberg, "Byzantine Parallels," *Art and Culture,* p. 169.

57. Clement Greenberg, quoted in John Rajchman, *Constructions,* p. 69. In chapter 4 of this book, Rajchman offers a critical view of Deleuze and Guattari's use of Pollock.

58. Clement Greenberg, "Byzantine Parallels," *Art and Culture,* p. 170.

59. Clement Greenberg, "The Case for Abstract Art," *The Collected Essays and Criticism, Volume 4 Modernism with a Vengeance,* p. 81.

60. Strangely enough, Greenberg also calls Pollock a "Gothic painter" ("The Present Prospects of American Painting and Sculpture," *The Collected Essays and Criticism, Volume 2, Arrogant Purpose, 1945–49*, p. 166) but, as Deleuze points out, "without seeming to give this term the full meaning it assumes in Worringer's analysis" (FB, 186/101).

61. Michael Fried, "Morris Louis," *Art and Objecthood, Essays and Reviews*, p. 106.

62. Michael Fried, "Three American Painters: Kenneth Noland, Jules Olitski, Frank Stella," *Art and Objecthood, Essays and Reviews*, p. 223.

63. Michael Fried, "Three American Painters: Kenneth Noland, Jules Olitski, Frank Stella," *Art and Objecthood, Essays and Reviews*, p. 223.

64. Michael Fried, "Three American Painters: Kenneth Noland, Jules Olitski, Frank Stella," *Art and Objecthood, Essays and Reviews*, p. 224–5.

65. Deleuze has elsewhere described the "American critics" definition of Abstract Expressionism as "the creation of a purely optical space" as "curious," and finally, in relation to his own work, as "a quarrel over words, an ambiguity of words" (FB, 106–7/99). This seems a very generous evaluation by Deleuze, and one that obscures the significant differences in their positions. Indeed, Deleuze puts it more bluntly in a subsequent passage when he writes: "By liberating a space that is (wrongly) claimed to be purely optical, the abstract expressionists in fact did nothing other than to make visible an exclusively manual space" (FB, 107/100).

66. As Timothy J. Clark notes, Fried's argument (and this applies equally well to Greenberg) only works when the viewer is an ideal distance from the work, at which the "surface volatizes." "At five feet away," he very practically points out, "it simply doesn't work." "Jackson Pollock's Abstraction," *Reconstructing Modernism: Art in New York, Paris, and Montreal 1945–1964*, p. 236.

67. For a criticism of Greenberg in these terms see Rosalind Krauss, *The Optical Unconscious*, p. 307–8.

68. The phrase comes from John Welchman's description of Pollock's work in *Modernism Relocated; Towards a cultural studies of visual modernity*, p. 45.

69. Michael Fried, "Three American Painters: Kenneth Noland, Jules Olitski, Frank Stella," *Art and Objecthood, Essays and Reviews*, p. 224.

70. Quoted in Irving Sandler, "Abstract Expressionism," *American Art in the Twentieth Century*, p. 78. Edited by C. M. Joachimides and N. Rosanthal, Munich: Prestal-Verlag, 1993.

71. John Welchman, *Modernism Relocated; Towards a cultural studies of visual modernity*, p. 226, italics added.

72. Pollock quoted in Nancy Jachec, *The Philosophy and Politics of Abstract Expressionism 1940–1960*, p. 83. This book gives a fascinating account of Pollock and Greenberg's development in terms of the intellectual context of post-War America. Of particular interest is their relation to the rise of

Existentialism, and its role in redefining Socialism as a politics of individual intervention within historical processes, unrelated to class interests or agency.

## NOTES TO CHAPTER FIVE

1. Walt Whitman, "Song of Myself," 26, *Leaves of Grass,* lines 598–610, M. Cowley ed., London: Penguin, 1959.
2. This term is left untranslated in the English translations of Guattari's work. It must be noted that this is the same word Deleuze and Guattari use in *A Thousand Plateaus,* and that we discussed in Chapter Four. Although this term is descriptive, and in itself does not carry any pejorative or positive sense, last chapter we saw its negative connotations developed, whereas in this one Guattari's use of the term takes on an affirmative sense.
3. Félix Guattari, "Subjectivities: For Better and for Worse," *The Guattari Reader,* p. 198. Clearly this statement prefigures the task of *Chaosmosis,* where it is repeated: "My perspective involves shifting the human and social sciences from scientific paradigms towards ethico-aesthetic paradigms" (Chaos, 10/24).
4. Félix Guattari "Institutional Schizo-Analysis," *Soft Subversions,* p. 271.
5. For Guattari the unconscious is what cannot be expressed in terms of the subject, and is what subjectivity represses. But the unconscious is nonetheless active, and is never figured as a lack. The unconscious is the virtual dimension of affect which fractalises the subject in processes of subjectivation. "[I]t is not necessary to oppose the basic logic of latent contents, to that of repression." Guattari writes, "It is possible to use a model in which the unconscious is open to the future and able to integrate any heterogeneous, semiotic components which may interfere. Then, meaningful distortions no longer arise from an interpretation of underlying contents. Instead they become part of a machinic set-up entirely on the text's surface. Rather than be mutilated by symbolic castration, recurring incomplete goals act instead as autonomous purveyors of subjectivation. The rupture, the breach of meaning, is nothing else than the manifestation of subjectivation in its earliest stages. It is the necessary adequate fractalisation which enables something to appear where the access before was blocked. It is the deterritorialising opening." "The Refrain of Being and Meaning; Analysis of a Dream," *Soft Subversions,* p. 233. ("Les ritournelles de l'Être et du Sens," *Cartographies Schizoanalytiques,* p. 235)
6. Deleuze and Guattari explain this fractal ontology in *A Thousand Plateaus:* "Fractals are aggregates whose number of dimensions is fractional rather than whole, or else whole and with continual variation in direction (ATP, 486/607). Subjectivation operates on this model, creating a "directional space" which "doesn't have a dimension higher than that which moves through it or is inscribed on it" (ATP, 488/609).

7.  Brian Massumi, "Chaos in the 'Total Field' of Vision," *Hyperplastik, Kunst und Konzept der Wahrnehmung in Zeiten der mental imagery*, p. 255.

8.  The affect is an "autopoietic" machine in precisely the sense the biologists Humberto Maturana and Francisco Varela first proposed the term: "the product of their operation is their own organisation." Quoted in Félix Guattari, *The Three Ecologies*, p. 102. As Maturana and Varela write, "an autopoietic machine continually generates and specifies its own organization through its operation as a system of production of its own components, and does this in an endless turnover of components under conditions of continuous perturbations and compensation of perturbation. [ . . . ] [A]utopoietic machines are unities whose organization is defined by a particular network of processes (relations) of production of components, the autopoietic network." Quoted in *The Three Ecologies*, p. 100. Guattari qualifies his use of Maturana and Varela's term however, inasmuch as they limit it to the unitary individuations of "living" or organic bodies. Against this limitation Guattari argues: "Autopoiesis deserves to be rethought in terms of evolutionary, collective entities, which maintain diverse types of relations to alterity, rather than being implacably closed in on themselves. [ . . . ] Thus we will view autopoiesis from the perspective of the ontogenesis and phylogenesis proper to a mecanosphere superposed on the biosphere" (Chaos, 39–40/62) This means that art can be understood as autopoietic, as Guattari specifically suggests (Chaos, 93/130). For an account of Maturana and Varela's relation to Deleuze and Guattari, see Ronald Bogue, "Art and Territory," *A Deleuzian Century? The South Atlantic Quarterly*, Summer 1997, Vol.96, No.3.

9.  This is another site of Guattari's break with Lacan. "Not only is I an other," he writes, "but it is a multitude of modalities of alterity. Here we are no longer floating in the Signifier, the Subject and the big other in general" (Chaos, 96/134).

10. Guattari describes the autogenetic properties of chaos as follows: "The chaotic nothing spins and unwinds complexity, puts it in relation with itself and what is other to it, with what alters it. This actualisation of difference carries out an aggregate selection into which limits, constants and states of things can graft themselves" (Chaos, 114–115/159).

11. Joyce writes, "every person, place and thing in the chaosmos of Alle anyway connected with the gobblydumped turkery was moving and changing every part of the time." James Joyce, *Finnegans Wake*, p. 118, London: Penguin, 1992.

12. Samual Butler, *Erewhon*, p. 219, London: Penguin, 1986. The machinic world of Erewhon, Deleuze and Guattari suggest, is not just a no-where, but simultaneously a now-here (WP, 100/96), meaning its utopian topos of virtual creativity does not transcend our world but continually infuses it with an immanent and revolutionary alterity.

13. Félix Guattari, "So What," *Chaosophy*, p. 18.

14. Gilles Deleuze and Félix Guattari, "Balance-Sheet Program for Desiring Machines," *Chaosophy,* p. 120–1.
15. Gilles Deleuze and Félix Guattari, "Balance-Sheet Program for Desiring Machines," *Chaosophy,* p. 128.
16. Gilles Deleuze, "Cold and Heat," *Photogenic Painting, Gerard Fromanger,* p. 64.
17. Gilles Deleuze, "On Gilbert Simondon," *Desert Islands and Other Texts 1953–1974,* p. 86. ("Gilbert Simondon, L'individu et sa genèse physico-biologique," *L'île desérte et autres textes 1953–1974,* p. 120)
18. Gilles Deleuze, *Seminar Session at Vincennes,* 27 February 1979.
19. Simondon argues that individuation is the result of the non-identity of being with itself. Being attempts to solve its non-identity through individuation, but this can never eradicate its constitutive difference, which keeps any individuation open and in progress (the power of repetition in Deleuze's terms). This inherent non-identity of being takes the form of a problem Simondon argues, a problem which is autopoietic inasmuch as it is that "by which the incompatibility within the unresolved system becomes an organising dimension in its resolution. "The Genesis of the Individual," *Incorporations,* p. 311. See also, Gilles Deleuze, "On Gilbert Simondon," *Desert Islands and Other Texts 1953–1974.* ("Gilbert Simondon, L'individu et san genèse physico-biologique," *L'île Déserte et Autres Textes 1953–1974*)
20. Georges Simondon, "The Genesis of the Individual," *Incorporations,* p. 311. For an account of Deleuze's use of Simondon see Ronald Bogue, *Deleuze and Guattari,* p. 61ff and Brian Massumi, "The Autonomy of the Affect," *Deleuze: A Critical Reader,* p. 227ff. Similarly, Guattari opposes a process of "automodelization" to that involving pre-existing models in "Institutional Schizo-Analysis," *Soft Subversions,* p. 268–9.
21. Félix Guattari, "Institutional Schizo-Analysis," *Soft Subversions,* p. 276.
22. Félix Guattari, "Subjectivities: For Better and for Worse," *The Guattari Reader,* p. 200.
23. The essay this quotation comes from, "The Exhausted" is not found in the French edition of *Critique et Clinique.* Deleuze's essay, 'L'Èpuisè' appears in Samuel Beckett, *Quad,* Paris: Minuit, 1992. The quotations come from p. 72.
24. Gilles Deleuze, "L'Èpuisè," in Samuel Beckett, *Quad,* p. 72.
25. Félix Guattari, "Subjectivities: For Better and for Worse," *The Guattari Reader,* p. 198–201.
26. Félix Guattari, "Subjectivities: For Better and for Worse," *The Guattari Reader,* p. 196.
27. This reading of Duchamp has been exhaustively developed by Thierry de Duve. De Duve argues that the readymade was Duchamp's ironic response to painting's contemporaneous re-foundation on pure color as the expression of an eternal language of abstraction. This was Kandinsky's argument in

*Concerning the Spiritual in Art,* one Duchamp was familiar with after his stay in Munich in 1912. The readymade is, on de Duve's account, the re-foundation of art on an act of pure nomination as an attack on the spiritual claims made by Kandinsky for modern abstract art. De Duve's Duchamp is the post-modern hero, the anti-painter. De Duve makes much of Duchamp claiming the tube of paint as the first readymade, and argues that in so doing Duchamp "switched from one regulative idea to another by giving that of his colleagues, the early abstractionists, an additional reflexive twist which turned it into a referent for his own idea. Their regulative idea was the specifically pictorial; his was *about* the specifically pictorial. Theirs was geared to establish their craft's name, *Malerei;* his was a philosophy *about that name,* a kind of pictorial nominalism" *Kant After Duchamp,* p. 165.

28. Duchamp's well-known statement is: "There is no art. Instead of choosing something which you like, or something which you dislike, you choose something that has no visual interest for the artist. In other words to arrive at a state of indifference towards this object; at that moment, it becomes a ready made." Quoted in J. Gough-Cooper and J. Caumont, *Marcel Duchamp,* unpaginated.

29. Félix Guattari, "Subjectivities: For Better and for Worse," *The Guattari Reader,* p. 198.

30. Alliez has developed this critique as part of his wider projection of an alternative direction to (post) modernism, a trajectory of "vital abstraction" that finds its most important exponent in the painter Henri Matisse. I attended Alliez's seminar, "On the Eye-Brain of Modernity" at the Akademie der bildenden Künste Wien, 2002–3, where he presented these arguments in detail. My account is heavily indebted to the work he developed there.

31. Éric Alliez points this out in "Rewriting Postmodernity (Notes)," unpublished translation by C. Penwarden and A. Toscano of an article which originally appeared in *Trésors publics 20 ans de création dans les Fonds régionaux d'art contemporain,* Paris: Flammarian, 2003. He also quotes another of Duchamp's interviews with Sweeney (1946) where he claims: "This is the direction that art must take: intellectual expression rather than animal expression."

32. Deleuze and Guattari's assumption of a productive chaos as the privileged ontological state has been criticised by Antonio Negri and Michael Hardt in their book *Empire* (Cambridge (Mass.): Harvard University Press, 2000). Given their attempt to reinvigorate a politics of the left in terms they take from Deleuze and Guattari, this criticism is important. Deleuze and Guattari, they write, "focus our attention clearly on the ontological substance of social production. Machines produce. The constant functioning of social machines in their various apparatuses and assemblages produces the world along with the subjects and objects that constitute it. Deleuze and Guattari, however, seem to be able to conceive positively only the tendencies

toward continuous movement and absolute flows, and thus in their thought too, the creative elements and the radical ontology of the production of the social remain insubstantial and impotent. Deleuze and Guattari discover the productivity of social reproduction (creative production, production of values, social relations, affects, becomings), but manage to articulate it only superficially and ephemerally, as a chaotic, indeterminate horizon marked by the ungraspable event" (p. 28). First, given the extensive development by Deleuze and Guattari of the "negative" pole of productivity in strata, faces, apparatus' of capture, etc., this criticism seems at least a little hasty. Second, it seems strange, and not a little strategic, that Hardt and Negri should call "superficial" one of the most important theoretical underpinnings of their own project (which they presumably correct and complete). Third, the indeterminable and ungraspable event has a specific philosophical meaning in Deleuze and Guattari which is only superficially reduced to their common meanings. The most chaosmic event may be "ungraspable," but it is, as we have seen, nevertheless entirely immanent to the actuality that expresses it. It is ironic that Hardt and Negri should criticise Deleuze and Guattari in this way when their own book seems to rest on just such an ungraspable event, the coming to power of the multitude. "The only event," Hardt and Negri tell us, "that we are awaiting is the construction, or rather the insurgence, of a powerful organisation. We do not have any models to offer for this event. Only the multitude through its practical experimentation will offer the models and determine when and how the possible becomes real" (p. 411). As almost the last words of their book, and as the culmination of their implied promises of a determinate and graspable production of the multiple, this is more than a little disappointing. Here, it seems as if Hardt and Negri finally accept Deleuze and Guattari's supposed commitment to an ontological revolution necessarily unknown, but nevertheless embodied, in Deleuze and Guattari's words, by a "people yet to come." This specific sense of Deleuze and Guattari's indeterminate and ungraspable event, which operates as the immanent ontological power unravelling stable structures, seems in fact very close to Hardt and Negri's own use of the term "multitude." "The deterritorialising power of the multitude," they write, "is the productive force that sustains Empire and at the same time the force that calls for and makes necessary its destruction" (p. 61). The multitude acts as the political expression of an ontological and affirmative matter/force which is forever over-coded by Empire, but which forever escapes it. As with Deleuze and Guattari's aesthetic paradigm, Negri and Hardt are also attempting an ontology of the social which would seek to express its most libratory immanent forces of creation. Their criticism of Deleuze and Guattari seems therefore, at best ungenerous, and at worst misleading, especially in relation to their own project.

33.  "That which is or returns has no prior constituted identity: things are reduced to the differences which fragment them, and to all the differences

which are implicated in it and through which they pass" (DR, 67/92). As a result: "The same is said of that which differs and remains different" (DR, 126/165). In this sense Deleuze and Guattari propose a rigorously Nietzschean readymade, a simulacrum or image without resemblance, which "attains the status of a sign in the coherence of eternal return" (DR, 67/93).

34. Gilles Deleuze, "On Nietzsche and the Image of Thought," *Desert Islands and Other Texts 1953–1974,* p. 138. ("Sur Nietzsche et l'image de la pensée," *L'île desérte et autres textes, 1953–1974,* p. 191)

35. Marcel Duchamp, quoted in Calvin Tomkins, *Duchamp, A Biography,* p. 159.

36. Félix Guattari and Antonio Negri, "Communist Propositions," *The Guattari Reader,* p. 255.

37. Fernando Pessoa, "The Keeper of Sheep," in *Selected Poems,* p. 81. Translated by J. Griffen, London: Penguin, 1974.

38. Nietzsche, *The Gay Science,* 367. Nietzsche discusses the painter Mirabeau's creative ability of forgetting in *On the Genealogy of Morals,* I, 10.

39. This is possibly the most direct statement of the vitalist and materialist 'permanent revolution' of the aesthetic paradigm. It is one they repeat: "Deformations destined to harness a great force are already present in the small-form refrain or rondo [ . . . ] the cosmic force was already present in the material, the great refrain in the little refrain, the great manoeuvre in the little manoeuvre" (ATP, 350/432).

40. Nevertheless, a number of commentators have claimed that Deleuze and Guattari are Romantics. Dana Polan for example, while pointing out that Deleuze "avoids a full romantic mythology of expressiveness," nevertheless calls Deleuze's book on Francis Bacon "quasi-romantic," and as such part of "the larger romantic project of Deleuze: to go beyond the surface fixities of a culture and find those forces, those energies, those fluxes, those sensations that specific sociohistorical inscriptions have blocked and reified into social etiquettes and stultifying patterns of representation" ("Francis Bacon, The logic of sensation," *Gilles Deleuze and the Theater of Philosophy,* p. 230). The problem here is not Polan's description of Deleuze's project, but its description as romantic. I hope the reasons for this will be obvious in what follows. In a more 'archaeological' mode John Sellers (in "The Point of View of the Cosmos: Deleuze, Romanticism, Stoicism" in *Pli* 8, 1999) argues that German Romanticism is a "central" influence on Deleuze and Guattari in its project of "following nature" (p. 1). Sellers traces connections from Deleuze and Guattari to Friedrich Schlegel's concepts of a "direct mediator," and a divine immanence as the "unity in multiplicity and multiplicity in unity" (p. 10). Although these connections are no doubt active in Deleuze and Guattari's work, Sellers strangely ignores their discussion of Romanticism in *A Thousand Plateaus,* and chooses to instead find evidence for the connections between Schlegel and Deleuze and Guattari in their shared interest in

the Stoics. Once again the problem is not the connections Sellers draws per se, but the lack of their critical assessment in light of what Deleuze and Guattari themselves write about Romanticism.

41. Immanuel Kant, *Critique of Pure Reason,* A68/B93.
42. Gilled Deleuze, *Third Lesson on Kant,* 28 March 1978.
43. Immanuel Kant, *Critique of Judgment,* ss. 26.
44. Gilled Deleuze, *Third Lesson on Kant,* 28 March 1978.
45. Kant writes: "The sublime may be described in this way: It is an object (of nature) the representation of which determines the mind to regard the elevation of nature beyond our reach as equivalent to the presentation of ideas" Immanuel Kant, *Critique of Judgment,* General Remarks upon the Exposition of Aesthetic Reflexive Judgments. Deleuze's reading of this movement can be found in *Kant's Critical Philosophy: The Doctrine of the Faculties,* p. 51–2.
46. Immanuel Kant, *Critique of Judgment,* General Remarks upon the the Exposition of Aesthetic Reflexive Judgments.
47. Gilles Deleuze, "The Idea of Genesis in Kant's Esthetics," *Desert Islands and Other Texts 1953–1974,* p. 62. ('L'idée de genèse dans l'esthétique de Kant,' *L'île Déserte et autres textes 1953–1974,* p. 88)
48. Immanuel Kant, *Critique of Judgment,* ss. 28.
49. Immanuel Kant, *Critique of Judgment,* ss. 28.
50. Gilled Deleuze, *Fourth Lesson on Kant,* 4 April 1978.
51. Deleuze specifically makes this point (C2, 18/29).
52. Gilles Deleuze, "The Idea of Genesis in Kant's Esthetics," *Desert Islands and Other Texts 1953–1974,* p. 62. ("L'idée de genèse dans l'esthétique de Kant," *L'île Déserte et autres textes 1953–1974,* p. 88)
53. Gilles Deleuze, *Fourth Lesson on Kant,* 4 April 1978.
54. Immanuel Kant, *Critique of Judgment,* ss. 28 and General Remarks.
55. As Deleuze and Guattari describe Romanticism: "It is certain that the Earth as an intense point in depth or in projection, as *ratio essendi,* is always in disjunction with the territory: and the territory as the condition of "knowledge," *ratio cognoscendi,* is always in disjunction with the earth" (ATP, 339/418).
56. Gustav Mahler, "Ich bin der Welt abhanden gekommen," *Ruckert Lieder.* Death is a recurring Romantic motif, and was often used as a description of the artist's journey from individual to universal consciousness.
57. Clement Greenberg, "Modernist Art," *The Collected Essays and Criticism, Volume 4, Modernism with a Vengeance,* p. 85.
58. Clement Greenberg, "Modernist Art," *The Collected Essays and Criticism, Volume 4, Modernism with a Vengeance,* p. 86. Greenberg writes: "The essence of Modernism lies, as I see it, in the use of characteristic methods of a discipline to criticise the discipline itself, not in order to subvert it but in order to entrench it more firmly in its area of competence" (p. 85).

59. Clement Greenberg, "'American-Type' Painting," *Art and Culture, Critical Essays,* p. 208.
60. Clement Greenberg, "Modernist Art," *The Collected Essays and Criticism, Volume 4, Modernism with a Vengeance,* p. 85.
61. Clement Greenberg, "Towards a Newer Laocoon," *The Collected Essays and Criticism, Volume 4, Modernism with a Vengeance,* p. 23.
62. Clement Greenberg, "Towards a Newer Laocoon," *The Collected Essays and Criticism, Volume 4, Modernism with a Vengeance,* p. 30.
63. Clement Greenberg, "Towards a Newer Laocoon," *The Collected Essays and Criticism, Volume 4, Modernism with a Vengeance,* p. 29. "The picture," Greenberg writes, "exhausts itself in the visual sensation it produces" p. 34.
64. That Greenberg regarded art after such abstraction as a decline is the most obvious symptom of his modernist teleology. See, Thierry de Duve, *Kant after Duchamp,* p. 216–248.
65. How, in other words, does art make these forces visible? Deleuze and Guattari often quote Paul Klee in this regard, particularly the line: "Art does not reproduce the visible; rather it makes visible." Paul Klee, *Creative Credo,* 1. Deleuze and Guattari's use of Klee as the spokesman for Modernism is ironic, considering the usual association of his work and thought (not least his own) with Romanticism. (See, Robert Rosenblum, "Other Romantic currents: Klee and Ernst," in *Major European Art Movements, 1900–1945*) But Klee's formulations that have been taken as Romantic are also open to Deleuze and Guattari's concept of Modernism. For example, Klee writes: "There, where the power-house of all time and space—call it brain or heart of creation—activates every function; who is the artist who would not dwell there?" (*On Modern Art,* p. 49). Obviously, space and time are not *a priori* categories, but elements of a creation that makes this there a here, and implies a brain and a creative chaosmos which are immanent to each other *in the production of art.* This reading is supported by Klee's rejection of what he calls the *"crass emotional phase of Romanticism,"* in favour of a "cool Romanticism," a "new Romanticism" which rejects the heroic solitude of the romantic artist in order to "embrace the life force itself," at "the source of creation" (*On Modern Art,* p. 49). Such an art would be, in Klee's words, "a Romanticism which *is one* with the universe" (*On Modern Art,* p. 43) and would find its definitively modern statement in the words Klee placed on his own tombstone: "I cannot be grasped in immanence." Finally, and importantly for Deleuze and Guattari, Klee will abandon romantic feelings of longing and disjunction, in realising that a "modern Romanticism" calls for the creation of a people to come (*On Modern Art,* p. 55).
66. This materialism would be the ground of Guattari's objections to post-modernism; that it fails to open itself to cosmic forces, to molecularise and deterritorialise itself sufficiently, and thereby accepts a romantic disjunction of discursive systems and what grounds them. That is, it is not materialist

enough. As a result, there is no true resistance in post-modernism because there is no true creation. "The virtual ethical and aesthetic abdication of postmodern thought," Guattari writes, "leaves a kind of black stain upon history." "Postmodernism and Ethical Abdication," *The Guattari Reader*, p. 116. The postmodern project of "deconstructing" cliché and opinion would not be the same as its absolute deterritorialisation, precisely because the first operation involves a supplemental dimension of irony and the second does not (Derridean differance cannot, I believe, be equated to Deleuzian difference, as they do not share the same ontological grounds). Deleuze and Guattari re-vitalise modernism rather than suggest a post-modernism, because they far prefer modernism's ontological ambition to post-modernism's epistemological pessimism. As Deleuze writes, paraphrasing D. H. Lawrence on painting, "the rage against clichés does not lead to much if it is content only to parody them; maltreated, mutilated, destroyed, a cliché is not slow to be reborn from its ashes" (C1, 211/284).

67. This is Deleuze and Guattari's version of the "death of the artist," and is extended by Deleuze's suggestion that the art work is a gravestone: "Art is defined as an impersonal process in which the work is composed somewhat like a *cairn*, with stones carried in by different voyages and beings in becoming" (ECC, 66/87).

68. In this sense, Modernism marks the point where "Art and philosophy converge," inasmuch as both, on Deleuze and Guattari's account, emerge at a point at which, "the constitution of an earth and a people that are lacking [are] the correlate of creation" (WP, 108/104). This is not to deny their very different materialities—concept and sensation—but to understand their common ontology, and their shared process of chaosmic construction/expression. Deleuze suggests, and here perhaps expresses his agreement with Guattari's privileging of art, that philosophy begins with sensation, inasmuch as 'the path that leads to that which is to be thought, begins with sensibility. [ . . . ] The privilege of sensibility as origin appears only in the fact that, in an encounter, what forces sensation and that which can only be sensed are one and the same thing" (DR, 144–5/188).

69. Walt Whitman, "Song of Myself," *Leaves of Grass,* lines 226, 505, and 136.

70. Deleuze and Guattari's terms of percept and affect involve a terminological reconfiguration in relation to the work of Spinoza, from where the term "affect" comes. As Deleuze and Guattari explain, what is here called "perception" and "affection" are what Spinoza had previously called "affection" and "affectus" (WP, 154/145–6), and what Deleuze and Guattari had in ATP called "affection" and "affect".

71. See B, 28–9/19–20 for a discussion of the percept in similar terms.

72. Deleuze and Guattari's association of Cubism with the plane of composition is perhaps even more ironic than their exploration of Klee's anti-Romanticism, and must be treated as a metaphor. Despite the Cubist's interest in Bergson and

Nietzsche, the well known Cubist "call to order" is an idealism rather than an empiricism, an attempt at 'objectivity' framed in the Kantian terms of a transcendental subject. For an art historical account of the Cubist interest in Bergson and Nietzsche see, Mark Antliff, *Inventing Bergson, Cultural Politics and the Parisian Avant-Garde,* Princeton: Princeton University Press, 1993. Especially chapter 2 "*Du Cubisme* between Bergson and Nietzsche."

73    Gilles Deleuze, *Negotiations 1972–1990,* p. 146–7.

74.   Gilles Deleuze, *Proust and Signs,* p. 97. (*Proust et les signes,* p. 54)

75.   Gilles Deleuze, *Proust and Signs,* p. 98. (*Proust et les signes,* p. 56)

76.   Some of Deleuze and Guattari's most beautiful passages evoke this creative mystical immanence: "The Cosmos is an abstract machine, and each world is an assemblage effectuating it. If one reduces oneself to one or several abstract lines that will prolong itself in and conjugate with others, producing immediately, directly *a* world in which it is *the* world that becomes, then one becomes-everybody/everything" (ATP, 280/343).

77.   Virginia Woolf, *Mrs. Dalloway,* p. 154–55, London: Penguin, 1996.

78.   Gilles Deleuze, "L'Èpuisè," in Samuel Beckett, *Quad,* Minuit, Paris, 1992. p. 77.

79.   Gilles Deleuze, "Having an Idea in Cinema," *Deleuze and Guattari New Mappings in Politics, Philosophy and Culture,* p. 18. (Qu'este-ce que L'acte de création, *Deux Régimes de Fous, Textes et Entretiens 1975–1995,* p. 300)

80.   This is a favourite set of images Deleuze often uses. In relation to Nietzsche: "There are dimensions here, times and places, glacial or torrid zones never moderated, the entire exotic geography which characterises a mode of thought as well as a style of life" (LS, 128/153). "It is up to us to go to extreme places, to extreme times, where the highest and the deepest truths live and rise up. The places of thought are the tropical zones frequented by the tropical man, not temperate zones or the moral, methodical or moderate man" (NP, 110/126). And in relation to German expressionist cinema: "It is the hour when it is no longer possible to distinguish between sunrise and sunset, air and water, water and earth, in the great mixture of a marsh or of a tempest" (C1, 14/26).

## NOTES TO CHAPTER SIX

1.    Deleuze and Guattari write: "An abstract machine is not physical or corporeal, any more than it is semiotic; it is diagrammatic" (ATP, 147/176).

2.    "The privilege of sensibility as origin," Deleuze writes, "appears in the fact that, in an encounter, what forces sensation and that which can only be sensed are one and the same thing." (DR, 144–5/188) Sensation marks the immanence of ontological and aesthetic dimensions, and is what must be thought, in painting as in philosophy.

3. This date refers to the appearance of a diagram or abstract machine. In ATP each plateau carries such a date, for example on November 28 1947 Antonin Artaud announces the Body without Organs (BwO). As we shall see, this is an important date for Deleuze's account of Bacon's diagram.

4. For a brief account of Riegl's concept of *Kunstwollen* see Chapter Four, note 43.

5. The chapter this quotation comes from, "Machinic heterogenesis" gives a good account of the machinic history Deleuze is employing in relation to Bacon's diagram. "It is at the intersection of heterogeneous machinic Universes, of different dimensions and with unfamiliar ontological textures, radical innovations and once forgotten, then reactivated, ancestral machinic lines, that the movement of history singularises itself" (Chaos, 41/63).

6. The diagram is "present," Deleuze and Guattari write, "in a different way in every assemblage, passing from one to the other, opening one onto the other, outside any fixed order or determined sequence" (ATP, 347/428).

7. For an interesting account of Bacon's "diagrammatic" use of Velázquez and Ingres see, Norman Bryson, "Bacon's Dialogues with the Past," in *Francis Bacon and the Tradition of Art*.

8. Deleuze writes: "Painting invents entirely different types of blocks. These are neither blocks of concepts nor blocks of movements/durations, but blocks of line/colors." Gilles Deleuze, "Having an Idea in Cinema," *Deleuze and Guattari New Mappings in Politics, Philosophy and Culture*, p. 15. ("Qu"est-ce que l"acte de création?," *Deux Régimes de Fous, textes et entretiens 1975–1995*, p. 293)

9. David Sylvester, *Interviews with Francis Bacon*, p. 16–7.

10. "Paintings eternal object is this:" Deleuze and Guattari write, "to paint forces" (WP, 182/172).

11. Spiritual or "geometric" abstraction, Deleuze argues produces a purely optical space without tactile connections, within which the "spiritual" (transcendent) values of the abstract forms signify according to a still classical model of representation. In "spiritual" abstraction color and form are understood in an entirely symbolic way, as representing higher truths (for example, Kandinsky's understanding of color in *On the Spiritual in Art*, or Malevich's understanding of form in Suprematism). Abstract expressionism is the other pole, and produces a catastrophe enveloping the entire canvas. Abstract Expressionism, Deleuze writes, "grounds itself in a scrambling" (FB, 117/111). Here, optical space disappears in favour of a manual line that produces a sensation that is "irremediably confused" (FB, 109/102). Deleuze's critique of "spiritual" abstraction and abstract expressionism, it must be noted, is specific to Deleuze's evaluation of Bacon's practice, and will not prevent Deleuze from affirming both diagrams elsewhere (he affirms both Pollock and minimalism as expressions of the Baroque fold (TF, 27/38, 160/168), and gives a positive evaluation of Mondrian (WP, 183/173). We

have already seen Deleuze and Guattari's affirmation of Pollock in ATP. The point is that different diagrams answer different questions, as Deleuze explains: "The important question is: Why did Bacon not become involved in either of the two preceding paths. The severity of his reactions, rather than claiming to pass judgement, simply indicate what was not right for him, and explains why Bacon personally took neither of these paths" (FB, 109/101–2). As a result, Bacon's "middle way" between geometric abstraction and abstract expressionism "is called a "middle" way only from a very external point of view" (FB, 118/111).

12.  We recall from Chapter Four that this is the aspect of Worringer's account of Egyptian art Deleuze and Guattari criticize.

13.  Deleuze takes the term "Figure" from Jean-Francois Lyotard's book *Discours,Figure.* Lyotard is primarily concerned with Freud's topological construction of the unconscious in which surface elements of a narrative appear as figurative transformations of an invisible system of unconscious relations. Lyotard argues that the unconscious production of conscious meaning does not occur through a process of interpretation—that is through the signifier—and this is the "importance" of the book for Deleuze ("Remarks (on Jean-Francois Lyotard)," *Desert Islands and Other Texts 1953–1974,* p. 214). (*L'île Déserte et Autres Textes, textes et entretiens 1953–1974,* p. 299) Instead, meaning emerges through an invisible "matrix" that exists outside of any laws of representation and discourse. For Lyotard the visible is structured by this invisible and unconscious matrix which becomes visible in the Figure, or "figural," *as* the deformation of figurative representations. The matrix, according to Lyotard, "resides in a space that is beyond the intelligible, [and] is in radical rupture with the rules of opposition; we can already see that this property of unconscious space, which is also that of the libidinal body, is to have many places in one place, and to block together what is logically incompatible. This is the secret of the figural: the transgression of the constitutive intervals of discourse and the transgression of the constitutive distances of representation" (Lyotard quoted in Yve-Alain Bois and Rosalind E. Krauss, *Formless A User's Guide,* p. 106–7). Deleuze, while adopting the deformative aspect of Lyotard's Figure, and acknowledging the "extreme importance" of his book (AO, 243/289) discards its psychoanalytic focus. This is because although Lyotard identifies the "figure-matrix" with desire, correctly in Deleuze and Guattari's opinion, he limits desire, and indeed "castrates" it (AO, 244/290) by bringing it back "toward the shores he has so recently left behind" in reducing the Figure to "transgressions" which remain secondary to what they deform (AO, 244/290). For an account of Deleuze's relation to Lyotard, see Ronald Bogue, *Deleuze on Music, Painting and the Arts,* p. 113–16.

14. In *A Thousand Plateaus* Deleuze and Guattari argue that the face finds its becoming-animal in a head-body. The head-body is composed of *"faciality traits,"* which "elude the organisation of the face" (ATP, 171/209).

15. That is, it considers painting as an ontological practice. See Maurice Merleau-Ponty, *The Visible and the Invisible* (references now found in the text following the abbreviation "VI"), and his essays "Eye and Mind," and "Cézanne's Doubt," in *The Merleau-Ponty Aesthetics Reader: Philosophy and Painting* (references to "Eye and Mind" are now found in the text following the abbreviation "EM").

16. Apart from Merleau-Ponty's work, Deleuze also draws on and discusses other phenomenological accounts of Cézanne, especially Erwin Straus, *The Primary World of the Senses,* and Henri Maldiney, *Regard, Parole, Espace.* For an account of Deleuze"s relationship to Straus and Maldiney see, Ronald Bogue, *Deleuze on Music, Painting and the Arts,* p. 116–121 (for Straus), and p. 139–145 (on Maldiney). For other accounts of Deleuze's relation to phenomenology see, Daniel W. Smith, "Deleuze's Theory of Sensation: Overcoming the Kantian Duality," in *Deleuze: A Critical Reader,* and Judy Purdom, "Mondrian and the destruction of space," in *Hyperplastik, Kunst und Konzepte der Wahrnehmung in Zeiten der mental imagery.*

17. Maurice Merleau-Ponty, "Cézanne's Doubt," *The Merleau-Ponty Aesthetics Reader: Philosophy and Painting,* p. 68.

18. As Merleau-Ponty writes, "it is not I who sees, not he who sees, because an anonymous visibility inhabits both of us, a vision in general, in virtue of that primordial property that belongs to the flesh, being here and now, of radiating everywhere and forever, being an individual, of being also a dimension and a universal" (VI, 142).

19. Merleau-Ponty's "pathic" flesh is clearly distinguished from Deleuze's "haptic" one in terms of this topology of absence. If we recall Merleau-Ponty's pathic topology of "the outside of its inside and the inside of its outside" (VI, 144), we can contrast this directly with Deleuze's haptic topology of a plane of composition which "is not internal to the self, but neither does it come from an external self or a non-self. Rather it is like the absolute Outside that knows no Selves because interior and exterior are equally a part of the immanent in which they have fused" (ATP, 156/194).

20. This is inevitable, Deleuze writes, for "A consciousness is nothing without a synthesis of unification, but there is no synthesis of unification without the form of the I, or the point of view of the Self" (LS, 102/124).

21. "The question of whether flesh is adequate to art," Deleuze and Guattari write, "can be put in this way: can it support percept and affect, can it constitute the being of sensation, or must it not itself be supported and pass into other powers of life?" (WP, 178/169).

22. Interestingly, Cézanne is more of a stopping place for Deleuze's recapitulation of Bacon, than for Bacon himself. As Bacon said of Cézanne: "I'm not

sure what place he has in the history of painting. I can see that he has been important, but I must admit I'm not madly enthusiastic about him, as many people are." Michael Archimbaus, *Francis Bacon. In Conversation with Michael Archimbaud*, p. 42.

23. Éric Alliez, "Some Remarks on Color in Contemporary Philosophy," unpaginated unpublished paper, given at the conference *Chroma Drama, Widerstand der Farbe*, the Akademie der bildenden Künste Wien, 2000. Alliez develops this idea here in some detail, writing, "Deleuze reverses the order in perceptions supposed in Merleau-Ponty's phenomenology of art and instead of the painter following the birth of the thing in its actualisation—a move from the virtual to the actual—has the painter dissolve the thing and move from the actual to the virtual. To the consistent material virtual discovered by the old Cézanne; to the matter and movement of paint as expressions of colors-constructions."

24. This independent light illuminating things obviously recalls our discussion of phenomenology. The separation of light from color introduces an optical space and implies a discrete eye to see it. We can understand Cézanne's relation to the Impressionists in this way, for although the Impressionists succeeded in dissolving form, this dissolution was achieved in light, Deleuze and Guattari argue, and depended on an "optical mixture of colors" in an autonomous eye (WP, 165/155). Cézanne said "Monet is but an eye," and this is no doubt a very Deleuzian criticism. Indeed, Deleuze expands on Cézanne's "lesson against the impressionists," writing that a sensation is not achieved through "the 'free' or disembodied play of light and color (impressions)." Rather, sensation emerges in the construction of colored planes, solid bodies of color that do not melt into the air. "Color," Deleuze writes, "is in the body, sensation is in the body, and not in the air" (FB, 35/40). The Impressionists then, not Cézanne, were the real painters of phenomenology.

25. For Goethe: "Two pure original principles in contrast are the foundation of the whole." *Theory of Colours*, 707. Goethe offers a whole range of terms to describe the differential relations of yellow and blue (*Theory of Colours*, 696) many of which describe the relations of forces—Repulsion/Attraction, Action/Negation. Deleuze generally sticks to hot and cold. See also Deleuze's discussion of the painter Gérard Fromanger in these terms, in "Cold and Heat," *Photogenic Painting, Gerhard Fromanger*.

26. Deleuze gives the example of the color "green: yellow and blue can surely be perceived but if their perception vanishes by dint of progressive diminution, they enter into a differential relation (db/dy) that determines green. And nothing impedes either yellow or blue, each on its own account, from being already determined by the differential relation of two colors that we cannot detect" (TF, 88/117).

27. Johann Wolfgang von Goethe, *Theory of Colours*, 805.

28. The forces of the earth (forces of folding, thermal and magnetic forces, forces of germination) emerge in Cézanne's paintings according to an abstract geometry. This abstract geometry, common to the mountains and to Cézanne's paintings, is what Deleuze and Guattari call "traits of content," with colors being their "traits of expression" (ATP, 141/176). The forces of the earth emerge in inseparable traits of content and expression, in Cézanne's paintings as in Nature, they form sensations (particle-signs).

29. Sensation, Deleuze says, is "irreducibly synthetic," because it is its nature "to envelop a constitutive difference of level" (FB, 37/41–2). Vision, in other words, is the differential calculus of Nature and gives an analogical expression of the becoming of its forces.

30. Here we are not far from Spinoza's formula for beatitude, a percept in which I think or experience God/Nature as God/Nature thinks itself.

31. Quoted in Éric Alliez, "Hallucinating Cézanne," p.185, in *Hyperplastik, Kunst und Konzepte der Wahrnehmung in Zeiten der mental imagery.*

32. Where Bacon remains Cézannean, Deleuze writes, "is in the extreme elaboration of painting as analogical language" (FB, 120/113).

33. "In Van Gogh, Gauguin, or today, Bacon," Deleuze and Guattari write, "we see the immediate tension between flesh and the area of plain, uniform color surging forth, between the flows of broken tones [*tons rompus*] and the infinite band of a pure, homogeneous, vivid and saturated colour" (WP, 181/171). More specifically, "Van Gogh and Gauguin, sprinkle the area of plain, uniform color with little bunches of flowers so as to turn it into wallpaper on which the face stands out in broken tones" (WP, 182/173). This is a device Gauguin frequently employs (*Sleeping Child,* 1884, Josefowitz collection, *Self portrait: "Les Miserables,"* 1888, Vincent van Gogh Foundation, Amsterdam, *La Belle Angele,* 1889, Musée d'Orsay, Paris). In Van Gogh the "wallpaper" tends not so much to the floral as to a swirling pattern (*Self-portrait,* 1889, Musée d'Orsay, Paris). Bacon also took other things from Gauguin and Van Gogh. The broken tones of Bacon's figures are much closer to Van Gogh's "malerisch" technique, while the flat colored grounds and the use of an armature to frame the figures is closer to Gauguin. In this latter respect Deleuze argues that Bacon shares a "cloissonism" with Gauguin which, for both, "recovers a function that is derived from the halos of premodern painting" (FB, 152/142). There is also a danger Bacon's "malerisch" period shares with the early Gauguin, that of a "blending" in the broken tones darkening the painting (FB, 143/134).

34. There are, for example, only "obvious" differences between Bacon and Cézanne, Cézanne paints landscapes and still-life's, Bacon does not, Cézanne paints Nature, Bacon interiors. But these differences are united, Deleuze argues, in their shared project, to *"paint the sensation"* (FB, 35/40).

35. This would be the only point at which my account of Deleuze's reading of Bacon differs from the otherwise immaculate description Ronald Bogue

gives in *Deleuze on Music, Painting, and the Arts.* "Sensation," Bogue argues, "registers directly on the nerves without passing through the brain" (p. 158). As we shall see this is perhaps simply a "quarrel over words."

36. Quoted in Éric Alliez, "Hallucinating Cézanne," p. 144. I have also taken the concept of the eye-brain which follows from Éric Alliez, who developed it in his seminar *On the Eye-Brain of Modernity,* at the Akademie der bildenden Künste Wien, 1999–2003. See Éric Alliez and Jean-Clet Martin, *L'Oeil-cerveau. De la peinture moderne,* Paris: Seuil, 2005.

37. "According to phenomenology," Deleuze and Guattari write, "thought depends on mans relations with the world—with which the brain is necessarily in agreement because it is drawn from these relations, as excitations are drawn from the world and reactions from man, including their uncertainties and failures. "Man thinks, not the brain"; but this ascent of phenomenology beyond the brain towards a Being in the world, through a double criticism of mechanism and dynamism, hardly gets us out of the sphere of opinions. It leads us only to an *Urdoxa* posited as an original opinion, or meaning of meanings" (WP, 209–10/197).

38. For Deleuze's account of the *spatium* as the intensive differenciation of spatio-temporal dynamisms particular to the Body without Organs, see DR, 251/323.

39. John Milton, *Paradise Lost,* book 1, line 124, in *The Complete English Poems,* p. 161, edited by G. Campbell, New York: Alfred A. Knopf, 1992.

40. Antonin Artaud, "To Have Done with the Judgement of God," *Selected Writings,* p. 571.

41. Antonin Artaud, "To Have Done with the Judgement of God," *Selected Writings,* p. 565.

42. The first quotation is Antonin Artaud, "Situation of the Flesh," *Selected Writings,* p. 111. The second is an unreferenced quotation of Artaud by Deleuze (C2, 165/215).

43. Antonin Artaud, "Situation of the Flesh," *Selected Writings,* p. 111.

44. Deleuze argues: "[Artaud] says that the cinema is a matter of neuro-physiological vibrations, and that the image must produce a shock, a nerve-wave which gives rise to thought, "for thought is a matron who has not always existed." Thought has no other reason to function than its own birth, secret and profound" (C2, 165/215).

45. Antonin Artaud, "Situation of the Flesh," *Selected Writings,* p. 110.

46. Antonin Artaud, final letter to Paule Thevenin, February 24 1948, *Selected Writings,* p. 585.

47. This is the theatre of what Deleuze calls dramatisation. A theatre both Artaud's and Bacon's, in which "It is intensity which is immediately expressed in the basic spatio-temporal dynamisms and which determines the 'indistinct' differential relation in a distinct quality and a distinguished extensity" (DR, 245/316). Deleuze calls this process "individuation," and in relation to Bacon

we could say it is the act of painting. "Individuation," he writes, "is the act by which intensity determines differential relations to become actualised, along the lines of differenciation and within the qualities and extensities it creates" (DR, 246/317).

48. Deleuze and Guattari discuss the "rhythmic character" in ATP, 318/391. Deleuze's discussion of the three different rhythms comes from the composer Olivier Messiaen.

49. It often appears as such, for example, in *Anti-Oedipus* Deleuze and Guattari write: "It must not be thought that the intensities themselves are in opposition to one another, arriving at a state of balance around a neutral state. On the contrary, they are all positive in relation to the zero intensity that designates the full body without organs. And they undergo relative rises or falls depending on the complex relationship between them and the variations in the relative strength of attraction and repulsion as determining factors" (AO, 19/25). Further down the page they mention Kant's theory of intensive quantity. Deleuze also discusses Kant's theory of intensity in DR, 231/298. The references in ATP have already been given.

## NOTES TO THE CONCLUSION

1. Thomas Pynchon, *Vineland*, p. 266–7, London: Minerva, 1990.
2. Gilles Deleuze, *Negotiations 1972–1990*, p. 145.
3. Gilles Deleuze, "Immanence: A Life," *Pure Immanence: Essays on A Life*, p. 27.
4. Félix Guattari, "Institutional Schizo-Analysis," *Soft Subversions*, p. 276.

# Bibliography

## GILLES DELEUZE—BOOKS

—— *Bergsonism,* translated by H. Tomlinson and B. Habberjam. New York: Zone Books, 1991.

—— *Le bergsonisme.* Paris: Presses Universitaires de France, 1966.

—— *Cinema1, The Movement Image,* translated by H. Tomlinson and B. Habberjam. Minneapolis: University of Minnesota Press, 1989.

—— *Cinema 1: L'Image-mouvement.* Paris: Minuit, 1983.

—— Gilles Deleuze, *Cinema 2, The Time-Image,* translated by H. Tomlinson and R. Galeta. Minneapolis: University of Minnesota Press, 1989.

—— *Cinéma 2. L'Image-temps.* Paris: Minuit, 1980.

—— "Coldness and Cruelty," *Masochism,* translated by J. McNeil. New York: Zone Books, 1991.

—— Gilles Deleuze and Claire Parnet, *Dialogues,* translated by H. Tomlinson and B. Habberjam. New York: Columbia University Press, 1987.

—— Gilles Deleuze and Claire Parnet, *Dialogues.* Paris: Flammarion, 1996.

—— *Desert Islands and Other Texts 1953–1974,* translated by M. Taormina. New York: Semiotext(e), 2004.

—— *L'île Déserte et Autres Textes, textes et entretiens 1953–1974.* Paris: Minuit, 2002.

—— *Deux Régimes de fous textes et entretiens 1975–1995.* Paris: Minuit, 2003.

—— *Difference and Repetition,* translated by P. Patton. New York: University of Columbia Press, 1996.

—— *Différence et Répétition.* Paris: Presses Universitaires de France, 1968.

—— *Essays critical and clinical,* translated by D. Smith and M. Greco. Minneapolis: University of Minnesota Press, 1997.

—— *Critique et Clinique.* Paris: Minuit, 1993.

—— *Expressionism in Philosophy: Spinoza,* translated by M. Joughin. New York: Zone Books, 1992.

—— *Spinoza et le problème de l'expression.* Paris: Minuit, 1968.

—— *The Fold: Leibniz and the Baroque,* translated by T. Conley. Minneapolis: University of Minnesota Press, 1993.

—— *Le Pli, Leibniz et le baroque.* Paris: Minuit, 1988

—— *Foucault,* translated by S. Hand. Minneapolis: University of Minnesota Press, 1988.

—— *Foucault.* Paris: Minuit, 1986.

—— *Francis Bacon: The Logic of Sensation,* translated by D.W. Smith. London and New York: Continuum, 2003.

—— *Francis Bacon logique la sensation.* Paris: Seuil, 2002.

—— *Kant's Critical Philosophy: The Doctrine of the Faculties,* translated by H. Tomlinson and B. Habberjam. Minneapolis: University of Minnesota Press, 1984.

—— *The Logic of Sense,* translated by M. Lester with C. Stivale, edited by C.V. Boundas. New York: Columbia University Press, 1990.

—— *Logique du sens.* Paris: Minuit, 1969.

—— *Negotiations 1972–1990,* translated by M. Joughin. New York: Columbia University Press, 1995.

—— *Nietzsche and Philosophy,* translated by H. Tomlinson. New York: Columbia University Press, 1983.

—— *Nietzsche et la philosophie.* Paris: Presses Universitaires de France, 1962.

—— *Nietzsche.* Paris: Presses Universitaires de France, 1965.

—— *Proust and Signs,* translated by R. Howard. London: Penguin, 1972.

—— *Proust et les signes.* Paris: Presses Universitaires de France, 1964.

—— *Pure Immanence, Essays on A Life,* translated by A. Boyman. New York: Zone Books, 2001.

—— *Spinoza: Practical Philosophy,* translated by R. Hurley. San Francisco: City Lights Books, 1988.

—— *Spinoza, Philosophie pratique.* Paris: Minuit, 1981.

## GILLES DELEUZE—ARTICLES

—— "Bergson's conception of difference," *The New Bergson,* edited by J. Mullarkey.

—— "Having an Idea in Cinema," *Deleuze and Guattari, New Mappings in Politics, Philosophy and Culture,* edited by E. Kaufman and K. J. Heller. ("Qu'est-ce que l'acte de création?," *Deux Régimes de Fous, textes et entretiens 1975–1995*)

—— "The Brain Is The Screen: An Interview with Gilles Deleuze," *The Brain is the Screen: Gilles Deleuze and the Philosophy of Cinema,* edited by G. Flaxman.

—— "Cold and Heat," *Photogenic Painting, Gerard Fromanger,* (English and French) translated by D. Roberts. London: Black Dog Publishing, 1999.

—— "L'Èpuisè," Samuel Beckett, *Quad.* Paris: Minuit, 1992.

## GILLES DELEUZE—SEMINAR TRANSCRIPTS (ALL FOUND AT WWW.IMAGINET.FR/DELEUZE)

—— *Seminar, The Nature of Flows,* 14 December 1971, translated by K.I. Ocana.

—— *Seminar Session On Scholasticism and Spinoza,* Vincennes, 14 January 1974, translated by T. S. Murphy.

—— *On Music,* Seminar Session 3 May 1977, translated by T. S. Murphy.

—— *Seminar Session of Spinoza,* 24 January 1978, translated by T. S. Murphy.

—— *Kant: Synthesis and Time,* seminar, 14 March 1978, translated by M. McMahon.

—— *Third lesson on Kant,* seminar, 28 March 1978, translated by M. McMahon.

—— *Metal, metallurgy, music, Husserl, Simondon,* seminar, 27 February 1979, translated by T. S. Murphy.

—— *Seminar Session on Spinoza,* 25 November 1980, translated by T. S. Murphy.

—— *Session on Spinoza,* seminar, 13 January 1981, translated by T. S. Murphy.

—— *Theory of Multiplicities in Bergson,* seminar, translated by T. S. Murphy.

## DELEUZE AND GUATTARI—BOOKS

—— *Anti-Oedipus, Capitalism and Schizophrenia,* translated by R. Hurly, M. Seem, and H. R. Lane. Minneapolis: University of Minnesota Press, 1983.

—— *L'Anti-Œdipe.* Paris: Minuit, 1972.

—— *A Thousand Plateaus,* translated by B. Massumi. London: Athlone, 1988.

—— *Mille Plateaux.* Paris: Minuit, 1980.

—— *What Is Philosophy?,* translated by H. Tomlinson and G. Burchell. New York: Columbia University Press, 1994.

—— *Qu'est-ce que la philosophie?.* Paris: Minuit, 1991.

## FÉLIX GUATTARI—BOOKS

—— *Cartographies Schizoanalytiques.* Paris: Galilée, 1989.

—— *Chaosmosis: an ethico-aesthetic paradigm,* translated by P. Baines and J. Pefanis. Sydney: Power publications, 1995.

—— *Chaosmose.* Paris: Galilée, 1992.

—— *Chaosophy,* edited by S. Lotringer. New York: Semiotext(e), 1995.

—— *Communists Like Us,* (with Antonio Negri), translated by M. Ryan. New York: Semiotext(e), 1990.

—— *The Guattari Reader,* edited by G. Genosko. Oxford: Blackwell, 1996.

—— *Molecular Revolution.* translated by R. Sheed. London: Penguin, 1984.

—— *La révolution moleculaire,* Fontenay-sous-Bois: Encre, 1977

—— *Soft Subversions,* edited by S. Lotringer. New York: Semiotext(e), 1996.

—— *The Three Ecologies,* translated by I. Pindar and P. Sutton. London: Athlone Press, 2000.

## OTHER BOOKS AND ARTICLES

—— Éric Alliez, *Capital Times: Tales from the Conquest of Time,* translated by G. Van Den Abbeele. University of Minnesota Press, Minneapolis, 1996.

—— Éric Alliez, *The Signature of the World, Or, What is Deleuze and Guattari's Philosophy?,* translated by E. Ross and A. Toscano. London and New York: Continuum, 2004.

—— Éric Alliez, "The Politics of *Anti-Oedipus*—Thirty Years On," *Radical Philosophy,* no. 124, march-april 2004.

—— Éric Alliez, "On Deleuze's Bergsonism," *Discourse* 20.3 (Fall 1998)

—— Éric Alliez, 'Midday, Midnight: The Emergence of Cine-thinking,' *The Brain is the Screen: Gilles Deleuze and the Philosophy of Cinema,* edited by G. Flaxman.

—— Éric Alliez, "Hallucinating Cezanne," *Hyperplastik, Kunst und Konzepte der Wahrnehmung in Zeiten der mental imagery,* edited by E. von Samsonow and E. Alliez. Vienna: Turia+Kant, 2000.

—— Éric Alliez, "The BwO Condition or, The Politics of Sensation," *Biographien des organlosen Körpers,* edited by E. von Samsonow and E. Alliez. Vienna: Turia+Kant, 2003.

—— Éric Alliez, "Rewriting Postmodernity (Notes)," an unpublished translation by C. Penwarden and A. Toscano which originally appeared in *Trésors publics 20 ans de création dans les Fonds régionaux d'art contemporain.* Paris: Flammarian, 2003.

—— Éric Aliez, "Some remarks on Colour in Contemporary Philosophy," unpublished paper given at the conference *Chroma, Widerstand der Farbe.* Vienna: Akademie der bildenden Künste, 2000.

—— David B. Allison editor, *The New Nietzsche: Contemporary Styles of Interpretation.* Cambridge (Mass.): MIT Press, 1977.

—— Louis Althusser, "The Only Materialist Tradition, Part One: Spinoza," *The New Spinoza,* edited by W. Montag and T. Stolze. Minneapolis: University of Minnesota Press, 1997.

—— Keith Ansell Pearson, *An Introduction to Nietzsche as Political Thinker.* Cambridge: Cambridge University Press, 1994.

—— Keith Ansell Pearson, "Towards the Ubermensch: Reflections on the Year of Nietzsche's Daybreak," *Nietzsche-Studien,* 23, 1994.

—— Keith Ansell Pearson, *Viroid Life, Perspectives on Nietzsche and the Transhuman Condition.* Routledge, London, 1997.

—— Keith Ansell Pearson, *Germinal Life, The difference and repetition of Deleuze.* London: Routledge, 1999.

—— Kieth Ansell Pearson, "Pure reserve, Deleuze, philosophy and immanence," *Deleuze and Religion,* edited by M. Bryden.

—— Michael Archimbaud, *Francis Bacon. In Conversation with Michael Archimbaud.* London: Phaidon, 1993.

—— Antonin Artaud, *Selected Writings,* edited by S. Sontag. Berkeley: University of California Press, 1976.

—— Antonin Artaud, *Watchfields and Rack Screams: Works from the Final Period,* edited and translated by C. Eshleman with B. Bador. Boston: Exact Change, 1995.

—— Alain Badiou, *Deleuze: The Clamour of Being,* translated by L. Burchill. Minneapolis: University of Minnesota Press, 2000.

—— Alain Badiou, "Gilles Deleuze: The Fold: Leibniz and the Baroque," *Gilles Deleuze and the Theatre of Philosophy,* edited by C. V. Boundas and D. Olkowski.

—— Alain Badiou, *Theoretical Wrtings,* edited amd translated by R. Brassier and A. Toscano. London and New York: Continuum, 2004.

—— Moshe Barasch, *Theories of Art From Plato to Winckelmann.* New York: New York University Press, 1985.

—— Moshe Barasch, *Theories of Art 3, From Impressionism to Kandinsky.* New York: Routledge, 2000.

—— Raymond Bellour, "Thinking, Recounting, The cinema of Gilles Deleuze," translated by M. McMahon. *Discourse* 20.3, (Fall 1998).

—— Henri Bergson, *The Two Sources of Morality and Religion,* translated by R. Audra and C. Brereton. London: Macmillan, 1935.

—— Henri Bergson, *Matter and Memory,* translated by N.M. Paul and W.S. Palmer. New York: Zone Books, 1998.

—— Henri Bergson, *Creative Evolution,* translated by A. Mitchell. New York: Henry Holt, 1911.

—— Ronald Bogue, *Deleuze and Guattari.* London: Routledge, 1989.

—— Ronald Bogue, *Deleuze on Music, Painting, and the Arts.* London: Routledge, 2003.

—— Ronald Bogue, "Gilles Deleuze: The Aesthetics of Force," *Deleuze: A Critical Reader,* edited by P. Patton.

—— Ronald Bouge, "Art and Territory," *A Deleuzian Century? The South Atlantic Quarterly,* (Summer 1997), Vol.96, No.3, edited by I. Buchanan.

—— Constantin Boundas, "Deleuze-Bergson: an Ontology of the Virtual," *Deleuze: A Critical Reader,* edited by P. Patton.

—— Constantin V. Boundas and Dorothea Olkowski editors, *Gilles Deleuze and the Theater of Philosophy.* New York: Routledge, 1994.

—— Mary Bryden editor, *Deleuze and Religion.* London: Routledge, 2001.

—— Norman Bryson, "Bacon's Dialogues with the Past," *Francis Bacon and the Tradition of Art.* Milan: Skira, 2003.

—— Michel de Certeau, "Mysticism," *diacritics,* 22.2, (summer 1992), translated by M. Brammer.

—— Michel de Certeau, *The Mystic Fable, Vol. One, The Sixteenth and Seventeenth Centuries,* translated by M. Smith. Chicago: University of Chicago Press, 1992.

—— Manolis Chadzadikas, *Byzantine Monuments in Attica and Boeotia.* Athens: Athens Editions, 1956.

—— Mark A. Cheetham, *Kant, Art, and Art History.* Cambridge: Cambridge University Press, 2001.

—— Timothy J. Clark, "Jackson Pollock's Abstraction," *Reconstructing Modernism: Art in New York, Paris, and Montreal 1945–1964,* edited by S. Guilbaut. Cambridge (Mass.): MIT Press, 1990.

—— Thomas Crow, "Saturday Disasters: Trace and Reference in Early Warhol," *Reconstructing Modernism: Art in New York, Paris, and Montreal 1945–1964,* edited by S. Guilbaut. Cambridge (Mass.): MIT Press, 1990.

—— Olivier Davies, "Thinking Difference, a comparative study of Gilles Deleuze, Plotinus and Meister Eckhart," *Deleuze and Religion,* edited by M. Bryden.

—— Thierry de Duve, *Kant After Duchamp.* Cambridge (Mass.): MIT Press, 1996.

—— Robert Delauney, "On the Construction of Reality in Pure Painting," *Art in Theory 1900–1990 An Anthology of Changing Ideas,* edited by C. Harrison and P. Wood. Oxford: Blackwell, 1992.

—— Jacques Derrida, *Spurs,* translated by B. Harlow. Chicago: University of Chicago Press, 1979.

—— John Dewey, *Art as Experience.* New York: Perigree, 1934.

—— Paul Douglas, "Bergson and Cinema: Friends or Foes," *The New Bergson,* edited by J. Mullarky.

—— Gregory Flaxman editor, *The Brain is the Screen: Gilles Deleuze and the Philosophy of Cinema.* Minneapolis: Minnesota University Press, 1999.

—— Gregory Flaxman, 'Cinema Year Zero', *The Brain is the Screen: Gilles Deleuze and the Philosophy of Cinema,* edited by B. Flaxman.

—— Hal Foster, *The Return of the Real, The Avant-garde at the End of the Century.* Cambridge (Mass.): MIT Press, 1996

—— Michael Fried, *Art and Objecthood, Essays and Reviews.* Chicago: University of Chicago Press, 1998.

—— John Gage, *Colour and Meaning. Art, Science and Symbolism.* London: Thames and Hudson, 1999.

—— John Gage, *Colour and Culture. Practice and Meaning from Antiquity to Abstraction.* London: Thames and Hudson, 1993.

—— Gary Genosko, "Guattari's Schizoanalytic Semiotics, Mixing Hjelmslev and Peirce," *Deleuze and Guattari: New Mappings in Politics, Philosophy and Culture,* edited by E. Kaufman and K. J. Heller.

—— Michael Goddard, "The scattering of time crystals: Deleuze, mysticism, and cinema," *Deleuze and Religion,* edited by M. Bryden.

—— Johann Wolfgang von Goethe, *Theory of Colours,* translated by C. L. Eastlake. Cambridge (Mass.): MIT Press, 1970.

—— Philip Goodchild, *Deleuze and Guattari, An Introduction to the Politics of Desire.* London: Sage, 1996.

—— Phillip Goodchild, "Why is philosophy so compromised with God?"*Deleuze and Religion,* edited by M. Bryden.

—— J. Gough-Cooper and J. Caumont, *Marcel Duchamp*. London: Thames and Hudson, 1993.

—— Clement Greenberg, *Art and Culture, Critical Essays*. Boston: Beacon Press, 1961.

—— Clement Greenberg, *The Collected Essays and Criticism, Volume 1, Perceptions and Judgements, 1939–44*, edited by J. O'Brian. Chicago: University of Chicago Press, 1985.

—— Clement Greenberg, *The Collected Essays and Criticism, Volume 2, Arrogant Purpose, 1945–1949*, edited by J. O'Brian. Chicago: University of Chicago Press, 1986.

—— Clement Greenberg, *The Collected Essays and Criticism, Volume 4 Modernism with a Vengeance*, edited by J. O'Brian. Chicago: University of Chicago Press, 1993.

—— Marcia Hall, *Colour and Meaning, Practice and Theory in Renaissance Painting*. Cambridge: Cambridge University Press, 1992.

—— Michael Hardt, *Gilles Deleuze An Apprenticeship in Philosophy*. Minneapolis: University of Minnesota Press, 1993.

—— Michael Hardt, "Exposure, Pasolini in the Flesh," *A Shock to Thought, Expressionism after Deleuze and Guattari*, edited by B. Massumi. London: Routledge, 2002.

—— Martin Heidegger, *Nietzsche Volume 1: The Will to Power as Art*, translated by D. Krell. New York: Harper and Row, 1979.

—— Paul Hills, *Venetian Colour: Marble, Mosaic, Painting and Glass 1250–1550*. New Haven: Yale University Press, 1999.

—— Peter Humphrey, *Painting in Renaissance Venice*. New Haven: Yale University Press, 1995.

—— Nancy Jachec, *The Philosophy and Politics of Abstract Expressionism 1940–1960*. Cambridge: Cambridge University Press, 2000.

—— Galen E. Johnson, "Ontology and Painting," *The Merleau-Ponty Aesthetics Reader: Philosophy and Painting*, edited by G. A. Johnson. Evanston: Northwestern University Press, 1993.

—— Fredric Jameson, "Marxism and Dualism in Deleuze," *A Deleuzian Century?, The South Atlantic Quarterly*, edited by I. Buchanan, (Summer 1997), Vol.96, No.3.

—— Immanuel Kant, *Critique of Pure Reason*, translated by N. K. Smith. London: Macmillan Press, 1933.

—— Immanuel Kant, *Critique of Judgement*, translated by W. S. Pluhar. Indianapolis: Hacket Publishing, 1987.

—— E. Kaufman and K. J. Heller editors, *Delenze and Guattari: New Mappings in Politics, Philosophy and Culture*. Minneapolis: University of Minnesota Press, 1998.

—— Paul Klee, *On Modern Art*, translated by P. Findley. London: Faber and Faber, 1948.

—— Paul Klee, *Creative Credo,* www.ubmail.ubalt.edu

—— Pierre Klossowski, *Nietzsche and the Vicious Circle,* translated by D. Smith. Chicago: University of Chicago Press, 1997.

—— Rosalind E. Krauss, *The Optical Unconscious.* Cambridge (Mass.): MIT Press, 1993.

—— Rosalind E. Krauss, *The Originality of the Avant-Garde and Other Modernist Myths.* Cambridge (Mass.): MIT Press, 1985.

—— Rosalind E. Krauss and Yve-Alain Bois, *Formless A User's Guide.* New York: Zone Books, 1997.

—— Raiji Kuroda, "Collapsing/Collapsed Discourse on Warhol, Regarding Two Elvis Series," *Andy Warhol 1956–86: Mirror of his Time.* Pittsburgh: Andy Warhol Museum, 1996.

—— Alphonso Lingis, "The Will To Power," *The New Nietzsche: Contemporary Styles of Interpretation,* edited by D. B. Allison.

—— Alex McIntyre, "Communion in Joy, Will to Power and Eternal Return in Grand Politics," *Nietzsche-Studien,* 25, 1996.

—— Pierre Macherey, "The Problem of the Attributes," *The New Spinoza,* edited by W. Montag and T. Stolze.

—— Pierre Macherey, "The Encounter with Spinoza," in *Deleuze: A Reader,* edited by P. Patton.

—— John Mullarkey editor, *The New Bergson.* Manchester: Machester University Press, 1999.

—— John Mullarkey, "Deleuze and Materialism: One or Several Matters?" *A Deleuzian Century?, South Atlantic Quarterly,* vol. 96, no. 3, 1997, edited by I. Buchanan.

—— Laura U. Marks, "Signs of the Time, Deleuze, Peirce, and the Documentary Image," *The Brain is the Screen: Gilles Deleuze and the Philosophy of Cinema,* edited by G. Flaxman.

—— Jean-Clet Martin, "Of Images and Worlds: Towards a Geology of the Cinema," *The Brain is a Screen: Gilles Deleuze and the Philosophy of Cinema,* edited by G. Flaxman.

—— Brian Massumi, *A User's Guide to Capitalism and Schizophrenia, Deviations from Deleuze and Guattari.* Cambridge (Mass.): MIT Press, 1992.

—— Brian Massumi, "The Autonomy of Affect," *Deleuze: A Critical Reader,* edited by P. Patton.

—— Brian Massumi, "Deleuze, Guattari, and the Philosophy of Expression," *Canadian Review of Comparative Literature,* Vol. XXIV, no. 3, (Sept. 1997).

—— Brian Massumi, "Chaos in the 'total field' of vision," *Hyperplastik, Kunst und Konzepte der Wahrnehmung in Zeiten der mental imagery,* edited by E. von Samsonow and Éric Alliez. Vienna: Turia+Kant, 2000.

—— Brian Massumi, "The Diagram as Technique of Existence," *Chroma Drama: Widerstand der Farbe,* edited by E. von Samsonow and Éric Alliez. Vienna: Turia+Kant, 2001.

—— Todd May, *The Political Philosophy of Poststructuralist Anarchism.* Pennsylvania: Pennsylvania University Press, 1994.

—— Maurice Merleau-Ponty, *The Visible and the Invisible,* edited by C. Lefort, translated by A. Lingis. Evanston: Northwestern University Press, 1968.

—— Maurice Merleau-Ponty, "Eye and Mind," *The Merleau-Ponty Aesthetics Reader: Philosophy and Painting,* edited by G. A. Johnson. Evanston: Northwestern University Press, 1993.

—— Maurice Merleau-Ponty, "Cezanne's Doubt," *The Merleau-Ponty Aesthetics Reader: Philosophy and Painting,* edited by G. A. Johnson. Evanston: Northwestern University Press, 1993.

—— Nick Millet, "The Third Eye," *The Journal of Philosophy and the Visual Arts,* No.6., edited by A. Benjamin. London: Academy Editions, 1995.

—— Nick Millet, "The Fugitive Body: Bacon's Fistula," *The Journal of Philosophy and the Visual Arts,* No.4, edited by A. Benjamin. London: Academy Editions, 1993.

—— W. Montag and T. Stolze editors, *The New Spinoza.* Minneapolis: Minnesota University Press, 1997.

—— Antonio Negri, "*Reliqua Desiderantur:* A Conjecture for a Definition of the Concept of Democracy in the Final Spinoza," *The New Spinoza,* edited by W. Montag and T. Stolze.

—— Antonio Negri, *The Savage Anomaly, the Power of Spinoza's Metaphysics and Politics,* translated by M. Hardt. Minneapolis: University of Minnesota Press, 1991.

—— Antonio Negri, *Insurgencies, Constituent Power and the Modern State,* translated by M. Boscagli. Minneapolis: Minnesota University Press, 1999.

—— Antonio Negri, *Time for Revolution,* translated by M. Mandarini. London and New York, Continuum, 2003.

—— Friedrich Nietzsche, *The Birth of Tragedy,* translated by F. Golffing. New York: Doubleday, 1956.

—— Friedrich Nietzsche, *Human, All Too Human,* translated by R. J. Hollingdale. Cambridge: Cambridge University Press, 1996.

—— Friedrich Nietzsche, *Daybreak,* translated by R. J. Hollingdale. Cambridge: Cambridge University Press, 1997.

—— Friedrich Nietzsche, *The Gay Science,* translated by W. Kaufmann. New York: Vintage, 1974.

—— Friedrich Nietzshe, *Thus Spake Zarathustra,* translated by R. J. Hollingdale. London: Penguin, 1961.

—— Friedrich Nietzsche, *Beyond Good and Evil,* translated by R. J. Hollingdale. London: Penguin, 1984.

—— Friedrich Nietzsche, *On the Genealogy of Morals,* translated by F. Golffing. New York: Doubleday, 1956

—— Friedrich Nietzsche, *The Case of Wagner,* translated by W. Kaufman. New York: Vintage, 1967.

—— Friedrich Nietzsche, *Twilight of the Idols,* translated by R. J. Hollingdale. London: Penguin, 1968.

—— Friedrich Nietzsche, *The Antichrist,* translated by R. J. Hollingdale. London: Penguin, 1968.

—— Friedrich Nietzsche, *Ecce Homo,* translated by R. J. Hollingdale. London: Penguin, 1979.

—— Friedrich Nietzsche, *Unpublished Letters,* translated and edited by K. Leidecker. London: Peter Owen, 1960.

—— Friedrich Nietzsche, *Selected Letters of Friedrich Nietzsche,* translated by C. Middleton. Chicago: University of Chicago Press, 1969.

—— Friedrich Nietzsche, *Selected Letters,* translated by A. N. Ludovici, edited by O. Levy. London: Soho Book Company, 1985.

—— Friedrich Nietzsche, *The Will to Power,* translated by W. Kaufmann and R. J. Hollingdale. New York: Vintage, 1967

—— Dorothea Olkowski, "Nietzsche's Dice Throw: Tragedy, Nihilism, and the Body Without Organs," *Gilles Deleuze and the Theater of Philosophy,* edited by C. V. Boundas and D. Olkowski.

—— John D. O'Meara, *Studies in Augustine and Eringena.* Washington: The Catholic University of America Press, 1992.

—— Paul Patton, *Deleuze and the Political.* London: Routledge, 2000.

—— Paul Patton editor, *Deleuze: a Critical Reader.* Oxford: Blackwell, 1996.

—— Paul Patton, "Anti-Platonism and Art," *Gilles Deleuze and the Theater of Philosophy,* edited by C. V. Boundas and D. Olkowski.

—— Vincent P. Pecora, "Deleuze's Nietzsche and Post-Structuralist Thought," in *Sub-stance,* vol.14, no.48, 1986.

—— Charles S. Peirce, *The Essential Peirce, Selected Philosophical Writings, Vol. 2 (1893–1913),* The Peirce Edition Project. Bloomington: Indiana University Press, 1998.

—— Charles S. Peirce, *76 Definitions of the Sign,* edited by R. Marty. http://www.door.net/arisbe/menu/LIBRARY/rsources/76defs.htm

—— Dana Polan, "Francis Bacon, The logic of sensation," *Gilles Deleuze and the Theater of Philosophy,* edited by C. V. Boundas and D. Olkowski.

—— Judy Purdom, "Mondrian and the destruction of space," *Hyperplastik, Kunst und Konzepte der Wahrnehmung in Zeiten der mental imagery,* edited by E. von Samsonow and Éric Alliez. Vienna: Turia+Kant, 2000.

—— John Rajchman, *Constructions.* Cambridge (Mass.): MIT Press, 1998.

—— John Rajchman, *The Deleuze Connections.* Cambridge (Mass.): MIT Press, 2000

—— Alois Riegl, *Late Roman Art Industry,* translated by R. Winkes. Rome: Giorgio Bretschneider, 1985.

—— Alois Riegl, *The Group Portraure of Holland,* edited by E. M. Kain and D. Briff. Los Angelus: Getty Research Institute, 1999.

—— Alois Riegl, "The Main Characteristics of the Late Roman *Kunstwollen*," *The Vienna School Reader, Politics and Art Historical Method in the 1930s,* edited by Christopher S. Wool.

—— Alois Riegl, "The Place of the Vapheio Cups in the History of Art," *The Vienna School Reader, Politics and Art Historical Method in the 1930s,* edited by Christopher S. Wool.

—— David Rodowick, *Gilles Deleuze's Time-Machine.* Raleigh: Duke University Press, 1997.

—— Robert Rosenblum, "Other Romantic Currents: Klee and Ernst," *Major European Art Movements 1900–1945, A Critical Anthology,* edited by P. Kaplan and S. Manso. New York: E. P. Dutton, 1977.

—— Emmachia Gustina Ruscelli, "An Examination of Late Venetian Painting Technique," http://wwwglar.gl/art-l.pdf

—— John Sellars, "The Point of View of the Cosmos: Deleuze, Romanticism, Stoicism," *Pli* 8, 1999.

—— Georges Simondon, "The Genesis of the Individual," *Incorporations,* edited by J. Crary and S. Kwinter. New York: Zone, 1992.

—— Danial W. Smith, "Deleuze's Theory of Sensation: Overcoming Kantian Duality," *Deleuze: A Critical Reader,* edited by P. Patton.

—— Danial W. Smith, "A Life of Pure Immanence": Deleuze's 'Critique et Clinique' Project," introduction to Gilles Deleuze, *essays critical and clinical.*

—— Daniel W. Smith, "The Place of Ethics in Deleuze's Philosophy: Three Questions of Immanence," *Deleuze and Guattari, New Mappings in Politics, Philosophy and Culture,* edited by E. Kaufman and K. J. Heller.

—— Daniel W. Smith, "The doctrine of univocality," *Deleuze and Religion,* edited by M. Bryden.

—— Benedict de Spinoza, *The Ethics,* "A Spinoza Reader," translated by E. Curley. Princeton: Princeton University Press, 1994.

—— David Sylvester, *Interviews with Francis Bacon.* London: Thames and Hudson, 1999.

—— *Titian,* exhibition catalogue. London: National Gallery, 2003.

—— Calvin Tomkins, *Duchamp, A Biography.* New York: Henry Holt, 1996.

—— Giorgio Vasari, *Lives of the Artists, volume 1,* translated by G. Bull. London: Penguin, 1987.

—— Arnaud Villani, "Deleuze et Whitehead," *Revue de Metaphysique et de Morale,* No.2, 1996.

—— Christopher Want, "Form without form: Revaluating Greenberg's Kant," *de-, dis-, ex-. Volume 1 Ex-cavating Modernism,* edited by A. Coles and R. Bentley. London: BACKless books, 1996.

—— Andy Warhol, *Andy Warhol 1956–86: Mirror of His time.* Pittsburgh: The Andy Warhol Museum, 1996.

—— Andy Warhol, *Andy Warhol: A Factory.* New York: Soloman R. Guggenheim Museum, 1999.

—— John Welchman, *Modernism Relocated, Towards a cultural studies of visual modernity.* Sydney: Allen and Unwin, 1995.

—— James Williams, "Deleuze on J. M. W. Turner, Catastrophism in philosophy?" *Deleuze and Philosophy: The Difference Engineer,* edited by K. A. Pearson. London: Routledge, 1997.

—— James J. Winchester, *Nietzsche's Aesthetic Turn, Reading Nietzsche after Heidegger, Deleuze, Derrida.* New York: SUNY Press, 1994.

—— Heinrich Wölfflin, *Principles of Art History, The Problem of the Development of Style in Later Art,* translated by M. D. Holtinger. New York: Dover, 1950.

—— Christopher S. Wool editor, *The Vienna School Reader, Politics and Art Historical Method in the 1930s.* New York: Zone Books, 2000.

—— Wilhelm Worringer, *Abstraction and Empathy, A Contribution to the Psychology of Style,* translated by M. Bullock. London: Routledge & Kegan Paul, 1967.

—— Wilhelm Worringer, *Form in Gothic,* translated by H. Read. New York: Schocken Books, 1967.

—— Yirmiyahu Yovel, *Spinoza and Other Heretics vol. 2, The Adventures of Immanence.* Princeton: Princeton University Press, 1989.

—— Francois Zourabichvili, "Six Notes on the Percept," *Deleuze: A Reader,* edited by P. Patton.

—— Francois Zourabichvili, "The Eye of Montage, Dziga Vertov and Bergsonian Modernism," *The Brain is the Screen: Gilles Deleuze and the Philosophy of Cinema,* edited by G. Flaxman.

# Index

## A

Absolute deterritorialisation; *see* Deterritorialisation

Abstract expressionism, 149, 193, 264 n.65

Abstraction, 9, 109–15, 118, 138, 140–50, 188, 205, 211, 221, 226; Geometric abstraction, 193, 275–6 n.11

*Abstraction and Empathy,* 142–3

Abstract line, 118, 138–49, 223, 274 n.76

Abstract machine, 119, 121–4, 135–8, 150, 168, 175, 180, 185, 188, 219, 221–2, 224, 227–8

Accident, 191–2, 210

Action-image, 85–6, 92, 98

Actual, 80, 92, 101–3, 110, 112–5, 154, 158, 177, 179–80, 225, 227; Actualisation, 121; Counter-actualisation, 225

Aesthetics, 3–10, 20, 28–9, 60, 64–5, 105, 223, 238 n.37; Aesthetic composition, 180–1; Aesthetic paradigm, 151, 154–7, 159, 163–7, 176, 181–3, 221, 223; *see* Onto-aesthetics Affect, 18, 31, 77, 86, 92–5, 100, 107, 124, 151–5, 157–60, 166–7, 172–3, 177–83, 200, 206–7, 210–11, 223–4, 253 n.27; Problematic affect, 152–3, 162; Sensory affect, 152–3; Spinozian affect, 45, 48–60, 63–7, 70, 73–4, 220–1, 224

Affection, 84, 86–7, 96, 118–9, 182–3, 253 n.27; Affection-image, 85–6, 91–4, 98; Spinozian affection, 50, 55, 58–9, 62–3, 65, 71–2

Affection-image; *see* Affection

Affirmation, 5–7, 9, 44–5, 49–51, 56–7, 59, 61, 64, 74, 81, 106, 117, 164, 181, 220, 222, 224, 227, 235 n.24; in Nietzsche, 12–4, 16–8, 20–1, 24–30, 33, 35–6

Alberti, Leon Battista, 132, 137

Alliez, Eric, 163, 200, 231 n.5, 237 n.32, 240 n.56, 255 n.44, 268 n.30, 278 n.23, 280 n.36

Analogy, 202, 205, 209–11

Anarchism, 164

Animal, 22–3, 25, 163, 183, 225; Animal-traits, 194; *see* Becoming-animal

*Anti-Oedipus,* 2, 124–6, 129, 133, 138, 140, 162, 209, 227, 245, 276, 281

Antonioni, Michelangelo, 100–1, 109–14, 119

Any-space-whatever, 94–5, 100, 109–11

Aquinas, Thomas, 46

Aristotle, 131–2, 156, 222

Armature, 193, 200

Art, 41–2, 48, 51–2, 55–7, 59–60, 63–6, 74–5, 97–8, 102, 104, 125, 151–159, 163–9, 171–3, 176, 178–83, 200, 219–21, 223–8; Art history, 187–8, 222; Art work, 51–2, 64–5, 152, 177–83, 187–8, 222–7; Modern art, 30–32, 35, 112, 138;

Artaud, Antonin, 51, 79, 108–13, 127, 207–12, 222, 245 n.25 and 28

Artisan, 126, 150, 177, 257–8 n.8; Cosmic artisan, 2, 4, 177